Britain's Black Past

Britain's Black Past

Edited and with an Introduction by
Gretchen H. Gerzina

LIVERPOOL UNIVERSITY PRESS

First published 2020 by
Liverpool University Press
4 Cambridge Street
Liverpool
L69 7ZU

Copyright © 2020 Liverpool University Press

British Library Cataloguing-in-Publication data
A British Library CIP record is available

ISBN 978-1-78962-160-0 cased
ISBN 978-1-78962-161-7 limp

Typeset by Carnegie Book Production, Lancaster
Printed and bound by CPI Group (UK) Ltd, Croydon CR0 4YY

Contents

Contents

Illustrations

Contributors

Caroline Bressey is Reader in Cultural and Historical Geography in the Department of Geography at University College London, where she founded the Equiano Centre, which ran from 2007 to 2017 to support research into the Black Presence in Britain. In 2009 she was awarded a Philip Leverhulme Prize. She is the author of *Empire, Race and the Politics of Anti-Caste* (Bloomsbury Academic, 2013), which won the 2014 Women's History Network Book Prize and the 2015 Colby Scholarly Book Prize.

Michael Bundock is the author of *The Fortunes of Francis Barber: The True Story of the Jamaican Slave Who Became Samuel Johnson's Heir* (Yale University Press, 2015). He is a director of Dr Johnson's House Trust and an Honorary Research Associate in the Department of English Language and Literature at University College London.

Vincent Carretta is Professor Emeritus of English at the University of Maryland and specializes in transatlantic historical and literary studies during the long eighteenth century. In addition to more than 100 articles and reviews on a range of eighteenth-century subjects, he has published two books on verbal and visual Anglophone political satire between 1660 and 1820 as well as authoritative editions of the works of Olaudah Equiano, Quobna Ottobah Cugoano, Philip Quaque, Ignatius Sancho and other eighteenth-century transatlantic authors of African descent. He recently edited *The Writings of Phillis Wheatley* (Oxford University Press, 2019).

Contributors

Kathleen Chater is an independent scholar. Her doctoral thesis was published as *Untold Histories: Black People in England and Wales During the Period of the British Slave Trade, c. 1660–1812* (Manchester University Press, 2009) and she has contributed entries about black Britons to the *Oxford Dictionary of National Biography*. She has also written numerous books and articles on aspects of genealogical research and history generally. Her latest work is *Henry Box Brown: From Slavery to Show Business* (McFarland, 2020), a biography of the American fugitive slave turned magician.

Ashley L. Cohen is Assistant Professor of English at the University of Southern California. She is the editor of *Lady Nugent's East India Journal, A Critical Edition* (Oxford University Press, 2014). Her articles and book chapters include 'Fencing and the Market in Aristocratic Masculinity', in *Sporting Cultures, 1650–1850* (University of Toronto Press, 2018), 'The Global Indies: Historicizing Oceanic Metageographies', in *Comparative Literature* (Winner of the Inaugural Srinivas Aravamudan Prize, 2017), and 'The "Aristocratic Imperialists" of Late Georgian and Regency Britain', in *Eighteenth-Century Studies* (2016). Her first monograph, *The Global Indies: British Imperial Culture, 1756–1815*, Yale University Press, is forthcoming Fall 2020.

Raymond Costello is a former Adviser for Racial Equality for Liverpool Education Authority Schools Inspection Department. He is an Honorary Research Fellow of the University of Liverpool School of Sociology, a Historical Associate for Merseyside Maritime Museum, National Museums Liverpool (NML) and a board member of the Centre for the Study of International Slavery (CSIS). He has been involved with many radio and television programmes and has a number of publications. His latest book is *Black Tommies: Soldiers of African descent in the First World War* (Liverpool University Press, 2015). He received an award from the Executive Professional Network Northern Chapter in 2002 and the Merseyside Black Police Association Community Award in 2008.

Madge Dresser, FRHS, RSA, retired as Associate Professor of History at the University of the West of England in 2016 and was subsequently appointed as Honorary Professor of Historical Studies at the University of Bristol. She has published widely in both the academic and public sphere on slavery and its memorialization and on the history of ethnic minorities and women in Britain. Her publications include *Black and White on the Buses* (Turnaround, 1986), *Slavery Obscured: The Social History of the Slave Trade in Bristol* (Continuum, 2001), *Bristol: Ethnic Minorities and the City, 1000–2000* (with Peter Fleming) (Phillimore, 2007) and *Slavery and the British Country House* (edited with A. Hann) (English Heritage, 2013). She has appeared in numerous broadcast documentaries in Britain and abroad, has acted as historical consultant for museums and is a trustee of several historical and social justice charities.

Christine Eickelmann is Research Associate at University of Bristol. She has completed the first known longitudinal study of an entire plantation population in the British Caribbean: *The Mountravers Plantation Community, 1734 to 1834* (available online). She co-authored *Pero, The Life of a Slave in Eighteenth-Century Bristol* (Redcliffe Press, 2004), wrote the biographies of Pero Jones and Frances (Fanny) Coker for the *Oxford Dictionary of National Biography*, and worked with Bristol Museum in interpreting their Georgian House Museum. She is currently researching the free black and coloured population of Nevis in the West Indies.

Charles R. Foy is Associate Professor, Emeritus, Early American & Atlantic History at Eastern Illinois University. Dr Foy has published more than a dozen articles on black mariners and is the creator of the Black Mariner Database, a dataset of more than 33,000 eighteenth-century black Atlantic mariners. He is completing a book manuscript, *Liberty's Labyrinth: Freedom in the 18th Century Black Atlantic*, that details the nature of freedom in the eighteenth century through an analysis of the lives of black mariners.

Gretchen H. Gerzina is the Paul Murray Kendall Professor in Biography and Professor of English at the University of Massachusetts Amherst. She is the author of *Black England: Life Before Emancipation* (John Murray, 1999) and *Mr and Mrs Prince: How an Extraordinary Eighteenth-Century Family Moved out of Slavery and into Legend* (Amistad, 2008), as well as biographies of Dora Carrington and Frances Hodgson Burnett. She is the editor of *Black Victorians/Black Victoriana*, and of three editions of *The Secret Garden*. She is currently completing a memoir about growing up biracial in the 1950s and 1960s in New England.

Raphael Hoermann holds a PhD in Comparative Literature from the University of Glasgow. He is Senior Research Fellow at the Institute for Black Atlantic Research (IBAR) and Lecturer in English Literature at the University of Central Lancashire. He has published on the genealogy of the Black Jacobin trope and the figure of the zombie and the Haitian Revolution. Currently he is completing a book manuscript on Transatlantic Gothic Narratives of the Haitian Revolution.

Paterson Joseph is a London-based actor and playwright. He has performed for most major theatre companies in the UK, including the National Theatre and the Royal Shakespeare Company. His work on screen includes *Timeless*, *The Leftovers*, *Peep Show* and the upcoming *Noughts & Crosses* for the BBC. He is the author of *Julius Caesar & Me—Exploring Shakespeare's African Play* (Methuen Drama, 2018), as well as performer and writer of *Sancho—An Act of Remembrance*.

Simon P. Newman is Sir Denis Brogan Professor of History at the University of Glasgow. He is the author of *A New World of Labor: The Development of Plantation Slavery in the British Atlantic* (University of Pennsylvania Press, 2013), which was awarded the British Association for American Studies Book Prize. He is director of the Runaway Slaves in Britain project (https://www.runaways.gla.ac.uk/).

Stephen Mullen completed a PhD at the University of Glasgow in 2014. He has published several articles on eighteenth-century Scotland and the Atlantic world. His monograph *The Glasgow Sugar Aristocracy in the British Atlantic World, 1775–1838* will be published in 2020 by the Royal Historical Society/Institute of Historical Research. He was awarded the University of Glasgow's Engaged Early Career Researcher of the Year prize (2016).

Nelson Mundell is a Leverhulme Trust-funded PhD candidate at the University of Glasgow and a member of the Runaway Slaves in Britain project, and he is completing his thesis on 'The runaway enslaved in eighteenth-century Britain'. The creator of a virtual plantation learning environment for school students, he is also co-creator of the project-based graphic novel *Freedom Bound* (BHP Comics, 2018).

Michael I. Ohajuru is a Senior Fellow of the Institute of Commonwealth Studies with honours degrees in Physics (Leeds, 1974) and Art History (Open University, 2008). He is Project Director and Chief Evangelist of *The John Blanke Project,* a contemporary art and archive project celebrating John Blanke, the black trumpeter to the courts of Henry VII and Henry VIII, and founder of *Image of the Black in London Galleries*, a series of gallery tours highlighting the overt and covert black presences to be found in the national art collections in London. He is also the co-convener of the Institute of Commonwealth Studies *What's Happening in Black British History* series of workshops fostering a creative dialogue between researchers, educationalists (mainstream and supplementary), archivists and curators, and policy-makers. He regularly writes and speaks on the black African presence in Renaissance Europe.

Anne Rainsbury is Curator of Chepstow Museum in Wales. She has been immersed in all aspects of its rich local history, uncovering its hidden histories and committed to keeping its stories 'alive' and relevant to the community, literally in the streets, and with events outside, as well as inside the museum. A major exhibition on Piercefield and Nathaniel Wells prompted extensive personal research, including on St Kitts. While still uncovering more details to add to Nathaniel and his family's story, her recent wider remit as Curator of Monmouthshire Museums is also bringing new West Indies links into focus. She is the author of *Chepstow & The River Wye* (The History Press, revised 2009); 'From Son of a Slave to a Proprietor of Piercefield' (*Heritage in Wales*, Cadw, Welsh Government, Spring 2007); and other articles.

Contributors

Alan Rice is Professor in English and American Studies at the University of Central Lancashire, Preston, and co-director of the Institute for Black Atlantic Research (IBAR). He has published *Radical Narratives of the Black Atlantic* (Continuum, 2003) and *Creating Memorials, Building Identities: The Politics of Memory in the Black Atlantic* (Liverpool University Press, 2010). He was co-curator of the Whitworth Art Gallery Manchester's 2007–8 exhibition *Trade and Empire: Remembering Slavery*. With Celeste Marie Bernier, Hannah Durkin and Lubaina Himid he has completed the first academic monograph on the Turner Prize-winning artist Lubaina Himid: *Inside the Invisible: Slavery and Memory in the Works of Lubaina Himid* (Liverpool University Press, 2019).

Theresa Saxon is based in the School of Humanities and Social Sciences at the University of Central Lancashire, Preston. She is one of the founder members of UCLan's Institute for Black Atlantic Research (IBAR). Her publications are responses to eighteenth- and nineteenth-century transatlantic theatre history, and research for her forthcoming book on Transatlantic Theatre was funded by the US Embassy in London, the British Academy Overseas Conference awards and the Eccles Centre for North American Studies at the British Library.

Sue Thomas is Emeritus Professor of English at La Trobe University, Melbourne, and a Fellow of the Australian Academy of the Humanities. Her books include *Telling West Indian Lives: Life Narrative and the Reform of Plantation Slavery Cultures 1804–1834* (Palgrave Macmillan, 2014), *Imperialism, Reform and the Making of Englishness in 'Jane Eyre'* (Palgrave Macmillan, 2008), *The Worlding of Jean Rhys* (Greenwood Press, 1999), and *England through Colonial Eyes in Twentieth-Century Fiction* (Palgrave, 2001), co-authored with Ann Blake and Leela Gandhi. She has published very extensively on nineteenth- and twentieth-century women writers, decolonizing literatures and nineteenth-century periodicals. Her scholarship on early Anglophone Caribbean life narrative has been funded by the Australian Research Council DP0987125.

Introduction

Gretchen H. Gerzina

The genesis of this book can be traced back to October 2016, when the Radio 4 series 'Britain's Black Past', which I presented, aired on the BBC every weekday for two weeks.[1] Each programme in the ten-part series took us to a different location, where I interviewed one or more experts about black people who had lived or worked there in the eighteenth or early nineteenth centuries. In Glasgow, three researchers talked about the database they were compiling of runaway slaves in Scotland and throughout the United Kingdom. In Liverpool, we walked along the docks and talked about early black sailors and the continuing community of people of colour. In Bristol, we walked through a Georgian house with two researchers who had separately investigated the lives of two very different enslaved people, a man and a woman, who had lived there. In a very windy Morecambe Bay, at low tide, we stood by the lonely grave of a boy who had died there, and whose grave has become a shrine. In Wales, we climbed a steep hill to the ruins of a country house once owned by a mixed-race heir and slaveowner. In London, we talked about the writers, activists and communities who had once lived there. It all came together in the studio, as the interviews were woven together, actors read the letters and words, and the music of a black eighteenth-century composer was added. The black past truly came alive again, and to most listeners that past was a revelation.

---

1 'Britain's Black Past', Loftus Productions, Executive Producer Elizabeth Burke. To listen, https://www.bbc.co.uk/programmes/b07yvszg.

Some time—perhaps a year or so—after the series aired, it occurred to me that it had brought together the recent work of so many who were able to shed new light on people and events from that past, including some that students of that period thought they knew, that their work deserved to be brought together in a book. So many of them were working separately to create new knowledge and a book could, as it were, put them in conversation with each other. Most of those I asked readily agreed, and a book also allowed me to include others who did not appear on the programmes, but whose work was exciting and revelatory, and would otherwise be scattered into various journals. This book project also could include those who were working outside academic institutions. Thus this volume features the work not only of historians and other academics but also of independent scholars, an actor and playwright, a lawyer who was also a biographer, and a museum curator. The writers are English, Scottish, German, Australian and American. They share a deep knowledge and respect for those who came before them.

People have, of course, been working on Britain's black past for many decades, and without their painstaking and ground-breaking research, none of what we know, and build upon, would be possible. One of the earliest was Edward Scobie (1918–1996), whose 1972 *Black Britannia: A History of Blacks in Britain* was crucial to an understanding of Britain's black past, and whose magazines *Checkers* (1948), *Tropic* (1960) and *Flamingo* (1961) spoke to Britain's black inhabitants and featured literary writers such as Samuel Selvon and George Lamming. Folarin Shyllon's 1977 book *Black in Britain 1555–1833* covered the years from the arrival of certain Africans to Britain to the abolition of West Indian slavery and apprenticeship. Peter Fryer (1997–2006) expanded these important earlier works to produce the magisterial *Staying Power* in 1985. My own *Black England: Life Before Emancipation* (1999) was indebted to their research, which guided the way to my own. These books are the broad and important shoulders on which so much of what is in the current volume rests. And their research in turn rests on the writings of early black Britons like Olaudah Equiano and Ignatius Sancho, whose work remains in, or has returned to, print today.

But what is fascinating is that the work continues, and new discoveries and interpretations continue to be made. As these chapters show, there was much we did not know about the men and women who lived back then, but thought we knew. As this research continues, new books continue to appear. In the past few years alone, new books by David Olusoga, Hakim Adi, Miranda Kaufmann and Ryan Hanley have been published on the subject, revealing Black Tudors, African women in Britain and others. New biographies of Samuel Johnson's servant and protégé, Francis Barber, and Olaudah Equino have appeared. This is not a stagnant area of research; in these hands, the past continues to expand. Nor is it only to readers that their work is aimed. Television and radio, art exhibitions, blogs and websites: all are keeping this past alive and bringing to wider audiences this growing sense that black people have been in Britain for far longer than they knew, and that this is not just a black past but a shared one.

The chapters in this book either build on this earlier knowledge, adding new discoveries and interpretations, or consist of new findings altogether. In its pages you will learn more about Mary Prince, whose narrative became an important abolitionist text; Sue Thomas is able to incorporate new findings and consolidate interpretations of Prince's life and narrative. Ashley Cohen lays out her astonishing discoveries about Julius Soubise, the one-time protégé of Ignatius Sancho, the London shopkeeper, letter writer and composer, and Soubise's previously unknown life in India. Actor Paterson Joseph recreates Sancho himself into a modern play, and recounts its genesis. Theresa Saxon too writes about a black actor, putting Ira Aldridge into a wider political context. Raphael Hoermann analyses the political speech of Robert Wedderburn, the firebrand activist. We move from the Tudors (Michael Ohajuru on the John Blanke Project), to television (Gretchen H. Gerzina on Dido Elizabeth Belle), to black heirs (Michael Bundock, the biographer of Francis Barber, and Anne Rainsford on Nathaniel Wells). As Madge Dresser and Christine Eickelmann show, the Bristol household of John and Jane Pinney held two enslaved people, Fanny Coker and Pero, whose lives were completely different yet lived under the same roof. The movement of black people appears in the chapters by Charles Foy (sailors) and Stephen Mullen, Nelson Mundell and Simon P. Newman (runaway slaves), and the importance of place is discussed by Ray Costello (Liverpool) and Alan Rice (Lancaster). Vincent Carretta discusses the backlash against his findings on Olaudah Equiano, and Caroline Bressey looks ahead to the nineteenth century. Finally, Kathleen Chater talks about research and researchers themselves, and the ways that scholars and genealogists work in different spheres, for different, and sometimes personal, reasons.

Increasingly, because current events show themselves to have parallels to those of the eighteenth and early nineteenth centuries, there is an urgency to keeping this past in the public consciousness. Recent events in Britain bear this out. In the few years since the series aired, black and brown British communities remain in the news in appalling ways. The tragic Grenfell Tower fire is the latest chapter in decades of complaints about the ways that black and brown lives seem to be expendable, but two and half centuries ago enslaved black people were tossed overboard in order for the slave ship owners to collect insurance on the loss; in the case of the fire, the council, made up primarily of members from a neighbouring affluent community, chose to have the building clad in an inferior, flammable material in order to save money. Yet, as early as 1980, the London reggae group Aswad pointed out the deaf ears of councils in their song 'African Children':

> The whole of the nation
> Living in these tenements,
> Crying and applying to their council
> For assistance every day
> Now that their tribulation so sad
> Now that their environment so bad
> High rise concrete
> No back yard for their children to play...

Many know of the arrival of Jamaican workers on the *Empire Windrush* in 1948, but they and their families and descendants did not anticipate the recent debacle surrounding the Windrush generation. Encouraged to relocate to Britain after the Second World War to work in factories and help rebuild the ravaged country, these British citizens from Jamaica and elsewhere in the Caribbean now find themselves classified as illegal immigrants by the very government that destroyed the papers proving their right to remain. Despite promises by the Home Office to fix the problem and offer financial restitution, not only has little changed but a number of those wrongly deported—often to countries that they left as small children and in which they know no one—have died in the resulting exile caused by the deliberate creation of a 'hostile environment'. Similarly, during the American War of Independence, the slaves of American patriots were encouraged by the British to work on the loyalist side, and promised freedom and a pension. When the war ended, many of them ended up destitute on the streets of London and other English cities, sparking the formation of the Committee for the Relief of the Black Poor and eventually a plan to ship as many of them as possible to Sierra Leone, where many of them perished. And, on a more romantic note, the marriage of Megan Markle to Prince Harry came only a few years after the release of the major motion picture *Belle*, a period drama that showed (and exaggerated) the life of Dido Elizabeth Belle, the mixed-race great niece of Lord Mansfield, raised in elegance in London and recently dubbed England's first black aristocrat.

When I wrote *Black England* many years ago, I imagined a readership that included both white Britons for whom this would be an important contribution to the notion of Britishness, and black British, either with a long history in Britain itself, or educated in a British system in the Caribbean. It wasn't until a student of mine, whose parents had moved from Nigeria to London before she was born, pointed out that this was also an unknown history for people like her that I realized that there was a much broader audience. This book, therefore, is aimed at multiple audiences: certainly both those descended from black ancestors who arrived centuries ago and those who are more recent arrivals, but also, importantly, all those who believe that black people arrived in Britain only after World War II. Erasing that essential British history has served to silence the voices of those who fought, argued, served, wrote and helped to create modern Britain. It is crucial to understanding both race today and Britishness. As genealogists are now showing, this past may not be embedded just in British history, but in British bodies. Not knowing the past, or denying it, has very real and dangerous consequences. This book, and the ongoing work of its contributors, is a recognition that knowing the past is one important way of shaping the future.

A word on nomenclature. The authors whose work appears here come from a variety of personal, scholarly, ethnic and national backgrounds, which is reflected in the language that they use to describe black people. Some of this is contextual; the term 'black' can refer to those from a variety of national origins, while 'African' can refer more specifically to those from the African continent, and 'Afro-British' to those of African background living in Britain. As editor, I have regularized some of these terms, but for the most part I have allowed the authors to self-select the terminology that they believe is most appropriate to the history and arguments that they are representing.

CHAPTER ONE

Before and After the Eighteenth Century: The John Blanke Project

Michael Ohajuru

Introduction

A Black[1] presence in a historical drama based in Tudor England has been claimed to be 'inaccurate and inauthentic' by Tim Bevan, producer of *Elizabeth* (1998).[2] This statement is historically incorrect and imaginatively impotent, lacking the intellectual curiosity to ask questions such as: What if there had been a Black presence at the Tudor court? How did it get there? What would have been the consequences?

The John Blanke Project[3] seeks to challenge such failures of the imagination. The Project commissions historians and artists to tell a real and unmistakably inclusive Tudor history and to show how history and imagination can work together by making connections between Black British history, then and now.

---

1 The following convention is used throughout the chapter: where Black has an upper-case B this refers to the people of the African diaspora; with a lower-case b it is simply the colour.
2 BBC Radio 4 *Presenting the Past—How the Media Changes History* (2016). Saturday 9 November 2013, 20:00, https://www.bbc.co.uk/programmes/b01mn4v4 (accessed 28 July 2018).
3 The John Blanke Project, http://www.johnblanke.com (accessed 28 July 2018).

John Blanke, the black trumpeter to the Tudor court, is the first person of African descent for whom we have both an identifiable image and documentation.[4] He makes a number of brief appearances in court records between 1507 and 1512. His fleeting presence in those records invites many questions: Was that his real name? Where did he come from? Whom did he marry? Where did he go after leaving Henry's court? The John Blanke Project asks contributors to address such questions as they imagine the black Tudor trumpeter, inviting them to respond in their chosen media. There are currently nearly eighty contributions to date, including work from historians, visual artists, poets, photographers, rappers, musicians and playwrights. The Project, with its strapline *imagine the black Tudor trumpeter*, encourages imaginative and creative thought about the Black presence—not just in Tudor history but in British history as a whole.

Background to the Project

The inspiration for the Project came from two sources. The first of these was a series of presentations I gave in 2013 with Dr Miranda Kaufmann, a fellow senior research fellow at the Institute of Commonwealth Studies. These presentations were based on a shared interest in the Black presence in fifteenth- and sixteenth-century Europe in general and England in particular. The second was the work of the visual artist Stephen B. Whatley. The presentations Kaufmann and I gave were entitled *Image and Reality: Black Africans in Renaissance England* (IRBARE).[5] I reviewed images of the Black by artists from the period, while Kaufmann presented the results of her doctoral research. Whatley was commissioned in 2000 to create a series of paintings on the history of the Tower of London and The Pool of London, in which he included a small image of John Blanke as a marginal,

---

4 Miranda Kaufmann, ed., 'Blanke, John (fl. 1507–1512), Royal Trumpeter', in *Oxford Dictionary of National Biography*, September 2017, http://www.oxforddnb.com/view/10.1093/ref:odnb/9780198614128.001.0001/odnb-9780198614128-e-107145 (accessed 28 July 2018).
5 Image & Reality: Black Africans in Renaissance England—IRBARE, http://irbare2013.weebly.com/ (accessed 28 July 2018).

supporting figure.[6] The black trumpeter can be found in the painting showing Henry VIII jousting before his queen, Katherine of Aragon, one of the series of thirty paintings Whatley produced to complete the commission. Together, IRBARE and Whatley's image were the stimulus for the John Blanke Project.

In IRBARE, Kaufmann introduced the audience to the lives of some of the 360-plus sub-Saharan African men, women and children she had found living in England and Scotland in the period.[7] Her evidence came from parish registers, church accounts, tax returns, household accounts, wills, diaries, letters and other documents. She found them living all over the UK, from Aberdeen to Truro. The references were most times quite fleeting, some might say buried, lost among so many other written records. For example, in the burial records of St Martin in the Fields for the year 1571 most deaths are recorded as single line. In September that year eight deaths are recorded, seven with just the name of the deceased. The entry for the burial on the 27th of that month includes not just the name 'Margureta', however, but also the note '... A Moore', from which Kaufmann deduced that Margureta was both a Christian and Black. Dr Kaufmann's evidence for the Black African presence in the Tudor period came almost entirely from equally brief, contemporaneous written records, from which she was able to piece together their lives. She could see what work they did, where and whom they married and generally how they survived and—in some cases—thrived.

John Blanke was the one exception in Dr Kaufmann's proof that there was a Black African presence in the Tudor period, as there was not just his written record in the court accounts of Henry VII and Henry VIII but also his image—he is pictured twice in the *Great Tournament Roll of Westminster*[8]—making him the exception.

6 *Henry VIII Jousting Before Queen Katharine of Aragon at the Westminster Tournament 1511*, by Stephen B. Whatley, 2000, oil on canvas, 102 × 152cm, Collection of HM Tower of London, http://www.stephenbwhatley.com/7_ henry-viii-jousting-before-queen-katharine-of-aragon-at-the-westminster-tournament-1511–2000-by-stephen-b-whatley (accessed 28 July 2018).

7 Details of Margureta come from Dr Miranda Kaufmann's unpublished doctoral thesis 'Africans in Britain, 1500–1644' (PhD, Oxford, 2011), which she was kind enough to share with me.

8 Workshop of Sir Thomas Wriothesley (d. 1534), *Westminster Tournament*

While Kaufmann had just two images of a known black African from the period to discuss, I had many hundreds, as the black magus or king in the biblical Adoration image was an established figure in European religious art, which dated back to the thirteenth century.[9] The black figure, as part of the Adoration scene, was to be found throughout Europe during the period, including England. The image of the black king would have been well known and understood at that time,[10] despite the fact that no African king visited Europe during the period.[11] The figure of the black king, along with much of the Adoration scene itself, was a conflation, interpretation and presentation of biblical study, courtly practice and artistic tradition. In reality, he never actually existed. I discussed the image of the Black King seen in Adoration pictures, what it meant religiously and socially and what it signified. His presence followed several established conventions: his position, his clothing, his stance and his gold earring[12] all acting as signifiers of 'the other' or 'not one of us'. In the process, a composition was created of one king and two kings—one black and two white—rather than three kings.[13] It can be argued that this difference was perhaps how one of the definitions of Whiteness, as a differentiator from Black, crystallized in Renaissance Europe at a time when black Africans were considered culturally to be barbarians and legally slaves.[14]

IRBARE made problematic contrasts between the image and reality of black Africans. On the one hand, we have the actual lived reality of black Africans as common, ordinary people—making a living in society

Roll, painted vellum, 1511, College of Arms, London; repro. in Sydney Anglo, ed., *The Great Tournament Roll of Westminster* (Oxford: Clarendon Press, 1968), vol. 2, plate 3, membranes 3–5; plate 18, membranes 28–9.

9 David Bindman and Henry Louis Gates Jr, eds, *The Image of the Black in Western Art, Volume II: From the Early Christian Era to the 'Age of Discovery', Part 2: Africans in the Christian Ordinance of the World* (Cambridge, MA: Harvard University Press, 2010), p. 52.

10 Paul H.D. Kaplan, *The Rise of the Black Magus in Western Art* (Ann Arbor: UMI Research Press, 1985), p. 21.

11 Thomas Foster Earle and Kate J.P. Lowe, eds, *Black Africans in Renaissance Europe* (Cambridge: Cambridge University Press, 2005), p. 23.

12 Richard C. Trexler, *The Journey of the Magi: Meanings in History of a Christian Story* (Princeton: Princeton University Press, 1997), p. 102.

13 Trexler, p. 102.

14 Earle and Lowe, p. 47.

1.1 Stephen B. Whatley, 'Tribute to John Blanke' (2015), charcoal on paper, A4.

as discovered from the archives. On the other, we see the fabricated image of the black African as part of an elite—a king depicted in one of the key images of the Christian Gospel, in which earthly kings pays homage to Jesus, the king of both Heaven and Earth. That image was to be found in churches throughout Europe. The contrast was emphasized by Kaufmann's two images of a real black African on the *Great Tournament Roll of Westminster* from the period—John Blanke—and the many hundreds of images of the black king I had to call upon, even though he never actually existed, underline the disparity between image and the reality of black Africans at that time.

Through my work with IRBARE I became aware of Stephen B. Whatley's monumental work on permanent display at Tower Hill tube station, where his paintings centred on the life and times of Henry VIII had been reproduced in a series of panels lining the walls of the underpass from the tube station to the Tower of London. Stephen took as his sources original historic documents, including the *Great Tournament Roll of Westminster* from the College of Arms. He took that document's central scene, Henry VIII jousting before his queen and the ladies of the court, completing one of the highest scoring 'tilts'. Surviving score cards[15] from the joust reveal that, although the king was quite successful, that score was never actually achieved. The image is artistic licence, flattering the king.

Whatley produces a stylized, modernist version of the scene in his distinctive and idiosyncratic colour palette of pastel greens, blues, pinks, reds and yellows, which wash into each other in his oil paintings like water colours, creating soft, muted edges between coloured forms in which he recreates the drama and movement of Henry's tilt before his queen. On the edge of Whatley's painting are the trumpeters, including John Blanke. We know it is John, as Whatley differentiates him by his facial colouring and a turban. The black musician was the only one of the troop of six trumpeters to wear any head covering and, as a consequence, his presence as depicted by Whatley is very distinctive.

I have had the opportunity to discuss with Whatley his depiction of John Blanke and, to my surprise, he was not looking to make any statements on the Black presence in Tudor times. He simply wanted to make

15 Anglo, 1968, p. xx.

an interesting composition based on the Tournament Roll. John Blanke's ethnicity did not preoccupy him at all in the way that it preoccupied me. I liked Whatley's work so much that I commissioned him to produce an A5 drawing of John Blanke from his Tower of London work, although he generously produced an A4 piece (Figure 1.1). It is a modernist drawing in which Whatley has captured the sound and movement of John Blanke from the *Great Tournament Roll of Westminster* as a black-and-white image. Whatley's work made me reflect on IRBARE, where Dr Kaufmann had just those two images of John Blanke in that one document the *Great Tournament Roll of Westminster*, now believed to be the only portrayal of a known black African in Britain in the period. This contrasted with the many hundreds, perhaps thousands, of images of the black king I have seen, despite the fact that John Blanke was real and the black king a fabricated conflation. It occurred to me that I might commission other artists to produce their imagined versions of John Blanke, based on his image and record from the archives, with a view to holding an exhibition of the produced images along with the original image from the *Tournament Roll*. Thus began The John Blanke Project.

History of the John Blanke Image

John Blanke's image lay ignored and forgotten in the archives from the courts of Henry VII and Henry VIII for almost half a millennium, and it took the detailed, persistent work of a dedicated academic and community historians to bring it to life. It was not until the mid-1950s that John Blanke was first revived by the diligent, systematic work of Dr Sydney Anglo, who, at the time, was doing post-doctoral research on early Tudor court festivals. At the then Public Record Office, working through the account books of John Heron, Treasurer of the Chamber, Anglo examined records covering the reigns of Henry VII and Henry VIII. There, under 7 December 1507, was the record that John Blanke was paid eight pennies (viijd) a day, twenty shillings (xxs) for the month. This was the first of several payments to John Blanke, 'the blacke trumpet': 'Item to John Blanke, the blacke trumpet for his month wages of Novembre last passed at viijd the day … xxs.'[16]

16 National Archive Exchequer E 36/214, f.109, 'The King's Book of Payments': John Blanke's wages, 7 December 1507.

At the same time, Anglo was studying manuscripts at the College of Arms, one of which was the *Great Tournament Roll of Westminster*, where he found two representations of a 'blacke trumpet' at the centre-rear of a troop of six trumpeters on horseback in two rows of three. He made the connection between 'the blacke trumpet' in the two documents—John Blanke in John Heron's accounts was the black trumpeter in the Tournament Roll. Anglo reintroduced John Blanke to the modern world within a footnote to this analysis of John Heron's accounts:

> I believe this John Blank [*sic*] was, in fact, a Negro in the Great Roll of the Tournament at Westminster in February 1511, preserved at the College of Arms, a negro musician is twice depicted amongst the king's trumpets. This I think was John Blank [*sic*], the 'blacke trumpet'.[17]

John Blanke might have remained a footnote only known to academics if not for the work of Audrey Dewjee and Ziggi Alexander, who brought the court musician to life for a second time. On this occasion it would be for a wider non-academic and community audience. In early 1980 they went to an exhibition of heraldry at the British Museum in an attempt to discover why so many coats of heraldic arms featured the heads of Africans. The centrepiece of the exhibition was the sixty-foot-long *Great Tournament Roll of Westminster* from the College of Arms. At the time, they were researching for an exhibition for Brent Library Service entitled *Roots in Britain: Black and Asian Citizens from Elizabeth I to Elizabeth II.* Audrey 'stopped dead in [her] tracks [and] could hardly believe [her] eyes'[18] when she saw that one of the six king's trumpeters depicted on the Tournament Roll was a black African.

As this was before digital reproductions could be exchanged by email or social media Audrey and Ziggi had to correspond by post with the College of Arms to ask and pay for the rights to use the image.

---

17 Sydney Anglo, *The Court Festivals of Henry VII: A Study Based on the Account Books of John Heron, Treasurer of the Chamber*, in *Bulletin of the John Rylands Library*, 43: 1, 1960, pp. 12–45.
18 John Blanke Project Historian: Audrey Dewjee, http://www.johnblanke.com/audrey-dewjee.html (accessed 29 July 2018).

Their exhibition *Roots in Britain* travelled the country for several years. In 1984 Peter Fryer wrote about John Blanke in his monumental, seminal book, *Staying Power: The History of Black People in Britain*, having first seen the John Blanke image in 1981 at the touring version of *Roots in Britain*. He acknowledged in his preface to *Staying Power* that he 'learnt much'[19] from their exhibition.

As mentioned earlier, it was Sydney Anglo who first recognized 'the blacke trumpet' in the archives. John Blanke goes on to appear in several other entries, as he is paid wages and takes part in the funeral of Henry VII and the coronation of King Henry VIII and Queen Katherine. He also successfully petitions the king for his wages to be doubled.[20] He appears in the Tournament Roll, leading the opening and closing of the jousting tournament that took place in February 1511 to celebrate the birth of Henry VIII's son on New Year's Day that year. His final mention in the records is in January 1512, when Henry VIII gives instruction for him to be given a gown of violet cloth, and also a bonnet and a hat as wedding presents.

The January 1514 listing of the court trumpeters makes no mention of John Blanke, so we can only assume he must have left the court before that date. His entry in Oxford notes his dates as 'fl. 1507–1512', where fl. stands for *floruit* (Latin for 'he/she flourished'), denoting a date or period during which a person was known to have been alive or active. So, we have some evidence from the court accounts of where and when he was active, as well as some indication of what he looked like from the Tournament Roll.

Those brief accounting entries and his two images, which are little more than caricatures, all raise more questions than answers. Some possible answers were to come from the imaginations of the contributors to The John Blanke Project.

---

19 Peter Fryer, *Staying Power: The History of Black People in Britain* (London: Pluto Press, 1984), p. x.
20 'John Blanke, Henry VIII's Black Trumpeter, Petitions for a Back Dated Pay', https://manyheadedmonster.wordpress.com/2015/07/27/john-blanke-henry-viiis-black-trumpeter-petitions-for-a-back-dated-pay-increase-2/ (accessed 30 July 2018).

The Project Overview

That original idea of an exhibition developed into *John Blanke Live!*, a series of individual events—an exhibition, symposia and workshops based on the contributions to the project. The activity was supported by the JohnBlanke.com website and its social media presence.

The contributions are split into two groups: historians and artists. The commissioning statement for the artists called for an A4 portrait-format drawing, following on from Whatley's initial contribution. Over time, however, the concept was expanded to offer commissions to photographers, rappers, musicians, playwrights and poets. None of the artists' works are online, with the exception of the Project's founding contribution, Whatley's *Tribute to John Blanke* (Figure 1.1). Instead, artists, in addition to their commissioned piece, are asked to make a statement beginning 'I imagined John Blanke as ...'. That statement, along with an image of the artist, is put on the Project's website. Ultimately these statements will form the basis of the Project's exhibition catalogue.

The historians are commissioned to write a thought piece of up to 300 words on some aspect, consequence or interpretation of John Blanke's life or presence that interests or intrigues them. Their complete contribution is made available on the website.[21] The historians include academic, community and independent historians, as well as writers, curators, teachers and tour guides.

Artists' Contributions

The Project's artists imagined John Blanke in a variety of ways. Many saw him as a musician who is part of the contemporary jazz musician's traditions and heritage: the visual artist Charmaine Watkiss imagined him as disciplined, focused jazz musician, for instance, while Phoebe Boswell went so far as to imagine him as the British jazz saxophonist Shabaka Hutchings and Keith Piper saw him as an 'advance guard' for the jazz trumpeter Miles Davis. Some artists envisaged him as a fellow member of the African diaspora, a relative from another time and place. The poet Roy Merchant imagined him as one of his ancestors,

21 John Blanke Project Artists, http://www.johnblanke.com/artists.html (accessed 28 July 2018).

while the visual artist Ebun Culwin wrote about him as a fellow member of the diaspora and parent. Others, such as vocal performer Randolph Matthews and visual artist Kimathi Donkor, imagined him as a talented, gifted musician with the will and confidence to be chosen by the king to play for him, while others, such as Seema Manchanda, concluded that, as one of the few Blacks at the Tudor court, he would have been lonely from time to time.

The poet John Agard imagines Blanke blowing 'not quite a fanfare for diversity, simply doing [his] bit for pomp and pageantry'. The late creative director and designer Jon Daniel imagined John Blanke as 'trump card' in a deck of cards in which Henry VIII was the king, while the poet Mark Thompson sees the rediscovered musician as a 'graphic crowbar' to prise open the cultural door to a better understanding of Black British history.

Each artist reimagined John Blanke in their own, often idiosyncratic, manner. Individually their works are creative interpretations of John Blanke from his image and his record, while collectively they demonstrate the ingenuity and invention within the artistic imagination. The complete statements of all the artists are to be found on the Project's website.

Historians' Contributions

The first historian I invited to contribute to the Project was Sydney Anglo, who modestly stated that he could not 'claim a great deal of perspicacity' when he first made the connection between the documents from the Public Record Office and the College of Arms archives during his post-doctoral research. I went on to commission other historians, encouraging them to see their contribution as acting as another—more detailed—layer to the responses of the artists. Their contribution was to be related to any part of John Blanke's history or elements of the Project that captured their imagination as an historian, based on some aspect of their knowledge, experience and expectations. Many of the historians focused on how tantalizing a brief historical record can be. Miranda Kaufmann was frustrated by John Blanke's imperfect record, which raised more questions than answers. Similarly, Temi Odumosu questioned how we can honour an entire life when there is so much we do not know. Hakim Adi saw that questioning was not a bad thing, but rather a chance to look for evidence that might challenge accepted wisdom. To that end, he saw John Blanke as an 'agent of change'.

The curator Jill Marsh pointed out how portraiture was new at the time and only for high-status individuals. For the common man to have a recognizable portrait was truly exceptional. Onyeka cautioned celebrating John Blanke's stardom, as making the trumpeter exceptional made his existence strange and marginalized him. This exceptionalism helps to maintain our prejudices.

The writer and historian Robin Walker questioned the value of that exceptionalism, arguing that for Black Africans to make history they must shape the world around them in African images and interests. Did John Blanke make those changes? The writer S.I. Martin considers how John Blanke changes us, seeing him as a mystery—a blank slate on which we project our duelling notions of Blackness and Britishness.

Change was a theme in several other contributions from historians. For educator Martin Spafford it was a change in attitudes to race, while teacher Dan Lyndon saw a change in how he taught history. The rapper and historian Phil Day argued that Blanke was an example of how migration drives change in history.

All the historians' statements are to be found in full on the Project's website. The variety of responses from the historians served to demonstrate the impact that John Blanke has on historical interpretation and imagination, which complemented the contributions of the artists to the Project.

John Blanke Live!

The *John Blanke Live!* Project extended the idea of the exhibition, adding John Blanke symposia and workshops with the strapline 'Art, Archive, Action'.[22] The sheer number of contributions and the size of the potential audience meant that initial ideas for a modest exhibition space have been abandoned.

The exhibition is now envisaged as an installation based on Modern Art Oxford's 2009 *Polaroids: Mapplethorpe*,[23] in which all the works

---

22 John Blanke Project Live! http://www.johnblanke.com/jbp-live.html (accessed 28 July 2018).
23 Modern Art Oxford (2009) *Polaroids: Mapplethorpe*, https://www.modern

were black-and-white and the same size, and were hung in one continuous line around the gallery space at eye level. All the Project's visual works are A4-size black-and-white drawings or photographs, while the poems will be printed at A4 and framed like the visual works, all in black A3 frames.

Together, the poems and drawings will be hung linearly, like Mapplethorpe's Polaroids. The 1,828cm-long/37.5cm-wide *Great Tournament Roll of Westminster*—original or copy—will be fully rolled out and will hang above the drawings, creating a dramatic contrast between its vivid colours and the black-and-white of the drawings and poems.

The search for a suitable exhibition space has begun. The goal is to find a space with the history, capability and willingness to hold the exhibition—*John Blanke: Imagine the Black Tudor Trumpeter*. Meanwhile, a workshop and symposia programme has been developed to bring the Project to its potential audiences and move it from the virtual space of its webpage and social media into a real-life setting.

Workshops

The workshops consist of two parts: the first a presentation on who John Blanke was and what he did, ending with an introduction to the Project; the second part an invitation for the audience to imagine their John Blanke in an A4 pencil or charcoal drawing workshop. To date there have been workshops for secondary and primary school pupils, for senior citizens and in a prison. The workshops have subsequently been developed to include one of the artists from the Project delivering a drawing class to assist the participants create their interpretation of John Blanke. Plans are in place to offer writing and music sessions led by contributors to the project as alternatives to a drawing session. The writing workshop will develop the 'storyseed' concept first described by Fiona Collins in *Tales, Tellers and Texts*:

Storyseed: It is the germ of a story from the past, present or future, a story which might end as fact, fantasy or fiction, a story

artoxford.org.uk/event/exhibition-59/ (accessed 28 July 2018).

about a place or a person you know, or you do not know or think you might know.[24]

The storyseed is used by the attendees to create their story in the Project's workshops. John Blanke would be used as the seed for their story, to be shared with the group at the end of the session. The output from each workshop is to be made into a book that will be on display at the same time as the exhibition.

Symposia

John Blanke Live! Symposia are open mic sessions in which approximately fifteen of the John Blanke Project contributors (a mix of historians, musicians, photographers, writers, poets, artists and rappers) share their interpretation of John Blanke. The artists develop and expand upon their 'I imagined John Blanke as ...' statements, while the historians present their view of John Blanke. To date there have been three Symposia: at the British Library, the College of Arms, and the National Trust property Sutton House. The latter two symposia were opened and closed by trumpet fanfares from Corporal Lawrence Narhkom, a black trumpeter in the British army currently in the band of the Grenadiers, whose presence reflects the continuity of the tradition of the black trumpeter over 500 years in the British army. Each of the symposia sold out and attracted much praise. More are planned for the future.

Imagination and The John Blanke Project

As mentioned earlier, the strapline for the Project is *imagine the black Tudor trumpeter*. Imagination is the fundamental concept to the Project, as it was a failure of the imagination that saw it as 'inaccurate and inauthentic' to portray a Black presence at the Tudor court. The inability to embark on any thought experiments or journeys that were described at the start of this paper has consequences. It leads to a mind closed to new ideas—in this instance, the reality of a Black presence in the Tudor court—when they do not fit with an established world

---

24 Gabrielle Cliff Hodges, Mary Jane Drummond and Morag Styles, *Tales, Tellers and Texts* (London: Cassell Education, 1999), pp. 49–56.

view. Such failures of the imagination have national implications, as university humanities departments are closed or restructured—not just in the UK but around the world. The departments favoured—principally Science, Technology, Engineering and Mathematics (STEM)—are perceived as more profitable or have been prioritized as the nation has a shortfall of employable expertise in these subjects.

This loss in the UK is also seen in secondary level education, where the report from the Department for Education published in June 2018 suggested that the number of arts subject teachers working in secondary schools in England has plummeted by 9,000 since 2011, a fall of almost a quarter (22 per cent).[25] These humanities losses at secondary school and university levels have a direct impact on the quality and quantity of the UK's creative outcomes, despite the contribution that the humanities (history, art, music, writing and other humanities subjects) make to the UK economy. The latest figures from the Arts Council indicate that the entire arts and culture industry in 2015 produced an estimated '£20 billion contribution to GDP, growing at 10% per year. Furthermore, the Government recoups £5 for every £1 spent on culture funding.'[26]

The philosopher and educationalist Martha Nussbaum, in her book *Not for Profit—Why Democracy Needs The Humanities*, argues that the study of humanities requires a fusion of 'searching critical thought, daring imagination, empathetic understanding of human experiences of many different kinds, and understanding of the complexity of the world we live in'.[27] Nussbaum's view can be developed into a representative model for the production of humanities-related creative outcomes such as films, books, plays or works of art. Those outcomes are not produced

---

25 National Statistics, *School Workforce in England: November 2017*, https://www.gov.uk/government/statistics/school-workforce-in-england-november-2017 (accessed 29 July 2018).

26 *Contribution of the Arts and Culture Industry to the National Economy: An Update of Our Analysis of the Macroeconomic Contribution of the Arts and Culture Industry to the National Economy*, report for Arts Council England July 2015, https://www.artscouncil.org.uk/sites/default/files/download-file/Contribution_of_the_arts_and_culture_industry_to_the_national_economy.pdf (accessed 30 July 2018).

27 Martha Nussbaum, *Not for Profit—Why Democracy Needs The Humanities* (Princeton: Princeton University Press, 2010), p. 7.

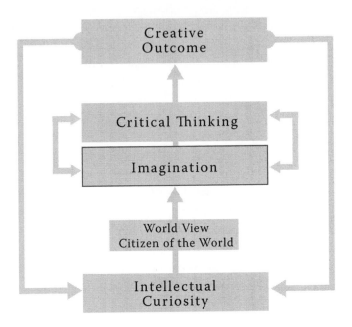

1.2 Creative Outcomes.

in isolation. Their source is a thought process that begins with intellectual curiosity, Socratic questioning based on a world view.

For The John Blanke Project, for example, those questions were asked at the beginning: Was that his real name? Where did he come from? Whom did he marry? Where did he go after leaving Henry's court? Such questions come from our knowledge of humanities—history, language, culture, religion and consideration of the sheer complexity of the world—rather than a constrained parochial or nationalist view. It is the view of a citizen of the world.

Once those questions have been raised, they must be interrogated in a feedback loop between critical thinking and the imagination (Figure 1.2), within which the critical thinking faculties continually challenge the output of the imagination for acceptability or viability—a potent, fruitful interaction. Eventually, an acceptable creative outcome is finally produced. Critical thinking can be considered as the check on or balance of the imagination, applying appropriate restraints where considered necessary. Having produced the creative outcome, intellectual curiosity can come back into play and the process continues, once again driven by Socratic questioning.

The naming of the Project's social media accounts—*WhoIsJohn-Blanke*[28]—is based on the Socratic questioning discussed earlier, which was initiated by the intellectual curiosity described above in the creative outcome model. Rather than dismiss the idea of the black Tudor John Blanke as 'inaccurate and inauthentic', his existence is imaginatively challenged. Possible answers to the question are to be found in that feedback loop between critical thinking and the imagination fed by ideas from one's world view and, in this case, one's knowledge of Spanish, English and Tudor histories. The search for an answer to the over-arching question 'Who is John Blanke?' could begin by asking more specific questions, such as: How could a black trumpeter appear in England in the Tudor court? How and where did he learn to play the trumpet? What evidence is there that he was well accepted at the Tudor court?

The analysis might go as follows: we know that there were black people in late fifteenth-century Spain, as 7.5 per cent of the population of Seville was reported to have been sub-Saharan African;[29] in 1475 King Ferdinand and Queen Isabell appointed a steward to look after their affairs;[30] and Henry VII's Treasurer of the Chamber paid a reward of £4 to '9 trumpets of Spain' shortly after Katherine of Aragon's arrival in England to marry his son.[31] We also know that 'African trumpeters [were] a very visible presence in many countries during the Renaissance',[32] evidenced, for example, by the troop of young black African musicians pictured in *The Engagement of St Ursula and Prince Etherius*, the altar piece of St Auta in Lisbon.[33] Thus, it is highly probable that John Blanke the black trumpeter came from Spain. From this basis

28 Twitter: WhoIsJohnBlanke, https://twitter.com/WhoIsJohnBlanke (accessed 23 August 2018); Facebook: WhoIsJohnBlanke, https://www.facebook.com/WhoIsJohnBlanke/ (accessed 23 August 2018).
29 David Northrup, *Africa's Discovery of Europe* (Oxford: Oxford University Press, 2014), p. 7.
30 Northrup, p. 7.
31 Miranda Kaufmann, *Black Tudors: The Untold Story* (London: Oneworld, 2017), p. 13.
32 Earle and Lowe, p. 39.
33 Bindman and Gates, p. 221.

John Blanke's character can be developed by creatively addressing the question: Who is John Blanke? This is what the playwright Ade Solanke does in her play *The Court Must Have a Queen*.[34]

Solanke has John Blanke returning to Henry VIII's court after an absence of twenty-five years, having spent time in Spain and travelled in the Caribbean as a member of the Spanish ambassador's entourage. That is clearly Solanke's creative imagination at work, based on the known possibilities for John Blanke and other black African trumpeters. As we have seen, it is quite possible that John Blanke might consider Spain as his home and could have been recruited from there as a trumpeter by the ambassador to be part of his embassy to the Caribbean. Through her imagination, coupled with critical thinking about John Blanke's probable life and times, Solanke makes his presence in her play set in the Tudor court demonstrably not 'inaccurate and inauthentic'.

Conclusion

To conclude, the Project has proven to be a novel and inclusive way of telling a piece of Black British history. The contributions have come from artists and historians from a range of ethnicities, genders and ages. Some of the contributors were academic, others non-academic or independent, including some based in the community. That rich diversity of minds and bodies is a core strength of the Project, enabling it to reach an equally diverse audience. I consider the Project a work in progress and will continue to invite selected contributions until the exhibition, which will mark fulfilment of the Project from the point of view of my own personal resources. Thereafter, I will be putting the works into storage and investigating the possibility of donating the collection to an archive.

The Project has demonstrated that when the archival record is exhausted or brief we need to look to the imagination to take things further, developing the story imaginatively based on the facts, allowing that potent feedback loop (Figure 1.2) between our imagination and critical thinking to take the story on. The creative potential of art,

34 Sam Curtis Lindsay (director), *The Court Must Have A Queen*, by Ade Solanke. Theatre performance, 29 June–2 September 2018, Hampton Court Palace, Great Hall, viewed 19 July 2018.

rap, poetry, music and other artistic media to breathe new life into an ephemeral history such as John Blanke's is reflected in the wide range of creative outputs from the Project. There are many such 'ephemeral histories' in Black British history, before and after the eighteenth century; some of those histories, such as Madge Dresser's Pero Jones or Alan Rice's Sambo, are told in other chapters here. They too have brief, incomplete biographies, which, like John Blanke's, have the ability to inspire historians and artists to reimagine their respective stories and relate them to our experience today, not only telling an authentic and accurate history but completing the circle and making the connections that enable Black British history to become real and relevant for us today.

CHAPTER TWO

The Slave and the Lawyers: Francis Barber, James Boswell and John Hawkins

Michael Bundock

Francis Barber (c.1742–1801) is one of the few black men or women in eighteenth-century Britain for whom a full biography is possible.[1] The sources for his life include the biographies of Samuel Johnson written by two lawyers who knew Johnson well, James Boswell and John Hawkins. Each included a portrait of Barber. They also made reference to him in other writings, published and unpublished, and correspondence between Boswell and Barber survives. These materials provide an insight into contemporary attitudes towards Francis Barber, his wife Elizabeth and their children, but they also exemplify the difficulties involved in the interpretation of such sources.

Barber was born into slavery in Jamaica in about 1742 and brought to England by his owner in 1750. After a period at school in Barton, Yorkshire, he was brought back to London, and in 1752 he became a servant in the household of Samuel Johnson, then at work on his *Dictionary of the English Language*. He was to remain there until Johnson's death in 1784, with the exception of two intervals. In 1756 he left the household, worked for an apothecary for two years and then served at sea for a further two years. He returned to Johnson's service in 1760, but left it again for about three years when Johnson sent him to be educated at Bishop's Stortford Grammar School.

1 Michael Bundock, *The Fortunes of Francis Barber: The True Story of the Jamaican Slave Who Became Samuel Johnson's Heir* (New Haven and London: Yale University Press, 2015).

In 1783 Barber married Elizabeth Ball. She was white, and both that fact and the birth of their mixed-race children excited hostile comment from some in Johnson's circle, while others (particularly Johnson) were supportive. The Barber family continued to form part of Johnson's household. On Johnson's death it was revealed that he had left Barber an annuity of £70 and also made him his residuary legatee: Barber inherited some £1,500. In 1786 the Barbers moved to Lichfield in Staffordshire, where for a time they were able to live comfortably, but the money ran out and Barber opened a small school—he may have been the first black schoolmaster in Britain. He died in some poverty in 1801.

James Boswell first met Francis Barber on 24 May 1763 when he called on Johnson at his home in the Inner Temple. Boswell recalled that he was 'shewn in by Francis Barber his faithful black servant'.[2] In Boswell's journals we glimpse Barber performing the typical tasks of domestic service—answering the door, serving at table, running errands and delivering messages.

Significantly, Barber is not anonymous to Boswell, who refers to him by name.[3] Their relationship was not one of social equals—Boswell was a gentleman and Barber was his friend's servant. But they were nonetheless pleased to meet each other. On 21 March 1772 Boswell met Barber, who had returned to Johnson's service following his three years at school. Boswell recorded that 'Frank and I were pleased to renew our old acquaintance.'[4]

Boswell decided to write Johnson's life at least as early as 1772, and

---

2 Marshall Waingrow, ed., *James Boswell's Life of Johnson: An Edition of the Original Manuscript in Four Volumes*, Vol. I (Edinburgh: Edinburgh University Press; New Haven and London: Yale University Press, 1994), p. 273. For the relationship between Barber and Boswell, see Michael Bundock, '"Pleased to Renew our Old Acquaintance": James Boswell and Francis Barber', *The New Rambler: Journal of the Johnson Society of London* 2015–16, series F, vol. XIX, pp. 53–66.

3 See, for example, Charles Ryskamp and Frederick A. Pottle, eds, *Boswell: The Ominous Years 1774–1776* (London: William Heinemann, 1963), p. 346 and Joseph W. Reed and Frederick A. Pottle, eds, *Boswell, Laird of Auchinleck 1778–1782* (Edinburgh: Edinburgh University Press, 1993), p. 139.

4 William K. Wimsatt and Frederick A. Pottle, eds, *Boswell for the Defence 1769–1774* (London: William Heinemann, 1960), p. 40; see also p. 165.

Barber was an obvious source for material.[5] On 19 May 1778 Boswell recorded that he had tipped Barber two shillings and asked him to save the proof-sheets and manuscripts of Johnson's *Lives of the Poets*, which Barber promised to do.[6] The following January Boswell wrote to Barber, reminding him of his promise.[7] Barber replied, confirming that he had kept what he could and that Johnson would let Boswell have a set of the *Lives*.[8]

On 29 May 1783 Boswell gave Barber five shillings (a generous tip when Barber's weekly wage was seven shillings) and 'bid him drink his master's health, or take good care of him'.[9] A few months later, still concerned about Johnson's health, Boswell wrote to Barber, requesting regular bulletins about 'how he is, who are with him, and in what manner his time is employed'.[10]

When Johnson died, on 13 December 1784, Boswell was in Scotland. Ten days later he wrote to Barber, asking him for information about Johnson's life.[11] On 31 December Barber called on James Boswell's brother, Thomas (often referred to as T.D. Boswell), bringing with him a large number of papers for Boswell. He gave Thomas his account of Johnson's last days, and the same day Thomas sent it to James in a letter.

Late the following year Boswell was back in London. On Thursday 22 December 1785 he recorded that he had met Barber by chance, and that he had promised to search for 'every scrap of his master's

5 Marshall Waingrow, ed., *The Correspondence and Other Papers of James Boswell Relating to the Making of the Life of Johnson*, 2nd edn, corrected and enlarged (Edinburgh and New Haven: Edinburgh University Press and Yale University Press, 2001), p. xlix (this edition is referred to in these notes as 'Waingrow').
6 Charles McC. Weis and Frederick A. Pottle, eds, *Boswell in Extremes 1776–1778* (London: Heinemann, 1971), p. 350.
7 Boswell to Barber, 22 January 1779, noted in Waingrow, p. 12.
8 Barber to Boswell, 19 February 1779, Waingrow, pp. 12–13.
9 Irma S. Lustig and Frederick A. Pottle, eds, *Boswell: The Applause of the Jury 1782–1785* (London: Heinemann, 1981), p. 154; Bundock, *The Fortunes*, p. 63.
10 Boswell to Barber, 30 January 1784, Waingrow, p. 17.
11 Boswell to Barber, 23 December 1784, noted in Waingrow, p. 26.

handwriting and give all to me'.[12] Barber kept his promise, sending Boswell all the letters he had.[13]

In the same letter Barber thanked Boswell for sending him a copy of the second edition of his *Journal of a Tour to the Hebrides*, a handsome gift that would have cost Barber six shillings.[14] It is striking that Barber was a recipient: so far as is known, Boswell distributed only seven presentation copies. One was to be presented to the king, although it is not known whether he ever received it.[15]

On 15 July 1786 Boswell sent to Barber, by then living in Lichfield, a questionnaire about Barber's life and about Johnson.[16] The answers are in Boswell's handwriting, so it seems that Barber returned the letter and Boswell later interviewed Barber face-to-face, writing down his replies.[17] Boswell used much of this material in his *Life of Johnson*, published in 1791.

Boswell's *Life*, however, was not the first major biography of Johnson to appear. Four years earlier, in 1787, John Hawkins published *The Life of Dr Samuel Johnson*. It was effectively the official life, as it appeared as the first volume of Johnson's works, of which Hawkins was the editor.[18] Later the same year the book was published separately in a revised edition, slightly retitled *The Life of Samuel Johnson, LL.D.*

12 Irma S. Lustig and Frederick A. Pottle, eds, *Boswell: The English Experiment 1785–1789* (New York: McGraw-Hill, 1986), pp. 18–19.

13 Barber to Boswell, 7 January 1786, Waingrow, p. 107.

14 Frederick A. Pottle, *The Literary Career of James Boswell, Esq.* (Oxford: Clarendon Press, 1929, rep. 1965), p. 119.

15 Bundock, *The Fortunes*, p. 111.

16 Boswell to Barber, 15 July 1786, Waingrow, pp. 127–31.

17 Waingrow, p. 128, n. 1.

18 John Hawkins, *The Works of Samuel Johnson, LL.D, Together with His Life and Notes on his Lives of the Poets in Eleven Volumes, Vol. I, The Life of Dr Samuel Johnson* (London, 1787). For this work see Bertram H. Davis, *Johnson Before Boswell: A Study of Sir John Hawkins' Life of Samuel Johnson* (New Haven: Yale University Press, 1960) and Martine W. Brownley, ed., *Reconsidering Biography: Contexts, Controversies, and Sir John Hawkins' Life of Johnson* (Lewisburg: Bucknell University Press, 2012). References in these notes to 'Hawkins, *Life*' are to Sir John Hawkins, *The Life of Samuel Johnson LL.D.*, ed. O M Brack Jr (Athens and London: University of Georgia Press, 2009).

Hawkins was well qualified to write such a book, by both his friendship of some forty years with Johnson and his experience as a writer. It is a substantial piece of work, 602 pages in the first edition. But the book was poorly received by the public, in part because it was flawed by lengthy digressions. More significantly, it did not hide Johnson's flaws and some of his friends took exception to what they regarded as an unsympathetic portrait.[19] When Boswell published his own *Life of Samuel Johnson* he lambasted Hawkins's work for its 'dark uncharitable cast' towards Johnson.[20] (He was also indignant that his own role in Johnson's life was minimized.[21])

Hawkins included in his *Life* a brief account of how Barber came to join Johnson as a servant. He then continued:

> Of this negro-servant much has been said, by those who knew little or nothing of him, in justification of that partiality which Johnson shewed for him, and his neglect of his own necessitous relations. The following particulars are all that are worth relating of him: He stayed with Johnson about five years, that is to say, till 1758, and then left him, but at the end of two years returned, and was taken again into his service.

According to Hawkins, Barber was, by nature, not fit to be educated and Johnson had wasted a substantial sum on his schooling:

> His first master had, in great humanity, made him a Christian; and his last, for no assignable reason, nay, rather in despite of nature, and to unfit him for being useful according to his capacity, determined to make him a scholar.
>
> He placed him at a school at Bishop-Stortford, and kept him

19 Bertram H. Davis, *A Proof of Eminence: The Life of Sir John Hawkins* (Bloomington and London: Indiana University Press, 1973), pp. 347–65.

20 James Boswell, *Life of Johnson*, ed. George Birkbeck Hill, rev. L.F. Powell (Oxford: Clarendon Press, 1934–64), Vol. I, p. 28. References in these notes to *Boswell's Life of Johnson* are to this edition.

21 James Boswell to William Temple, 5 March 1789, Chauncey Brewster Tinker, ed., *Letters of James Boswell* (Oxford: Clarendon Press, 1924), Vol. II, p. 361.

there five years; and, as Mrs. Williams was used to say, who would frequently reproach him with his indiscretion in this instance, expended three hundred pounds in an endeavour to have him taught Latin and Greek.[22]

Later in the book, at the point where he is discussing Johnson's will, with its generous provision for Barber, Hawkins renews his attack:

It was hinted to me many years ago, by his master, that [Barber] was a loose fellow;[23] and I learned from others, that, after an absence from his service of some years, he married. In his search of a wife, he picked up one of those creatures with whom, in the disposal of themselves, no contrariety of colour is an obstacle. It is said, that soon after his marriage, he became jealous, and, it may be supposed, that he continued so, till, by presenting him with a daughter of her own colour, his wife put an end to all his doubts on that score.[24]

Hawkins is openly hostile towards both Barber and his wife, Elizabeth. Unpicking the threads of this antipathy is not easy: a number of factors are at work. The first is that there are a number of factual errors in his account of Barber. Although not very significant in themselves, they suggest that Hawkins was not completely familiar with Barber's history and the detail of his relationship with Johnson.[25]

22 Hawkins, *Life*, pp. 197–8.

23 In marked contrast of tone (if not content) to 'loose fellow', Mrs Piozzi recounted that Johnson had told her that Barber had been 'eminent for his success among the girls'; see Hesther Lynch Piozzi, *Anecdotes of the Late Samuel Johnson*, ed. Arthur Sherbo (London: Oxford University Press, 1974), p. 130.

24 Hawkins, *Life*, pp. 356–7, note.

25 Barber was brought to England in 1750, not 1752; he did not go to live with Dr Bathurst on the death of Dr Bathurst's father; he joined Johnson's household in 1752, not 1753; he left the household in 1756, not 1758; he returned after four years, not two; he was at Bishop's Stortford Grammar School for three years, not five; he was not absent from Johnson's service for some years before he married, having returned eighteen months before his marriage.

Then there is Hawkins's attitude towards Elizabeth Barber. Hawkins never dignifies her by using her name: indeed, she is scarcely an individual, but rather a type, 'one of those creatures' for whom a different skin colour is not an obstacle to marriage. His hostility towards interracial marriage in general (not just in this case) is manifest and the vitriolic condemnation of a white woman marrying a black man is reminiscent of Edward Long or, in a later generation, William Cobbett.[26]

Hawkins's attitudes are further complicated by the fact that he believed that Elizabeth Barber had had an adulterous relationship with a white man, who was the father of her first daughter. (In the first edition of his *Life of Dr Samuel Johnson* Hawkins alleged that Francis Barber was not the father of either of Elizabeth's daughters, an allegation he omitted from the revised edition.[27]) It is impossible to know whether there is any basis in fact for this story, though Hawkins was not alone in believing it to be true, and Johnson may have shared his belief.[28]

Another matter that greatly exercised Hawkins was Johnson's provision for the Barbers, both in welcoming the family into his household and in effectively making Francis Barber his heir:

> Johnson, in the excess of indiscriminating benevolence, about a year before his death, took the wife and both the children, into his house, and made them a part of his family; and, by the codicil to his will, made a disposition in his favour, to the amount in value of full fifteen hundred pounds.

In doing so, according to Hawkins, Johnson was guilty of 'ill-directed benevolence' and 'ostentatious bounty'.[29] Hawkins developed these criticisms further in a remarkable postscript to his book.

Shortly after his comments on the will, Hawkins sets out his account of Johnson's last night, which was appalling. Johnson was desperate to live and believed that draining the fluid from his hugely

26 Bundock, *The Fortunes*, pp. 144, 148.
27 Hawkins, *The Life of Dr Samuel Johnson* (1st edn, 1787), p. 586, note.
28 Bundock, *The Fortunes*, pp. 150–1.
29 Hawkins, *Life*, pp. 356–7, note, 362, 366.

swollen limbs might help. In spite of the efforts of Barber and John Desmoulins[30] to restrain him, Johnson seized a lancet and stabbed himself in the legs and scrotum.[31] It was to no avail, and he died the next day, 13 December 1784.

Hawkins names Barber as the source of his information about the matter, writing, 'I interrogated him very strictly concerning it'.[32] It is a revealing sentence. Barber had just lost his master and friend of thirty-two years in shocking circumstances and was deeply distressed. (When he recounted the details to Thomas Boswell, 'the poor man ... cryed bitterly'.[33]) The very next day Hawkins, displaying astonishing insensitivity, subjected Barber to severe cross-examination—and later published the fact that he had done so.

The main part of Hawkins's *Life* closes with the text of Johnson's will and its codicil. There then follows a postscript (seven pages long in the first edition), which is devoted to attacking Barber. The postscript is in part motivated by Hawkins's conviction that servants are hardly ever 'to be preferred to those who are allied to the testator in blood or by affinity'.[34] Hawkins describes at length Johnson's failure to make provision for 'a relation ... Humphrey Heely' and 'a first cousin, Elizabeth Herne, a lunatic'. In fact Heely was hardly a close relation: he had once been married to Johnson's cousin, Elizabeth Ford, but had remarried after her death. Herne was Johnson's first cousin once removed, towards whose maintenance in an asylum he had paid £15 a year. Johnson left £100 in trust for her, but the trustee, a wealthy clergyman who had agreed to provide for Herne, renounced the legacy.[35]

Barber is portrayed as crafty, selfish and ungenerous, refusing to share any of his good fortune with the impoverished Heely. More seriously, Hawkins accuses Barber of dishonestly trying to ensure that the estate did not pay a bill for Herne's care that Johnson had incurred:

---

30 Son of Elizabeth Desmoulins, a former member of Johnson's household.
31 Bundock, *The Fortunes*, pp. 170–1.
32 Hawkins, *Life*, p. 358.
33 T.D. Boswell to James Boswell, 31 December 1784, Beinecke Rare Book and Manuscript Library, Yale University, GEN MSS 89, C 506.
34 Hawkins, *Life*, p. 356, note.
35 For discussion of these legacies, see Bundock, *The Fortunes*, pp. 179–82.

according to Hawkins, Barber 'pretended that he could bring a woman to swear that there was nothing due'.[36]

How is the modern reader to evaluate the unfavourable portrait that Hawkins paints of Barber? It was a perspective shared by Hawkins's daughter, Laetitia-Matilda, for whom 'the immortalised Frank ... could scarcely, I think, less deserve the reflected credit given him.' She was present at one clash between John Hawkins and Barber, so her views cannot be said to be wholly derived from her father.[37] Unless one is simply to dismiss Hawkins's allegations as untrue, then his concerns about Barber's character have to be taken seriously.[38] There is no doubt, however, that Hawkins's attitudes are significantly influenced by the fact that Barber is black. The postscript (and the book) close with the following paragraph:

> The above facts are so connected with the transactions of Dr. Johnson in the latter days of his life, that they are part of his history; and the mention of them may serve as a caveat against ostentatious bounty, *favour to negroes*, and testamentary dispositions *in extremis*.[39]

Hawkins's account of Barber was widely publicized in the newspapers.[40] Boswell saw an opportunity to gain an advantage over his rival biographer and on 29 June 1787 he wrote to Barber:

> Sir John Hawkins having done gross injustice to the character of the great and good Dr. Johnson, and having written so injuriously of you and Mrs. Barber ... I cannot doubt of your inclination to

---

36 Hawkins, *Life*, pp. 365–6, note.

37 Laetitia-Matilda Hawkins, *Memoirs, Anecdotes, Facts, and Opinions* (London: Longman, etc., 1824), Vol. I, p. 153. See also p. 222.

38 Compare Davis, *Johnson before Boswell*, p. 59 with Greg Clingham, 'Hawkins, Biography, and the Law', in Brownley, *Reconsidering Biography*, pp. 137–54 at 143–8.

39 Hawkins, *Life*, p. 366. The italic for '*favour to negroes*' was introduced in the revised edition.

40 Davis, *Johnson Before Boswell*, pp. 15–16.

afford me all the helps you can to state the truth fairly, in the Work which I am now preparing for the press.[41]

Barber was in a position to be able to help Boswell. Hawkins was in possession of Johnson's diaries (to which Barber was entitled) and Boswell wanted them to use in his own work. So he enclosed a draft of a letter to be signed by Barber and sent to each of Johnson's executors, John Hawkins, Joshua Reynolds and William Scott. The letter demanded that all papers or books in Johnson's handwriting be handed over.

Boswell concluded his letter to Barber on a more personal note: 'Be assured that I am ever sincerely concerned for your welfare. I send my compliments to Mrs. Barber and am with much regard, Dear Sir, Your steady friend'[.]

Barber's reply left Boswell in no doubt of his willingness to assist:

I have not had the mortification to fall in with that impious production of Sir John Hawkins relating to the Life of my Dear Master, but assure yourself Dear Sir it will be to me a subject of the greatest happiness to render abortive the unworthy and false proceedings of the above mention'd Gentleman and from hence you may justly infer that fuller exposition of that basest of Mortals in as much as he has reflected not only on me and my consort, but on the unsullyed Character of the best of beings my affectionate and unparallel Master ... .[42]

Barber sent Boswell the authorization, and on 20 July 1787 Hawkins handed over some of the papers.[43] Eight months later, Boswell returned to the subject, requesting that Barber provide another instruction to Hawkins to hand over to Thomas Boswell Johnson's diplomas and any other papers. Boswell concluded: 'I shall be glad to hear particularly how you go on, and I send my compliments to Mrs. Barber.'[44]

41 Boswell to Barber, 29 June 1787, Waingrow, p. 173.
42 Barber to Boswell, 9 July 1787, Waingrow, pp. 176–7.
43 Lustig and Pottle, *The English Experiment*, p. 143.
44 Boswell to Barber, 3 March 1788, Waingrow, p. 211.

Barber replied, thanking Boswell for 'the friendly part which you have took in favour of my poor decease'd Master'.[45] A few days later Boswell wrote to Barber again, enclosing a copy of the funeral sermon Johnson had composed for his wife, Elizabeth.[46] The letter begins, 'Dear Sir'. When Boswell writes to Barber he addresses him as 'Mr. Francis' or 'Good Mr. Francis' or 'Dear Sir'. In contrast, Boswell's letters to his own senior servants address them by first name only or use no salutation at all.[47]

On 2 April 1788 Barber replied, enclosing the demand. He also took the opportunity to ask Boswell for a loan of £10 to assist with medical expenses and rent.[48] It was a substantial sum (almost exactly what he had earned in a year in the Navy), but Boswell promptly replied, enclosing the money. Boswell had also given some thought to ways in which Barber could improve his financial position. He wrote:

> Some of your old Master's friends have thought that your opening a little shop for a few books and stationary wares in Lichfield might be a good thing for you. You may consult, and consider of it. I am, Dear Sir, your sincere friend.[49]

On 16 December 1789 Boswell wrote again to Barber, seeking further information about Johnson.[50] Barber replied a few days later, providing more details and enclosing a copy of the inscription that Johnson had composed to keep with his wife's wedding ring. Boswell used Barber's account of the ring (and reproduced the inscription) in his *Life of Johnson*.[51]

In several letters over the years Barber had expressed concern about both his health and his finances. On 29 September 1790 he wrote to

---

45 Barber to Boswell, 12 March 1788, Waingrow, p. 213.
46 Boswell to Barber, 20 March 1788, Waingrow, pp. 214–16.
47 James J. Caudle and Michael Bundock, *The Runaway and the Apothecary: Francis Barber, Edward Ferrand and the Life of Johnson* (privately printed for The Johnsonians, 2011), p. 26, n. 12.
48 Barber to Boswell, 2 April 1788, Waingrow, p. 215.
49 Boswell to Barber, 11 April 1788, Waingrow, p. 216.
50 Boswell to Barber, 16 December 1789, noted Waingrow, p. 228.
51 Barber to Boswell, 20 December 1789, Waingrow, pp. 228–9 and 229, n. 6; *Boswell's Life of Johnson*, Vol. I, p. 237.

Boswell in despair about his situation: 'I wish I never had come to reside at this Place.' He had more medical bills to pay and had also spent heavily on his children's education, 'as it is my wish, upon my Master's Account, to see them Scholars'. He had other debts too. In the picture he painted he had at first been welcomed in Lichfield by local tradesmen who, doubtless knowing of the legacy, had been eager to extend him credit. But that had all come to an end:

> ... several with whom I dealt, hasteily have sent in their Bills, pressing immediate payment, as if in a manner they would eat me at once, and as my Quarterly payment (as it becomes due) will not be sufficient to discharge the same and to leave me a farthing in Pocket to subsist upon, and having no friend here to assist me, or confide in; beg you will assist me in my distressed situation[.][52]

Barber asked Boswell for another loan, this time of £20, to be repaid at eight guineas plus interest per quarter. He also hoped for assistance in finding work.

Boswell had helped Barber out before, but he now had substantial debts of his own, as well as five growing children to provide for.[53] In his reply he declined to lend him more money, but pointed out that the repayment terms Barber was offering Boswell would in fact be sufficient to satisfy Barber's creditors. There was a note of reproach in his response. The original letter has not survived but Boswell summarized its contents in his register of letters:

> Reminding him that his worthy Master was attacked for the extraordinary liberality of the provision which he left to him. It would be a sad thing if the World should know that even that does not maintain him decently; advising him against leaving Lichfield which his Master recommended as his residence—there he can live much cheaper, and with fewer temptations than in London.[54]

---

52 Barber to Boswell, 29 September 1790, Waingrow, pp. 261–2.
53 Waingrow, p. 264; Marlies K. Danziger and Frank Brady, eds, *Boswell: The Great Biographer 1789–1795* (London: Heinemann, 1989), pp. 108–9.
54 Boswell to Barber, 11 October 1790, summarized in Boswell's register of letters, Waingrow, p. 264.

It is the last known correspondence between Barber and Boswell. Perhaps there were further letters which have not survived, or maybe communication ceased: we do not know.

Boswell's *Life of Johnson* was published in 1791. In it Boswell wrote:

> That [Johnson's] sufferings upon the death of his wife were severe, beyond what are commonly endured, I have no doubt, from the information of many who were then about him, to none of whom I give more credit than to Mr. Francis Barber, his faithful negro servant, who came into his family about a fortnight after the dismal event.[55]

The reader is immediately struck by Boswell's tribute to Barber. He does not merely acknowledge Barber as a source: he goes further in asserting his creditworthiness. At other places in his narrative Boswell again acknowledges Barber as a source for the *Life*.[56]

At the point where Barber joins Johnson's household Boswell adds a biographical note that is clearly based on the answers to his questionnaire. It outlines (accurately) Barber's life, and states that he was in Johnson's service from 1752 until Johnson's death with the exception of two intervals, 'So early and so lasting a connection was there between Dr. Johnson and this humble friend'.[57]

Barber often appears respectfully in the text as 'Mr. Barber', 'Mr. Francis Barber', or 'good Mr. Francis'.[58] In his relationship with Johnson he is portrayed as a loyal servant, frequently (if conventionally) described as 'honest' or 'faithful'.[59] Boswell shows Johnson, for his part, thinking of Barber with affection. The reader is told of his 'sincere regard for Francis Barber, his faithful negro servant'.[60] Writing of Johnson's concern, late in his life, to provide financially for Barber, Boswell records:

55 *Boswell's Life of Johnson*, Vol. I, p. 239.
56 *Boswell's Life of Johnson*, Vol. I, p. 241, Vol. IV, p. 417. Barber is also identified as an indirect source (Vol. I, p. 235).
57 *Boswell's Life of Johnson*, Vol. I, p. 239, n. 1.
58 *Boswell's Life of Johnson*, Vol. IV, p. 404; Vol. I, p. 237; Vol. III, p. 222.
59 *Boswell's Life of Johnson*, Vol. I, pp. 235, 237, 239; Vol. II, pp. 5, 62, 376; Vol. IV, pp. 370, 401, 417.
60 *Boswell's Life of Johnson*, Vol. I, p. 239.

> Having no near relations, it had been for some time Johnson's intention to make a liberal provision for his faithful servant, Mr. Francis Barber, whom he looked upon as particularly under his protection, and whom he had all along treated truly as an humble friend.[61]

The repeated reference to Johnson's 'humble friend' is significant. It asserts the difference in social status between the two, while at the same time recognizing the depth of the relationship between them. In the discussion of Johnson's provision for Barber (and of the latter's actions as residuary legatee) Boswell also takes the opportunity to defend Barber against the attack published by John Hawkins: 'I am enabled fully to refute a very unjust reflection, by Sir John Hawkins, both against Dr. Johnson, and his faithful servant, Mr. Francis Barber.'[62] (Indeed, the positive portrait of Barber throughout Boswell's *Life* provides an implied response to Hawkins's hostile one.)

Elsewhere Boswell is more subtle in his defence of Barber against criticism. In her *Anecdotes of the Late Samuel Johnson* (1786) Hester Thrale Piozzi had recounted a story about Johnson going out himself to buy oysters for Hodge the cat, 'that Francis the Black's delicacy might not be hurt'. Boswell tells the same story in his *Life of Johnson*, but he silently revises it, replacing Piozzi's sneer at Barber's 'delicacy' with 'lest the servants ... should take a dislike to the poor creature'.[63]

Boswell included in the *Life of Johnson* several of Johnson's affectionate letters to Barber, and others that refer to him and Elizabeth in a similar tone: 'Remember me kindly to Francis and Betsy', 'tell Frank I hope he remembers my advice' and 'give my love to Francis'.[64] (In all the many hundreds of surviving letters written by Johnson, this is the only occasion on which he sends his love to anyone.) But the most striking references to Barber appear in Boswell's discussion of the last day of Johnson's life. Boswell prints, almost verbatim, an extract from the

---

61 *Boswell's Life of Johnson*, Vol. IV, p. 401.
62 *Boswell's Life of Johnson*, Vol. IV, p. 370.
63 For further discussion, see Bundock, *The Fortunes*, pp. 148–9.
64 For letters to Barber, see *Boswell's Life of Johnson*, Vol. II, pp. 62–3, 115–16. For letters referring to him, see Vol. II, pp. 282, 386 and Vol. III, p. 92.

letter that his brother Thomas had sent him on 31 December 1784,[65] passing on Barber's account of that last day:

> Of his last moments, my brother, Thomas David, has furnished me with the following particulars:
>
> 'The Doctor, from the time that he was certain his death was near, ... often said to his faithful servant, who gave me this account, "Attend, Francis, to the salvation of your soul, which is the object of greatest importance:" he also explained to him passages in the scripture, and seemed to have pleasure in talking upon religious subjects.
>
> On Monday, the 13th of December, the day on which he died, a Miss Morris, daughter to a particular friend of his, called, and said to Francis, that she begged to be permitted to see the Doctor, that she might earnestly request him to give her his blessing. Francis went into his room, followed by the young lady, and delivered the message. The Doctor turned himself in the bed, and said, "God bless you my dear!" These were the last words he spoke.—His difficulty of breathing increased till about seven o'clock in the evening, when Mr. Barber and Mrs. Desmoulins,[66] who were sitting in the room, observing that the noise he made in breathing had ceased, went to the bed, and found he was dead.'[67]

At this crucial point in the biography Barber features prominently. He is given credit as Thomas Boswell's source, receives frequent instruction from Johnson concerning his salvation and is the guardian of the door who can give (or withhold) 'permission' to see Johnson. Barber and Miss Morris are the only people to hear Johnson's final words. Last, but far from least, Barber is one of only two people present at the very moment of Johnson's death.[68]

---

65 T.D. Boswell to James Boswell, 31 December 1784, n. 33 above.
66 Boswell's mistranscription of 'Mr' Desmoulins; see T.D. Boswell to James Boswell, 31 December 1784 and Gordon Turnbull, 'Not a Woman in Sight', *Times Literary Supplement*, 18–25 December 2009, pp. 19–21.
67 *Boswell's Life of Johnson*, Vol. IV, pp. 417–18.
68 The prominence that Boswell accords to Barber in his account of Johnson's

In short, the picture of Barber in Boswell's *Life of Johnson* and the account he presents of the relationship between Barber and Johnson are sympathetic and respectful. They reflect Boswell's generally positive attitude towards Barber himself and towards the Barber–Johnson relationship. But, in penning it, Boswell is also reacting against the account of John Hawkins, sometimes consciously so.

Boswell and Hawkins paint dramatically different portraits both of Barber and of his relationship with Johnson. Where Hawkins is contemptuous, Boswell is well-disposed. For Hawkins, Johnson was foolishly over-indulgent towards the undeserving Barber: for Boswell, Johnson acted generously towards a loyal servant and friend. As I have suggested, it is not always easy to evaluate these accounts and to judge what drives their authors.

Boswell was in part motivated by his rivalry with Hawkins and his wish to obtain material for the *Life of Johnson*, while Barber stood to gain from Boswell's support and assistance. But there was much more to their relationship than mere self-interest: between the two men there was genuine respect and affection. Marshall Waingrow captures the balance well when he writes that 'the element of calculation—on both sides—is outweighed by good feelings—on both sides'.[69]

Hawkins's concerns about Barber's character were genuine, but they existed alongside his denunciation of 'contrariety of colour' in marriage and '*favour to negroes*'. Such attitudes do not necessarily make Hawkins an unreliable witness, but they do mean that in judging the value of his testimony we have to somehow take account of both his racism and the likelihood that his critique of Barber's behaviour had some basis in fact.[70]

The sources, of course, are fragmentary. There are occasions when perhaps only fiction could now capture the true force of the moment. In the entry in his journal for Tuesday 7 April 1778 Boswell recorded:

death makes it difficult to accept Lisa Berglund's contention that at this point Boswell minimizes Barber's role (Berglund, 'Oysters for Hodge, or, Ordering Society, Writing Biography and Feeding the Cat', *Journal for Eighteenth-Century Studies*, 33: 4, 2010, pp. 631–45 at p. 640).
69 Waingrow, p. 12.
70 See especially the careful discussion in Clingham, 'Hawkins, Biography, and the Law'.

Then Dr. Johnson's. I bid Frank get buns. Comfortable breakfast....
Read him [Johnson] Lord Hailes on Negro. He liked it.[71]

'Lord Hailes on Negro' was the judgement of Lord Hailes in the Scottish case of *Knight v Wedderburn*. On 15 January 1778 the Court of Session had upheld the ruling of John Swinton, Sheriff-Depute of Perth, that slavery was inconsistent with the principles of Scots law.[72] It may be that Barber was present when Boswell read out that judgement. We know that Johnson 'liked it'. But what might it have meant to the former slave, Francis Barber?

---

71 Weis and Pottle, *Boswell in Extremes*, pp. 244, 246.
72 John W. Cairns, 'The Definition of Slavery in Eighteenth-Century Thinking: Not the True Roman Slavery', in Jean Allain (ed.), *The Legal Understanding of Slavery: From the Historical to the Contemporary* (Oxford: Oxford University Press, 2012), pp. 61–83 at p. 80.

CHAPTER THREE

Revisiting Olaudah Equiano, or Gustavus Vassa

Vincent Carretta

Facts are stubborn things; and whatever may be our wishes, our inclinations, or the dictates of our passions, they cannot alter the state of facts and evidence.[1]   (*John Adams*)

Scholars have long considered the significance of *The Interesting Narrative of Olaudah Equiano, or Gustavus Vassa, the African. Written by Himself,* first published in London in 1789. But, in emphasizing only parts of the text, rather than trying to assess the whole, the various disciplinary approaches to the *Interesting Narrative* are reminiscent of the parable of the elephant and the blind men. Nineteenth-century commentators were often more concerned with the fact *that* Equiano wrote, than with *what* he wrote; African-Americanist literary critics have usually concentrated on whatever elements in Equiano's *Interesting Narrative* seem to anticipate those in Frederick Douglass's 1845 *Narrative*; Africanist literary critics have recognized Equiano as a forefather of Anglophone-African, particularly Anglophone-Nigerian, literature; cultural anthropologists seeking the fullest account of eighteenth-century Igbo ethnography have considered just the first

---

1 John Adams, argument in defence of British soldiers during the Boston Massacre trials, 4 December 1770.

two chapters of Equiano's autobiography; and most historians of the transatlantic slave trade have shown little interest in the *Interesting Narrative* beyond Equiano's description of the Middle Passage.[2] The reception history of the significance of the *Interesting Narrative* since its initial publication has largely been dependent upon assumptions about its author's veracity. Baptismal and naval records that say that Vassa/Equiano was born in South Carolina, however, require us to revisit the author's claims about his national and personal identities.[3] The recently discovered records have raised questions about the true identity of the author of the *Interesting Narrative* that have understandably elicited often passionate, albeit occasionally intemperate, responses from the various stakeholders in the continuing debate over the significance of the *Interesting Narrative* and its author.

Olaudah Equiano/Gustavus Vassa tells us that he was born in Africa in 1745, enslaved in 1756 and forced across the Middle Passage to the Caribbean and then Virginia, where Michael Henry Pascal, an officer on leave from the Royal Navy, purchased him. His new owner renamed him Gustavus Vassa and brought him to England, where he was baptized at St Margaret's, Westminster, in February 1759. He served under his owner during the Seven Years' War. He learned to read and write in the schools that were open to all crewmembers aboard the larger ships in the Royal Navy. Pascal sold Equiano into West Indian slavery in 1762, as the war was ending. After he purchased his freedom in 1766 he went on voyages of commerce and adventure

---

2 Although the legal name of the polynymic author of the *Interesting Narrative* was Gustavus Vassa, I refer to him here and below as Equiano, the mononym that literary scholars and historians most commonly use to refer to him.

3 I first revealed the documentary evidence in endnotes to my edition of Olaudah Equiano's *The Interesting Narrative and Other Writings* (New York: Penguin, 1995; rev. edn 2003), and subsequently in a series of elaborations of the evidence and its possible implications: 'Olaudah Equiano or Gustavus Vassa? New Light on an Eighteenth-Century Question of Identity', *Slavery and Abolition*, 20, 1999, pp. 96–105; 'More New Light on the Identity of Olaudah Equiano or Gustavus Vassa', in Felicity Nussbaum (ed.), *The Global Eighteenth Century* (Baltimore: The Johns Hopkins University Press, 2003), pp. 226–35; *Equiano, the African: Biography of a Self-Made Man* (Athens, GA: The University of Georgia Press, 2005; paperback edition, Penguin Putnam, 2007).

to North America, the Mediterranean and the West Indies, as well as towards the North Pole. He subsequently experienced a spiritual rebirth as a Methodist. After briefly being involved with the project to send the Black Poor in London to settle in Sierra Leone, he published newspaper articles opposing the transatlantic slave trade. He designed the *Interesting Narrative* in part to further that cause.

The significance of Equiano's autobiography was appreciated as soon as it was published (Figure 3.1). It was widely and positively reviewed during his lifetime. In 1792 he married an Englishwoman, with whom he had two daughters. Profits from the sales of the nine editions of Olaudah Equiano/Gustavus Vassa's autobiography between 1789 and 1794 made him probably the wealthiest person of African descent in Britain when he died on 31 March 1797. His surviving daughter inherited £950 in 1816, the equivalent in 2016 to (roughly) £90,280, or about $122,000, which derived primarily from the sales of his *Interesting Narrative* to the more than 1,100 subscribers of its nine editions.

The financial success and political influence of Equiano's *Interesting Narrative* depended upon its author's rhetorical *ethos* and his credibility as the first purported enslaved survivor of the Middle Passage to describe that experience. Opponents and supporters of the transatlantic slave trade knew that, prior to the publication of Equiano's autobiography, the only extensive accounts of the Middle Passage were either by Europeans engaged in the trade or by fictional characters. Apologists for the trade argued disingenuously that if the Middle Passage was as horrific as abolitionists claimed its survivors would have said so. Defenders of the trade could not afford to let Equiano go unanswered. In 1792 a London newspaper challenged Equiano's identity, and hence his credibility, by claiming that he was actually born in the West Indies. He thus would not have been able to provide the abolitionist movement with the needed voice of a survivor of the Middle Passage. Equiano responded in subsequent editions of his *Narrative* with a letter addressed 'To the Reader' denouncing the 'invidious' attempt 'to hurt my character, and to discredit and prevent the sale of my Narrative ...'.[4] He was as concerned for his pocketbook as he was for his integrity. Questions about Equiano's identity would arise

---

4 Equiano, *The Interesting Narrative*, 5. All subsequent references to this edition of Equiano's autobiography are noted parenthetically below.

3.1 Frontispiece to Equiano's *Interesting Narrative.*
Courtesy of the John Carter Brown Library at Brown University.

again two centuries later. Much remains at stake in the controversy over whether he reclaimed or invented an African birth, and whether he experienced the Middle Passage.

Through the posthumous republications of his autobiography, Equiano's contributions to the abolitionist and later emancipationist causes, as well as to literary history, have been as great after his death as they had been while he was alive. Following the legal abolition in 1807 by Britain and in 1808 by the United States of their own respective transatlantic slave trades, many Britons sought to extend the abolition to other nations. The British government established a policy of actively trying to suppress the transatlantic trade by intercepting slave ships and transporting their now-liberated Africans to the British colony of Sierra Leone. With its classic account of the horrors of the Middle Passage, the *Interesting Narrative* was an obvious piece of evidence to use in this international abolitionist campaign. Hence, a new edition of the autobiography was published in Belper, England, in 1809. When an international campaign was mounted to pressure France to abolish its own transatlantic slave trade further British editions appeared in Halifax (1813, 1814, 1819), Leeds (1814) and Penryn (1815). France reluctantly ended its trade in 1815.

Directly and indirectly, the most influential nineteenth-century transmission of Equiano's reputation and the knowledge of his autobiography was Henri Grégoire's publication in Paris in 1808 of *De la littérature des Nègres, ou, Recherches sur leurs facultés intellectuelles, leurs qualités morales et leur ouvrages literature; suives de Notices sur la vie et les ouvrages des Nègres qui se sont distingués dans les Sciences, les Lettres et les Arts* [*Concerning the Literature of Negroes, or Research on Their Intellectual Faculties, Their Moral Qualities, and Their Writings; Followed by Accounts of the Life and Works of Negroes Who Have Distinguished Themselves in the Sciences, Letters, and Arts*]. To gain a wider audience, Grégoire arranged to have translations of his book published in Germany (1809) and the United States (1810). Hoping to influence prominent Americans to accelerate what he mistakenly thought was progress towards the abolition of slavery in the United States, Grégoire sent a copy of his original French edition of *De la littérature des Nègres* to Joel Barlow, who received it enthusiastically. He also sent a copy to Thomas Jefferson, who disingenuously assures Grégoire that no person living wishes more sincerely than I do, to see a complete refutation of the doubts I have myself entertained and expressed on the grade of understanding allotted to them [the enslaved], and to find in that respect they are on a par with ourselves.

Jefferson further contends that 'whatever be their degree of talent it is no measure of their rights. Because Sir Isaac Newton was superior to others in understanding, he was not therefore lord of the person or property of others.'[5] Jefferson nevertheless continued to act as 'lord and master of the person or property of others'.

But Grégoire's greatest effect on the development of nineteenth-century abolitionism was less direct. Once the transatlantic trade was legally abolished, attention in both Britain and the United States turned to trying to abolish the institution of slavery itself, particularly in North America. Later abolitionist writers, such as Abigail Mott in *Biographical Sketches and Interesting Anecdotes of Persons of Colour* (New York, 1826) and Lydia Maria Child in her *Appeal in Favor of That Class of Americans Called Africans* (New York, 1836), freely and explicitly cited and quoted Grégoire's work in their own attacks on slavery rather than on the slave trade. American abolitionists hoped that recounting Equiano's life would help to eradicate slavery in North America as well.

Nineteenth-century European abolitionists acknowledged the part that Equiano played in both the abolition of the transatlantic slave trade in 1807 and the abolition of slavery in Britain's colonies in the West Indies in 1838. Because of Equiano's extended account of various types of slavery in Europe, the Middle East and the Americas, his autobiography was an obvious choice for the growing number of British and American emancipationists, now increasingly called abolitionists, to invoke against the defenders of slavery. The evolution of both the nineteenth-century transatlantic pro- and anti-slavery movements is reflected in the posthumous reception history of the reprints, redactions, abridgements and summaries of *The Interesting Narrative*.

5 'Jefferson to Grégoire, 25 February 1809' in Merrill D. Peterson (ed.), *Thomas Jefferson, Writings* (New York: Library of America, 1984), p. 1202.

Nineteenth-century references to Equiano were usually in the context of life under slavery, rather than of the Middle Passage. At mid-century Henry Gardiner Adams only very briefly recounts Equiano's movement from Africa to the Americas because the 'horrors of "the middle passage" have been so often described, that we need not sicken and disgust our readers with the account here given of them … .'[6] Although the Middle Passage plays a slightly larger role in the account of Equiano's life in Abigail Mott's *Narratives of Colored Americans* (New York, 1875), Reverend William J. Simmons's virtual erasure of the episode in his *Men of Mark: Eminent, Progressive and Rising* (Cleveland, 1887) is far more typical of the ways that nineteenth-century abolitionists appropriated the story of Equiano's life for their cause. When John Wesley Edward Bowen mentioned 'Gustavus Vassa, a learned Englishman' at the end of the nineteenth century, he says nothing about the Middle Passage episode.[7]

Abolitionists of African descent contributed to keeping Equiano's name and reputation alive. Equiano was increasingly celebrated as an example of the intellectual achievements of people of African descent. On 18 May 1827, in *Freedom's Journal* (New York), the first African-American newspaper in the United States, Samuel Cornish and John Brown Russworm briefly summarized the life of 'Gustavus Vasa [*sic*], whose African name was Olando [*sic*] Equiano'. Frederick Douglass published an advertisement on 17 March 1848 in his newspaper, *The North Star* (Rochester, New York), for Wilson Armistead's *A Tribute for the Negro: Being a Vindication of the Moral, Intellectual, and Religious Capabilities of the Colored Portion of Mankind; with Particular Reference to the African Race* (Manchester and London, 1848), which emphasized the book's portraits of Douglass and Equiano. And W.E.B. Du Bois's recognition in 1913 of the status of the *Interesting Narrative* in literary history has been unquestioned since: '[Equiano's] autobiography … was the beginning of that long series of personal appeals of which Booker T. Washington's *Up from Slavery* is the latest.'[8]

---

6 Henry Gardiner Adams, *God's Image in Ebony* (London, 1854), p. 64.

7 John Wesley Edward Bowen, *Africa and the American Negro* (Atlanta, 1896), p. 171.

8 W.E.B. Du Bois, 'The Negro in Literature and Art', *Annals of the American*

Equiano's *Interesting Narrative* has experienced a renaissance of interest in popular culture, as well as in historical and literary studies, since the 1960s. Equiano has been the subject of television shows, films, comic books and books written for children. The story of his life is part of African, African-American, African-British and African-Caribbean popular culture. Excerpts from Equiano's book now appear in every anthology and on any website covering American, African-American, British and Caribbean history and literature of the eighteenth century. The most frequently excerpted sections are the early chapters on his life in Africa and his experience on the Middle Passage crossing the Atlantic to America.

Despite the pervasive circumstantiality of the *Interesting Narrative*, no one before 1995 attempted to verify or falsify the dates, places and names that Equiano mentions throughout his autobiography. The discovery of records that say that the author of the *Interesting Narrative* was born in South Carolina obligates us to revisit the questions first raised during his lifetime about who he was and about what the *Interesting Narrative* is. The title that he chose for his book foregrounds the question of whether he was either Olaudah Equiano *or* Gustavus Vassa, *or* both at once. That question requires his readers to consider whether he experienced the Middle Passage from Africa to the Americas; the extent to which he ever considered himself to be an African American; whether Vassa revealed or invented his identity as Equiano; and why he waited until the late 1780s to embrace that identity.

Why in his autobiography might Equiano have created an African nativity and disguised an American birth? Before 1789 the abundant evidence and many arguments against the transatlantic slave trade came from white voices alone. Opponents of the trade initially did not recognize the rhetorical power an authentic African voice could wield in the struggle. Equiano knew that to continue its increasing momentum the anti-slave trade movement needed precisely the kind of account of Africa and the Middle Passage he could supply. An African, not an African-American, voice was what the abolitionist cause required. Equiano recognized a way to do very well financially

Academy of Political and Social Science, 49, 1913, pp. 862–7, and in Nathan Huggins (ed.), *W.E.B. Du Bois, Writings* (New York: Library of America, 1986), p. 863.

by doing a great deal of good in supplying that much-needed voice. He may have forged a part of his personal identity, and created an Igbo national identity *avant la letter*, to enable himself to become an effective spokesman for his fellow diasporan Africans. If indeed he did so, he risked being exposed as an imposter, and thus discrediting the abolitionist cause. But the financial and rhetorical success of his book demonstrated that it would have been a risk well worth taking.

Scholars have long acknowledged that Equiano's conception of an eighteenth-century Igboland is anachronistic, rendering his claim to an Igbo national identity problematic. Cultural anthropologists and historians of Africa nonetheless value Equiano's 'unique first-hand account of eighteenth-century Igboland' so highly because so little other direct information exists about the mid-eighteenth-century ancestors of contemporary *Igbo*.[9] What little other information exists came through white intermediaries or observers. Hence, Equiano's representation of Igbos was very difficult for his contemporaries to falsify. But scholars and critics have increasingly come to recognize that the apparent uniqueness of Equiano's account does not guarantee its reliability and authenticity.[10] One of the most judicious commentators on Equiano's

9 Elizabeth Isichei, *A History of the Igbo People* (New York: St. Martin's Press, 1976), p. 21. John Thornton, *Africa and Africans in the Making of the Atlantic World, 1400–1800* (Cambridge: Cambridge University Press, 1992; rev. edn 1998), p. 310, notes that 'Almost all we know about the [Igbo] region in the eighteenth century comes from the testimony of Olaudah Equiano, an Igbo who was enslaved as a youth around 1755.'

10 S.E. Ogude, 'Facts into Fiction: Equiano's *Narrative* Reconsidered', *Research in African Literatures*, 13, 1982, pp. 30–43 at p. 32, argues that because an eleven-year-old was very unlikely to have the almost total recall Equiano claims, 'Equiano relied less on the memory of his experience and more on other sources' in his account of Africa. And Ogude, 'No Roots Here: On the Igbo Roots of Olaudah Equiano', *Review of English and Literary Studies*, 5, 1989, pp. 1–16, denies that the linguistic evidence Catherine Acholonu offers in 'The Igbo Roots' supports Equiano's account. Despite Ogude's scepticism about Equiano's veracity, he does not question Vassa/Equiano's fundamental identity as an African. In her review in *Journal of African History*, 33, 1992, pp. 164–5, of Paul Edwards, *The Life of Olaudah Equiano*, and Catherine Acholonu, *The Igbo Roots of Olaudah Equiano*, Elizabeth Isichei remarks of Equiano's description of Africa, 'I have come to believe that it is a palimpsest, and that though he was indeed an Igbo (though

assertion of an African-born Igbo identity observes that '[a]fter reading *The Interesting Narrative*, one of the first things that strikes the critical scholar is how scanty and muddled Equiano's "recollection" of Igbo society is.'[11] And, as Nobel Laureate Chinua Achebe observed, the consciousness of the Igbo national identity that Equiano asserts is a quite recent phenomenon.[12]

Unsurprisingly, raising questions about Equiano's claim to a personal African identity has evoked impassioned responses from commentators for whom Equiano is an essential founder of African literature, as well as from anthropologists and historians who accept his *Interesting Narrative* as a preeminent primary source. My publication of the documents has elicited from fellow academics attempted refutations, dismissals, misrepresentations, vilifications, denunciations, accusations and threats of assault. Several members of the audience at a conference in England in 2003 made physical threats. I have been accused of being a methodologically naïve self-promoting racist. One linguist calls me an *'enfant terrible* hungry for fame, with loads of vested interests and ulterior motives'.[13] A cultural anthropologist accuses me of 'impugning ethnographic research results' because I have expressed scepticism about the afore-mentioned linguist's

---

even this has been questioned) he fused his own recollections with details obtained from other Igbo into a single version' (165). Katherine Faull Eze, 'Self-Encounters: Two Eighteenth-Century African Memoirs from Moravian Bethlehem', in David McBride, LeRoy Hopkins and C. Aisha Blackshire-Belay (eds), *Crosscurrents: African Americans, Africa, and Germany in the Modern World* (Columbia, SC: Camden House, 1998), pp. 29–52, considers 'Equiano's Igbo past [to be] mostly a reconstruction of European or Colonial American travel narratives, most obviously, Anthony Benezet's *Some Historical Account of Guinea*', pp. 33, 50fn22.

11 Adiele E. Afigbo, *Ropes of Sand: Studies in Igbo History and Culture* (London: University Press Limited, 1981), p. 151. Despite his reservations, Afigbo accepts Equiano's claim to an African birth.

12 Chinua Achebe, *Morning Yet on Creation Day: Essays* (London: Heinemann, 1975), p. 177.

13 Catherine Obianuju Acholonu, 'The Igbo Roots of Olaudah Equiano', in Chima J. Korieh (ed.), *Olaudah Equiano and the Igbo World: History, Society and Atlantic Diaspora Connections* (Trenton, NJ, and Asmara, Eritrea: Africa World Press, Inc., 2009), pp. 49–66, at p. 61.

methodology.[14] I confess to finding suspect any methodology that depends on the testimony of 150-year-old witnesses.

One literary critic suggests that the misrecordings of 'Vassa' as 'Feston' and 'Weston' on the 1773 muster lists of the *Racehorse* cast doubt on the age and South Carolina place of birth recorded for him on the same lists.[15] The critic offers several other candidates as possible men miscalled Feston/Weston. But neither the future soldier nor criminal that this critic identifies would have been among the best seamen available in peacetime for a dangerous government-sponsored voyage, rather than the experienced and demonstrably multi-talented Vassa/Equiano. This critic seems to imply that Equiano fabricated his participation in the expedition. Another literary critic accuses me of rendering Equiano a 'huckster' because I note his business acumen and argue that he successfully sought to do well by doing good. She calls my 'justification for Equiano's greatness ... far more offensive than the insinuation of mendacity'. The critic ironically chose the journal *Novel: A Forum on Fiction* in which to publish her refusal to accept the possibility that Equiano may have engaged in fiction-making.[16]

Most academics have been far more receptive to acknowledging the evidence and evaluating its significance. Historians of the transatlantic

---

14 Dorothy Chinwe Ukaegbu, 'Igbo Sense of Place and Identity in Olaudah Equiano's Interesting Narrative', in Chima J. Korieh (ed.), *Olaudah Equiano and the Igbo World*. Trenton, NJ: Africa World Press, 2009, pp. 67–92 at p. 70.
15 John Bugg, 'The Other Interesting Narrative: Olaudah Equiano's Public Book Tour', *PMLA*, 121, 2006, pp. 1424–42 at p. 1425.
16 Cathy N. Davidson, 'Olaudah Equiano, Written by Himself', *Novel: A Forum on Fiction*, 40, 2006, pp. 18–51 at pp. 42, 37, 42, 43.
One commentator turns to fiction in response to the problematic baptismal and naval records. In his review in *Journal of American History*, 93, 2006, pp. 840–1, of my biography of Equiano, Ugo Nwokeji apparently believes in the validity of 'alternative facts'. (Kellyanne Conway, US counselor to the president, promoted the concept of 'alternative facts' during a Meet the Press interview with Chuck Todd on 22 January 2017.) After dismissing as essentially fake news the records that say that Equiano was born in South Carolina, Nwokeji faults me for ignoring alleged records that no one else has ever seen, and whose sources Nwokeji understandably fails to cite. As the late Daniel Patrick Moynihan noted, we all have a right to our own opinions, but we do not have a right to our own facts.

slave trade have a vested interest in the veracity of Equiano's account of the Middle Passage because they consider it a *locus classicus*. According to one historian,

> Equiano has become a canonical text because it has the ring of authenticity. ... If it is not a first-person account of the travails of an African, then its appeal diminishes considerably. Indeed its appeal declines so much that we can no longer use Equiano as a guide to the Middle Passage ... .[17]

However, this historian takes his argument a step too far when he writes that

> once we doubt whether Equiano was an African, it becomes harder, contra, Carretta, to believe him in other areas. I have, for example, always had my doubts about the provenance of his name: I have surveyed thousands of slave names in Jamaica and have never come across a name as outlandish as Gustavus Vassa.[18]

All the available evidence, however, demonstrates that there should be no doubt that Gustavus Vassa and the man now better known as Olaudah Equiano were one and the same.

Another historian deems the implications of the baptismal and naval records to be stimulating: 'Whatever is not strictly "true" in [Equiano's] narrative—whatever he did not actually see or do what he said he did—becomes a kind of larger Truth in its universalism.' As this historian notes, Equiano may have been 'acting as a kind of oral historian, a funnel or repository for communal memory'. Unlike those to whom he gave a voice, because of the training and education

---

17 Trevor Burnard, 'Good-bye, Equiano, the African', in Donald A. Yerxa (ed.), *Recent Themes in the History of Africa and the Atlantic World: Historians in Conversation* (Columbia: University of South Carolina Press, 2008), pp. 100–5 at p. 103.

18 Burnard, 'Good-bye, Equiano', pp. 103–4. Gustavus Vassa, or Gustavus I (1496–1560), was a noble Swede who led his people to freedom from Danish rule in 1521–3 and went on to become a very successful king of liberated Sweden.

he gained during and after his years with the Royal Navy Equiano never experienced the grinding agricultural existence endured by the vast majority of his enslaved contemporaries. Paradoxically, because Equiano's own life was so extraordinary, his voice is representative of the millions of fellow people of African descent who suffered the Middle Passage and its equally horrific aftermath. This historian and I agree that, if Equiano engaged in self-fashioning, his life and *Interesting Narrative* raise 'complicated questions' about the choices of identity available to diasporan Africans.[19]

Answers to those questions continue to be sought. The most prolific defender of Equiano's veracity is Paul Lovejoy, writing in 2006.[20] Recognizing that the older Equiano was when Pascal bought him the more credible Equiano's account of his earlier life would be, Lovejoy takes a deductive approach to the available internal and external evidence. Lovejoy is not the first person to try to square Equiano's age with his reliability. The anonymous editor of the posthumous 1814 edition of the *Interesting Narrative* argues that Equiano was able to recall events in his childhood so circumstantially because they were so traumatic, and because he probably subsequently described them repeatedly. The question of Equiano's credibility is greatly compounded, however, if he was as young when he came under Pascal's control as his baptismal and naval records indicate. Lovejoy simply revises the evidence to fit the conclusion:

> What appears to establish his place of birth as South Carolina disappears when the chronology of his narrative is more carefully

---

19 Jon Sensbach, 'Beyond Equiano', in Donald A. Yerxa (ed.), *Recent Themes in the History of Africa and the Atlantic World: Historians in Conversation* (Columbia: University of South Carolina Press, 2008), pp. 106–10 at pp. 108, 110.

20 Paul Lovejoy, 'Autobiography and Memory: Gustavus Vassa, alias Olaudah Equiano, the African', *Slavery and Abolition*, 27, 2006, pp. 317–47. For what I consider to be significant flaws in Lovejoy's argument and methodology, and Lovejoy's reaction, see my 'Response' and his 'Rejoinder', *Slavery and Abolition*, 28, 2007, pp. 115–25. 'Olaudah Equiano or Gustavus Vassa: What's in a name?' in Toyin Falola and Matt Child (eds), *Igbo in the Atlantic World: African Origins and Diasporic Destinations* (Bloomington: Indiana University Press, 2016), pp. 199–217.

deciphered, suggesting that Vassa was likely two or three years older than he thought. ... Hence his account of his homeland and the terror of the 'Middle Passage' should be considered as being derived from his memory.[21]

Lovejoy's latest contribution to the conversation about Equiano's identity relies on Equiano's references to the practice of circumcision in Africa, which he does not say he himself experienced. If Equiano was not born in Africa, Lovejoy asks, 'Why did he mention circumcision so much if the memory of the ritual and the context were not important to him?'[22] A probable answer can be found in the way that Equiano called upon biblical and theological evidence to argue against the enslavement of Africans.

In the face of the small but increasingly influential number of contemporaneous believers in polygenesis, who argued that God created various types of human at different times, Equiano's description of 'Eboe' supports the orthodox Christian monogenetic belief that all humans descended directly from Adam and Eve.[23] He links monogenesis and the contemporaneous stadial theory of social development to contend that Africans are as capable of progress as Europeans. Equiano portrays the customs of his purported African homeland as analogous to those of ancient Jews. 'Eboan Africans' (44) are as innocent of the truth of Christian revelation as Old Testament Hebrews were: Africans because of geographical isolation; Hebrews because of historical distance. Equiano elaborates his analogy between Africans and Old Testament Jews to make his monogenetic point, while also implying that Africans are fully prepared for Christian Revelation.

Equiano does not compare Africans *culturally* to eighteenth-century Jews, who were isolated and treated as aliens by their Christian neighbours because they refused to embrace Christianity and its customs.

21 Lovejoy, 'Autobiography and Memory', p. 347.
22 Lovejoy, 'Olaudah Equiano or Gustavus Vassa', pp. 199–217, at p. 210.
23 The most significant contemporaneous proponent of polygenesis was Edward Long, whose atypical eighteenth-century arguments in his *History of Jamaica* (London: T. Lowndes, 1774) anticipate dominant nineteenth-century pseudo-scientific racism.

Rather, Equiano's repeated references to the practice of circumcision in Africa rhetorically underscore his contention that the Igbo are culturally and religiously *pre-Christian*, comparable to 'the Israelites in their primitive state' (44). Equiano carefully avoids associating the Igbo use of circumcision with that of eighteenth-century Jews. To do so would imply to his contemporaneous readers that the Africans were anti-Christian.

Lovejoy briefly mentions a recently discovered letter that Equiano wrote on 6 May 1780 to the prominent abolitionist and emancipationist Granville Sharp (200). In thanking Sharp for having given him several of his anti-slavery writings, Equiano may here also inform the ongoing conversation about the truthfulness of his later claim to have experienced the Middle Passage.[24]

---

24 The letter is in the University of Illinois at Chicago, Special Collections: Gustavus Vassa to Granville Sharp, 6 May 1780, in Anti-slave trade movement—Great Britain—Correspondence, Sierra Leone Collection, Series VI, Supplement 1, Box 1, Folder 1:

To Granville Sharp Esqr.
In old jewry Chepside
[verso]
Most Worthy and Benevolent
        And Truly Favoured Sir.__
Thus with my inmost, & utmost Respect, Gratitude, & Thanks to you for all your kindnesses: Sir. Not having time before to Read the three Last good Books You was so kind to Give me till with in this week, I first have Read the just Limitation of Slavery, & the Law of Passive Obedience with Very Great Satisfaction: I Now have Read the Law of Retribution which I think is Quite Ravishing, for which I do Request the pray hearing God to hear my prayers & Infinitly Reward you & all yours: for all your Labours, pains, and Love to the poor, and very much Afflected Brethren of mine: may the Good Lord Reward you aboundently for these four pages in the Law of Retribution, which I thinks is Exceedingly striking. Viz. all the 149th page, & all of the 151st & page 320th & Lastly the four Last Lines But two in page 331st. __ if God speares me I shall Read the next week the Law of Liberty: & if god spares me to Visit you again I will be Glad to Beg of you: the Tract of the Law of Nature & principles of Action in man. Thanks to the Lord I have good Deal time to Read in this place I am now in.
my present master is a mile [*sic*] man, But a fornicator, & how soon I may be Removed from his Service I knows not as I am not much in favour with the fornicatress who has the Ruling of him & the whole house.

Most Worthy & Benevolent Sir, &c. I Conclude in Praying & in wishing you & all yours Every blessings of the Old & New Testment, may you all shine in Glory here after. Aman.

I am with Respect & Gratitude &c. &c.

yours hum^{ble} Servt

Gustavus Vassa, at M^r

Delamain wine merchant

N° 67. Berners Street oxford

Road __ Saturday May the 6th __ 80.

The letter is prefaced by a note by baronet Sir Thomas Phillipps (1792–1872), of Middle Hill, Worcestershire, a collector of books and manuscripts. He was the illegitimate only child of Thomas Phillipps (1742–1818), senior partner in Phillipps, Nash, Lowe & Co., manufacturers and printer of calico in Manchester. The note reads, 'Gustavus Vasa 6 May 1780 A Black & an African, who wrote his own life He fell into fits if any one pronounced his real name, which was Olaudah Equiano My Father knew him—T Phillipps of MiddleHill.' Lovejoy does not comment on the possible implications of Vassa's reportedly agitated reaction to the sound of 'his real name'. Phillipps, however, could have heard of his 'fits' only at second hand.

Equiano had known Sharp at least since April 1774, when he sought Sharp's help in his unsuccessful attempt to save his friend John Annis from being kidnapped back into slavery. The letter demonstrates that Equiano and Sharp had maintained a connection since then. Equiano mentions several of Sharp's books, which Sharp had recently given him: *The Just Limitation of Slavery in the Laws of God, Compared with the Unbounded Claims of the African Traders and British American Slaveholders* (London, 1776); *The Law of Passive Obedience, or Christian Submission to Personal Injuries: Wherein Is Shewn, that the Several Texts of Scripture, which Command the entire Submission of Servants or Slaves to their Masters, Cannot Authorize the Latter to Exact an Involuntary Servitude, nor, in the least Degree, Justify the Claims of Modern Slaveholders* (London, 1776?); *The Law of Retribution; or, a Serious Warning to Great Britain and her Colonies, Founded on Unquestionable Examples of God's Temporal Vengeance against Tyrants, Slave-holders, and Oppressors* (London, 1776). Equiano mentions looking forward to reading Sharp's *The Law of Liberty, or, Royal Law, by which all Mankind will Certainly be Judged! Earnestly Recommended to the Serious Consideration of all Slave-holders and Slavedealers* (London, 1776), and *A Tract on the Law of Nature, and Principles of Action in Man* (London, 1777).

The London Directory for the Year 1780, 15th edn (London: Printed for T. Lowndes, No. 77, in Fleet Street, 1780) includes 'Delamain Henry and Son, *Mer.* 67 Berner's street'. Henry Delamain (1729–1822) was the father of John Henry Delamain (1756–1811), one of the original subscribers to Equiano's *Interesting Narrative* in 1789.

The four 'Exceedingly striking' pages of Sharp's *Law of Retribution* that Equiano cites all mention slave insurrections, the first three during the Middle Passage. Equally striking in Equiano's letter is the absence of any reference to his having personally experienced the Middle Passage. Although he may have previously told Sharp of his own experience, the omission here is at the least a noteworthy lost opportunity to offer an eyewitness corroboration of the accounts of the shipboard sufferings of his 'very much Afflected Brethren'.

If the author of the *Interesting Narrative* invented an alternative identity to serve the abolitionist cause, should we approach his book as a novel, rather than as an autobiography? Every autobiography is an act of re-creation. Wherever Equiano was born, he represents himself as African British, not African American. Unlike today, eighteenth-century autobiographers were not under oath when they reconstructed their lives. Furthermore, an autobiography is an act of rhetoric designed to influence the reader's impression of its author, and often, as in the case of the *Interesting Narrative*, also to affect the reader's beliefs or actions. Rather than being assumed to be transparent, the author of the *Interesting Narrative* should be recognized as being as adept an autobiographer as Benjamin Franklin and Frederick Douglass, or like Daniel Defoe, whose fiction and true stories often crossed literary lines.

Trying to identify the author of the *Interesting Narrative* requires us to draw conclusions from imperfect evidence, which is often at best circumstantial or dispositive, rather than decisive. Biographers, historians and literary scholars are rarely able to meet the prosecutor's

---

Equiano's 'present master'— that is, his employer—was George Pitt (1721–1803), who added the surname Rivers when he was created Baron Rivers in 1776. Rivers subscribed for two copies of Equiano's *Interesting Narrative* in 1789. Equiano mentions in his *Interesting Narrative* that sometime between March 1779 and 1783 he 'served a nobleman in the Dorsetshire militia' (223). Rivers was colonel of the Dorset militia from 1757. He was lord lieutenant of the county of Glamorgan when Equiano wrote this letter to Sharp. Six days later Rivers was appointed lord lieutenant of the county of Southampton, a position he held until 1782. Horace Walpole calls Rivers a 'brutal half mad husband' to his wife, from whom he had separated in 1771. Equiano's characterization of his employer as 'a fornicator' is consistent with the reputation Rivers had of being 'debauched'; http://www.historyofparliamentonline.org/volume/1754–1790/member/pitt-george-1721–1803.

standard of proving a case 'beyond a reasonable doubt'. But they may be able to discover a preponderance of evidence to support a convincing resolution, even if the nature of that evidence renders a decision necessarily inconclusive. Whether or not Equiano fabricated an African identity is certainly disputable, but he undeniably had the means, motive and opportunity for inventing an African birth. That identity rendered him the credible survivor of the Middle Passage that both sides called for in the late eighteenth-century argument over the abolition of the transatlantic slave trade. Arguments about the national and personal identities of the author of the *Interesting Narrative*, as well as the significance of his account of the Middle Passage, will undoubtedly continue to be revisited as relevant new primary evidence is discovered and dispassionately evaluated.

CHAPTER FOUR

Britain's Black Tars

Charles R. Foy

On a wintery day in December 1779 Amos Anderson entered HMS *Loyalist* as an able-bodied seaman. The Rhode Island-born black did not find service in the Royal Navy to his liking, deserting the frigate at Charleston the following November.[1] Anderson's time on land proved short-lived; he was impressed back onto the *Loyalist* on 31 March 1781. Three months later, while off Cape Henry, the British frigate was captured by *L'Aigrette*. Anderson reappears in the historical record in April 1784, when his service on the *Loyalist* was the subject of a trial at the Old Bailey. John Moseley, a black on the *Loyalist*, was charged with impersonating Anderson in 1783 so as to obtain his wages for serving on the *Loyalist*.[2] Moseley was able to impersonate Anderson because his shipmate had been 'sold at Martinico' after the *Loyalist* had been captured and was not in England when Moseley engaged in his fraud. Fortunately for Anderson, he was able to escape enslavement, get back to Rhode Island and from there sail on Captain Aaron Sheffield's merchant ship to London in December 1783. Once in England Anderson convinced authorities to arrest and prosecute his former ship mate. Anderson

1 'Black' refers to a person of African ancestry.
2 Anderson's life is detailed in: HMS *Loyalist* Muster, 1779–1780, The National Archives (TNA), ADM 36/8201; Old Bailey Online, https://www.oldbaileyonline.org/browse.jsp?div=t17840421–17; Thomas Binsteed, 11 April 1784, TNA ADM 106/1282/284; HMS *Vengeance* Muster, 1791–1793, TNA ADM 36/11231; HMS *Zealous* Muster, 1799–1800, TNA ADM 36/12511; Wills of Amos Anderson, TNA ADM 48/1/132 (1793) and TNA ADM 48/2/89 (1800); 24 March 1813 Baptism, St Alsege, Greenwich (reference provided by Audrey Dewjee).

subsequently re-entered naval service in the 1790s, was baptized as an Anglican and at the end of his life was a Royal Hospital pensioner.[3]

Anderson's life, with its range of maritime experiences—volunteer seaman, deserter, impressed sailor, prisoner, Prize Negro, maritime fugitive and pensioner—helps illustrate the nature of British blacks' lives at sea, the critical role black mariners played in Britain's eighteenth-century Atlantic empire and three paradoxes critical to understanding black tars' lives in Britain.[4] The first paradox was that, although British identity was, in part, based upon the legal right to move where one wanted, many British blacks were compelled to work at sea, whether by slave masters, press gangs or Admiralty Court judges.[5] Secondly, while many enslaved people in Britain's Atlantic empire viewed the United Kingdom as a 'land of liberty', black sailors migrating to the British Isles faced a significant barrier to obtaining economic independence; when they worked at sea many whites viewed them as appropriate subjects of profit who could be sold as slaves, making long careers at sea a risky endeavour. And, although Britain offered blacks freedom and better legal treatment than they experienced elsewhere in Britain's empire, many black sailors who migrated to the British Isles found that they often lacked the connections critical to obtaining social and economic independence.

3 Cassandra Pybus believes Anderson came to England in 1783 on HMS *Loyalist* with Moseley and was there 'shanghaied and taken to the West Indies to be sold'. *Epic Voyages of Freedom: Runaway Slaves of the American Revolution and Their Global Quest for Liberty* (Boston: Beacon Press, 2006), p. 85. However, the *Loyalist* was out of service by 1781, and at the Old Bailey trial Anderson testified he had been sold in Martinique the same year, Captain Sheffield testified that Anderson returned to England on his merchant ship in December 1783 and no witness testified that Anderson had been coercively carried away from England. Given the prevalence of British black sailors sold into slavery, it appears likely that Anderson was condemned by his French captors as a prize good and sold in 1781 into slavery. See, for example, Historical Society of Pennsylvania, MSS Coll. Box 11A, Folder 1B ('seven prize negroes' sold at Martinique in June 1779).

4 'Prize Negroes' refers to Blacks captured at sea who were then sold by their captors as prize goods. 'Maritime fugitives' refers to enslaved individuals who sought freedom by fleeing via the seas.

5 Jack P. Greene, ed., *Exclusionary Empire: English Liberty Overseas, 1600–1900* (Cambridge: Cambridge University Press, 2010), p. 3.

The Centrality of Black Seamen to Britain's Atlantic Empire

The most prominent image of blacks at sea in the eighteenth century was the 1787 print of the *Brookes*. It depicts hundreds of Africans lying flat tightly packed into the British slave ship's hold. While for millions of Africans their chief experience of being at sea was the horrific Middle Passage, the *Brookes* image does not capture the totality of maritime experiences of British blacks. Rather than objects being moved, considerable numbers of blacks worked as seamen, pilots, canoemen, cabin boys and ordinaries who moved commodities that were the lifeblood of Britain's Atlantic empire. They worked on Liverpool merchant ships, Bermudian blue sea vessels, Bristol slave ships, Jamaican drogers, Royal Navy men-of-war, Rhode Island coasters and Royal African Company sloops.[6] With the eighteenth century marked by almost continual warfare, manning the Royal Navy and Britain's merchant and fishing fleets was 'the most serious problem' facing the British government.[7]

The foundation of Britain's eighteenth-century Atlantic empire was its maritime sector. Britain's imperial power was predicated upon its blue water policy of maintaining an extensive merchant fleet while undertaking considerable expansion of the Royal Navy during wartime. This meant having sufficient numbers of seamen in time of war to man Royal Navy ships as well as Britain's merchant fleet. As Denver Brunsman has noted, 'no sailors, no navy; no navy, no empire'.[8] What often has been overlooked in histories of Britain's eighteenth-century empire is that black seamen were often critical to Britain's mercantile and naval successes, particularly in the Western Atlantic and Africa.[9] And what helped shape the lives of British black tars was

6 Philip D. Morgan, 'Introduction, Maritime Slavery', *Slavery & Abolition*, 31: 3, 2010, p. 311.
7 Daniel A. Baugh, *Naval Administration in the Age of Walpole* (Princeton: Princeton University Press, 1965), p. 22.
8 Denver Brunsman, *The Evil Necessity: British Impressment in the Eighteenth-Century Atlantic World* (Charlottesville: University of Virginia Press, 2013), p. 9.
9 Charles R. Foy, 'The Royal Navy's Employment of Black Mariners and Maritime Workers, 1754–1783', *International Maritime History Journal*, 28: 1, 2016, pp. 8–9.

the nature of the British empire: a commercial and political system predicated upon the exploitation of coerced labour, almost unceasing warfare throughout the eighteenth century and transatlantic connections that made the empire successful.

From Francis Drake's early forays into the Atlantic to the large-scale movement of indentured servants to the Americas and the development of the transatlantic slave trade, Britain's Atlantic empire relied heavily on coerced labour. Its overseas colonies depended upon bonded labour, such as indentured servants working in Philadelphia and black slaves toiling in Caribbean sugar fields. To transport the millions of labourers upon which British colonies and national wealth depended, Britain's blue water policy required large numbers of seamen to man British merchant and fishing ships, privateers and Royal Navy vessels. Many of these men also found themselves coercively forced to work, being impressed during wartime. And yet, despite both merchant and naval captains' best efforts, in regions such as Africa and the West Indies, where white seamen died at an alarming rate, there were often insufficient numbers of whites to man British ships. The result was that in the Western Atlantic and on the African coast British vessels were frequently manned with large numbers of blacks. Initially the Royal African Company, and then later private slave traders, regularly employed blacks, such as Jack Prince, to help reef sails and steer ships carrying Africans to enslavement in the Americas.[10] In the Western Atlantic hundreds of Blacks sailed on British merchant ships from British colonial ports. In 1743 alone a census of North American ships at Kingston, Jamaica, disclosed forty-one blacks among the vessels' 135 seamen. In Antigua, Bermuda and South Carolina, black boatmen and sailors were often a majority of crews moving tobacco, rice and sugar to markets.[11] In

10 Emma Christopher, *Slave Ship Sailors and Their Captive Cargoes, 1730–1807* (Cambridge: Cambridge University Press, 2006), App. 2.
11 Edward Trelawyne letter to Lords of Admiralty, 21 December 1743, TNA ADM 1/3917; David Barry Gaspar, *Bondsmen and rebels: A Study of Master–Slave Relations in Antigua* (Baltimore: The Johns Hopkins University Press, 1985), pp. 110–13; Michael Jarvis, *In the Eye of All Trade: Bermuda, Bermudians, and the Maritime Atlantic World, 1680–1783* (Chapel Hill: The University of North Carolina Press, 2010), p. 106; Philip D. Morgan, *Slave Counterpoint: Black Culture in the Eighteenth-Century*

Virginia, Thomas Jefferson and other planters regularly employed slave watermen. And the Royal Navy also employed large numbers of black tars; the *Black Maritime Database* contains records on almost 1,700 black Royal Navy seamen. At the beginning of the eighteenth century there were relatively few blacks, such as Captain John Symonds's servant or the free sailor John Guavas, on naval ships.[12] But over the course of the century the numbers of black tars increased significantly and came to include Olaudah Equiano, author of a bestselling personal narrative, Joseph Emidy, who became a well-known Cornwall composer, and Francis Barber, Samuel Johnson's servant, as well as lesser-known men, such as the trumpeter James Scipio who served on HMS *Pompee* in 1800.[13]

A considerable number of the blacks who served on British ships were maritime fugitives. Enslaved peoples perceived ships as 'swift-winged angels' that could take them far from their slave masters.[14] Particularly in wartime, ship captains showed little hesitation in hiring escaped slaves. Whether Antiguan runaways, English house servants such as Francis Barber or Rhode Island fugitives, British ship captains valued these men's muscle and skill over their enslaved status. And, in

Chesapeake & Low Country (Chapel Hill: University of North Carolina Press, 1998), pp. 337–42.

12 *The Slave Families of Thomas Jefferson*, Vol. I, pp. 23, 35, 212, 266–7, 363; *Post-Boy* (London), 6 July 1701; *London Post with Intelligence Foreign and Domstick*, 6 March 1700. The Black Mariner Database (BMD) is a dataset developed by the author that contains records for more than 33,000 Black mariners and maritime fugitives. The BMD has fifty-one fields of data from archives across the Atlantic and provides 'information we need to assess the typicality' of Blacks' lives in the Atlantic. Geoffrey Plank, 'Sailing with John Woolman', *Early American Studies*, 7: 1, 2009, p. 51 n. 15. The BMD is not, however, a static dataset. Given the paucity and nature of records concerning Black mariners, it is anticipated that conclusions regarding individual sailors will be modified as new information is obtained and integrated into the dataset.

13 BMD; HMS *Namur*, Muster, TNA ADM 36/6253; Registers of Allotments, 1797–1799, TNA ADM 27/2/237. The French navy also had considerable numbers of Black seamen. *Providence Journal and Town and Country Advertiser*, 21 August 1799.

14 W. Jeffrey Bolster, *Black Jacks: African American Seamen in the Age of Sail* (Cambridge, MA: Harvard University Press, 1995), p. 1.

being given berths, maritime fugitives became a critical component in the maritime sinew of British imperial power.[15] The practice of hiring runaways was so prevalent that the *Black Maritime Database* contains references to more than 6,200 maritime fugitives, the vast majority of whom were enslaved in British colonies, although more than 120 fled slave masters in England.

An Anxious Atlantic

While Britain's need for maritime labour provided opportunities for Blacks to work at sea, particularly in the Americas and Africa, British black tars' dark skin put them at risk of being enslaved whenever they went to sea. This could happen by being kidnapped, captured at sea and sold as prize goods, being returned to their former slave masters by the Royal Navy or being caught in the web of American Seamen's Acts. Such legislation authorized local officials to imprison black sailors while their ship was in port, whether or not they had freedom papers. A single sheet of paper that could be easily lost or stolen, such as manumission papers, was often all that kept black sailors from enslavement. The nature of a world in which they could be enslaved, based on whites' desire for profit, created for British black tars an Anxious Atlantic.

Even experienced black sailors could find themselves victims of whites taking advantage of the legality of slavery in much of the Atlantic basin to kidnap and sell into slavery British black seamen. Former slave William Jackson is a good example of this. Having fled his Virginia master in the mid-1750s, Jackson made his way to Great Britain. Living in Liverpool for eight years, he 'followed the Sea'. In 1763 Jackson choose to sail with Captain McDaniel from Liverpool to Chesapeake Bay. Upon reaching Maryland, McDaniel placed Jackson in the custody of the local sheriff to be returned to his former slave master. Like a number of other ship captains,

---

15 HMS *Stag* Musters, 1758–1759, TNA ADM 36/6755; *Boston Post-Boy*, 9 April 1759; *Newport Mercury*, 8 April 1776; John Brewer, *The Sinews of Power: War, Money and the English State, 1350–1750* (Cambridge, MA: Harvard University Press, 1990).

Captain McDaniel looked upon blacks in his crew as a means for private profit.[16]

Whites viewing black seamen as objects of profit began on the African coast, where British traders regularly kidnapped African canoemen and sailors.[17] This viewing of black seamen as a means to private wealth came to be widespread in the Anglo-American Atlantic. Kidnappings of black seamen occurred even in regions such as New England, where in the last decades of the eighteenth century abolitionism was strong.[18] As one South Carolinian observed, 'many are kidnapped' and brought to Charleston to be sold.[19] And, despite the efforts of Obadiah Brown and other abolitionists to protect them, British black sailors such as Harry Monroe were regularly kidnapped in the Americas.[20] This view that black seamen could be the means to private fortune was not limited to Africa or the Western Atlantic, however: as Equiano so poignantly described in his *Interesting Narrative* and as the abolitionist Granville Sharp's correspondence evidences, kidnapping of black seamen also occurred in the British Isles.[21]

Kidnapping was something the noted abolitionist Granville Sharp knew first-hand. Sharp regularly sought writs of *habeas corpus* to prevent coercive takings of blacks and maintained contact with seamen he assisted. As Sharp noted in discussing a case where he sent an attorney by coach late at night from London to Deal to catch up with a ship that was coercively transporting a Black to Barbados, 'a delay of even a single minute' could be the difference in preventing coerced

16 *Maryland Gazette*, 24 August 1763.

17 Randy Sparks, 'Gold Coast Merchant Families, Pawning, Awning, and the Eighteenth-Century British Slave Trade', *William & Mary Quarterly*, 70: 2, 2013, pp. 325–7.

18 *Massachusetts Gazette* (Boston), 15 February 1788. The BMD contains more than sixty instances of Black seamen being kidnapped.

19 *New-York Packet*, 13 March 1786.

20 Obadiah Moses Brown Papers, Series I, Correspondence, Rhode Island Historical Society (RIHS).

21 *London Chronicle*, 27 April 1774; Equiano, *Interesting Narrative*, 142; Granville Sharp Commonplace Books, Gloucester Records Office (GRO), D3549/13/4/1.

transportation of a black tar from England to enslavement in the Americas.[22]

While the possibility of being kidnapped caused British black seamen dread, they probably suffered greater anxiety about being captured and sold as prize goods. With both British and American courts presuming that Blacks captured at sea were slaves and putting the burden on Blacks to prove otherwise, and other nations also declaring captured enemy Black sailors prize goods, hundreds of captured black seamen were sold into slavery during the eighteenth century.[23] Privateers and Royal Navy crews alike viewed black sailors as potential objects of profit. As the Vice-Admiralty Court in Barbados observed in 1795, 'the practice ... has been to consider Negroes captured from the Enemy as property and consequently condemnable as Prize.'[24] And although most captured black seamen were sold as Prize Negroes in the Western Atlantic, some, such as the Negro Boy 'taken as a prize' by a Royal Navy vessel off Florida, were sold into slavery in England.[25]

British black sailors also found themselves re-enslaved as a result of the actions of the Royal Navy. As a 'guarantor of the whole system of British Atlantic commerce', the Royal Navy protected slave forts, slave ships and slave colonies, including assisting in the suppression of slave revolts. Naval officers often felt bound by local customs in Britain's colonies, including respecting slave owners' claims to their runaways.[26] The result was that fugitives who obtained berths in the Royal Navy could find themselves discharged for 'being a slave'. John Incobs, Kingston, Black Jack, Coffee, James Dick (Figure 4.1), Dublin, Polydore

---

22 1 August 1787 letter, Granville Sharp letters to Archbishop of Canterbury, Granville Sharp Papers, GRO D3549/13/C3.

23 Charles R. Foy, 'Eighteenth Century Prize Negroes: From Britain to America', *Slavery & Abolition*, 31: 3, 2010, pp. 379–93; Deposition of Joseph Dickinson, 5 July 1732, *Bermuda Historical Quarterly*, 12: 3, 1955, pp. 82–3.

24 Nathaniel Whitting Records, 1773–74, Mss 9001-W, RIHS; Edward Long Vice Admiralty Judge to William Henry Lyttleton, 10 January 1762, TNA CO 137/61, ff. 82–3; Our Lord the King v Twenty-Eight Negroes, 2 February 1793, National Maritime Museum, Greenwich, CAL 127.

25 *Daily Advertiser* (London), 6 October 1743.

26 Vincent Brown, *The Reaper's Garden: Death and Power in the World of Atlantic Slavery* (Cambridge, MA: Harvard University Press, 2008), p. 15.

4.1 HM Galley *Arbuthnot* muster, 1783–6
TNA ADM 36/10426. Photograph by the author.
Courtesy of the National Archives, Kew, United Kingdom.

and other black Royal Navy tars thus found themselves returned to enslavement throughout the Atlantic.[27]

In the years after the American Revolution British black seamen who came ashore in the southern United States also faced a loss of their freedom as a result of Seamen's Acts. If unable to pay prison fees, blacks could find themselves flogged in a 'merciless' manner. To avoid being imprisoned, black seamen often avoided voyages that required disembarking in southern American ports.[28] Laws such as North Carolina's 1788 enactment that allowed for the recapture of manumitted slaves still in the state resulted in black seamen being 'pursued by men with dogs and arms'.[29]

Simply put, when at sea British black sailors were at risk. They entered a world in which whom they could trust was unclear, leaving them constantly on guard: did they have freedom papers with them; would their captains protect or sell them; and would enemies treat them as prisoners of war or chattel to be sold? The anxiety these issues caused black sailors reinforced their status as 'lesser' at a time (the eighteenth century) and in a world (the Anglo-American Atlantic) where blackness left one vulnerable.

27 HM Galley *Arbuthnot* Musters, 1783–1786, TNA ADM 36/10426; *Daily Courant* (London), 23 January 1710; HM Galley *Scourge*, Musters, 1779–1785, TNA ADM 36/10427; Letter of Francis Holburne, Portsmouth, 18 December 1758 to John Cleveland, TNA ADM 1/927.
28 *The Oracle of the Day* (Portsmouth, NH), 9 January 1794; Limbo Robinson, 1798, Welcome Arnold Laborer Books, Vol. 7, John Carter Brown Library, Providence, Rhode Island; *City Gazette and Daily Advertiser* (Charleston), 17 September 1788.
29 Gary B. Nash, *Race and Revolution* (Lanham, MD: Rowman & Littlefield, 1990), pp. 185–8.

British Black Tars' Maritime Opportunities

Regular warfare during the eighteenth century and the resultant burgeoning maritime labour market provided plentiful opportunities for Blacks to find work at sea. Yet these opportunities were not equal to those enjoyed by whites found on Britain's ships. Instead, Blacks faced strong limits to their advancement and encountered racist attitudes among their ship mates.

Among the almost 1,700 blacks known to have served in the eighteenth-century Royal Navy, only one, Jack Perkins, was a captain, and only three others were midshipmen. These men were exceptional. Perkins and Edward Young, a black midshipman on the ill-fated HMS *Bounty*, each had patrons who pushed higher ups in the Admiralty to recognize the men's talents. Most blacks were not so fortunate. Lacking both the navigational and literacy skills required to become officers, most blacks also did not have connections with elites, such as Commodore Ford, to support their careers. The barriers to blacks' advancement became even more significant when in the early nineteenth century the Admiralty issued a directive 'to dismiss from the service all Midshipmen, surgeons, etc. of colour', formally barring blacks' advancement in the Navy.[30]

In addition to rarely being given supervisory roles, blacks also were frequently assigned as officers' servants, stewards, cooks or rowing galleys. Service as servants, stewards and cooks, typically considered 'feminine' labour, reinforced perceptions of black mens' lower status. Similarly, the 170 blacks assigned to British naval galleys were compelled to perform work that in other navies was typically done by enslaved individuals. Ironically, many of the seamen impressed onto Royal Navy galleys were free blacks. Performing such servile work starkly reinforced for them how thin

---

30 Kathleen Chater, *Untold Histories: Black People in England and Wales During the Period of the British Slave Trade, c. 1660–1807* (Manchester: Manchester University Press, 2009), p. 80; Douglas Hamilton, '"A most active, enterprising officer": Captain John Perkins, the Royal Navy and the boundaries of slavery and liberty in the Caribbean', *Slavery & Abolition*, 39: 1, 2017, pp. 80–100; Foy, 'The Royal Navy's Employment', pp. 15–16.

a line there was in the Anglo-American Atlantic between free and coerced labour.[31]

Black sailors' opportunities were also limited by racial antagonism among whites on British ships. In 1780 Barlow Fielding requested a transfer owing to the crew on HMS *Orpheus* having 'taken a Dislike' to his 'Colour' and the ship's captain believing it impossible 'for me to remove [this] Particular Prejudice'. Similarly, at the beginning of the century a black tar was reprimanded for use of 'provoking words' to a Captain whom the records imply had abused the sailor. While common interests and the need for team work among seamen may have created a greater bond among white and black sailors than between workers on shore, whites' racial animus towards blacks did not disappear when men were employed at sea.[32] To counter such hostility, black seamen often shared messes on board. When blacks worked on a ship in numbers, such as the six who did on HMS *Stag* in 1762, this offered some support for individual black tars.[33]

One benefit British black seamen could receive that land-based Britons did not was pension and disability benefits. Paying six pence a month to the Greenwich Hospital fund made them eligible for such benefits. However, while Briton Hammon wrote of receiving a pension for his maritime service and Amos Anderson was an in-pensioner at the Greenwich Hospital, they were the rare blacks

---

31 David Kazanjian, '"Ship as Cook": Notes on the Gendering of Black Atlantic Labor', *Radical Philosophy Review*, 5: 1/2, 2002, pp. 12–13; Charles R. Foy, 'Compelled to Row: Blacks on Royal Navy Galleys During the American Revolution', in Don N. Hagist (ed.), *Journal of the American Revolution: Annual Volume 2019* (Yardley, PA: Westholme Publishing, 2019), p. 261. The 170 Blacks serving on galleys was more than twice blacks' representation on other Royal Navy vessels in the Americas.

32 Philip D. Morgan, 'Black experiences in Britain's maritime world', in David Cannadine (ed.), *Empire, the Sea and Global History: Britain's Maritime World, c. 1763–c. 1840* (New York: Palgrave Macmillan, 2007), pp. 122–3; Court Martials, TNA ADM 1/5261, ff.273–6; Peter Linebaugh and Marcus Rediker, *The Many-Headed Hydra: Sailors, Slaves, Commoners, and the Hidden History of the Revolutionary Atlantic* (Boston: Beacon Press, 2000), pp. 228–34, 328; Arne Bialuscheski, 'Black People under the Black Flag: Piracy and the Slave Trade on the West Coast of Africa, 1718–1723', *Slavery and Abolition*, 29: 4, 2008, p. 469.

33 HMS *Stag* Muster, 1761–1762, TNA ASDM 36/6759.

who benefited from making Seamen's Sixpence payments. A more common experience was that of black seaman Joseph Johnson, who was denied a pension because he had not served in the Royal Navy. The records for Greenwich Hospital, Chatham Chest, as well as local Trinity Hospitals, contain few references to blacks receiving benefits for their maritime labours.[34]

Migration of Black Tars to Britain and Their Lives There

The overwhelming majority of black seamen working on British ships in the Atlantic were born, lived and or worked in Africa or the Americas, regions in which most of them were enslaved. Over the course of the eighteenth century increasing numbers of blacks migrated to the British Isles, such that in the second half of the eighteenth century there were an estimated 10,000 blacks in the United Kingdom. The overwhelming majority of these blacks appear to have come to the British Isles not as slaves but as seamen and soldiers.[35] Justice Mansfield's 1772 *Somerset* decision holding that slave masters in England lacked the power to detain and deport their slaves, may not, as some contemporaries contended, have caused slaves from the Americas to 'flock over in vast numbers'. However, in the three years after the *Somerset* decision the number of maritime fugitives in the Americas more than tripled from the prior three years. Men such as Bacchus, a nineteen-year-old Virginia runaway, 'imagine[d]' that he would 'be free' in England. He and many other maritime fugitives attempting to reach England did so having learned of the *Somerset* decision from colonial newspapers.[36] So too did enslaved black tars, such as the four sailors on the *Lawrence*,

34 Foy, 'The Royal Navy's Employment', pp. 17–18; John Thomas Smith, *Vagabondia, or Anecdotes of Mendicant Wanderers through the Streets of London* (London, 1817), Guildhall Library, Corporation of London, pp. 33–4; Records of Scarborough Trinity House, 1752–1775, ZOX 10/1 North Yorkshire Records Office.
35 There is much uncertainty regarding the size of Britain's eighteenth-century Black population. Kathleen Chater, *Untold Histories: Black People in England and Wales During the Period of the British Slave Trade, c. 1660–1807* (Manchester: Manchester University Press, 2009), pp. 25–34.
36 *Virginia Gazette* (Purdie & Dixon), 30 September 1773; *Virginia Gazette* (Purdie & Dixon), 30 June 1774.

who in 1776 upon docking in Portsmouth harbour quickly asserted perceived rights to freedom under *Somerset*.[37]

England as a land of liberty held a strong hold on the imagination of enslaved peoples in British Atlantic colonies. In 1797 Jack Ghost was an Antiguan slave whose master sent him in a canoe to get turtle grass and put it on board the ship *Broot*. After doing so 'a tho't struck him, that such an opportunity would probably never offer again for his getting to England'. Having made two voyages to Liverpool as a seaman, Jack believed that getting to England would secure him freedom. Serendipitously stowing away on the ship, Jack secreted himself in an empty water barrel. Upon being discovered, the captain put Jack's prior maritime experience to advantage, having the stowaway work as a seaman on the *Broot*. Five decades earlier a Virginian slave named James similarly set out to 'get a passage in some vessel to Great Britain'.[38]

Definite information on the background of eighteenth-century black British seamen is hard to come by. However, newspapers, ship musters, court records and parish records do offer us a window into their lives by which we can draw some conclusions regarding the nature of life for British black tars. A number of black seamen became residents of Britain after having deserted ships on which they served as enslaved sailors. Cambridge and Cuffee, who in 1758 deserted ships in London two weeks apart, are typical of this cohort.[39] These black tars were part of a larger group of enslaved sailors who took the opportunity to flee in ports throughout Europe, particularly in the second half of the eighteenth century when the legal status of slavery in Europe came under increasing scrutiny. Flight by slave seamen, such as the unnamed Negro on the *Windsor Prize* found hiding in Ireland, was not uncommon. The attempts of enslaved seamen to find freedom in British ports led some American slave owners, such as Aaron Lopez of Newport, to avoid having slave sailors work on ships sailing to Britain in the years before the American Revolution.[40]

---

37 Charles R. Foy, '"Unkle Somerset's" Freedom: Liberty in England for Black Sailors', *Journal for Maritime Research*, 13: 1, 2011, pp. 21–36.
38 *The Gazette of the United States* (Philadelphia), 7 February 1798; *Maryland Gazette*, 17 August 1749.
39 *Public Advertiser* (London), 14, 28 November 1758.
40 *London Evening Post*, 18 March 1758; Aaron Lopez Papers, Jewish History

Although black seamen eagerly fled British colonies in the Americas for life in Great Britain, they often found that freedom in the British Isles did not always equate with greater economic opportunities. This is evident in the lack of opportunities for blacks to progress up the British maritime hierarchy. Black ship captains were a rarity in ships sailing from the British Isles. The only black ship captain discussed in a British newspaper was a master named Bell. When the unfortunate skipper's snow was wrecked off the Isle of Wight in 1760, the *Somerset Weekly Advertiser or Lewes Journal* reported that he had been 'driven to the last Extremity' and had hanged himself. Nor did blacks, with the exception of Jack Perkins, serve as captains in the Royal Navy.[41] In contrast to this almost complete absence of black commanders in ships from British ports, in British American colonies black ship masters were common. Tony, Ben, Simon and Steven were among the scores of Patroons who directed rice and tobacco schooners along the rivers of the Carolina Lowcountry and the Chesapeake. In the West Indies blacks commanded pilot boats and privateer ships, while in Halifax they served as captains of merchant vessels. The willingness of slave masters in British colonies to have blacks command their vessels is reflected in how they spoke of their 'negro Patroon[s]' as a 'skillful honest fellow[s]' or as 'well acquainted with the Bay and most of the Rivers in Virginia and Maryland'.[42]

While slavery did not have the same legal status in the British Isles that it did in the Americas, particularly after the *Somerset* decision,

Center, New York.

41 Chater, *Untold Histories*, p. 236; Foy, 'The Royal Navy's Employment', pp. 15–16.

42 Philip D. Morgan and George D. Terry, 'Slavery in Microcosm: A Conspiracy Scare in South Carolina', *Southern Studies*, 21: 2, 1982, p. 132; *South-Carolina Gazette* (Timothy), 29 July 1745 and 20 August 1753; *South Carolina Gazette and American Country Journal*, 10 November 1767; *Virginia Gazette* (Purdie and Dixon), 11 April 1771; *South Carolina Gazette*, 29 October 1737; *Maryland Gazette*, 17 November 1791; *Salem Gazette*, 9 February 1798; *New-York Weekly Journal*, 8 July 1734; Kenneth J. Donovan, 'Slaves in Île Royale, 1713–1760', *French Colonial History*, 5, 2004, p. 32. Blacks also captained British vessels on the African coast. David Eltis, 'Europeans and the Rise and Fall of African Slavery in the Americas: An Interpretation', *American Historical Review*, 98: 5, 1993, p. 1401.

black sailors did encounter hostility in Britain. This hostility, which occasionally may have been race-based, was more frequently based upon class or xenophobic attitudes.[43] And yet, while overt racism toward black mariners may have been limited, some black tars undoubtedly encountered in Britain the hostility Ukawsaw Gronniosaw experienced from whites who resented having to economically compete with Blacks. This hostility can be seen in 'Anglicanus' expressing concern that blacks were replacing white workers as well as efforts to bar all foreigners or non-natives from apprenticeships in London. Such barriers resulted in blacks experiencing difficulties finding regular work. Thus, although many black tars who came from the Americas had experience in ship yards, naval dockyards in Great Britain employed very few of them. By the mid-1780s there were considerable numbers of black seamen among London's close to 2,000 destitute blacks. Former black tars, such as Joseph Johnson, took to busking at London's markets in order to survive.[44]

Despite these considerable hurdles to achieving economic independence for black tars in eighteenth-century Great Britain, communities of black seamen did develop in Britain's larger ports. The *Black Mariner Database* has records for seventy-four black Bristol seamen, forty-three Liverpool black tars and 147 London black sailors. Among these men were cooks, foremast men and ordinaries. Although some, such as the Bristol seamen Antonio Franario and John Quaco, who spent fourteen and twenty-one years at sea, found regular employment on ships, most black sailors appear to have been to sea for only one or two voyages.[45] Thus, the stability of their economic lives appears to have been, for the most part, shaky.

While often struggling economically, British black tars engaged in public action to assert political rights. Whether it was Negro London,

---

43 Chater, *Untold Histories*, pp. 164–72; Gerzina, *Black England*, p. 27.

44 Ukawsaw Gronniosaw, *Wonderous Grace Display'd in the Life and Conversion of James Albert Ukawsaw Gronniosaw* (Bath, 1770), 1712; *Gentleman's Magazine*, XXXIV (1764), p. 495; Foy, 'The Royal Navy's Employment', p. 19; Foy, '"Unkle Somerset's" Freedom', p. 30; Chater, *Untold Histories*, pp. 231–2; Gerzina, *Black England*, p. 140.

45 Stephen D. Behrendt, 'Human Capital in the British Slave Trade', in David Richardson, Suzanne Schwarz and Anthony Tibbles (eds), *Liverpool and Transatlantic Slavery* (Liverpool: Liverpool University Press, 2007), p. 79; Bristol Musters, Muster #156, 1777–1778, Bristol Records Office SMV/9/3/1/8.

who in 1721 took part in a mutiny complaining of having to 'work too hard', or Sam in 'sailor's habit' who was among the mob of seamen who in 1768 protested after the Massacre of St George Field, black tars in Britain made efforts to have their voices heard.[46] Being able to do so without the threat of a master's lash clearly distinguished their lives in Britain from that they and their fathers experienced in the Americas. However, it was not until the Reform Act of 1832 that a few of them would have access to the ballot box.

A chief characteristic of life for British black seamen was that many of them lacked family connections. Very few black men migrated to Great Britain in the eighteenth century with family members. Black men of all occupations had a lack of black female companions—approximately 80 per cent of black Britons were men. In port cities with large populations of black mariners the number of women was even smaller.[47] The result was that many, if not most, black tars were single and those that did marry, such as Olaudah Equiano or Adam Darkman of HMS *Lenox*, often married white women.[48] Nor did many black seamen have family members accompany them to the British Isles. In this respect, Amos Anderson was typical. Cut off from his Igbo mother and never knowing his father, Anderson lacked kinship connections in England. Like most black seamen, Anderson resided in a large port. Rare was the black tar, such as Robert Slaves of Scarborough, who resided in a small British port.[49] As did many British black tars, Anderson turned to shipmates, black and white, for

---

46 Jesse Lemish, 'Jack Tar in the Street', *William and Mary Quarterly*, 25: 3, 1968, pp. 371–407; New Cross Radical History Walk, https://www.gold.ac.uk/calendar/?id=11353 (accessed 8 November 2019); *Gazetteer and New Daily Advertiser* (London), 9 June 1768.

47 Chater, *Untold Histories*, p. 30; Stephen D. Berrendt and Robert A. Hurley, 'Liverpool as a Trading Port: Sailors' Residences, African Migrants, Occupational Change and probated wealth', *International Journal of Maritime History*, 29: 4, 2017, p. 889 (12.05 per cent of 639 Blacks in Liverpool parish records were women).

48 Equiano, *Interesting Narrative*, pp. 386–7. Darkman married Mary Ann Wicherly at Halverstroke in 1771. Information regarding Darkman's marriage was provided by John Ellis.

49 *Brotherly Love* Muster, 1757–1758, Scarborough Muster Rolls, 1754–1765, TNA CUST 91/112.

companionship and community. The two wills he executed, one in 1793 and a second in 1800, reflect this. In each, Anderson bequeathed his worldly possessions to his shipmates John Horton and John Raymond, men who he deemed 'trusty friends'.[50]

When migrating across the Atlantic to Great Britain black tars shed the shackles of slavery. To do so, they often gave up family, kin and connections that had supported them. Thus, while free in ways they never could be in the Americas, they needed to form new connections and identities to sustain them. Becoming members of religious communities in Britain was one method many, such as Amos Anderson, chose. A second method that all black tars engaged in was the creation and presentation of identities of their own choosing. Some, such as Olaudah Equiano, emphasized being African. Many others chose surnames that reflected the names of Royal Navy ships they served on, as did the Congo-born Thomas Arbuthnot of HM Galley *Arbuthnot*.[51] In doing so, they, as had Joseph Johnson when busking with a headdress of HMS *Victory* on his head, clearly asserted their Britishness based upon having served the king. These men understood that their status in British society was tenuous and sought to cement their place in Britain by reminding others of their central role in the creation of Britain's maritime empire.

50 Wills of Amos Anderson, TNA ADM 48/1/132 (1793) and TNA ADM 48/2/89 (1800).
51 HM Galley *Arbuthnot* muster, 1780–1782, TNA ADM 36/10213.

CHAPTER FIVE

Black Runaways
in Eighteenth-Century Britain

Stephen Mullen, Nelson Mundell and Simon P. Newman

This essay is based upon extensive research into thousands of eighteenth-century Scottish and English newspapers, a database of seventy-five newspaper notices offering enslaved people for sale and 831 advertisements for freedom-seeking bound and enslaved people who had escaped from their masters and mistresses. These surviving records hint at the existence of a larger number of people who escaped but were not advertised for, and an even larger number who did not run away. As this essay will demonstrate, many of those who were enslaved, who were bought and sold and who escaped, were children or young adults, and the essay will explore the story of Jamie Montgomery, a young enslaved runaway in Scotland.[1]

Enslaved people were far from unusual in Georgian Britain, as suggested by an advertisement placed in 1719 by a young London craftsman, who may well have owned the unnamed enslaved boy or acted on behalf of his owner:

> There is a Negro Boy of 8 or 9 Years old, to be sold, of a very good black Complexion. Enquire at Mr. Perchard's, Pewterer, the Corner of Abchurch-lane, Cannon-street.[2]

1 This essay builds upon the Leverhulme Trust-funded research project 'Runaway Slaves in Britain: bondage, freedom and race in the eighteenth century', https://www.runaways.gla.ac.uk/.
2 *Daily Courant* (London), 20 November 1719, p. 2.

'For sale' notices such as this one, along with those advertising for the capture and return of escaped enslaved and bound labourers, were an everyday feature of English and Scottish newspapers, appearing alongside the day-to-day commercial notices that filled the burgeoning newspapers of Georgian Britain. Together they demonstrate not only that there was an enslaved population in Britain but, perhaps more significantly, that trafficking of enslaved people was routine.

Sometimes such advertisements featured enslaved people who were new or recent arrivals from the colonies or even from Africa, as in the case of

A WINDWARD COAST BLACK BOY,
[Ap]pears to be under 14 Years old, well looking and tractable having been three Months in England.[3]

The named contact person for this advertisement was the publisher of the leading Liverpool newspaper *Williamson's Liverpool Advertiser and Mercantile Register*. Robert Williamson often acted as broker in the sale of enslaved people, and in this case he sought out an unnamed boy who had endured one of the more than 7,000 British transatlantic slave-trading voyages which shipped some 1.75 million enslaved people from West Africa to the Americas during the first three quarters of the eighteenth century.[4] Perhaps this boy had become a favourite of the ship's captain or a senior officer, who then retained him as a personal servant, thereby enabling him to avoid plantation slavery, the fate of the vast majority transported from Africa.

This did not mean a full reprieve, however, for enslaved people who were brought to Britain were never more than one sale away from a return to colonial plantation slavery. They existed in a liminal state between the harsh racial slavery of the colonies and the more benign working conditions for white and black people alike in the British Isles.

3 *Williamson's Liverpool Advertiser and Mercantile Register* (Liverpool), 17 August 1765, p. 3.
4 According to *Voyages: The Trans-Atlantic Slave Trade Database*, between 1701 and 1800 British ships carried an estimated 2.5 million enslaved people from Africa to the New World colonies. http://www.slavevoyages.org/assessment/estimates (accessed 30 September 2018).

A return to the terrors of New World bondage was always possible, as one mid-eighteenth-century advertisement made clear:

> To be SOLD,
> A Pretty little Negro Boy, about nine Years old, and well limb'd.
> If not disposed of, is to be sent to the West Indies in six Days Time.
> He is to be seen at the Dolphin Tavern in Tower Street.[5]

A well-known tavern in central London, the Dolphin was a stone's throw from the Tower of London and no more than a couple of hundred yards from the wharves from which ships regularly departed for the American and Caribbean colonies. No doubt the Dolphin was frequented by ship captains who could easily sell a healthy young enslaved boy in Jamaica, Virginia or other colonies for a handsome profit.[6] When enslaved people were returned to the plantation colonies they were subject to colonial slave codes and the brutal violence of the slave regime. When one 'Negroe Servant' in England was 'threatened by his Master, for some Misconduct, to be sent to the Plantations', the threat was sufficiently terrifying for the man to hang himself in his owner's coal cellar.[7]

A sample of seventy-five newspaper notices advertising the sale of eighty-nine enslaved people highlights some interesting points. Of those whose gender is known only eight (10.3 per cent) were female, while 70 (89.7 per cent) were male. More remarkable was the fact

---

5 *Daily Advertiser* (London), 11 December 1744, p. 2.

6 The Dolphin Tavern was listed in such sources as *New Remarks of London Or, A Survey of the Cities of London and Westminster, of Southwark and Part of Middlesex and Surrey ... Collected by the Company of Parish Clerks* (London: for E. Midwinter, 1732), p. 5.

7 'Any Lady or Family going to the West-Indies', *Public Advertiser* 24 March 1768; 'A likely Black BOY', *The Public Advertiser* 19 July 1764, p. 3; 'Yesterday a Negroe Servant', *Derby Mercury* (Derby), 22 June 1753, p. 2. In only three cases were prices specified: a fifteen-year-old male was advertised at thirty guineas in 1764, a boy at £40 in 1768, and a ten–eleven-year-old boy for fifty guineas in 1769: see 'A likely Black BOY', *Public Advertiser* 19 July 1764, p. 3; 'For sale' *Edinburgh Evening Courant* 18 April 1768; 'A NEGRO BOY, To be disposed of', *Public Advertiser*, 8 April 1769.

that virtually all enslaved people offered for sale in Great Britain were children or young adults. While two were described as men, one as a 'young fellow' and twelve (16.2 per cent) were aged between nineteen and twenty-two, the other fifty-nine (79.7 per cent) were aged between one and seventeen. Almost one-third (twenty-four, 32.4 per cent) were children aged between eight and twelve.[8]

These essential characteristics of people advertised for sale in British newspapers are indicative of the demographic characteristics of the enslaved population in England and Scotland, a population that was strikingly different from white British servants and enslaved plantation workers. White British men and women hired themselves out as agricultural workers, although women dominated the ranks of domestic servants.[9] In the colonies, planters sought out 'prime' male and female fields hands aged between their late teens and early thirties to carry out the physically demanding tasks of planting, tending, harvesting and processing staple crops such as sugar, rice and tobacco. Throughout the eighteenth century it was the men and women in these age groups who dominated the human cargoes of the thousands of British slave ships; most of the deadly plantation societies had relatively few enslaved children and even fewer late-middle-aged or elderly enslaved people.[10]

However, when planters, merchants, lawyers, colonial officials, doctors, clerics and naval and army officers selected enslaved people to accompany them to Great Britain they rarely chose them from the great mass of plantation labourers. Instead, they tended to take trusted

8 The ages (or estimated ages) of sixty-two were specified in newspaper advertisements; eight were described as 'boys' and one as a 'girl', one as a 'young fellow' and two as 'men'.

9 Perhaps 80 per cent of domestic servants in eighteenth-century Britain were female. See Carolyn Steedman, *Labours Lost: Domestic Service and the Making of Modern England* (Cambridge: Cambridge University Press, 2009), p. 28, pp. 36–41; Bridget Hill, *Servants: English Domestics in the Eighteenth Century* (Oxford: Clarendon Press, 1996), pp. 6–7, pp. 101–4; Paula Humfrey, *The Experience of Domestic Service for Women in Early Modern London* (Farnham: Ashgate, 2011), pp. 25–9. See also Tim Meldrum, *Domestic Service and Gender, 1660–1750: Life and Work in the London Household* (Harlow: Pearson Education, 2000).

10 For a discussion of the plantation work forces, see Simon P. Newman, *A New World of Labor: The Development of Plantation Slavery in the British Atlantic* (Philadelphia: University of Pennsylvania Press, 2013), pp. 189–242.

domestic attendants, or young boys and occasionally girls who had become favourites. Some enslaved people in Britain were craftsmen, and others were seamen, but most were personal and domestic servants, often dressed in smart livery and living emblems of the wealth of their owners. While it was West Africa's young men and women who toiled on the plantations of the Americas, it was children who attended to masters and mistresses in the British Isles.[11] Many enslaved adults resisted their enslavement on plantations, occasionally participating in large-scale rebellions but more commonly seeking short- or long-term escape, but in Britain it was often enslaved children and young adults who resisted by trying to escape, in search of a very different kind of freedom in the British Isles.

Table 1. Ages of freedom-seeking runaways in Britain, 1700 to 1780

Age Range	Number	%
6 to 14 (including 'boys')	105	16.9
15-19 (including 'young')	216	34.7
20 to 30	266	42.8
31 and older	35	5.6

Source: 'Runaway Slaves in Britain' https://www.runaways.gla.ac.uk/database/ (accessed 5 July 2018)

The demographic profile of freedom-seeking runaways in Britain was quite distinctive from that of the colonies, and those who sought freedom in England and Scotland were younger and more likely to be male than fugitives in the Americas (Table 5.1). Among 622 whose

11 While the vast majority of enslaved and bound children in Britain were African in origin, some were South Asian and a few indigenous American. The only work to date focusing on enslaved children in eighteenth-century Britain is Dolly MacKinnon, 'Slave Children: Scotland's Children as Chattels at Home and Abroad ion the Eighteenth Century', in Janay Nugent and Elizabeth Ewan (eds), *Children and Youth in Premodern Scotland before the Nineteenth Century* (Woodbridge: The Boydell Press, 2015), pp. 120–35.

actual or approximate age was specified in the newspaper advertisements placed by their masters, a remarkable 321 (51.6 per cent) were no more than teenagers, aged between six and nineteen.[12] Moreover, 105 (16.9 per cent) British runaways were aged fourteen or less (or were described as 'boys'), exactly three times as many as were aged thirty-one or older. Just as significantly, these freedom-seekers were overwhelmingly male and, of 820 fugitives whose gender is known, 758 (92.4 per cent) were male and only sixty-two (7.6 per cent) were female.

By way of comparison, a database of Jamaican runaways during the eighteenth and early nineteenth centuries revealed that almost one-quarter of 948 fugitives whose gender was identified were female:[13] 231 (24.4 per cent) female runaways meant that the proportion of female runaways in Jamaica was between three and four times larger than in Britain. The age of runaways revealed a similar disparity, for in Jamaica the proportion of young runaways was significantly lower, with ninety-three (36.9 per cent) of those whose age was known being nineteen or younger. Significantly, many of the Jamaican children who eloped ran away with parents or family members as part of group escapes, or on occasion escaped to try and reunite with parents, siblings or other family members, so the number of children who escaped in Jamaica alone and on their own initiative was even lower. Family elopements were virtually unknown in Britain, as most of the enslaved taken to England and Scotland were children who had been separated from their families in Africa, the American and Caribbean colonies or South Asia, and who were alone in Britain.

To a master, the act of selecting a young boy, removing him from the plantation fields and allowing him better food and clothing and the lighter physical labour of domestic work could feel like an act of great kindness. For example, one planter who returned to Britain, John

12 Four runaways described as 'boy' and fourteen as 'young' have been included in the 321 who comprise the youngest cohort; one 'man' has been included in the twentythirty age cohort; and three 'middle-aged' and one old are included in the oldest cohort.

13 This database has been compiled by Simon P. Newman, and included 1,000 Jamaican advertisements from between 1775 and 1823. It is the basis of 'Hidden in Plain Sight: Escaped Slaves in Late Eighteenth- and Early Nineteenth-Century Jamaica', *William and Mary Quarterly*, 3rd ser., digital edition (June 2018).

Wedderburn, testified that he 'took a liking' to an enslaved African boy named Joseph Knight and consequently made Knight 'his personal servant and have upon all occasions... treated him with particular kindness and favour'.[14] To white masters the act of bringing favoured enslaved children to Britain might appear the culmination of such largesse: freeing them from the experience and influences of American and Caribbean slavery, and immersing them in the day-to-day life of domestic service in Georgian Britain.

The surviving family portraits of elite British families attended by liveried enslaved are intended to show domestic harmony in the context of imperial and mercantile success, and they attest to the ways in which youthful enslaved domestics might display the wealth and accomplishments of owners. Yet the portraits reveal nothing of the interior mental world of these enslaved children, of the horrors they had experienced, the dislocation and trauma. Whether born in Africa or the Americas, these boys and girls had been ripped from parents and community and taken to live and work in the overwhelmingly white and alien British Isles. Some, like twelve-year old Occorro, had endured the Middle Passage from Africa to the Americas, and the trauma of that experience was then compounded by further removal to Britain.[15] Thirteen-year-old Somerset was branded both on his arm and his forehead, the latter perhaps a punishment for resistance or escape in the past. He may have been a cabin boy, for the advertisement seeking his capture encouraged anybody who took up the boy to return him to naval officers, either to Captain Fish or Lieutenant Masters.[16] Fifteen- or sixteen-year-old Vernon may also have been African-born, given the African country marks described as 'scars on his forehead'. Only about four feet nine inches tall, he had 'but little of the English language'. Vernon was described as 'lame' having 'lost some of his toes', though whether this was the result of

14 Sir John Wedderburn of Ballindean, 'Deposition before the Sheriff of Perth', 15 November 1774, National Records of Scotland (hereafter NRS), CS 235/2/2.

15 Occoro was described in a runaway advertisement as having 'three Scars on each side of his Face', Country Marks applied in West Africa and thus evidence of his African birth. See 'Went away on Sunday Night last ...' *Daily Advertiser* (London) 4 January 1745, p. 2.

16 'ELOP'D or Stolen ...' *Daily Advertiser* (London), 12 April 1760, p. 2.

injury or illness is unclear.[17] Given his African day-name, sixteen-year-old Quoshy was quite possibly African-born, and he was branded on his breast with the letters EA, the initials of his master Captain Edward Archer.[18] Some runaways were even younger: Bacchus, an eight-year-old 'little Negro Boy', was, when he escaped, wearing old and worn clothing and shoes, and was hampered by the loss of toes from both feet.[19]

What drove such bound and enslaved young people to escape into a foreign environment? In most cases the only evidence we have is the short newspaper advertisement placed by masters, owners or their agents, thus reflecting more of the perceptions and objectives of white masters than of the fugitives themselves.

Occasionally, however, additional records beyond these runaway advertisements reveal more about the children who attempted to escape from slavery in eighteenth-century Britain. Jamie Montgomery was almost certainly born in Virginia about 250 years ago and, given the massive forced migration of enslaved Africans to Virginia during the mid-eighteenth century, it is quite possible that one or even both of Jamie's parents had been born in Africa. We do not know exactly how old Jamie was, but when he arrived in Scotland he was probably a young teenager who had grown up in a fairly large community of enslaved Africans working on the tobacco plantations of Joseph Hawkins. Hawkins first established a plantation in Spotsylvania County around 1740, and was successful until his death, at which the *Virginia Gazette* carried an advertisement for the sale of his 'EIGHTY likely Virginia born SLAVES'.[20]

---

17 'STOLEN or STRAY'D ...' *London Daily Post and General Advertiser* (London), 27 July 1741, p. 2.

18 'A Negro, named Quoshey', *London Gazette* (London), 30 December 1700, p. 2. Quoshey appears to be a variant of either the Twi or the Ndyuka name Kwasi, the day name for Kwasiada or Sunday. See David DeCamp, 'African Day Names in Jamaica', *Language*, 43: 1, 1967, pp. 139–49.

19 'WHEREAS a little Negro Boy', *Daily Advertiser* (London), 20 May 1742, p. 2.

20 Hawkins' will makes clear that he had already established his son, also named Joseph, on his own plantation. Joseph Sr. left his slaves and household goods to his daughters Lucy and Sarah. Neither had yet married, and the sale of the slaves would have provided them with sizeable dowries. See 'Will

The owners of new tobacco plantations and farms in western Virginia found it difficult and expensive to purchase goods from and send crops back to ports on the Atlantic coast. Scottish merchants and factors—many of them representing Glasgow firms—neatly filled this need by establishing trading houses close to the new plantations, and soon these Virginia planters found themselves enmeshed in Glasgow's Atlantic economy. The large majority of Virginia's tobacco came through Glasgow and its Clyde ports, and the city grew wealthy from this trade. The largest tobacco merchants, such as Andrew Buchanan, Archibald Ingram, Alexander Oswald and John Glassford, have left an indelible impression on the city.[21] Several Scottish trading houses were based in Fredericksburg, the Spotsylvania county seat and a fast-growing town on the Rappahannock River, which provided access to the coast.[22]

Like most of the tobacco planters of Spotsylvania County, Joseph Hawkins frequently visited Fredericksburg in order to conduct

of Joseph Hawkins, 30 March 1769, Spotsylvania County, VA RECORDS, 1761–1772, Will Book D (MF Reel 27), p. 525; 'To be SOLD ... by Joseph Hawkins', *Supplement to the Virginia Gazette* (Williamsburg, Virginia), 26 April 1770, p. 1.

21 J.H. Soltow, 'Scottish Traders in Virginia, 1750–1775', *The Economic History Review*, 12: 1, 1959, pp. 83–98; Robert D. Mitchell and Warren R. Hofstra, 'How do settlement systems evolve? The Virginia backcountry during the eighteenth century', *Journal of Historical Geography*, 21: 2, 1995, pp. 123–47; Warren R. Hofstra, *The Planting of New Virginia: Settlement and Landscape in the Shenandoah Valley* (Baltimore: The Johns Hopkins University Press, 2004); Alan L. Karras, *Sojourners in the Sun: Scottish Migrants in Jamaica and the Chesapeake, 1740–1800* (Ithaca: Cornell University Press, 1992), pp. 118–69; T.M. Devine, *The Tobacco Lords: A Study of the Tobacco Merchants of Glasgow and their Trading Activities, c. 1740–90* (Edinburgh: John Donald, 1975); Simon P. Newman, 'Theorizing Class in an Atlantic World: A Case Study of Glasgow', in Simon Middleton and Billy G. Smith (eds), *Class Matters: Early North America and the Atlantic World* (Philadelphia: University of Pennsylvania Press, 2008), pp. 16–34.

22 For a discussion of Scots factors and merchants in early Fredericksburg see R. Walter Coakley, 'The Two James Hunters of Fredericksburg', *The Virginia Magazine of History and Biography*, 56: 1, 1948, pp. 3–21. Jacob M. Price, 'The Rise of Glasgow in the Chesapeake Tobacco Trade, 1707–1775', *William and Mary Quarterly*, 3rd ser., 11: 2, 1954, p. 197, pp. 179–81.

business.[23] One of Hawkins' business transaction occurred on 9 March 1750. For a price of £56 12s 5d Virginia currency, Hakwins sold 'One Negro Boy named Jamie' to a Scottish merchant named Robert Shedden.[24] No record of Jamie survives in Virginia, and we know of this transaction only because the original bill of sale—the legal proof of ownership—is today held by the National Archives of Scotland.

We know a little more about Robert Shedden, the Scot who purchased Jamie. He was one of many Scottish sojourners who sought their fortunes working for merchant and trading houses in Britain's Chesapeake and Caribbean colonies. Robert was the second son of John and Margaret Shedden, who owned the Marsheland property in the parish of Beith, Ayrshire.[25] Shedden was at the heart of the expanding tobacco trade in western Virginia, and he worked with leading Glaswegian merchants such as John Murdoch, William Crawford Jr and Andrew Cochrane: indeed, Shedden would later describe himself as a 'Merchant in Glasgow'.[26]

It was not unusual for successful Scottish factors and merchants to purchase slaves who would undertake physical labour in their trading houses, but this was not why Shedden purchased Jamie. Shedden planned to send Jamie to Scotland, where he would be apprenticed to a joiner, and then return the skilled and thus more valuable boy back to Virginia and sell him back to Hawkins for a healthy profit.[27] White

---

23 William Armstrong Crozier, ed., *Spotsylvania County Records, 1721–1800: Being Transcriptions, From the Original Files at the County Court House, of Wills, Deeds, Administrators' and Guardians' Bonds, Marriage Licenses, and Lists of Revolutionary Pensioners* (Baltimore: Southern Book Company, 1955), pp. 160, 165, 167, 174, 179.

24 Bill of Sale, dated Fredricksburgh, 9 March 1750, NRS, CS234/S/3/12. The purchaser's name appears as either Shedden or Sheddan in different records.

25 James Dobie, *Memoir of William Wilson of Crummock* (Edinburgh, privately printed, 1896), p. 67.

26 Petition of Robert Shedden to the Lords of Council and Session, 9 August 1756, NRS, CS234/S/3/12. Some of Shedden's business dealings are revealed in the records of his estate following his death in 1759: see NRS, CC9/7/64/379.

27 Shedden described this arrangement in *Memorial for Robert Sheddan of Morrice-hill, Late Merchant in Glasgow* (9 July 1756), 2, Advocates Library, Session Papers, Campbell's Collection, p. 1; for discussion of this practice in comparative context, see John W. Cairns, 'Enforced Sojourners: Enslaved Apprentices in Eighteenth-Century Scotland', in E.J.M.F.C. Broers and

craftsmen were expensive to hire in western Virginia, and planters were eager to have their own enslaved boys trained in artisanal crafts.

Shedden's younger sister Elizabeth was married to Robert Morrice, a skilled carpenter in their home town of Beith, and late in 1752 Shedden sent Jamie from Virginia to Scotland.[28] In Spotsylvania County Jamie had been part of a large community of black people: a generation later, the First Federal Census recorded that the nearly 6,000 enslaved people in Spotsylvania County constituted over half of the county's population.[29] It is very likely that Jamie had spent much of his early childhood mainly in the company of people whose skin was the same colour as his. His parents or others in this community would have told him tales of their own earlier lives in West Africa, and perhaps of the horrors of the Middle Passage, and with them he would have shared the vestiges of West African culture as well as the food and the developing language and culture of the emerging African American community of Virginia.

However, Ayrshire was a long, long way from Virginia. Midway between Paisley and Ardrossan, Beith was a small but growing town surrounded by arable and dairy farmland, and in 1759 the town was home to almost 700 'examinable persons'. These included a wide number of skilled craftsmen, including masons, saddlers, shoemakers, smiths, coopers and carpenters, and Jamie was settled into the household of Robert and Elizabeth Morrice, where he began his apprenticeship.[30] How unfamiliar this small town in Scotland must have seemed to a young African American boy torn from his family and community in Virginia. Arriving late in the year, the dark days, the food, the language—everything must have seemed alien to Jamie.

R.M.H. Kubben (eds), *Ad Fontes: Liber Amicorum Prof. Beatrix van Erp-Jacobs* (Nijmegen: Wolf Legal Publishers, 2014), pp. 67–81.

28 The family connection is revealed in various family trees, and in the documents concern Shedden's estate following his death, NRS, CC9/7/64/57–60. In some documents Morrice's name is spelled as Morris.

29 This number refers to those eligible for church membership. *Heads of Families at the First Census of the United States Taken in the Year 1790: Records of the State Enumerations: 1782–1785. Virginia* (Washington: Government Printing Office, 1908), p. 9.

30 John Sinclair, *The Statistic Account of Scotland. Drawn from the Communications of the Ministers of the Different Parishes. Volume Eight* (Edinburgh: William Creech, 1793), pp. 317, 320.

Robert Shedden paid Robert Morrice £40 as Jamie's apprenticeship fee and a further two shillings per week for Jamie's bed, board and clothing. It is unclear whether or not the two men had agreed upon a formal indenture.[31] We do not know if Jamie was Morrice's only apprentice, but it is likely that he was one of several in a larger business, and he would have lived and worked alongside these white boys, and eaten his meals and slept with either Morrice's apprentices or his children. It would also appear that Jamie attended church with the Morrice family, along with most residents of Beith. This was quite probably the first time Jamie had ever been inside a church, for Virginia had fewer than 100 clergymen and only one church per 1,000 white residents: organized Christianity in mid-eighteenth-century Virginia was a white affair.[32]

Two years into Jamie's apprenticeship his owner Robert Shedden returned home to Scotland. Having made his fortune, Shedden had purchased the estate of Morrisill, near Beith, and shortly after his return he then married Elizabeth Simson.[33] For reasons that are unclear Shedden reclaimed Jamie from Robert Morrice and brought him into the Shedden household. Jamie's subordinate status was confirmed by Shedden's decision to rename him 'Shanker', almost certainly a derogatory appellation, and to take him away from his professional training and his home with the Morrice family. Jamie would later assert that Shedden employed him:

> in the most slavish and servile business, his only occupation being the sawing of wood, and other laborious works, which requiring neither skill nor ingenuity, but sinews and strength,

31 *Memorial for Robert Sheddan of Morrice-hill, Late Merchant in Glasgow* (9 July 1756), 2, Advocates Library, Session Papers, Campbell's Collection, p. 2.
32 John M. Murrin, 'Religion and Politics in America from the First Settlements to the Civil War', in Mark A. Noll and Luke E. Harlow (eds), *Religion and American Politics From the Colonial Period to the Present* (Oxford: Oxford University Press, 2007), p. 41; Mark A. Noll, Nathan O. Hatch, George M. Marsden, David F. Wells and John D. Woodbridge, eds, *Christianity in America: A Handbook* (Grand Rapids, MI: Lion Publishing, 1983), p. 76.
33 Dobie, p. 69; James Paterson, *History of the County of Ayr, With a Genealogical Account of the Families of Ayrshire*, Vol. I (Ayr: John Dick, 1847), p. 276.

were therefore judged proper for a Person of [his] complexion, and of his unusual strength and vigour.[34]

This language is significant. While Jamie had left the colonies as a Virginia-born enslaved African American, after several years in Scotland he had begun to think of himself as a skilled craftsman who was qualified for more than menial manual labour. Why did Shedden treat Jamie this way? Shedden was a wealthy man, so it was unlikely to be a cost-cutting measure. Perhaps Shedden had realized that Jamie was growing into his later teens away from the violent discipline of slave society and that, having lived, worked and worshipped alongside white people, the teenage boy was beginning to think of himself as an individual deserving of certain rights.

The fact that Jamie had been baptized by John Witherspoon, minister of the church in Beith, might support this interpretation. Shedden believed that Jamie 'got it into his Head, that by being baptized he would become free', and Shedden opposed Jamie's baptism because of 'the Fancies of Freedom which it might instill into his Slave'. Witherspoon provided Jamie with some basic religious instruction and in April 1756 the minister provided the young black man with a certificate testifying to the bearer's good Christian conduct: Witherspoon proved ready and willing to welcome Jamie into his congregation on nominally equal terms, and to give him a certificate that recognized his independent agency as a Christian believer.[35]

Shedden and Jamie told different stories about what happened next, and these survive in their contradictory accounts in the National Records of Scotland. Robert Shedden's brother Matthew was due to sail to Virginia in the spring of 1756, and Robert decided to honour his agreement with Joseph Hawkins and send Jamie back to Virginia and sell him at a profit. According to Shedden, Jamie went willingly to the ship at Port Glasgow, eager to see his family once again. In contrast, Jamie recalled that he had been forcibly taken from his bed by Shedden, his brother James and two other men. With his hands tied Jamie was

---

34 *Memorial for James Montgomery—Sheddan* [*sic*]; *Against Robert Sheddan* (23 July 1756), pp. 1–2. Advocates Library, Session Papers, Campbell's Collection, V.

35 Deposition by Shedden, dated Morrishill, 22 June 1756, NRS, CS 234/S/3/12.

tethered to a horse and dragged from Beith to Port Glasgow, 'not upon the King's high way, but thro' muirs or lonely places, and other by-roads'. If Jamie is right, it is possible that Shedden did not want friends and neighbours to see how he was treating Jamie. In Port Glasgow the Virginia-bound ship was not yet ready, and Jamie was imprisoned and guarded by his captors, but he was allowed to walk along the quay, 'which was necessary for the recovery of his health'. Jamie seized this opportunity to escape and made his way to Edinburgh.[36]

Jamie had no intention of returning to Virginia. This was a momentous decision for the young man, as it was for other young runaways in Britain. Escaping from Shedden and asserting his freedom made it highly unlikely that Jamie could ever again return to Virginia and see his parents, siblings, family and community. During his years in Scotland Jamie's life, work and community had become familiar and comfortable, and apparently he had no desire to return to a land where he would only ever be property.

Following Jamie's escape, Shedden placed advertisements in Glasgow and Edinburgh newspapers, including one that appeared in the *Edinburgh Evening Courant* (Figure 5.1):

RUN Away from the Subscriber, living near Beith, Shire of Ayr, ONE NEGRO MAN, aged about 22 years, five feet and a half high or thereby. He is a Virginian born Slave, speaks pretty good English; he has been five years in this country, and has served sometimes with a joiner; he has a deep Scare [*sic*] above one of his eyes, occasioned by a stroke of a horse; he also has got with him a Certificate, which calls him Jamie Montgomerie, signed, John Witherspoone [*sic*] Minister. Whoever takes up the said Run-away, and brings him home, or secures him, and gets notice to his master, shall have two guineas reward, besides all other charges paid by me.

ROB. SHEDDEN[37]

---

36 *Memorial for Robert Sheddan of Morrice-hill, late Merchant in Glasgow* (9 July 1756) Advocates Library, Session Papers, Campbell's Collection, p. 2; *Memorial for James Montgomery—Sheddan* [*sic*]; *Against Robert Sheddan* (23 July 1756), Advocates Library, Session Papers, Campbell's Collection, V, pp. 2–3.
37 *The Glasgow Courant*, 3–10 May 1756, p. 3; *Glasgow Journal*, 3 May 1756, p. 3; *Edinburgh Evening Courant* (Edinburgh), 4 May 1756.

RUN away from the Subfcriber, living near Beith, Shire of Ayr, ONE NEGROE MAN, aged about 22 Years, five Feet and a half high or thereby. He is a Virginia born Slave, fpeaks pretty good Englifh; he has been five Years in this Country, and has ferved fometime with a Joiner; he has a deep Scare above one of his Eyes, occafioned by a Stroke from a Horfe; he has alfo got with him a Certificate, which calls him James Montgomerie, figned, John Witherfpoone Minifter. Whoever takes up the faid Run-away, and brings him home, or fecures him, and gets Notice to his Mafter, fhall have two Guineas Reward, befides all other Charges paid, by me
ROB. SHEDDEN.
Morrifhill, April 26th 1756.
N.B. The Negroe run away the 21ft inft.

5.1 Advertisement placed by Robert Shedden in
Edinburgh Evening Courant, 4 May 1756.
Reproduced by permission of the National Library of Scotland.

This was the first time that Jamie appeared in any kind of public document or record. Jamie's status as 'a Virginian born Slave' was brashly and publicly asserted by Shedden, who clearly felt no shame in asserting his right of ownership of another human being in the pages of Scotland's leading newspapers. A good number of Scots either had interests in businesses concerned with the trade in goods produced by slaves or owned slaves themselves, and at this point few, if any, Scots opposed slavery: the movement to abolish the transatlantic slave trade would not exist for another generation. But, while asserting Jamie's enslaved status, Shedden's advertisement also revealed how acclimatized Jamie has become: he had lived in Scotland for five years, spoke English well, had been baptized and had apprenticed with a joiner.

Moreover, Shedden admitted that Jamie carried with him a certificate given him by the Rev. John Witherspoon 'which calls him Jamie Montgomery'. These few words speak volumes about the many battles over ownership of a human that were inherent in slavery. By renaming

Jamie as 'Shanker' Shedden had asserted absolute control over the young slave, not only by the act of renaming but also by the use of a name not normally applied to people. Renaming enslaved people was a common practice by slaveholders. Some enslaved people, such as Olaudah Equiano, were given several different names in their lifetimes. Perhaps Shedden resented the fact that Jamie had appropriated a surname: at this point enslaved people in Virginia generally were recorded with only first names, for surnames gave lineage and legal identity to those whose status as property made such individuality impossible. We do not know why Jamie had chosen the name Montgomery, although we do know that it was a fairly common surname in Ayrshire. Perhaps the choice was inspired by Elizabeth Montgomerie, the young wife of John Witherspoon, in whose home Jamie had received religious instruction.[38]

The certificate given by Witherspoon to Jamie Montgomery was typical of those given by ministers to parishioners who were moving, and by demonstrating religious identity and affiliation they could be utilized in other parishes as evidence of good Christian standing. Witherspoon had therefore validated Montgomery's belief that he was more than enslaved property. But property is what Jamie Montgomery was, at least as far as Robert Shedden was concerned. Shedden would later assert that he had 'paid *L. 56 Virginia* Currency' for Montgomery, as well as 'considerable Sums for his Apprentice Fee, his Board, Clothing, and the Expence of recovering him, &c', and Montgomery was not, Shedden believed, entitled to *Habeus Corpus*, 'for by *Magna Charta* only a Freeman is intitled thereto'.[39]

Somehow Montgomery made his way across Scotland to Edinburgh, and once there he was able to use his training and church certificate to secure work as a journeyman joiner in Peter Wright's workshop. Montgomery's apprenticeship had given him a skill and a professional identity, and thus a means by which to subsist. It appears that he thought that he could live, work and worship alongside Scotsmen, practising

---

38 J. Walter McGinty, *'An Animated Son of Liberty': A Life of John Witherspoon* (Bury St Edmunds: Arena Books, 2012), p. 8.

39 *Memorial for Robert Sheddan of Morrice-hill, Late Merchant in Glasgow* (9 July 1756) Advocates Library, Session Papers, Campbell's Collection, pp. 15, 17.

his craft and living as a free man. Perhaps, too, he thought of one day settling down, marrying and having a family, for other black men were able to marry into the community and make lives for themselves and their families in mid-eighteenth-century Scotland and England. These were all aspirations that would have been unthinkable back in Virginia, where an escaped slave would have had few prospects for work and an independent life. In Virginia, working alongside white craftsmen as a free and equal man and marrying into white society were illegal.

Unfortunately for young Jamie Montgomery, Shedden's reward of two guineas plus expenses proved his undoing. At the bottom of the original bill of sale for Jamie an officer of the Baillie Court named John Braidwood wrote a receipt for £2 2s dated 13 May 1756, paid to him 'for apprehending one Negro Black boy named James Montgomerie'.[40] No doubt Shedden had brought the receipt with him to Edinburgh as proof of his ownership of Jamie, and had then had Braidwood write a receipt for the reward money on this same document.

Shedden petitioned the Edinburgh courts to have Montgomery returned to him, but the judges authorized Robert Gray, the procurator fiscal of their court, to act for Montgomery. Gray responded to Shedden's petition asking 'upon what principle can the pursuer pretend that *Jamie Montgomery* is a slave?'[41] Sadly Edinburgh's Tolbooth jail was a dirty and disease-ridden place, and the unfortunate Jamie died before his case could be heard.

Jamie Montgomery chose to escape only when he was threatened with a return to Virginia and a degrading of his perceived rights. He represents the experience of many of the enslaved children brought to Britain. While their passage to England and Scotland may have been highly traumatic, residence in Britain gave some an opportunity to develop a life with new opportunities. For Montgomery, familiar with the violence and work regimen of Virginia slavery, life as a skilled carpenter and church-member in Scotland afforded him a taste of a kind of life that it would have been nearly impossible for him to enjoy in Virginia.

---

40 Bill of Sale, 9 March 1750 and receipt, 13 May 1756, NRS CS 234/5/3/12.
41 *Memorial for James Montgomery—Sheddan* [sic]; *Against Robert Sheddan* (23 July 1756), pp. 16–17. Advocates Library, Session Papers, Campbell's Collection, V.

In North America and the Caribbean a great many enslaved people ran away in order to reunite with family members or to find refuge within welcoming communities of African Americans, whether free or enslaved. In Britain, Jamie Montgomery and many others like him did not, indeed could not, do this. By running away on the eve of his return voyage to Virginia, Jamie knew that successful escape meant never again seeing kith and kin and eschewing any opportunity to find solace within African American society and culture. Some 3,000 miles from his native Virginia, he instead sought something entirely different in Scotland. The great irony of the transportation of enslaved children to Georgian Britain is that it could be a deeply traumatic dislocation and yet offer the opportunity to escape into a society in which plantation slavery did not exist. As Jamie Montgomery discovered, there were no guarantees of success in an attempt to find freedom in Georgian Britain. But for him and for other enslaved children and youth, the act of great cruelty and psychological harm in separating them from family and community and taking them to Britain might yet present these enslaved young people with opportunities to create lives for themselves away from the racism, the violence and the horror of racial slavery in Britain's American and Caribbean colonies.

CHAPTER SIX

The Making of a Liverpool Community: An Elusive Narrative

Raymond Costello

On 25 January 2010 a newspaper ran an article suggesting the implementation of a national 'Windrush Day' as a fitting way to celebrate what it called 'Britain's immigrant population'.[1] It carried the implication that black settlement was a new phenomenon in Great Britain, and in doing so perhaps inadvertently subscribed to the commonly held image of black people born in the United Kingdom as being the descendants of quite recent settlers. On 22 June 1948 the SS *Empire Windrush* had brought 492 Jamaican workers into Tilbury Dock in response to governmental requests to the colonies for willing hands to help the British economy following the Second World War.[2] This event, possibly the largest influx of black settlers experienced on any one particular occasion, gave rise to the creation of the '*Windrush* Myth', the belief held by some that this was the beginning of the history of black settlers in Britain. Numbers were small at first, but West Indian settler numbers increased, adding to an already more diverse Britain than is popularly thought.

Black communities have existed in Britain for at least five centuries, some of them dying out only to arise again at a later date. However, in the north-west of England, the Liverpool Black community differs from that of other cities because of its continuity, with some of its families

---

1 Patrick Vernon, 'Windrush Day: A Fitting Way to Celebrate Our Immigrant Population', *The Guardian*, 25 January 2010.
2 Fryer, *Staying Power*, pp. 304–9.

dating back many generations. Freed slaves, black servants and children of African rulers visiting the port as free African students arrived from at least the 1730s. Later, the American War of Independence caused a small number of free Black Loyalists to settle in the growing township, adding to the numbers and creating a true community. While London has had a black presence since at least the Tudor period, over the centuries it has had a greater degree of transience than that of Liverpool. Although some black settlers may have arrived later, this port has had an uninterrupted black population for some two and a half centuries.[3]

Although black populations of other port cities, such as London and Bristol, may have reduced at various times, there is unlikely to have been a time when they have disappeared entirely. Some reduction was caused by transience, but this is not the only reason for black population reduction in ports; the 'bloodline' of some early black settlers may have simply disappeared into the general population of the British Isles. Liverpool, with its old black population, has possibly experienced this genetic assimilation more than any other part of the country prior to the twenty-first century. Some visibly white residents may even be unaware of their racial heritage.

Now native to England for centuries, this group still faces difficulties of identification, and the names and stories of earlier settlers remain elusive even to fellow Liverpudlians. Although there seems to be popular tacit agreement on the existence of an old community of African ancestry in Liverpool, and documentary evidence is available, both scholars and interested members of the public find it difficult to locate any contiguous group narrative of the early Liverpool black community. The fact that some black Liverpudlians are able to trace their roots in Liverpool for many generations is hard to find in history books, leading to an invisibility surrounding both the way that this unique community, the oldest black community in Europe, came about and the many peoples who have contributed to it over the centuries. Some of them are, however, hidden in plain sight.

Records show what are possibly the first black children being born (or at least baptized) in Liverpool by the mid-eighteenth century. A baby, Peter Smith, the son of Mercury (described as 'Mr. Reed's Negro') and

---

3 Ray Costello, *Black Liverpool: The Early History of Britain's Oldest Black Community 1730–1918* (Liverpool, Picton Press, 2001).

Mary Smith, was baptized at St Peter's church on 15 December 1752,[4] while in the dockland area around Liverpool's first dock, now Canning Place, entries in a section of the baptismal records of St James Church showing only black people include Thomas, the son of Jack Brown, described as 'a native of Savannah'.[5] Jack Brown was by no means the only African American in Liverpool in the eighteenth century. Some African Americans chose to serve Britain when the North American colonies openly rebelled against colonial British rule. In 1775 Lord Dunmore, the British royal governor of Virginia, promised freedom to all slaves who opposed their American masters and joined the British forces sent to deal with the insurrection.[6] At the war's end many of these black loyalists followed British forces and shipped out of such American ports as Savannah and Charleston after the British surrender to the Americans.[7] In the baptismal records of St James Church around the time of the evacuation of black loyalists in the 1780s is to be found, 'Peter Salisbury, Negro from Baltimore, Maryland, was baptized September.'[8] It is not clear if he was among the black loyalists, viewed baptism as a protection against enslavement, or was an adult or a child.

One of the largest single contributions to the Liverpool Black population came from black sailors settling in the port. Several free black seamen are to be found in the port of Liverpool during the late eighteenth century and it is possible there may have been many more; indications of race in British ships' records are only occasionally made, so that names or the geographical location of seafarers' births are often the only clues. Some seventy-six black sailors are listed as working on Liverpool slave ships in Board of Trade papers for the years 1794 to 1805, recruited directly in Liverpool or their homelands in Africa or the West Indies.[9] Later, when one American captain sailed into

4 *St. Peter's Baptisms*, Liverpool City Records Office.
5 *St. James Old Registers, Baptisms, 1775–1813*, Liverpool City Records Office.
6 Blackburn, Robin, *The Overthrow of Colonial Slavery 1776–1848* (London, Verso, 1988), p. 103.
7 Blackburn, *The Overthrow*, pp. 114–16.
8 *St. James Old Registers, Baptisms, 1775–1813*, Liverpool City Records Office.
9 Christopher, *Slave Ship Sailors*, Appendix 1, 231–33; Appendix 2, 1794–1805, pp. 234–3.

Liverpool in 1857 with an all-white crew, he exchanged them for an all-black crew, while another captain claimed they were 'the best men they had'.[10]

The elusive narrative of the black presence in Liverpool makes it difficult to articulate a sense of a true racialized community in those early years. The rise of the port of Liverpool over its rival ports of London and Bristol in the second half of the eighteenth century saw people of African descent speaking many languages and from a variety of disparate cultures,[11] raising the question, 'What scope was there for the development of a community drawn from an aggregate of people of different origins and social classes?' In our time, although the colour of the skin of people of African descent living in close proximity might engender the formation of community or brotherhood among black settlers in Liverpool, it should not always be taken for granted that racial background operated that way in the distant past. Other factors, such as class (or caste), literacy and cross-racial relationships, need to be considered. The fact that the majority of early settlers were of slave origin and denied the right to an education makes any evidence of their relationships in Britain largely dependent upon others. Black individuals fortunate enough to break those strictures were able to provide a useful source of written evidence. Oral testimony could be transcribed by others. Former slaves lucky enough to gain the friendship of wealthy patrons or European commentators, such as members of the rising British abolitionist movement in the late eighteenth century, were also potential sources of evidence about early black settlers' lives.

As one of a select group of literate former slaves visiting or resident in Britain, Olaudah Equiano, one of the better-known black commentators, unfortunately does not mention the Liverpool black community in his autobiography, although he did visit the port.[12] Another potential group of informants capable of providing evidence of any commonality of feeling among early black individuals in European society included

10 Bolster, *Black Jacks*, p. 218.
11 Gomer Williams, *History of the Liverpool Privateers and Letters of Marque with an Account of the Liverpool Slave Trade, 1744–1812* (Liverpool University Press, repr. 2004 [1897]), p. 471.
12 Equiano, *Interesting Narrative*.

Africans who were the children of African rulers and had been sent to Britain for a European education. Unlike Equiano, they had never been enslaved and belonged to a more privileged group. John Naimbanna arrived in England in 1791 and stayed until June 1793. On one occasion Naimbanna was present at the House of Commons during a debate on the slave trade and heard someone speaking in favour of the trade; while he was well aware of the trade, he was outraged to hear comments he found very derogatory and 'degrading to the characters of his countrymen'. Leaving the House, he exclaimed loudly:

> I will kill that fellow wherever I meet him, for he has told lies of my country; [...] If a man should rob me of my money, I can forgive him; if a man should shoot at me I can forgive him: if a man should sell me and all my family to a slave ship, so that we should pass all the rest of our lives in slavery in the West Indies, I can forgive him; but if a man takes away the Character of the people of my country, I never can forgive him.[13]

Naimbanna was well aware that such racist rhetoric resulted in the permanent categorization of black people as inferior to Europeans, even when their individual circumstances and caste may differ from each other.

Naimbanna's visit to England coincided with the development of the pseudo-scientific racism used to justify African slavery, already associated with blackness, exemplified in such authors as the virulent racist Jamaican planter and slave owner Edward Long, who believed that black people in the Americas were characterized by the same 'bestial manners, stupidity and vices which debase their [African] brethren', embodying 'every species of inherent turpitude'.[14] Naimbanna's 'community' were those similarly maligned Africans, rather than the localized community of a single English city.

---

13 Anon., 'The Black Prince: A True Story being an Account of the Life and Death of Naimbanna, an African King's Son', *Cheap Repository Tracts* (1796), pp. 8–9.
14 Long, *History of Jamaica*, vol. 2, p. 476; Elof Axel Carlson, *The Unfit: A History of a Bad Idea* (Cold Spring Harbor, NY: Cold Spring Harbor Press, 2001), pp. 286–8.

Otto Ephraim, an African student whose father was one of the late eighteenth-century rulers of the Efik country, of the Calabar 'Oil Rivers' region of the Niger delta, received his education in Liverpool, living in George Street in the township's centre. When he eventually returned to West Africa his letters show the value of closer trading relations based on personal friendship rather than business, which was the aim of the British in bringing chiefs' sons to England. Ephraim apparently remembered the family he grew up alongside with some affection, ending one letter to Ambrose Lace, a Liverpool merchant, with 'P.S. Remember me to your Wife and your son Joshua Ambrose William and Polly.'[15] Nevertheless, none of his correspondence reveals a consciousness of fellow-feeling with known Africans of a different station living in the English port. Perhaps, as a 'well-heeled' black scholar, his social class kept him from forming a sense of community with enslaved people and sailors. The opportunity for recording any pan-black feeling was not necessarily scarce, however. Some fifty to seventy wealthy African children, who would also have had the ability to commit their thoughts to paper, were at school in Liverpool in the 1780s.[16]

The notion of 'community' is worth scrutiny and has recently attracted the attention of scholars. In examining the assumption that people of the same race, religion, culture or language sharing a geographic area might inevitably see themselves as a community, Anthony Cohen has defined community as a largely mental construct given credibility by objective manifestations in locality or ethnicity,[17] but Elizabeth Frazer's examination of community links as a virtual entity or ideal concluded that any 'material density of social relations that has traditionally been thought to be a necessary element of the concept community' can sometimes be eclipsed and manifested in

15 Williams, pp. 548–9.
16 Carl Bernhard Wadström, *An Essay on Colonization Particularly Applied to the Western Coast of Africa with Some Free Thought on Cultivation and Commerce, Vol. 1* [1794] (Newton Abbot: David and Charles Ltd., 1968 reprint), pp. 94–5.
17 Robbie Aitken and Eve Rosenhaft, *Black Germany, The Making and Unmaking of a Diaspora Community, 1884–1960* (Cambridge: Cambridge University Press, 2013), p. 6. The quote from Anthony P. Cohen, *The Symbolic Construction of Community* (London: Routledge, 1985), is on p. 109.

6.1 Florence and Mora James, c.1870s. Author's family collection.

other ways.[18] The term 'Black community' has become increasingly common in the British press and public debate following the riots that took place in several cities in the UK in the early 1980s, particularly in the Toxteth area of black settlement in Liverpool. Paul Gilroy believed that the riots led to a self-conscious rhetoric of community based on the realities of daily experiences, everyday neighbourhood matters and networking through political organizations. The concept of 'blackness' might perhaps then be seen as a social construct derived from the situated experience of otherwise disparate groups finding themselves in a particular circumstance; a political response[19] often structured by external perceptions in addition to internal practices and articulations of identity.[20] Any suggestion that the 1981 riots may have been the origin of a self-awareness of black people seeking common cause as a group in Liverpool is not the case, however; a student's club known as the Ethiopian Progressive Association had existed at Liverpool University as early as 1906 and other examples can be seen below.[21]

Naimbanna's fears did come to pass: black people of all stations in Britain came to be seen in the same light. This created distance between poor blacks and their white fellows, since the latter had a somewhat greater potential for social mobility. As the nineteenth century progressed, official and private documents related to individual black Liverpudlians, rather than a wider community. Evidence of the existence of poor blacks in Liverpool can be found in the writings of such commentators as Henry Mayhew and Charles Dickens, and is well-rehearsed by modern historians to counter the stereotypes of black people in Britain. Mayhew wrote in 1861 that

---

18 Elizabeth Frazer, *The Problem of Communitarian Politics. Unity and Conflict* (Oxford: Oxford University Press, 1999), pp. 76, 81.

19 Aitken and Rosenhaft, pp. 5–6, quoting Paul Gilroy, *'There Ain't no Black in the Union Jack': The Cultural Politics of Race and Nation* (Chicago: University of Chicago Press, 1991), pp. 223–50.

20 Aitken and Rosenhaft, quoting Diane Frost, *Work and Community among West African Migrant Workers since the Nineteenth Century* (Liverpool: Liverpool University Press, 1999), pp. 187–96.

21 Louis R. Harlan, 'Booker T. Washington and the White Man's Burden', *American Historical Review*, LXXI, 1965–6, p. 464.

It is only common fairness to say that negroes seldom, if ever, shirk work. Their only trouble is to obtain it. Those who have seen the many negroes employed in Liverpool, will know that they are hard-working, patient, and too often underpaid.[22]

In 1858 Charles Dickens made a similarly brief comment resulting from what was effectively a 'pub crawl' of the Toxteth dockland slums with a police superintendent friend during which he encountered a public house with a mixed, but predominantly black, clientele, where a 'jolly black landlord presided over a scene of and dancing with childish good-humoured enjoyment'. His friend commented that, 'They generally kept together, these poor fellows … because they were at a disadvantage singly, and liable to slights in the neighbouring streets.'[23] However, in spite of the ghetto feeling of the area, 'the Black community' has always been multiracial, black people living alongside whites.

Throughout the nineteenth century newer black settlers arrived in Britain following each of Britain's wars, bringing to Liverpool their own languages, cultures and religions. This has masked the true age of the community, perpetuating a popular view of local black people as exotic and un-English. Each time, the most recent wave of black immigration was seen as representative of the Liverpool black community. The anthropologist Jacqueline Nassy Brown found that there was a tendency for Liverpool-born Black locals to assume the corporate 'genealogy' of the group. By asserting their 'birth here for generations'—meaning the group rather than their own family—she felt that they were lamenting the fact that their existence as a group was still unacknowledged.[24] This should not necessarily negate the idea of a continuous presence, as there has been a good deal of intermarriage with older settlers, despite the belief by some that the 'old community' has died out, breaking that continuity. An example of the obscuring of the longevity of older black family lineage is the family of Henry Brew,

22 Douglas Lorimer, *Colour, Class and the Victorians* (Leicester: Leicester University Press, 1978), p. 41.
23 Ian Law and June Henfrey, *A History of Race and Racism in Liverpool, 660–1950* (Liverpool: Merseyside Community Relations Council, 1981), p. 25.
24 Jacqueline Nassy Brown, *Dropping Anchor, Setting Sail: Geographies of Race in Black Liverpool* (Princeton: Princeton University Press, 2005), p. 92.

who settled in Liverpool between the world wars. Although he was a Gold Coast West African, he married a woman whose black family in Liverpool dated from the Crimean War, a continuity often forgotten.[25] Few of the younger generation had a real understanding of the longer community past, even though Brown refers a number of times to the community's 'origin story'.

Members of the old, well-established black community have had a long history of misidentification. George William Christian (1872–1924) was a member of a very able black family; both he and his brother trained as clerks for the John Holt shipping line, a firm with a tradition of employing black seamen. The firm may have thought he was well-suited to the climate of West Africa and sent him out to their Nigerian office in a clerical role. Excelling at trade, he was soon in the position to set up his own merchant trading business in Nigeria and Cameroon, employing both Europeans and local Africans—an unusual position at that time. This caused him some difficulties, as he occupied a role characteristic of colonial whites, yet was not a locally born African, normally referred to by the colonial masters as 'natives'. As a British-born black, Christian had to take the powerful Liverpool-based Elder Dempster shipping line to court in England after they refused to ship the produce of his oil-exporting business in West Africa; the shipping firm was bewildered that a 'native', as they thought Christian was, seemed to be cutting out the middleman by organizing his own affairs. This was not the only occasion. Christian was arrested and fined for failing to register a land title in German-held Cameroon, which was necessary for native-born German African subjects. The MP for Toxteth, supported by the British Foreign Office, intervened on his behalf, pointing out to the German authorities that George Christian was not a German colonial subject.[26]

At the conclusion of the First World War approximately 200,000 black people living in Britain faced hostility from mostly poor whites,

25 Ray Costello, 'A Hidden History in Liverpool: The James Family', in *North West Labour History: Black Presence in the North West* (Salford, North West Labour History Group, 1995), pp. 41–3.
26 Jeffrey P. Green, 'George William Christian: A Liverpool "Black" in Africa', *Transactions of the Historical Society of Lancashire and Cheshire*, 134, 1986, pp. 141–6.

disappointed that the prime minister Lloyd George's promises of better conditions in their daily lives, 'homes fit for heroes', had been slow in implementation. Recently demobilized indigenous black servicemen living in the ports were readily, and incorrectly, identified as possible 'aliens' and in May 1919 severe riots broke out during which white rioters attacked individual blacks in the streets of Britain and burned their homes and lodgings. In Liverpool, mobs many thousands strong ransacked the Elder Dempster shipping line's hostel for black seamen, the David Lewis Hostel for black ratings and houses in the heart of the Liverpool Black settlement area.[27] The Liverpool black population have traditionally lived in close proximity to available work, invariably associated with shipping. Originally centred on the South Dock area of the city from the mid-eighteenth century onwards, the black settlement in Liverpool increased as ships engaged in the West Africa trade docked in this area. Later in the nineteenth and twentieth centuries such shipping lines as the Elder Dempster Line and the Blue Funnel line built their own lodging houses in the South Docks area to provide accommodation for black seafarers whose contracts terminated in Liverpool, thus supplementing the private lodging houses and accommodation in the homes of already settled countrymen and kinsmen.[28]

The riots of 1919 reached a climax in early June when, after being discharged in March, Charles Wotten, a young Bermudan ship's fireman living at 18 Upper Pitt Street, a boarding house for black seamen in the dockland area, was murdered. Police raiding the boarding house saw Wotten struggling to get away from a large crowd and running down an entry towards Queen's Dock, where the pursuing crowd of several hundred stoned him to death in the dock.[29] Wotten's death certificate gave the cause of death as 'Drowning; how he got into the water the evidence is not sufficient to show.'[30] On 11 June, under the heading 'Colour Riots—700 Blacks Take Refuge in Bridewell' (the local lock-up), the *Evening Express* continued to describe horrific scenes

---

27 *Evening Express* (Liverpool), 9 June 1919, p. 3.
28 Ola Uduku and Gideon Ben-Tovim, *Social Infrastructure Provision in Granby/Toxteth* (Liverpool: University of Liverpool, 1997), p. 11.
29 *Evening Express* (Liverpool), 10 June 1919, p. 3.
30 TNA Death Certificate, No. 148, 5 June 1919, HC 132030.

as families begged to be locked up for safety,[31] the irony being that, as one writer put it, 'while whites viewed blacks as foreign, different and inferior, blacks viewed themselves as citizens and defenders of the British Empire.'[32]

Members of the black community became politicized in the early twentieth century. Black people of many generations living in the port of Liverpool had a ready-made champion in the Liverpool-born Black John Richard Archer (1863–1932), mayor of Battersea in 1913. Archer, the son of a Barbadian ship steward and an Irish-born mother, dedicated his life to the cause of socialism and on November 1913 was nominated as Progressive candidate for mayor in Battersea, amidst a media circus. Ignorance of the old Liverpool Black population caused some confusion in the press about his origins, commenting on his 'keen contest with an Englishman'.[33] At the conclusion of the First World War John Archer was only too aware of the difficulties faced by black people in his home city:

> I am the son of a man who was born in the West Indian islands. I was born in England, in a little obscure village that probably never was known until this evening, the City of Liverpool. I am a Lancastrian born and bred, and my mother—well she was my mother. She was not born in Rangoon and she was not Burmese. She belonged to one of the greatest races on the face of the earth. My mother was an Irishwoman, so there is not much of the foreigner about me after all.[34]

On 16 June 1919 Archer led a deputation to meet Liverpool's deputy mayor to plead the case of the local black community, as many former black servicemen were unable to obtain employment and, turned out of their lodgings onto the streets, were pressing for repatriation. Archer's intervention was welcome, as attempts to enlist the help of the local

---

31 *Evening Express*, 11 June 1919, p. 5.
32 Michael Rowe, 'Sex, Race and Riot in Liverpool 1919', *Immigrants & Minorities: Historical Studies in Ethnicity, Migration and Diaspora*, 19: 2, 2000, pp. 55–70 at p. 66.
33 *Daily Mail*, no. 5, 486, 5 November 1913, p. 5.
34 *Daily Express*, 11 November 1913.

authorities had proved difficult.[35] The Board of Trade repatriation scheme was principally offered to black sailors who had come to Britain during wartime by the marine department of the Board of Trade and had been in operation since February 1919,[36] but in Liverpool the cry of former servicemen, 'We want to go home!'[37] was hardly a solution to difficulties faced by families of the locally born black community of many generations. The passage of time had turned most into what one commentator called 'black Englishmen',[38] with no more connection with their ancestral homelands than early twentieth-century British families of French Huguenot ancestry might have had with France.

The government showed some confusion not only about how to deal with demobbed black servicemen but regarding where to place black soldiers of the old Liverpool black community during the First World War. Private A. Francis was a volunteer soldier under the Derby Scheme, but was posted to a colonial force stationed in Britain, the British West Indies Regiment, rather than a regular British unit. He is mentioned in correspondence as 'a man of colour who was discharged after two years seven months service on account of amputation Right Arm sustained on active service in France.'[39] The problem was that soldiers of the British West Indies Regiment were pensioned according to the Royal Warrant 19114, Article 1162, which paid less than European soldiers. Under that scheme, Private Francis was eligible for a life pension at the rate of only 1/6 a day. Francis complained by letter to the Ministry of Pensions that he been resident in England since 1898, and was earning good wages in a shipyard in Liverpool, but since his discharge in October 1918 had been unable to return to his former job because of his disability. A senior civil servant, Sir Laming Worthington Evans, appears to have supported Francis's complaint, as he mentioned in the replying correspondence that a mistake in Francis's posting should not prejudice his case and the issue of a pension under the correct warrant

35 *Evening Express*, 10 June 1919, p. 1.
36 TNA MT 4/761, Marine Department, Board of Trade letter to all Mercantile Marine offices, 7 February 1919.
37 *Evening Express*, 10 June 1919, p. 1.
38 P.C. and G.W. Brown, 'We too were at Cardiff', *The Keys*, III/1, July–September 1935, p. 4.
39 TNA T1/12482, Letter from the Ministry of Pensions to the Treasury 9 February 1920.

at the rate of 28/- per week should be continued while he continued to live in the British Isles.[40]

Private Francis's case was successful, but is symptomatic of the way in which British-born or long-domiciled black people were considered as 'aliens' at points in the long history of the Liverpool black settlement. The Manual of Military Law in 1907 had spelt out the policy towards black recruits to enable troops raised in African protectorates to serve outside their boundaries: 'under the Naturalization Act, 1870, a naturalized alien has the same privileges as a British subject, and therefore is capable of being enlisted to serve His Majesty.'[41] Enlistment 95. (1.) stated:

> Any person who is for the time being an alien may, if Negroes &c. (etc.) [...] be enlisted in His Majesty's regular forces, so, however, that the number of aliens serving together at any one time in any corps of the regular forces shall not exceed the proportion of one alien to every fifty British subjects, and that an alien so enlisted shall not be capable of holding any higher rank in His Majesty's regular forces than that of a warrant officer or non-commissioned officer:
>
> (2.) Provided that, notwithstanding the above provisions of this section, any inhabitant of any British protectorate and any negro or person of colour, although an alien, [...] shall, while serving in His Majesty's regular forces, be deemed to be entitled to all the privileges of a natural-born British subject.[42]

Throughout the manual, the terms 'negroes' and 'aliens' seem to be used as synonyms, but, nevertheless, the fact that the rights of serving black soldiers were enshrined within British military law provided a useful precedent in the case of Private Francis and others. The frequent confusion regarding the categorization of black people placed black servicemen living in post-war Britain facing a different

40 TNA T1/12482, Letter 9 February 1920.
41 'Enlistment', Ch. X, 28, *Manual of Military Law 1907*, War Office, Great Britain, War Office, Edition 6 (London: HMSO, 1907), p. 190.
42 'Special provisions as to Persons to be Enlisted. Enlistment 95', ARMY ACT, *Manual of Military Law 1907*, p. 358.

'firing line': the Aliens Restriction (Amendment) Act of 1919 and the stronger Aliens Order of 1920. Rather than viewing the recently returned unemployed black servicemen as part of the same working class, the Seamen's Union seemed as confused as those who had written the Manual of Military Law. The Union's inclusion of Black servicemen in their own anti-alien agitation resulted in the 1920 Order, followed by the Special Restrictions (Coloured Alien Seamen) Order of 1925, which required 'coloured' British citizens of the empire to register with the police as aliens. Police were enabled to impose restrictions on 'aliens' who could not prove British nationality as colonial subjects, but in practice even black British ex-servicemen and those long-resident in the UK found themselves forced to comply. British-born blacks with proof of British nationality in such older settlements as Cardiff, Tyneside and Liverpool were, once again, the most aggrieved.[43] The reluctance to classify them as both black and British stemmed from an inability or refusal to recognize their citizenship, an issue that unfortunately often persists to this day.

Before and after the First World War there were concerted efforts by black residents of Liverpool to organize themselves into community groups. The period following the Second World War was a replay of the 1919 riots for Black Liverpudlians, and returning black servicemen faced unemployment and hostility from former neighbours again. Although Paul Gilroy mentions that the 1981 riots may have increased a feeling of community under pressure, black organizations certainly existed prior to that date. Meeting at the Manchester Pan-African Congress in 1945, Liverpool Black Community selfhelp organizations, including the Negro-Welfare Association and the Coloured Workers Association, made links with national organizations, such as the League of Coloured Peoples, founded in 1931.[44]

The Liverpool black community is nevertheless very much an example of a community that has emerged from crisis. New black communities arising in the UK out of Britain's slave trade and Empire were distinct from individuals' older allegiances in their countries

---

43 Jacqueline Jenkinson, 'The 1919 Race Riots in Britain: A Survey', in Rainer Lotz and Ian Pegg (eds), *Under the Imperial Carpet: Essays in Black History 1780–1950* (Crawley: Rabbit Press, 1986), p. 198.
44 Fryer, p. 350.

of origin, and could include communities based on newer images of occupations, social class, religion and culture, in spite of the seemingly overwhelming salience of skin colour in our time. In Ephraim's and Naimbanna's time, the notion of a self-conscious 'black diaspora' was yet to be articulated by people of African descent and even more recent investigators of 'black community' point out the possibility of modern communities being divided and even antagonistic towards component elements within the greater group.[45]

For example, collaborating with Arthur Creech Jones, the Labour Party's colonial affairs spokesman during the Second World War, Pastor G. Daniels Ekarte of the African Churches Mission in Liverpool complained that black crewmen recruited in Liverpool were being discharged in West African ports and fresh hands taken on who were considered largely 'raw Africans', who knew little of the skills necessary in discharging a seaman's job.[46] This exchange was the result of local black seamen in the port being paid as though they too were untrained recruits, a derisory £6 a month, rather than being paid on an equal footing with white firemen, who could earn £16. Had African firemen signed on in Liverpool, they would have received £12, causing Liverpool-born blacks to be even more aggrieved.[47] Models of black community must take into account the relationship between the politics and culture of the working class, but it is not inevitable that difficulties faced by people living in areas of black settlement should be automatically viewed through the prism of class struggle or communal solidarity.

It would seem that, over the course of three centuries, black Liverpudlians have lacked a popular narrative, or shared origin story, outside of knowing that they are part of the oldest black community in England. Narrative therapists believe that what people think they are, and what is told about them, are important in building a sense of identity and a

45 Gilroy, *'There Ain't No Black in the Union Jack'*, pp. 223–50.
46 Marika Sherwood, '"Strikes! African Seamen, Elder Dempster and the government, 1940–42', in Diane Frost (ed.), *Ethnic Labour and British Imperial Trade: A History of Ethnic Seafarers in the UK* (London: Frank Cass, 1995), pp. 130–45, at p. 136.
47 Tony Lane, *The Merchant Seamen's War* (Manchester: Manchester University Press, 1990), p. 160–1.

sense of what is possible for themselves.[48] During the 1970s and 1980s narrative therapy, a form of psychotherapy, was developed largely by an Australian social worker Michael White and David Epson of New Zealand with the aim of helping build identity.[49] Their belief was that by identifying their own values people are able to source the necessary skills and knowledge needed to confront problems of daily life they might face,[50] challenging any destructive negative popular imagery that may impinge upon their lives. Many Liverpool black people lack this necessary narrative.

For recent immigrants, visualizing the Liverpool black community is difficult without a knowledge of the longer history. One of the factors that may have also contributed to this larger group identity has sometimes been a self-elected, if pragmatic, solution of Liverpool black individuals tagging themselves on to whichever 'pure' national group they happen to have descended from, but are no longer necessarily in touch with. In the search for their own identity, they follow prevalent fashions and culture currently popular in the Caribbean, Africa and America, rather than finding that group identity more locally. Children of the present-day Liverpool population descended from the old black community may not fit neatly into these categories based on newer migration stories. Those descended from the older settlement, as well as newer arrivals may require consideration in the school curriculum. In addition, over the years, intermarriage with the local white population has produced a heterogeneous community with varied but distinct cultural and ethnic identities.

It is as though this well-established and interesting group within British society does not exist, creating the potential for negative outcomes adding to existing levels of poverty, including loss of grants, funding implications and moves to implement equal opportunity programmes. The physical presence of a community native to Liverpool

48 Vincent Fish, 'Post Structuralism in Family Therapy: Interrogating the Narrative/Conversational Mode', *Journal of Family Therapy*, 19: 3, 1993, pp. 221–32.
49 Catrina Brown and Tod Augusta-Scott, *Narrative Therapy: Making Meaning, Making Lives* (London: Sage Publications, 2007), p. 36.
50 Salvadore Minuchin, 'Where is the Family in Narrative Family Therapy?' *Journal of Marital & Family Therapy*, 24: 4, 1998, pp. 397–40.

remains vague in official documents. The most recent UK census, in 2011, recorded a diverse general population of Liverpool of 466,400.[51] Until recently, the vast majority of Liverpool's non-white ethnic minorities lived in the Toxteth area, but since the 1981 riots, the population also lives in the Kensington area, east of the city centre. The 2001 census gives some 38 per cent of the population of Granby Ward, 37 per cent of Princes Park Ward and 27 per cent in Central Liverpool Ward as being non-white.[52] The census also showed that 92.79 per cent of Liverpool's residents (including the Liverpool-born black population) were born in England, only 3.27 per cent being from elsewhere in the world.[53] In 2001 a mere 500 Liverpool residents were born abroad, including in the Republic of Ireland, China, Hong Kong, Germany and India; only a very small percentage of this already paltry figure was of African descent, mostly from Somalia and Nigeria.[54] The greater part of the old black population has origins directly in Africa, rather than the Caribbean. An analysis in 2009 estimated that approximately 5,000 Liverpudlians were of mixed white and black Caribbean origin, compared with more than 6,900 of full or partial black African origin.[55] This figure is surprisingly small, the identity of the old Liverpool black community possibly lost between the general figure for Liverpool residents born in England and citizens who just happen to be of mixed race, however transient.

The individual constituent, and very real, needs of newer black Liverpudlians, such as language, housing, religion and culture, may be easier to identify than those of Liverpool-born black people, resulting in another effect of non-recognition: being considered a perpetual immigrant. This could be seen as a serious setback to racial integration, as it perpetuates both the myth of black immigration as a

---

51 'Resident Population Estimates, All Persons', *Office for National Statistics.* Retrieved 15 January 2010. https://www.ons.gov.uk/help/localstatistics
52 'Area Granby (Ward)', *Office for National Statistics.* Retrieved 26 November 2015. https://www.ons.gov.uk/help/localstatistics
53 'Neighbourhood Statistics: Country of Birth', *Office for National Statistics.* Retrieved 16 January 2010. https://www.ons.gov.uk/help/localstatistics
54 'Area: Liverpool (Local Authority)', *Office for National Statistics.* Retrieved 22 September 2015. https://www.ons.gov.uk/help/localstatistics
55 "Neighbourhood Statistics: Country of Birth', *Office for National Statistics.* Retrieved 16 January 2010. https://www.ons.gov.uk/help/localstatistics

recent phenomenon, with assimilation and acculturation curing all of society's problems of racism, and the belief that the key to integration lies in learning English and knowing about British culture rather than in recognizing a local culture that has existed for hundreds of years.

Although the old Liverpool black community may be thought by some to be only a generation or two old, in common with other black settlements in Britain following the two world wars—that popular misconception, the 'Windrush Myth'—it is a population which, having stripped away all the supposed causes of disadvantage (language, religious and cultural differences) presents a possible model for future generations of a multi-racial Britain in other cities to follow, which can be understood and hopefully embraced and celebrated as part of a rich, diverse country.

CHAPTER SEVEN

Pero's Afterlife: Remembering an Enslaved African in Bristol

Madge Dresser

Who was Pero? The answer to that question remains tantalizingly elusive, for only the bare bones of his life, which ended in 1798, are documented in the historical record. Even these remained largely forgotten until the end of the twentieth century. This chapter therefore seeks first to recount what is known about Pero's life, and then to reconstruct a more rounded picture of the man himself. It will do so by considering him in relation to other working people (both black and white) in late eighteenth-century Bristol and asking what the surviving evidence might suggest about his inner life.

The second aim of this chapter is to examine what we might call Pero's afterlife. Since the late 1990s Bristol's slaving past has been subject to increased public scrutiny and Pero has been invoked as emblem of Bristol's black presence and the city's reliance on the Atlantic slave trade. How did this come about and what have been the political and cultural implications of his belated memorialization? In other words, what does Pero's afterlife tell us about racial divisions in the city and about the formation of black British identity?

I am indebted to Professor Gretchen H. Gerzina, Dr Edson Burton, Sue Giles and Christine Williams for reading through and commenting on the draft of this chapter. Any shortcomings in the final text are entirely my own responsibility.

The Historical Pero

Pero (also known as Pero or William Jones) (1753–1798) was the personal servant of John Pretor Pinney, a Nevis plantation owner and sugar merchant who lived in Bristol from the 1780s and built a fine mansion in Great George Street Bristol in 1791. By the time Pero arrived in England he was in his mid-thirties and had served as Pinney's slave since the age of twelve. Pinney first purchased him and his sisters Nancy and Sheba in 1765 for £115 to work on his Montravers plantation in Nevis. Pero was born in the Caribbean and probably in Nevis. He certainly spent his youth there, we know that his father and another sister Eva lived on another plantation on the island and that Pero kept in contact with them throughout his life.[1]

It is evident that Pero impressed Pinney as trustworthy and quick to learn, as he singled him out from his 150 slaves to be his personal manservant. Unusually for an enslaved worker, Pero was literate and, by the time he was fourteen, Pinney paid a substantial fee to board him out for sixteen months to a white tradesman to learn 'how to shave and cut hair'. It was traditional for white British boys (and some girls) to be apprenticed and similarly boarded out at fourteen, and although this was not part of a formal apprenticeship by which Pero could qualify as a master barber, it was more substantial 'than 6 months barbering training afforded to his enslaved contemporary Olaudah Equiano'.[2]

By his twenties Pero was permitted to travel on his own to St Kitts, which, given the restrictions on slave mobility at the time, indicates that he enjoyed Pinney's trust. In Nevis Pero was also allowed to transact

---

1 Much of this first section builds on the pioneering research of Christine Eickelmann and David Small. For more information on Pero's birth family in Nevis see 'The Mountravers Plantation Community', Part 2, Chapter 4, pp. 324–5 in Montavers plantation (Pinney's Estate), Nevis, West Indies at https://seis.bristol.ac.uk/~emceee/mountravers~part2chapter4.pdf. See also Christine Eickelmann and David Small, *Pero: the life of a slave in eighteenth-century Bristol* (Bristol: Redcliffe Press, Bristol Museums and Art Gallery, 2004). See also 'John Pinney' and 'Pero Jones' in the *Oxford Dictionary of National Biography* (henceforth *ODNB*).
2 'The Montravers Plantation Community', p. 327 at https://seis.bristol.ac.uk/~emceee/mountravers~part2chapter4.pdf (accessed 9 November 2019).

business on Pinney's behalf, carrying as much as £50 (a large amount of cash for slaves to handle) to Pinney's business associates.[3] The enterprising Pero also did business of his own, presumably pocketing the proceeds, and 'sold Pinney a sheep, a goat, and dungbaskets and hired at his own expense an old enslaved woman' to assist him.[4] In 1772 Pero and his sister Nancy also travelled to Philadelphia, when Pinney and his new wife Jane Weekes visited there for their honeymoon. On his return to Nevis Pero's skill set was further enhanced when he was boarded out to a man named Mial (probably an enslaved man belonging to Pinney's mother-in-law)[5] to learn how to pull teeth, as tooth decay was rife on sugar plantations.

Yet, despite his relative autonomy, Pero was still a slave and had no choice but to leave Nevis to move to England when the Pinneys decided to return there with his family in 1783. For Pero, this meant leaving his birth family behind, even though Mrs Pinney's freed maidservant Frances (Fanny) Coker also came with them. Pero first stayed in London, where Pinney's meticulous business records show that he was at least on one occasion paid £1 1s in wages. The very fact that Pero received wages at all did not mean, however, that he was now formally free, for the status of enslaved people on the British mainland was, even after the Mansfield Judgement of 1772, still being contested.

Bristol's population at the time was under 60,000. Though socially stratified, it was still a face-to-face society. Merchants, even those such as Pinney who were not members of Bristol's elite Society of Merchant Venturers, were in contact with each other or knew of each other through their social networks. As Pinney's trusted personal servant, Pero had a special status in the Pinney household. There are no paintings of him, so we don't know quite how he was dressed, but we do know that Pinney laid out a substantial sum to ensure he wore some good boots. Pero would have frequently interacted with Pinney's associates, friends and relatives (including Pinney's relative and former plantation manager, William Coker, at whose Dorset farm Pero stayed in 1783). Serving at meals, attending to visitors and

---

3 £50 in the 1770s would be worth over £4300 in today's money, according to http://www.nationalarchives.gov.uk/currency-converter/.
4 Eickelmann and Small, pp. 21, 29–30.
5 Eickelmann and Small, p. 32.

waiting on Pinney while he entertained, Pero would have heard their conversations and the records suggest that he knew about their social circumstances.

Though the records incline us to see him only in relation to the white elite, Pero also would have met with those servants who accompanied their masters to the Pinney household and would have been closest to those servants and people of colour with Nevis connections. James Tobin, Pinney's Bristol business partner, whom Pinney knew from Nevis, was a constant presence in the household, and his black servants George Evans and Priscilla Gould, also from Nevis, lived only a few streets away in Berkeley Square. Another Nevisian, Ann (reportedly Tobin's mixed-race illegitimate half-sister) was in the city by 1780. In 1785 Kate Coker (originally the slave of Pinney's plantation manager William Coker) had accompanied Pinney's eldest children back to England in 1778 and visited Bristol again in 1780 as a free black servant attending the wife of a Nevis minister known to the Pinneys. It was through these connections that Pero was able to communicate, albeit indirectly, with his family back in Nevis.[6]

Other Bristol associates of Pinney, such as the Bushes, the Baillies, the Crugers and the Cobhams, also had black servants, some of whom, like those employed by Baillie, lived around the corner from Pero. Though enjoying a more comfortable position as an upper servant in a prosperous family than the majority of the city's labouring poor, it is hard to think that Pero did not interact with Bristol's lower orders, particularly those few people of colour in the city who worked there as mariners, musicians and casual workers. It seems that he made additional money, too, by lending money at interest to other servants, some if not most of whom would have been white.[7]

Pero's personal opinions are lost to history, but by focusing on the wider political climate of the day we might begin to discern the debates and conversations that Pero witnessed and by which his own views may have been shaped. By 1788, when the abolitionist movement took off in Bristol, discussions about slavery would have been hard to

6 Pinney's own ships travelled back and forth to Nevis and Pinney engaged his own aunt to sell some sundry articles on Pero's behalf on the island: Eickelman and Small, p. 44.
7 Eickelmann and Small, p. 58.

avoid in the Pinney household.[8] Both Pinney and Tobin (who wrote pamphlets from 1785 defending slavery and condemning 'race mixing') were not only members of the recently formed Bristol branch of the West India Association but also part of an organized anti-abolitionist coalition consisting of other sugar refiners, merchants, manufacturers and absentee planters, which first met in April 1789.[9]

But, given that Pinney's social networks also included those with opposing views, Pero may have also heard abolitionist views as well. Anti-slave trade campaigners Thomas Clarkson, John Wesley and Hannah More were all in Bristol at the time and the school More ran with her sisters was on Park Street, where the Pinneys still resided until they moved around the corner to Great George Street in 1791.[10] Unusually for a man of his colour and social position, Pero was literate (though we don't know precisely how literate), so it is also possible that he was exposed to these issues through the city's flourishing press and broadside culture. With this in mind, it is intriguing to think that Pero as Pinney's valet probably accompanied his master on a trip to Germany in 1789, which took them through France shortly after the Bastille fell, the Declaration of the Rights of Man had been proclaimed and the future of slavery in France was being fiercely debated.[11]

On their return to Bristol plans were afoot for the family to visit Nevis, and Mrs Pinney returned first, insisting that Pero's fellow servant Fanny Coker return with her. Her husband and Pero joined them later in 1790 where they remained for a stay of six months. This was the first time in seven years that Pero would have seen his family and his

---

8 See Pinney's letter to William Coker in February 1788 regarding the threat posed by abolition in Peter Marshall, 'The Anti-Slave Trade Movement in Bristol', in Patrick McGrath (ed.), *Bristol in the Eighteenth Century* (Newton Abbot: David & Charles, 1972), pp. 194–5; and his letter of the 31 October 1790 to Tobin on the same theme in 'The Mountravers Plantation Community, Part 2 Chapter 5, p. 630 at https://seis.bristol.ac.uk/~emceee/welcome.html (accessed 1 July 2018).

9 Madge Dresser, *Slavery Obscured: The Social History of Slavery in An English Provincial Port* (London and New York: Continuum, 2001; reprinted by Redcliffe Press 2007 and Bloomsbury Academic Press 2013), pp. 147–9.

10 Dresser, *Slavery Obscured*, pp. 146.

11 Eickelmann and Small, p. 42; email from David Small to Madge Dresser 18 July 2018.

continuing emotional attachment to them is evidenced by the fact that, on his return to Bristol, he sent parcels for his nephew William Fisher as well for his father, his sister and two enslaved friends, including a woman named Bridget with whom he seemed to have formed an attachment. These gifts can be seen as an early example of the remittances by which West Indian and later immigrants traditionally support and maintain their connections with their families back home.[12]

These travels occurred at a time when the Bristol to which Pero returned was in a febrile state, with reformers pushing for abolition and wider political reforms followed by government repression as Britain sought to suppress radicals at home and insurgent people of colour in the French colonies.[13] It was in this atmosphere that Pero made his second visit to Nevis in 1794 with Pinney. They briefly visited Martinique, which had just been captured from the French by the British navy. For reasons that remain unclear, this trip seems to have proved a watershed in Pero's life. The Pero who returned to Bristol was a different man from the one who had left.

Pero, the enterprising and tractable manservant, had become increasingly addicted to drink and kept 'dissolute company'. Pero's drinking took its toll, and the family became increasingly exasperated by his unreliability. Pinney's family wanted Pero banished back to Nevis:

> almost ever since he left Nevis in 1794 his conduct has been very reprehensible ... every branch of my Family have urged me to discharge him and to send him back to Nevis with an annual allounces [*sic*]: provided his behaviour there should have deserved it.[14]

Pinney resisted his family's wishes, citing a deep fondness for Pero, 'who waited on my person for upward of 32 years'. But, fondness aside, it tells us much about the status of enslaved people that the Pinneys would even contemplate forcing Pero back to Nevis (well after the Mansfield Judgement) and cutting off any means of support should

12 Eickelmann and Small, p. 44.
13 'Slave Resistance Gains Momentum 1790–1791', *History of Haiti 1492–1805*, https://library.brown.edu/haitihistory/4.html.
14 Eickelmann and Small, pp. 55–8.

he continue to drink. However, when he fell severely ill by the end of May 1798 (probably due in part to his heavy drinking), he was taken to lodgings just outside Bristol for a 'change of air'.[15] There, various members of the Pinney family did their duty, reportedly visiting him 'three or four times a week' until his death sometime later that year.[16]

Pero died a broken man, but precisely why remains unclear. Was he depressed by having to leave his Nevis family yet again? Plantation records suggest that he had fathered one or two daughters while on the visit. Or was his behaviour a more generalized expression of resentment against his enslaved status and slavery in general?[17] Did Pero hear how slavery was under fire from conversations in the Pinney household? Was he influenced by radical abolitionists who may well have been part of the 'dissolute company' with whom his master complained he now fraternized? Certainly, by 1795 John Pinney's son Azariah and Tobin's son James Webbe Tobin kept company with abolitionist campaigners such as the radical romantic poet Samuel Taylor Coleridge, who had delivered a fiery and much-reported anti-slavery lecture in Bristol that June, and who visited the Pinney household shortly thereafter.[18]

Whatever the backstory, Pero's alienation and decline were evident and Pinney admits that his death came as a relief to the family. Mrs Pinney dutifully sent a box of his clothes for his father and nephew in Nevis, sold his watch to purchase a pair of gold earrings for each of his three sisters and divided the ten guineas in his possession among his family. The money he was thought to have accrued from his money-lending activities was unrecorded and so lost to his family.[19] Pero was probably buried in the graveyard of St Augustine the Less (now

---

15 Eicklemann and Small suggest that he was taken to Ashton in Somerset; Eickelmann and Small, pp. 55–8; but Peter Martin (aka 'Pirate Pete'), a Bristolian and local tour guide, informed me in July 2018 that there is a tradition that he stayed at Marshfield, Gloucestershire.
16 Eickelmann and Small, p. 58.
17 Eickelmann and Small, p. 55.
18 *Western Daily Press* (henceforth *WDP*), 27 April 1950; George Whalley, 'Coleridge and Southey in Bristol, 1795', *The Review of English Studies*, 1: 4, 1950, pp. 327–8.
19 Eickelmann and Small, p. 58.

underneath the Royal Marriott Hotel in Bristol) under the name of William Jones.[20]

Pero Forgotten?
The Black Presence in Bristol since Pero's Death

In 1807, less than a decade after Pero's death, the British slave trade was declared illegal and by 1834 the Slave Emancipation Act formally proclaimed an ending to enslavement in the British colonies. But the exploitation of cheap black labour continued and the trade with West Africa, the slave states of the USA and the West Indian colonies continued to dominate Bristol's economy.

Acknowledging Bristol's slaving past became an embarrassment as liberal values increasingly informed British political discourse. By the 1860s conservative Bristolians, especially those allied to the city's Society of Merchant Venturers, preferred to play down their historic role in promoting the slave trade and opposing slave emancipation,[21] while those of a more liberal persuasion generally preferred to focus on those in Bristol who had campaigned against the slave trade or for emancipation.[22] Both sets of responses would

20 Eickelmann and Small, p. 58. An anonymous source involved in the renovation of the Royal Marriott Hotel suggested that he was buried there.

21 See Madge Dresser, 'Bristol', in David Dabydeen and John Gilmore (eds), *Oxford Companion to Black British History* (Oxford: Oxford University Press, 2007); Dresser, 'Remembering Slavery and Abolition in Bristol', *Slavery and Abolition*, 30: 2, 2009, pp. 223–7; Bristol's continuing dependence on slave-produced cotton and tobacco meant that the city was divided over whom to support during the American Civil War.

22 Aside from frequent references to Bristol's associations with Thomas Clarkson, Hannah More and John Wesley, the work of Bristol Quaker and Baptist anti-slavery campaigners during the emancipation campaign was also remembered. See *WDP*, 14 July 1933: reference to the 1835 portrait of the anti-slavery campaigner Rev. Thomas Roberts by James Curnock showing him beside slave manacles. The portrait was purchased by the Bristol Museum and Art Gallery in 1999. https://artuk.org/discover/artworks/reverend-thomas-roberts-188407); Dresser, 'Remembering Slavery', pp. 223–7.

continue to characterize the civic discourse on the subject until the late twentieth century.[23]

The descendants of the old merchant families with their colonial connections remained highly influential in the city well into the late twentieth century[24] and the records implicating them in the slave-based economy remained largely in the private domain.[25] However, in 1939 three things happened to lay the groundwork for Pero's eventual resurrection in the public consciousness: the donation of the Pinney family papers to the University of Bristol;[26] the publication of C.M. MacInnes's *Bristol: A Gateway to Empire*, detailing the city's role in the Atlantic slave system;[27] and the gifting of the Pinney mansion to the city's museum service.[28]

But, for the time being, Pero's story still remained forgotten. An informal luncheon preceding the official launch of the Georgian House (as 7 Great George Street would now be called) was convened in October 1939 by the Royal Empire Society at their Bristol headquarters in Whiteladies Road. The opening of the house was celebrated as a 'Great West India Occasion', to which various notables, including the president of the still extant West India Committee of London, had been invited. At the luncheon, Bristol's then sheriff (Col. E.W. Lennard)

23 Bristol Central Reference Library (BCRL). Mounted MM718 'Slavery'. Contains various press cuttings including *WDP* 14 April 1932, 27 October 1933, *Evening World* (nd but 1933); Dresser, 'Remembering Slavery', pp. 223–7.
24 See Patrick McGrath, *The Merchant Venturers of Bristol: A History of the Society of Merchant Venturers of the City of Bristol from its Origin to the Present Day* (American Society of Civil Engineers, 1975); Roger Clements, *Local Notables and the City Council* (London: Macmillan, 1969), pp. 31–50.
25 BCRL, Various press cuttings including *WDP*, 14 April 1932, 27 October 1933, *Evening World*, nd but 1933 in 'Slavery', folder 718.
26 R.W. Pretor Pinney donated a large swathe of the Pinney family papers to the University of Bristol Library in September 1939. Thanks to Hannah Lowery of the University of Bristol Library's Special Collection for this information.
27 C.M. MacInnes, *Bristol: A Gateway of Empire* (Bristol: J.W. Arrowsmith, 1939 and Newton Abbot: David and Charles Ltd., 1968), which was origi-nally dedicated to the Society of Bristol Merchant Venturers; see also C.M. MacInnes, *England and Slavery* (Bristol: Arrowsmith, 1934).
28 Re Pinney Mansion being given to the city by Canon R.T. Cole, see *WDP*, 9 February 1939.

proudly cited Bristol's centuries-long connections with the West Indies and described such early Bristol slave traders and buccaneers as Woodes Rogers and Edmund Teach as 'worthy adventurers' who had 'played great parts in the colonial history of the Caribbean'. At a time 'when all too many of the city's West Indian memorial and landmarks were fading or disappearing the retention of Pinney's mansion would now serve', said the sheriff, as a fitting memorial to 'a great merchant and planter'.[29]

Descriptions of the city's new acquisition focused in true connoisseurship tradition on the aesthetics of its architecture, portraits and furniture. The role of the enslaved labourers whose enslavement made this possible was sidelined.[30] And, in all this, Pero's presence in the house remained invisible. Pero's afterlife only truly began in 1950, when the academic Richard Pares briefly mentioned him as Pinney's slave and valet in his book *A West India Fortune*, based on the Pinney family papers.[31]

In the early 1960s local press coverage of the Pinneys and the Georgian House did begin to acknowledge the family's role in slavery, but usually in the most sanitized way ('slavery was brutal' but Pinney was 'just' and even on occasion 'shrewdly kind' in his treatment of his plantation slaves). In the house itself no mention was made of any black servants in Bristol, nor did any feature in the 'charming model' of John Pinney and his family positioned in a glass case in the entrance hall suggest such a presence.[32]

Yet somehow, in the popular imagination at least, the spectre of Pero or his counterparts lingered. Marguerite Steen's immensely popular post-war blockbuster about a Bristol slave trader, obviously grounded in conversations with old Bristol families and local historians, featured 'Africa', a loyal and much put-upon house servant employed in a great

29 BCRL, Folder 'Mounted Material MM114,' 'The Georgian House, Number 7 Great George Street', Folder 114.
30 BCRL, Folder 'Mounted Material MM114,' 'The Georgian House, Number 7 Great George Street', 11 February 1939 et al. in Folder 114.
31 Richard Pares, *A West India Fortune* (New York: Longmans Green, 1950), p. 130.
32 BCRL, Folder 'Mounted Material MM114,' 'The Georgian House, Number 7 Great George Street', nd but probably 1962 in 'The Georgian House', Folder 114, p. 30; *Evening Post*, 26 April 1962, Folder 114, p. 44.

house in the vicinity of Great George Street, and speaking with a Caribbean accent.

The arrival of the Windrush generation of immigrants from the Caribbean to Bristol after the war, and the racism, deprivation and discrimination they faced, added a new dynamic to the way the city dealt with its slaving history. But Paul Boateng, one of the few black students attending the University of Bristol in the 1970s, remembers thinking 'Bristol was still in denial about slavery' at that time, a view that Tony Benn, then MP for Bristol South East, also held.[33] Boateng recalls passing by the Georgian House in those days wondering about the black presence in the Pinney house. A 1976 ITV fantasy series 'The Georgian House', which was actually filmed at 7 Great George Street, attempted to acknowledge this connection, albeit in ways that said more about white liberalism than historical reality. In the series, Brinsley Forde played an enslaved servant (described as 'a Negro boy with supernatural powers') who is freed by time-travelling white university students who, while acting as guides in the house, had found themselves transported back to the eighteenth century.[34]

By the 1980s the expansion of historical work on Britain's (and Bristol's) slaving past,[35] increasing numbers of people of African-Caribbean ancestry born in the city and the expansion of higher education and cultural industries generated an increased interest in some quarters in both the city's black presence and its historic links with slavery. The St Paul's uprising of 1980 had shaken the city out of

33 Telephone interviews with Paul Boateng in July 2018 and with Tony Benn in 1987, who spoke to me off the record but who later confirmed this view more publicly.
34 *WDP*, 27 December 1975. Brinsley Forde, then a child actor, went on to become a founder member of the Reggae band ASWAD: Wikipedia (https://en.wikipedia.org/wiki/The_Georgian_House.)
35 There is a vast literature on this subject but, for our purposes, the most notable publications relating specifically to Bristol and published in the 1970s were C.M. MacInnes, 'Bristol and the Slave Trade' (Bristol Historical Association Pamphlet, University of Bristol 1968), http://www.bris.ac.uk/Depts/History/bristolrecordsociety/publications/bha007.pdf, and Peter Marshall, 'The Anti-Slave Trade Movement in Bristol' (Bristol Historical Association Pamphlet, University of Bristol, 1968) http://www.bris.ac.uk/Depts/History/bristolrecordsociety/publications/bha020.pdf.

its complacency about race relations and when Paul Boateng, now a qualified civil rights lawyer, returned to the city to defend (successfully) those charged with riot, he felt that the need for Bristol to come to terms with its past was more essential than ever, given that the hostility shown to the city's African-Caribbean inhabitants was grounded in that earlier history.

In the early 1980s David Small, a local secondary history schoolteacher who was teaching about the Georgian House as part of a Schools Council project, also took issue with the way official Bristol publications skirted around the subject. He recalls visitors to the Georgian House being presented with a leaflet that, though it mentioned Pinney's sugar plantations, referred to slavery only by stating that Pinney 'continued to take a "lively interest in the running of the estates and the welfare of his negro slaves" and made no mention of Pero or any other particular slave'.[36]

Small began to do research on the slavery connections of the Pinneys and their enslaved workforce both in Bristol and Nevis. In 1991 he and his partner Christine Eickelmann (who had worked as a community organizer in St Paul's in Bristol, and whose chapter on Fanny Coker, who also lived in the Pinney house, appears in this book) went to Nevis and gathered information from the descendants of the Pinney and Tobin families about Pero and other enslaved workers. Armed with new evidence about Pero and other enslaved Africans owned by Pinney, Small made repeated approaches in the early 1990s to persuade the Georgian House to alter its leaflet and include a permanent exhibition about Pero and plantation slavery, but to no avail.

From the late 1980s into the early 1990s the pioneering research of economic historians such as David Richardson and Ken Morgan established beyond doubt just how central slave trading and slave-produced labour was to Bristol's history, and Philippa Gregory's 1995

---

36 Email from David Small to Madge Dresser, 30 July 2018. His recollections accord with my own. But the only exhibition concerning slavery in that decade was a small temporary one in 1983 at the Queen's Road Museum, which focused on Bristol's role in the abolition. His recollections of the way in which Georgian House's relationship to slavery was glossed over accord with my own and Art Gallery (Queens Road), Bristol Archives (henceforth BRO) 40482/O/DE/1/191.

Bristol-based novel *A Respectable Trade* popularized these themes to a wider public. Yet all this was ignored in the International Festival of the Sea (1996) and the 500th anniversary of Cabot's 'discovery' of Newfoundland (1997), both of which were deafeningly silent about the city's historic involvement in slavery. Protests ensued and the Bristol Slave Trade Action Group (BSTAG) was set up to pressure for the public acknowledgement of Bristol's slaving past.[37] BSTAG members tended to come from outside Bristol and from a range of ethnic backgrounds, and did not share the same defensive mindset discernible among many of Bristol's longer-established white residents.[38] Stephen Price, who became Director at Bristol's Museum and Art Gallery in 1996, and Sue Giles, the ethnography curator there, worked with BSTAG to devise a phased reconfiguration of the museum service's approach to the city's involvement in slavery and its historic black presence, and engaged me as their academic history advisor.

In 1997, as part of their plan, a small exhibit researched by David Small was installed in the Georgian House. Located on the top floor of the museum, the exhibit detailed for the first time not only Pinney's role as slave owner and sugar merchant but Pero's position in the household. In addition, a panel charting Bristol's involvement in the slave trade (as opposed to plantation history) was placed downstairs in the main hall, but this mysteriously vanished within the year, indicating the internal resistance on the part of some museum staff to highlighting Bristol's slaving history. As Stephen Price and his team nervously prepared for the city's first-ever major exhibition on the slave trade at the main museum in Queen's Road, the Georgian House became the site of a guerrilla intervention.

In 1998 four African-American actors, appearing in a 'controversial' play on race at the Bristol Old Vic, visited the Georgian House. They

37 For a fuller account of this process see Sue Giles, 'The Great Circuit: Making the Connection between Bristol's Slaving History and the African-Caribbean Community', *Journal of Museum Ethnography*, 13, 2001, pp. 15–21 and Dresser, 'Remembering Slavery and Abolition', pp. 223–46.
38 Early members of BSTAG included Peter Courtier of the Bristol Council for Racial Equality (later Bristol Racial Equality Council [BREC]), Cllr Pat McLaren, Mikey Dread, Annia Summers, Cllr. Ray Sefia, Kwesi Ngosi. See BRO, 43129/Adm/R/25 BREC *Newsletter*, 214, December 1996/January 1997, pp. 5–6. Thanks to Peter Courtier and Sue Giles for references.

were outraged by what they saw as the 'pathetic' inadequacy of the exhibition, hidden away in what was virtually the attic of the house. Evidently unaware that the museum services were also preparing a slavery trail and the above-mentioned exhibition, and that the house had been used as the location of the television series of Gregory's novel *A Respectable Trade*, they staged a dramatic protest to which they invited the local press. 'Draped in chains, they enacted a short theatre piece in the Georgian House's "slave trade" room to tell the true story.' Ejected from the museum after a few minutes, they continued their performance just outside the house.[39] Their gesture, oblivious as it was to the 'sensitive state of city politics', had, according to one commentator, a polarizing effect on public opinion, arguably alienating those who might have been amenable to a more inclusive interpretation of the house's history.[40]

However, the case still remained that, aside from a small plaque put up privately by Ian White (then an MEP) and the novelist Philippa Gregory in 1997, there was no public monument acknowledging the role enslaved Africans played in Bristol's prosperity.

Pero's Bridge

All this coincided with a major redevelopment of Bristol's Harbourside, where a new footbridge across St Augustine's Reach had been commissioned. First planned in 1994, the bridge was the product of an unprecedented collaboration between the developers (JT group), the engineers Ove Arups, Bristol City Council and the 'Irish Sculptress' Eilis O'Connell. Its metal structure, intended to reflect the city's industrial history, and its innovative cantilevered design with its horn-shaped counterweights made it strikingly distinctive. As the £900,000 bridge neared completion in May 1998, the public was invited to suggest possible names through the *Bristol Evening Post*.[41]

---

39 *WDP*, 26 October 1998; http://jeremymcneill.tripod.com/georghouse.html (accessed 28 July 2018). Charles Dumas was one of the actors involved. http://www.personal.psu.edu/faculty/c/x/cxd28/ (accessed 28 July 2018).
40 Elizabeth Kowaleski Wallace, *The British Slave Trade and Public Memory* (New York: Columbia University Press, 2006), p. 50.
41 Bristol Museums and Art Gallery (henceforth BMAG) folder *Bristol*

Paul Stephenson, the veteran civil rights campaigner and by then the honorary president of the West Indian Parents and Friends Association, along with the MEP Ian White and Peter Courtier of the Bristol Racial Equality Unit, vigorously lobbied for the name of Pero.[42] At the time, little had been written about Pero except that he was Pinney's enslaved servant, so few knew much more about him. Stephenson and his allies saw singling out Pero as a way to draw attention to the city's historic black presence and to acknowledge its dependence on slave-produced wealth.

In the event Pero came second in the *Evening Post* poll, with more of the 110 respondents preferring to name the bridge after the recently deceased Bristol philanthropist John James. Tellingly one respondent suggested naming the bridge 'We Bristolians Are All Very Sorry for Everything Bridge,' which expressed the resentment still felt in some quarters about the focus on Bristol's slaving history, a point underlined by the way so many Bristolians refer to it as 'the Horned Bridge'.[43]

Ultimately, Pero prevailed as a name at least partly because it was thought to suit the wider interests of the City Council and the JT Development Group, headed by JT Pontin, himself a Bristol Merchant Venturer. Naming the bridge after Pero and launching it to coincide with the opening of the major exhibition on Bristol's slave trade would show Bristol as acknowledging its slaving past without having to go to the expense of a dedicated monument or otherwise address some of the deeper issues around the representation of race and history in the city. One did not have to be a racist to dismiss it as 'gesture politics'.[44] But some advocates for the naming of Pero's bridge did so from genuine motives.

Evening Post (BEP), 17 November 1998; Leisure Services Committee Report 17 November 1998 Sue Giles's folders on Pero; BCRL Bridges-General; BRO 428/PM/34BCRL, Pero's Bridge in Local Architecture File.

42 BMAG folder *BEP*, 17 November 1998; Leisure Services Committee Report, 17 November 1998; Sue Giles's folders on Pero; BCRL Bridges-General; BRO 428/PM/34.

43 BCRL, *BEP*, 14 March 1998, 14 July 1998 and other press cuttings in Pero's Bridge in Local Architecture File P–Z; Simon Birkbeck, 'Pero's Bridge, Bristol', in 'Bridges General' Folder, 568; BMAG, Folder on Slavery: Pero's Bridge.

44 *BEP*, 17 November 1999.

Paul Boateng, by then an MP (one of the very first of African descent), and a junior minister for culture under the Labour government, was asked (on Stephenson's suggestion) to officiate. Given his past associations with Bristol and his subsequent friendship with Stephenson through the anti-apartheid campaign, he was happy to come. If Pero was hardly a symbol of explicitly direct defiance, for both Stephenson and Boateng he served as a symbol of survival. Photos of the launch show the crowd attending contrasted with those at the Festival of the Sea or the John Cabot quinquennial, being more racially diverse and drawn from the more progressivist circles of Bristol's population. Sherri Eugene, Bristol's first black female television presenter, was asked to cover the event for HTV, Peter Baidoo, from the black writers' group, read some poems and an unnamed black actor in eighteenth-century dress posed as Pero for photos with Stephenson, who later that year invited the High Commissioner of the Gambia to view the bridge.[45]

The 'controversial' bridge soon attracted adverse press coverage and hostile letters in the press, ostensibly on account of its expense and various maintenance and design problems; but even when these were resolved some, if not most, Bristolians continued to call it the Horned Bridge, implicitly and sometimes explicitly resisting its official associations with Pero and slavery.[46] The small plaque put up to explain who Pero was and why the bridge was named in his honour was hard to see and generally ignored.[47]

After the millennium Pero's story was disseminated beyond Bristol through various new books, broadcasts and websites charting Bristol's involvement in Atlantic slavery.[48] In 2004 the museum published

45 BRO, 42840/CD/29,30 152, 154, 42840/PM/34; 43129/GA/BSTAG/7; 43609/Ph 17, 17/2 and 17/12.
46 BCRL, Press cuttings such as 'the 'orned bridge', nd, in 'Local Architecture File, P–Z'; https://www.opendemocracy.net/beyondslavery/madge-dresser/ obliteration-contextualisation-or-guerrilla-memorialisation-edward-colst; *BEP*, 3 November 1998; *Evening Post*, 14 March 2000.
47 Noted by Stuart Butler in his poem on Pero's bridge, http://radicalstroud. blogspot.com/2015/09/the-bristol-slavery-trail.html (accessed 9 November 2019) and by Michael Jenkins, interviewed 19 July 2018.
48 See 'The Georgian House', in Madge Dresser and Sue Giles, *Bristol and Transatlantic Slavery* (Bristol Museums and Art Gallery, 2000); (www. portcities.org) and Dresser, *Slavery Obscured*; see also 'Under the Bridge', by

Eickelmann and Small's *Pero: The Life of a Slave in Eighteenth Century Bristol*, which set out for the first time the outlines of Pero's life and the circumstances of his illness.

But, like all good symbols, Pero became a polysemic figure onto which people projected their own interpretations. The Bajan-born artist Graeme Evelyn used an Arts Council grant to stage 'Two Coins', a multimedia meditation on slavery past and present originally intended to be projected onto Bristol's Colston statue. To this end he made four small films shot variously in Africa, the Caribbean and Bristol. The last film used an actor to play a stylized servant based loosely on Pero, attending his master in a stylized sequence set in the Georgian House.[49]

The rendering of Pero's story at the Georgian House has evolved over the past decade as the new research has been integrated into the museum programme and a more diverse visitor base actively sought. The actor Angus Brown, who appeared in Evelyn's 'Two Coins' film in 2007, was engaged in 2012 to impersonate Pero at the Georgian House during the UN International Slavery Remembrance Day (Figure 7.1). His instructions were to interact in character with museum visitors.[50] Four years later the house was used for a broadcast on 'Pero Jones and Fanny Coker' as part of Gretchen H. Gerzina's Radio 4 series 'Britain's Black Past'.[51] And, in 2017, a new website and revamped exhibit on Pero, Pinney and slavery, using the newest findings of Eickelmann and Small, was installed in the house as part of a wider programme of performances and events about slavery-related themes.[52]

Pero's bridge itself has been portrayed by increasing numbers of artists but often with little or no reference to slavery or Pero's story. One

Shawn Sobers and Rob Mitchell (HTV: 2001), the first television documentary on the memorialization of slavery in Bristol (which was also the first such programme made by two black British filmmakers), now available at time of publication at https://vimeo.com/11471392 (accessed 9 November 2019).

49 Dresser, 'Remembering Slavery and Abolition', p. 237; see also http://graemeevelyn.com/the-two-coins/ (accessed 9 November 2019); telephone conversation with Graeme Evelyn, 15 July 2018.

50 Telephone interview by Madge Dresser with Angus Brown. 15 July 2018.

51 https://www.bbc.co.uk/programmes/b07wtd6y.

52 https://www.bristolmuseums.org.uk/blog/bristol-transatlantic-slave-trade/; https://seis.bristol.ac.uk/~emceee/welcome.html and https://seis.bristol.ac.uk/~emceee/bristoldevelopments.html; email from Edson Burton, 2 August 2018.

7.1 Angus Brown as Pero in a reconstruction at the
Georgian House Museum c.2007.
Credit: *Evening Post*, Photographer Jon Kent

of the ironies is that since 2014 the bridge has become a repository for padlocks put up as romantic tokens by couples oblivious to its slavery associations.[53] Others have used the bridge as a site to commemorate the suffering of enslaved people and celebrate racial diversity and human rights.[54] Amid various recent campaigns to 'decolonize' Bristol's public monuments, Pero's bridge has come under criticism for choosing to celebrate an apparently deferential servant rather than those enslaved Africans who actively challenged the slave system.

Pero Resurrected

Some contemporary artists and commentators of colour have begun to confront Pero's ambiguous and difficult image in order to explore the possible connections between his alcoholism and his position as an enslaved man in a white city. Ros Martin's performance piece 'Being Rendered Visible in the Georgian House' eloquently imagines Fanny Coker engaging in a dialogue with an ancestral spirit to meditate on the occasion of Pero's death:

> The Old Slave draws on his pipe.
> 'Maybe, just maybe, William didn't mean to …'
> [Fanny Coker] 'Drink and kill himself? Just wanted to be rendered useless? Who would ever believe that of Pero?' She says.
> [Old Slave:] 'Precisely.'
> [Fanny Coker]: 'Pero the tooth extractor, Pero the trader, Pero the money lender, Pero the loyal valet who serves Mr Pinney nigh on 32 years, now ungratefully and wantonly gives up. Why?'
> [Old Slave:] '… Maybe, just maybe, he wished to be returned to Nevis, to comfort, to raise his motherless daughter, be reunited with his beloved sisters.'
> [FC:] 'Only, how would that ever happen?!' retorts Fanny.[55]

---

53 https://www.bristol247.com/news-and-features/news/biggest-love-lock-yet-on-peros-bridge/.
54 See, for example, the 'Hands Across the City' event in October 2017 at https://journeytojustice.org.uk/projects/bristol/#link-location.
55 http://www.bristol.ac.uk/media-library/sites/arts/research/documents/being-rendered-visible-ros-martin.pdf.

Paul Boateng, drawing on his own personal experience, makes the point that Pero's isolation as one of the few black faces in an overwhelmingly white city 'must have inevitably impacted on his own mental state' and may help to explain 'his descent into alcoholism'.[56]

It is that very sense of alienation, of being in but not part of the city, that most particularly resonates with a whole new generation of young Bristolians of African or partially African descent. Their search for identity, for a sense of belonging, is crucial both to their individual well-being and to the future of a healthy society. Those young people interested in their historic roots reportedly glean their information from Facebook groups and uncorroborated websites. If, in consequence, they do not often find source-based material that is accurate, accessible and nuanced they will form a distorted view of their past. There is, for example, a good degree of historical misunderstanding about the black presence in Bristol that the invocation of Pero can actually help to entrench, since one commonly held misconception is that he represents a large population of enslaved Africans living in Bristol. In truth, the story of British slavery is a transnational one and, while the profits and slave-produced goods accrued to ports such as Bristol, enslaved Africans living there constituted only a tiny fraction of the many more who lived in Africa, the Americas and the Caribbean.[57]

Yet the haunting nature of Pero's story, when we take the time to reflect upon on it in all its tragic complexity—derives in part from its association with a particular house and a particular city. Edson Burton's 2017 poem 'A Slave's Reverie' pictures Pero in the Georgian House awoken from his tortured memories of the Caribbean by the ringing of the servant's bell.[58] In that sense Pero is truly, as Michael

---

56 Paul Boateng interview.

57 I am grateful for the insights of the filmmaker Michael Jenkins of 8th Sense Media and of Tayo Lewin, a history undergraduate of the University of Bristol, interviewed on 19 July 2018 and 13 July 2018 respectively.

58 ... Through ice clad corn street
    Along eerily silent Old Market I press
    Slim and stout inns and abodes
    Mark city's edge I step beyond
    City's boundary. The air suddenly sweet
    Hibiscus shoots break layered snow
    Warm blast teeming with gossamer

Mayerfeld Bell puts it, 'a ghost of place', an ancestral spirit, which, along with those of John Pinney, Kate Coker and even Edward Colston, combine to imbue Bristol with its unique aura. As he writes,

> the rightful possession of a place depends in part upon our sense of the ghosts that possess it, and the connections of different people to those ghosts. Which spirits we choose to resurrect is a political choice. Because they are our ghosts, what we make of them is what counts.[59]

> Wings, swarm downwind, I spin.
> Lizard swerve between dry grass
> Mongoose runs in search of rodent
> Black faced monkey calls from bush.
> Home- horn blow and dirge song
> Iron glint in sun chopping cane stem
> Field hand cut eye upon me in livery.
> The canefield and great house a land and ocean
> Liberty a mystery hidden in forested hills
> Shrouding the estate behind us both.
> The bell echoes through the house:
> Master Pinney I turn from the window
> Saved from tortured dreams.'

Thanks to Edson Burton for permission to use his poem.

59 Michael Mayerfeld Bell, 'The Ghosts of Place', *Theory and Society*, 26: 6, 1997, p. 832. BRO, 43129/Adm/R/25 BREC *Newsletter*, 214, December 1996/ January 1997, pp. 5–6. Thanks to Peter Courtier for this reference.

CHAPTER EIGHT

Within the Same Household: Fanny Coker

Christine Eickelmann

Frances (Fanny) Coker, born enslaved and raised in the West Indies, worked for almost four decades in John and Jane Pinney's Bristol home, now the Georgian House Museum. She was freed, trained and educated, and employed by the very people who 'owned' her family on their plantation, but through her own abilities was able to rise from a low-status job to that of an upper servant. While she had to negotiate complex relationships in Bristol, throughout her life she stayed in touch with family and friends in the West Indies either directly or through visitors to Bristol—black and white, free and enslaved.

Fanny Coker belonged to a group of women who so far have remained largely invisible in British history: plantation-born female domestic servants. Paintings of the Georgian era depict many more black male than female servants, and nowadays much is known about several male servants, such as Olaudah Equiano, Francis Barber, Cesar Picton, and Jack Beef. Some of these men have written their own life stories (as had Mary Prince) but, since Fanny Coker did not leave any written material, her life had to be pieced together from official documents and what her employer noted about her. Given the paucity of information about black women servants, her story is an important contribution to our understanding of black servants' lives in Georgian England, but until more research is carried out into black women servants we will not know how typical her life was.

Fanny Coker was born on 26 August 1767 on Mountravers sugar plantation on the island of Nevis, the oldest of five children born to an enslaved woman known as Black Polly (Figure 8.1). Her mother was bought in 1765 at the age of twelve by John Pinney, who owned Mountravers. Black Polly, born in Africa and identified by Pinney as an 'Egbo' (Igbo, from present-day Nigeria), became a seamstress.[1] Fanny's father almost certainly was Pinney's white plantation manager William Coker.[2] Her siblings were black, except for Billey Jones (born in 1773), who was, like her, a 'mulatto' and probably Pinney's son. She also had two white brothers—Coker's children with his wife Frances. Mrs Coker was one of Mrs Pinney's aunts, and Fanny was therefore Mrs Pinney's cousin-by-marriage.

Fanny Coker was the only enslaved person from Mountravers known to have been baptized in the eighteenth century,[3] and she was among the few enslaved girls whose education Pinney financed.[4] Fanny first trained as a seamstress and was then schooled with another enslaved girl, Mulatto Polly, and two Pinney children, probably the oldest, John Frederick and Betsey. By the time Fanny completed her education almost five years later, she had been freed. Pinney manumitted her on 15 September 1778.[5]

For some years John Pinney had wanted to return to England and in 1783 he was finally able to leave Nevis with his wife Jane and their two-year-old son Pretor. The older children, John Frederick, Betsey and Azariah, were at school in England already. Another daughter, Alicia, had died during an outbreak of fever at the age of four. Fanny, dressed in black callimanco and wearing a 'black trimmed hat', brown stockings and shoes, had attended Alicia's funeral in January 1780.[6] In 1783 Fanny Coker, by then aged almost sixteen, left Nevis with the

---

1 The Letterbooks (LB), Accountbooks (AB) and Domestic Boxes mentioned below are in the Pinney Papers (PP), held in the University of Bristol Library Special Collections (BULSC).

LB 3 List of Negroes purchased by Jn. Pinney, 1769.

2 AB 20 Wm Coker's account (a/c) (Black Polly's delivery accounted for).

3 AB 17: 30 June 1770 (Fanny's baptism accounted for).

4 AB 17: 29 December 1775; AB 20 and AB 21 Expense a/c; AB 26 Mary Keep's a/c (Fanny's education accounted for).

5 Eastern Caribbean Supreme Court Registry, Nevis (ECSCRN), Common Records (CR) 1777–78 f.129.

6 PP, DM 1173 Nevis Ledger 1780–1790 ff.8–12 Expense a/c Nevis (Fanny's mourning attire accounted for).

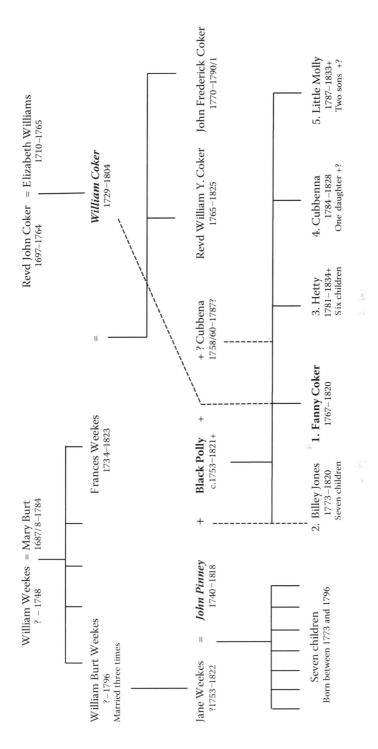

8.1 Fanny Coker's family tree.
Created by the author.

Pinney family and parted from her own: her mother, her brother Billey and her two-year-old sister Hetty. The travellers included John Pinney's thirty-year-old black enslaved manservant Pero Jones. In 1765 Pinney had purchased Pero, then twelve years old, and had him trained as a barber and tooth puller.

The Pinneys and their servants had an easy passage of just under six weeks, landed at Dover and went to lodge in London.[7] They celebrated Christmas at Woodcutts, William Coker's estate in Dorset (the Cokers had also left Nevis), and the following spring the Pinneys and their servants settled down in Bristol in rented accommodation not far from the harbour. Originally from Dorset, Pinney had always wanted to live in a 'pleasant and convenient situation in the West' and, since his wife was 'so avers [sic] to live in the country and so desirous of settling in some Town',[8] he chose Bristol, with its commercial and social opportunities. Bristol was no longer the leading slaving port in Britain, as it had been in the 1730s, but it still took an active part, and many of its inhabitants were involved in the African and West Indian trades: they built and crewed the ships, financed and insured voyages, manufactured or supplied the export wares, and from the colonies imported the slave-produced commodities.

Jane Pinney, a Nevis-born Creole, or island-born person, had to establish her place in Bristol society; white Creoles were often looked down upon by British-born whites. She may have been guided by another Nevis Creole, Kitty Nisbet. Slave-born but freed,[9] Kitty had worked as a servant in England for over a decade and knew the country's ways and customs. She became 'Mrs Pinney's woman', but soon after the Pinneys had moved to Bristol Kitty's former employer was preparing to return to Nevis and enquired after her. Although Mrs Pinney was 'extremely sorry to part from her',[10] Kitty left and Jane Pinney engaged a new maid.[11] Fanny, meanwhile, sewed and mended and also looked after Pretor, the youngest Pinney offspring until the births of Mary in 1786 and Charles in 1793.

---

7 AB 34, AB 33 Memos.
8 LB 4 Pinney to George Warry, 13 June 1778 and 10 June 1779.
9 ECSCRN, CR 1757–62 f.446.
10 LB 5 Pinney to Walter Nisbet, 25 March 1784.
11 PP, Miscellaneous Volumes 8 Pinney's Journal, Memo (1785).

John Pinney set up in business as a sugar factor with his friend from Nevis, the planter James Tobin. Their company exported plantation supplies, such as building and boiling lime, nails, 'negroe clothing', cart wheels and herrings,[12] and imported West Indian slave-produced sugar and rum. While they firmly believed that the slave trade was vital for the plantation economy, the wider population was beginning to question this, particularly after news spread of the barbaric murder at sea of over 130 African captives on the ship *Zong*, in late 1781, in order to collect insurance money.[13] Their consciences stirred, citizens became concerned about conditions on slaving vessels and on the plantations and, sensitive to the change in public opinion, Tobin set out to defend colonial interests. In pamphlets he argued that free black people would not work in the fields and compared favourably the enslaved people's living conditions with those of the labouring poor in Britain. The growing number of children born in England to white women and black men he dismissed as a 'contaminated breed'—a racial slur that would have hurt Fanny and also Tobin's mixed-race sisters.[14] No doubt they, Fanny and also Mrs Pinney saw the irony in his claim that on the plantations it was the hired managers and overseers who fathered the mixed-race children, rather than the gentlemen planters.[15]

The Pinneys' home in Park Street was close to the local parish church and the cathedral, but Fanny chose to worship further away, in the Broadmead Baptist Church. The Baptists may have met her social and religious needs, but it is also likely that their politics appealed to her; its leaders were among the founder members of the Bristol branch of the Society for Effecting the Abolition of the Slave Trade.[16] The

12 LB 37 Pinney to John Julius, 12 October 1787.

13 James Walvin, *The Zong, A Massacre, the Law and the End of Slavery* (New Haven: Yale University Press, 2011).

14 David Small, 'James Tobin', *Oxford Dictionary of National Biography* (*ODNB*) (Oxford: Oxford University Press, 2004).

15 Fanny and Mrs Pinney would have known that Tobin's mixed race sisters Anne and Lydia had lived in Bristol (ECSCRN, CR 1769–71 ff.315–17, CR 1778–83 f.594; V.L. Oliver, *Caribbeana* (London: Mitchell Hughes & Clarke, 1914), Vol. 5, p. 3).

16 Timothy Whelan, 'Robert Hall and the Bristol Slave-Trade Debate 1788–1789', *Baptist Quarterly*, 38, 2000, pp. 212–24; Roger Hayden, 'Caleb Evans and the Anti-Slavery Question', *Baptist Quarterly*, 39, 2001, pp. 4–14.

abolitionist cause gathered such momentum in the city that in January 1788 hundreds of people attended an abolition meeting and, along with citizens all over the country, eagerly signed petitions condemning the trade. Under pressure, in July the British government passed legislation to regulate conditions on British slaving vessels, the Dolben Act. This so rattled the Bristol pro-slavery lobby that they founded their own organization to counter the new national mood. Headed by the Society of Merchant Venturers and funded by levies on slave-produced sugar, the Bristol West India Association sought to defend the trade in enslaved Africans as vital to British and colonial prosperity. Pinney foresaw the new Act as 'an omen of a general abolition'[17] and, fearing that this would damage their commercial interests, he and Tobin swiftly joined.[18]

It was against this background of polarizing views that Fanny Coker pledged herself to the Baptist church and, according to its principles, on the evening of 10 March 1789 publicly declared her faith. The church records state that 'Frances Coker the descd.t of African ancestors, gave a most intelligent and pleasing acc.t of the work of God upon her soul, and was accepted as a candidate for baptism.'[19] Some months later she underwent baptism and with it began her lifelong commitment to the Baptist church.[20]

If the Pinneys, as Anglicans, disapproved of her choice, they did not hold it against her. Their new house in Bristol was being built and, with a trip to Nevis planned, they gave up their rented accommodation and dismissed all servants except Fanny and Pero. Mrs Pinney wanted to take her 'sympstress alias nursemaid' to Nevis and, once again, Fanny Coker displayed her independence of mind. She refused to go. Her reasons for this are not known. She may have been terrified of the hazardous Atlantic crossing—earlier in the year the packet from Antigua had been feared lost[21]—or she may have dreaded returning to a society grounded in plantation slavery. Given the unstable political situation, she may have feared being abducted by pirates or French invaders; two enslaved men

17 LB 37 Pinney & Tobin to George Webbe, 3 July 1788.
18 John Latimer, *The Annals of Bristol in the Eighteenth Century* (Frome: Butler & Tanner, 1893), pp. 476–7.
19 Bristol Archives (BA), 30251/BD/M1/3.
20 BA, 30251/BD/R1/4a, 4c(i), 4c(ii) and 30251/BD/M1/4.
21 LB 37 P & T to Mrs Arthurton, 16 January 1789.

from Mountravers had already been stolen off the island. Whatever her reasons, she stood firm, even when threatened with dismissal. Pinney suggested giving her a reference so that she could 'procure a place in some respectable family'[22] in England and, being free, Fanny could have left her employment. Her fellow servant from Nevis, however, was still enslaved and did not have such a choice. If Pero wanted to work elsewhere, Pinney had to approve and either sell or free him. Although enslaved people could not be forced to return to the West Indies, they could still be bought and sold in England. Fanny, with her skills and her contacts in Bristol and London, would easily have found a position in another household, yet she decided to travel with the Pinneys after all and, sensibly, asked one of John Pinney's female cousins to mediate.

In Nevis Fanny saw for the first time her five-year-old brother Cubbenna and her two-year-old sister Molly. Both later became field hands and the other sister, Hetty, a domestic, while Billey was apprenticed to a cooper. Although during her seven-month visit Fanny would have worked for the Pinneys, she would have seen much of her family, as they lived nearby, on the plantation. It is likely that she supported her mother financially; after the visit Black Polly bought wooden shingles and boards to upgrade her house.[23]

On their return journey to England the Pinneys took with them a ten-year-old enslaved girl, Christianna Jacques. Her mother, Mulatto Polly, wanted her to be trained in England and agreed to finance her daughter's three-year-apprenticeship at £10 a year (worth about £1,100 in 2017).[24] No doubt on the voyage home it fell to Fanny to look after Christianna. When the party arrived back in Bristol in September 1790, the Pinneys' new house was not yet finished. For six months the family and their servants first stayed with the Tobins and then took lodgings until they could move into Great George Street. These changes made it harder for Christianna to adjust to her new environment, and she

---

22 LB 8 Pinney to Elizabeth Pinney, 27 October 1789.

23 AB 43 Plantation a/c.

24 BULSC, DM1705 Richard Pares's Notes for *A West India Fortune*, 233: Pinney Family Letterbooks, Box D-6 f.258: Pinney to James Williams, 17 January 1797; https://www.measuringworth.com/calculators/ppoweruk/ Lawrence Officer and Samuel Williamson, 'Five Ways to Compute the Relative Value of a UK Pound Amount ...', accessed 17 June 2018.

became so difficult to manage that Pinney considered sending her back to Nevis,[25] but she settled down and remained in England.

The Pinneys engaged new staff in addition to Fanny and Pero, making do with relatively few: a cook, a housemaid, an upper servant, a coachman and a stable boy. Employers could choose from a large, ever-changing pool of domestics; one contemporary estimate put their number in England and Wales at 910,000, of whom the majority were female.[26] Servants tended to change employers if better opportunities arose elsewhere,[27] and over the years various people worked for the Pinneys. For the household to run smoothly newcomers had to integrate themselves into the household, but it is impossible to assess to what extent these 'Black and white servants lived and worked side by side, enjoying each other's company and sharing a common social and economic life.'[28] Fanny and Pero, the only foreign-born servants, but also Mrs Pinney,[29] had brought with them West Indian expressions, manners and customs, which may have united these Creoles while distancing them from the rest of the household.

Fanny's relationship with her fellow servants was complicated by her relationship with her employers. Pinney stated that his family had treated her 'from her infancy, with great tenderness' and that she was 'never considered ... in the light of a menial servant, but as one who had a claim to our protection and support'.[30] In this he suggests that he thought of her almost as dependent kin, which made her neither wholly 'upstairs' nor wholly 'downstairs'. By contrast, he still considered

25 LB 9 Pinney to T.P. Weekes, 5 March 1791.

26 Bridget Hill, *Women, Work & Sexual Politics in Eighteenth-century England* (London: UCL, 1994), p.126, quoting Patrick Colquhoun, *A Treatise on Indigence* (1806), p. 253.

27 D.A. Kent, 'Ubiquitous but Invisible: Female Domestic Servants in Mid-Eighteenth Century London', *History Workshop Journal*, 28, 1989, p. 120, quoting J. Jean Hecht, *Domestic Servants*, p. 81.

28 Paul Edwards and James Walvin, *Black Personalities in the Era of the Slave Trade* (London: Macmillan, 1983), p. 46.

29 Pares, *A West India Fortune*, p.75; Chloe Aubra Northrop, *White Creole Women in the British West Indies: From Stereotype to Caricature* (Denton: University of North Texas, 2010), pp. 18–19, quoting J.B. Moreton, *West India Customs* (1793), pp. 121, 108, 118.

30 LB 8 Pinney to Elizabeth Pinney, 27 October 1789.

Pero—born enslaved in Nevis and nominally free in Britain—as his property. Like other live-in staff, Pero had free board and lodging plus some perquisites, such as a livery and tea and sugar, but he received no wages; only occasional sums of money.[31] Such discrimination was legal; in 1785 Judge Mansfield ruled that slaves from abroad were not entitled to wages unless they could prove their employers' promise of payment.[32] In contrast to Pero, Fanny and Pinney's other servants enjoyed a contractual relationship, with fixed pay and perks. However, everyone's time off would have been irregular and at their employers' discretion, thereby underlining their dependent status.[33]

Fanny and most of the other servants in the Pinney household were on annual contracts and paid quarterly. This bound them more closely to their employers than those on weekly or daily rates, while providing some security if they became sick and unable to work: anyone born outside the parish who received wages and remained with their employer for more than a year became entitled to claim parish poor relief.[34] Pero, not being waged, would not have qualified. If he fell ill he could only hope that his employer would maintain him. As it happened, Pero's health declined and he became incapable of doing his duties. The Pinneys supported him until he died in 1798.[35]

Although originally employed as a seamstress with responsibility for the young Pinney children, Fanny became Mrs Pinney's lady's maid. This made her the highest-ranked among the female staff, but in the early 1800s she was not yet the highest-paid. Men generally earned more than women and the highest-paid member of staff was Pero's replacement, a footman. He earned £26 a year, the coachman £14 14s 0d, the cook £13 2s 6d, Fanny £12 and the housemaid £8 18s 6d. The lowest grades, a kitchen maid and a washer woman, were on daily rates.[36] As Fanny

---

31 For instance, AB 17: 25 December 1783; AB 33 Cash a/c. It is not known whether their different legal positions affected Fanny's and Pero's relationship.
32 William R. Cotter, 'The Somerset Case and the Abolition of Slavery', *History*, 79: 255, 1994, p. 42.
33 LB 9 Pinney to T.P. Weekes, 24 January 1791.
34 Kathleen Chater, *Untold Histories: Black People in England and Wales during the Period of the British Slave Trade, c.1660-1807* (Manchester: Manchester University Press, 2011), p.139.
35 LB 14 Pinney to James Williams, 12 November 1798.
36 PP, DM1173 Pinney Somerton and Bristol Expense Book, 1801–1804 f.16.

became more proficient in her job, over time her wages rose to £26 a year.[37] When she was travelling she received an additional allowance for a maid to do her washing, which meant that, in effect, one female upper servant employed another of lower status. The hierarchy below stairs reflected British society's preoccupation with class[38]—or, as it was then called, rank—and presumably Fanny, like her contemporaries, would have viewed 'less-polished lower servants ... as [her] inferiors'.[39] If she found fault with the way the maid did her laundry, she had to handle any complaints sensitively lest the relationship turned sour. Employers did not tolerate squabbling servants.

As lady's maid Fanny had to attend to her mistress at all times. Her duties were to help Mrs Pinney dress and undress: lacing stays, tying ribbons and arranging layers of undergarments and gowns. She had to style hair and prepare cosmetics from ingredients such as castor oil and scent. The wardrobe needed to be in perfect order, including the many bonnets, bags, slippers, shoes, gloves, jewellery, fans and decorative feathers. Cleaning and maintaining these required a good knowledge of the different materials so as not to spoil any through improper handling. Although rich, the Pinneys were not extravagant, and Fanny's seamstress training meant she could alter garments cheaply by adding fashionable touches. As to her own clothes and linens, she possessed three trunks full[40]—more than servants generally owned.

In addition to understanding style and etiquette, lady's maids were expected to conduct themselves with propriety, speak in refined tones and be educated beyond mere reading; they had to be able to read out loud in a pleasing manner.[41] Given such requirements, these servants tended to come from genteel but impoverished backgrounds—clergymen's

Pinney's servants earned about as much as those in London: around 1800 lady's maids received between £10 and £20 a year and cooks between £7 and £15, while house and kitchen maids were usually on less than £10. However, wages varied greatly according to employer (Hill, *Women, Work*, p. 133).

37 AB 65 Mrs Pinney's a/c.

38 Hill, *Women, Work*, pp. 132, 146; Chater, *Untold Histories*, p. 225.

39 John R. Gillis, 'Servants, Sexual Relations, and the Risks of Illegitimacy in London, 1801–1900', *Feminist Studies*, 5: 1, 1979, p. 152, quoting John Burnett, ed., *Useful Toil* (London: Allen Lane, 1974), pp. 150–3.

40 Domestic Box C1–7, Jane Pinney to Charles Pinney, 21 February 1821.

41 Hill, p. 230.

daughters and the like[42]—and the fact that Fanny was able to rise from seamstress to lady's maid demonstrates her intelligence and her ability to adapt. Servants were rarely promoted within a household; those who wanted to progress usually moved on,[43] yet Fanny decided to remain. Wealthy women generally preferred personal attendants who also provided companionship,[44] and Fanny and Mrs Pinney, with their common West Indian background, may have enjoyed each other's company despite the differences in their social and economic standing. The women certainly spent a lot of time together; maids tended to accompany the lady of the house on all excursions. Mrs Pinney, fourteen years Fanny's senior, enjoyed walking, and she and Fanny would often have strolled to Jack's Coffee House, where Mrs Pinney was a member.[45] Mrs Pinney was also an energetic traveller, and over the years Fanny visited many different places with her mistress. Part of the summer they spent at the Pinney's new country house, Somerton in Somerset. On long trips Fanny took with her the one truly private item all servants possessed: a lockable trunk for personal belongings.

Occasionally Fanny was in charge of looking after Racedown, the Pinneys' old country residence in Dorset. While enjoying greater freedom on her own, she would have had to adjust to a quiet rural life. One summer she had with her a woman called Nancy.[46] On their return to Bristol, with fifty hilly miles ahead, Nancy travelled with the coachman in the gig and Fanny rode Miss Pinney's horse. The gig broke down and they returned to Racedown for extensive repairs. When they set off again, the women swapped places: Fanny sat with the coachman, 'and Nancy on horseback went on tow'.[47] Fanny also travelled alone by public coach,[48] demonstrating that she was an organized, independent woman.

Although she and her mistress spent a lot of time together, in England there was a greater distance between them than there would

---

42 Chater, *Untold Histories*, p. 224, quoting Hecht, *Domestic Servants*, pp. 60–3.
43 Gillis, p. 148.
44 Chater, *Untold Histories*, p. 224.
45 AB 49 f.15.
46 This may have been Fanny's friend Ann/Nancy Seymour.
47 AB 2 Gill's Racedown Account: 1 and 20 September 1794.
48 AB 42 f.63: 8 April 1795.

have been had they remained in the West Indies. There servants still slept in hallways and on landings in the old-fashioned manner, or in their master's or mistress's bedroom; John Pinney called this 'the West-India mode of making two beds in a room'.[49] In Great George Street the servants' spaces were the attic, where they slept in dormitory-style bedchambers, and the two lowest floors, with its kitchen and cellars. To move about, they used a discrete staircase, not the main stairs.

West Indian produce regularly arrived from Nevis: rum, sugar and many tropical fruits, but also staples such as yams, cassava bread and arrow root, as well as pumpkins and roast cashew nuts, which Mrs Pinney ordered from Fanny's mother, Black Polly. She also requested calabashes, whereas Mr Pinney asked for turtles, distilled orange flower water, castor oil, guava jelly and pickled peppers. While these luxuries were for the Pinneys, Fanny's family and friends would also have sent her presents, possibly through ships' crews, certainly through visitors. In turn, she gave these people items to take to Nevis, or Pinney forwarded them in his ships. Some are documented—a parcel and a box for her mother,[50] iron hoops for her brother's coopering business,[51] a locket with hair work,[52] a handkerchief she sent to a friend[53] and a cloak and bonnet she had made for one of Mrs Pinney's aunts (for which she was paid)[54]—but there would have been many more unrecorded transactions. She also sent money,[55] an early form of remittance. This was not unusual; many servants endured homesickness, irregular working hours and curtailed personal freedom in order to support their families.[56]

Fanny was able to stay in touch with goings-on in Nevis; travellers carried across the Atlantic not just presents and perhaps goods for trading but also news and gossip. The Pinneys, with an extensive

49 Domestic Box S4, Pinney to Governor Burt, 12 May 1777.
50 LB 16 Pinney to James Williams, 11 February 1801; LB 17 Pinney to James Williams, 6 March 1802.
51 LB 18 Pinney to Henry Williams, 15 December 1803.
52 LB 19 Sundry Account to Anthony Henderson.
53 LB 9 Pinney to T.P. Weekes, 31 October 1790.
54 AB 37 f.33.
55 LB 9 Pinney to Ann Weekes, 30 October 1791.
56 Gillis, p. 150, quoting Charles Booth, ed., *Life and Labour of the People in London* (London: Macmillan, 1903), Vol. 4, p. 224.

network of friends and business contacts, often received visitors from the island and also hosted several free black and mixed-race women. They generally came as servants, accompanying lady and gentleman travellers, children crossing the Atlantic on their own, and also families: Kate Coker attended on a clergyman's wife and her daughter;[57] on another occasion Ann Seymour brought this woman's luggage and then stayed on a while,[58] and Nanny Weekes, recently freed by one of Mrs Pinney's aunts, escorted Mrs Pinney's orphaned nephews to Bristol.[59] Christianna Jacques's mother, Mulatto Polly, who by then had been freed,[60] accompanied a planter and his family as a servant. When he failed to pay her wages and passage home, Mulatto Polly remained in Bristol for over a year. During this lengthy stay she saw her daughter, who in the meantime had got married and moved to Chatham.[61] Mulatto Polly visited Bristol at least three more times.[62] She was not the only servant left penniless; one free woman, Ritta Erskine, turned to the Pinneys for help after her mistress had died *en route* from Nevis. Pinney's firm provided her with wages, mourning clothes and passage home.[63]

Fanny looked after these visitors and may have introduced them to other people from the West Indies who worked in Bristol for various planters and merchants. James Tobin's domestics George Evans and Priscilla Gould, for instance, lived just up the road in Berkeley Square. Fanny would also have known the black servant who worked for Tobin's father-in-law in Bristol, and the man Tobin's brother-in-law brought from Falmouth on his visits. However, no doubt, she would have been in touch with many others, including independently living

57 LB 37 Pinney & Tobin to William Jones, 16 June 1785.
58 LB 16 Pinney to Frances Jones, 27 November 1800; AB 42 Mary Pinney's a/c.
59 AB 22 f.64.
60 ECSCRN, CR 1794–97 f.620.
61 LB 46 Pinney and J.F. Pinney to William Scarborough, 1 and 12 November 1806. Christianna was last mentioned in 1810 (AB 65 Expense a/c).
62 LB 23 Pinney to P.T. Huggins, 13 October 1810; Pinney to J.C. Mills, 10 October 1811, 16 October 1812; Domestic Box C1 Bundle 6, Jane Pinney to Charles Pinney, 25 October 1820.
63 LB 22 Pinney to James Tobin, 20 September 1808.

free women such as Maria Herbert, the mistress of the president of the Nevis Council.[64]

Among the people who visited the Pinneys was Mrs Pinney's father, William Burt Weekes. Fanny knew him well; after leaving Nevis he sometimes stayed at Great George Street, but last lived in Wraxall, near Bristol, with his nephew William Young Coker, one of Fanny's white brothers, who had become a clergyman; the other, John Frederick, died aged twenty. When old Weekes died in 1796[65] everyone from Great George Street attended his funeral in Wraxall and the 'hearse, a chariott and four-two coaches ... with [Pinney's] carriage and servants made up the procession'.[66] In 1804 Fanny's father died at his family home, Woodcutts.[67] John Pinney had taken Woodcutts into his possession after Coker had failed to repay mortgages, and his widow went to live in Somerset with their son William and his family.

Just as servants might attend family burials, they partook in weddings, albeit at a distance. When Pinney's heir John Frederick got married, in a typically paternalist gesture Pinney provided strong beer, wine and music for 'workmen servants and others'.[68] On Betsey's marriage Fanny also received a cash gift, but for the other servants her wedding was a quieter affair, while Mary's went almost unnoticed.[69] These three Pinney children married into families with strong slaving connections.[70] In complete contrast, James Webbe Tobin, the son of the pro-slavery campaigner James Tobin, married the niece of an anti-slavery campaigner and member of the Broadmead Baptist Church.[71]

64 LB 12 Pinney to John Herbert, 28 May 1795.
65 Somerset Archives (SA), D/P/Wraxall Burials 2/1/3.
66 LB 12 Pinney to Ann Weekes, 16 January 1797.
67 Dorset History Centre, D-PIT/F/99 Burial Certificate.
68 AB 42 John Frederick Pinney's a/c.
69 AB 42 Elizabeth Pinney's a/c; Memo.
70 John Frederick Pinney married Frances Dickinson, Betsey Peter Baillie and Mary Jeremiah Ames. For the Dickinson family's involvement in slavery, see SA, Dickinson Papers DD\DN. For the Baillies' and Ames's, see Anon, *Historical Research Report, Predecessor Institutions Research Regarding Slavery and the Slave Trade* (Royal Bank of Scotland Group/Citizens Financial Group, May 2006, updated May 2009), Appendix 4 and 5; Sheila Lambert, ed., *House of Commons Sessional Papers of the Eighteenth Century* (Delaware: Scholarly Resources, 1975), Vol. 72 pp. 637–40.
71 David Small, 'James Webbe Tobin', *ODNB*.

After moving with his wife to Nevis, it was James Webbe Tobin who brought to public attention an atrocity that had been committed against enslaved people on Mountravers. Despite earlier misgivings, in 1808 the Pinneys had sold Mountravers and most of its enslaved people to Edward Huggins, a Nevis planter with a reputation for cruelty. When the plantation workers defied the new owner's methods he retaliated by having thirty-two men and women publicly and very brutally flogged. Although Huggins was tried on a charge of cruelty, he was acquitted by a rigged jury. James Webbe Tobin was so outraged that he informed the Governor and, through abolitionists, publicized the case in Britain.[72] Fanny would have read about these shameful events in *The Times*,[73] but whether the repercussions of selling to Huggins strained her relationship with the Pinneys is not known. Her own family and a number of other, favoured people escaped Huggins's regime because Pinney had not sold them with the plantation but reserved them for his own use. While he rented the group to a seemingly well-disposed planter, he allowed Black Polly, Billey Jones and his wife and their younger children to live independently in Charlestown, the island's capital. Pinney sent goods for trading to Black Polly and also to Mulatto Polly 'per agreement': soap, candles, flour, firkins of butter and barrels of pork. In addition, the women bought items from the plantation, which they sold on their own accounts.[74] While the father of Mulatto Polly's children paid for her to be freed, Pinney left Black Polly in a legal limbo. He considered her free[75] and 'exempt from all labor on [his] account',[76] but he did not legally free her. This became an issue later when all enslaved people in the British colonies had to be officially registered.

Surprisingly, there is nothing in the records to suggest that Fanny ever urged Pinney to free her mother, or that she tried to buy her mother's freedom or that of other family members. She is known, however, to have pressed Pinney 'to send a fresh supply' of goods

---

72 The National Archives (TNA), CO 152/96 Huggins Case (Correspondence).
73 *The Edinburgh Review or Critical Journal*, May 1811 to August 1811 Vol. XVIII, pp. 323–5; The *London Statesman*, 21 September 1811, quoted in *The Times*, 17 June 1811; *Connecticut Journal*, 2 January 1812 (courtesy of Vincent Hubbard).
74 For instance, AB 39 Black Polly a/c; AB 50 Plantation a/c.
75 LB 45 Pinney to Samuel Laurence, 7 February 1810.
76 LB 22 Pinney to J.W. Stanley, 15 August 1807.

while allowing her mother extended credit for items he had sent her.[77] Pinney, in turn, at least twice used Fanny as an intermediary: once, after hearing about Billey misbehaving, he 'desired Fanny to write to her mother' about this;[78] another time to stop her mother and brother claiming that Billey was Pinney's son.[79]

Pinney's firm also supplied Billey Jones with goods from Bristol. When he failed to pay a substantial debt, Pinney threatened to sell him while confirming that Billey's two oldest children were to remain hired out to the plantation where the other reserved people worked. When Billey Jones applied to buy his children Pinney refused the request.[80] No doubt Fanny would have lobbied Pinney on her family's behalf. After all, living in the same house as the man who owned her mother and her siblings meant she could try and influence events in Nevis. This sense of responsibility may have underpinned her decision to remain with the Pinneys. While her long service could be interpreted as inertia, her early actions show her to have been feisty and energetic, determined to shape her own life. It may well be that she was sufficiently satisfied with the arrangements. Certainly, the Pinneys benefited from having a respectable, long-serving member of staff; Fanny provided stability and the experience to instruct new domestics.

As a live-in servant Fanny could spend her earnings as she pleased and, being thrifty, by 1802 she was able to invest £60 in stock.[81] John Pinney arranged this; he also invested money on behalf of two other servants. Half-yearly dividends of between £1 4s and £1 10s boosted Fanny's income,[82] and over time her stock holdings rose to £100. Her long-term financial position was secured after Pinney's death in January 1818, when he willed her an allowance of £30 a year on the condition that she remained in Mrs Pinney's service or left with her permission.[83] He was protecting his ageing widow from perhaps having to adjust to a new attendant; strong bonds connected

77 LB 14 Pinney to James Williams, 12 November 1798.
78 LB 12 Pinney to James Williams, 15 November 1796.
79 LB 17 Pinney to James Williams, 6 March 1802.
80 LB 24 Pinney to J.C. Mills, 8 March 1814, 4 April 1814.
81 LB 17 Pinney to Messrs. Williams & Sons, 11 December 1802.
82 PP, DM1173 Pinney Cash Ledger, 1803–1806.
83 ECSCRN, Book of Wills, 1805–18 ff.386–7.

mistress and maid after years of daily close physical and emotional contact.[84]

As if prompted by her employer's death, three months later Fanny Coker made her will, which two fellow servants witnessed. She appointed as executors Charles Pinney and her brother Billey, allocated money and her personal possessions and, tellingly, left £5 'for the missionary belonging to the Baptist'.[85] Since 1814 the Bristol Baptists had been sending missionaries to Jamaica and, as they had worshipped at the Broadmead Church, news would have reached her of their successful efforts to convert enslaved people to their faith.[86] Her bequest is evidence of her support.

When she made her will in April 1818 Fanny was 'in perfect health of body and of sound mind', but by February 1820 she was 'severely ill'. She suffered from a 'liver affection' and Mrs Pinney hired a nurse to care for her.[87] Fanny Coker died on 12 April 1820. She was fifty-two years old. According to the Baptist records she had 'lived honourably and died comfortably'.[88] On 17 April Frances Coker, a 'woman of colour', was buried in the Baptist Burial Ground in Redcross Street, with Revd Thomas Roberts conducting the funeral.[89] Later a tomb stone was placed on her grave.[90]

Charles Pinney carried out his duties as executor, having Fanny Coker's will proved and her possessions valued. At £3 3s the single most valuable item was her metal watch. He sold her investments to cover her legacies and accounted for the expenditure.[91] Her will had

---

84 Pinney's stipulation was not unusual; see Chater, *Untold Histories*, pp. 88, 227.

85 TNA, PROB 11/1645/245.

86 Gordon Catherall, A 'Bristol College and the Jamaican Mission', *Baptist Quarterly*, 35: 6, 1994, pp. 296–9. William Knibb, who, like his brother Thomas, also rose through the Bristol Baptists, was to play an important role in the struggle for abolition in Jamaica.

87 Domestic Box C1–6, R.E. Case to Charles Pinney, 19 April 1820; AB 65 Mrs Pinney's a/c.

88 BA, 30251/BD/M1/3.

89 BA, 30251/BD/RS/5(a)5. Revd Roberts joined the Committee of the Bristol Auxiliary Anti-Slavery Society, which was set up in 1823.

90 AB 70 Frances Coker a/c.

91 For a summary of Fanny Coker's legacies and Charles Pinney's actions as

stipulated that, if her 'dear mother Polly' died before her, the £30 Fanny bequeathed her was to go to her eldest brother, but, as it turned out, Billey Jones had died shortly before Fanny. To him she had left £20, her watch and all her silver spoons and other plate; to her other three siblings she had left £10 each and they were to share her clothes and bed linen. She remembered her friend Ann Seymour with a personal gift, her 'best tea chest', valued at 10s. Just as Mrs Pinney had sent Pero's belongings to his family in Nevis, she sent three trunks to Black Polly 'with her poor daughter Fanny's clothes'.[92]

Mrs Pinney did not replace her maid and, living with her daughters, kept only a male servant.[93] She died in 1822. While a plaque in Somerton church pays tribute to her,[94] there is no memorial to Fanny Coker; her tomb stone is lost. After the Baptist Burial Ground became disused her grave was moved with others to a single site in Greenbank Cemetery, Bristol. No individual names were recorded.[95] However, her memory lived on in Nevis; her brother Billey's daughter and grand-daughter were called Fanny. She was survived by her mother, her sisters Hetty and Little Molly, her brother Cubbenna and fourteen nephews and nieces.

The account of Fanny Coker's life arose out of a longitudinal study of the enslaved population on Pinney's Mountravers plantation. One of its aims was to recognize these people as individuals and to remember them, to give them their place in history. Fanny Coker was one of more than 900 enslaved people studied and, although in many ways she was an ordinary woman leading an ordinary life, her story nevertheless yields some surprising details. Through the many different visitors from Nevis, the travelling to and fro of her employers and their import and export business, she was able to maintain contact with her enslaved family and became part of a network of information and economic exchange across the Atlantic. In Bristol she, no doubt, belonged to the

executor, see Domestic Box 1814–45, particularly Stamp Office Forms 1–3. Similar in Domestic Box H Bundle 31.

92 Domestic Box C1, Jane Pinney to Charles Pinney, 2 February 1821.

93 LB 28 Charles Pinney to John Hyde, 8 January 1822.

94 St Michael and All Angels Church, Somerton.

95 Pers. comm., J. Norman, Bereavement Services Officer, Bristol City Council, 7 January 2000.

wider black servant community (as yet largely unresearched), and to a religious congregation linked to the abolition of the slave trade and to missionary activity in the West Indies. Free to leave her employment, she chose to remain, loyally working for her slave-owning employers for nearly forty years. Hers is not a straightforward narrative of oppression, exploitation and drudgery. Her horizons went well beyond the confines of the servants' attic; educated, skilled, well-travelled and financially comfortable, Fanny Coker had agency and managed to shape her own life.

CHAPTER NINE

The Georgian Life and Modern Afterlife of Dido Elizabeth Belle

Gretchen H. Gerzina

Over the past few decades there has been a fascination with the story of Dido Elizabeth Belle, the mixed-race great-niece of William Murray, the first earl of Mansfield, partly raised by him and his wife at Kenwood House in north London. The double portrait of Dido and her cousin Elizabeth Murray (Figure 9.1) graced the cover of my book *Black England* (published in the US as *Black London*),[1] but now can be seen on numerous websites, in other books and now even on drinks coasters sold in the Kenwood House gift shop, where the portrait hung for many years until it was moved to Scone Palace in Scotland, the home of later and current earls of Mansfield. A copy still hangs prominently in Kenwood House.

Over the years, historians, archaeologists, art historians, independent scholars and others have been tracking down and filling out the story of Dido Elizabeth Belle. While some facts remain sparse, their important work gives a much fuller picture of her life than was known earlier. For example, we now know that her mother was a property owner in Pensacola, Florida; where Dido and her husband lived in Pimlico, London; where their sons are buried in Hampstead, London; that the

---

1 Gretchen H. Gerzina, *Black England: Life Before Emancipation* (London: John Murray, 1995). Both the UK and US editions are out of print, but it is available as a free digital download at https://www.dartmouth.edu/~library/digital/publishing/books/gerzina1995/.

9.1 Dido Elizabeth Belle and her cousin Lady Elizabeth Murray
at Kenwood House. © Earls of Mansfield, Scone Palace.

portrait was not painted by Johann Zoffany, as previously asserted; and
that, despite repeated assertions that Dido was a former slave, she was
in fact born free.

This chapter brings together that research, but also looks at modern
media portrayals of her. In 2013 Amma Asante directed the 2014 film
Belle, which, despite taking great liberties with Dido's story, brought
her to international attention as, according to one newspaper article,
'Britain's First Black Aristocrat'.[2] Starring some of the best-known
British actors, as well as the then less well-known Gugu Mbatha-Raw
as Dido, it was available on Netflix, reaching an even wider audience
than it did in its original cinema release. And, in August 2018, the BBC

2 'Britain's First Black Aristocrat', *The Telegraph*, 6 July 2016.

programme *Fake or Fortune* dedicated part of an episode to tracking down the actual painter of the famous portrait. That episode, airing in Series 7, examined two unrelated double portraits featuring black girls or young women, the first the famous one of Dido and her white cousin Elizabeth, and a slightly later double portrait of two enslaved, or formerly enslaved, black girls. Continually linking the paintings not only by their depictions of racialized subjects but also by its repeated insistence that Dido had been born a slave, the programme, which can now be seen on YouTube, ends with a definitive statement of the artist of Dido and Elizabeth's painting. However, although the family accepted that attribution, it is still in part questioned by those who have been researching it for far longer. This chapter will look at that research, but also ask why, at this particular moment, the story of Dido Elizabeth Belle is experiencing a media resurgence.

Dido's origins

It has been known with certainty for centuries that Dido was the natural daughter of Sir John Lindsay, the nephew of William Murray, later Lord Mansfield, and an African woman named Maria Belle. Born in Scotland in 1737, Lindsay had early and sustained success in the British navy, where he received his first ship command on the *Pluto* before the age of twenty.[3] He went to have a career full of action and travel, including tours in the Caribbean and Florida, often on the ship *Trent*, in which he captured ships and their prizes for the British government and bounties for his crews. He was knighted in 1764 and went on to become an admiral.[4]

Dido was not his only mixed-race child. Before his marriage to Mary Milner on 17 September 1768 Lindsay fathered 'a brood of' children, of whom Dido was the eldest.[5] These other children were the short-lived John Edward, born to Mary Vellet, 'a mulatto', in 1762;

3 Paula Byrne, *Belle. The Slave Daughter and the Lord Chief Justice* (New York: Harper Perennial, 2014), p. 16.
4 Joanne Major, 'Dido Elizabeth Belle—We Reveal NEW Information about her Siblings' (blogpost), in *All Things Georgian*, 26 June 2018, https://georgi-anera.wordpress.com/author/joannemajor/.
5 Major, 'Dido Elizabeth Belle'.

Ann, born in Jamaica in 1766 to 'Sarah Gandwell, a free negro'; another daughter, Elizabeth, born just a month later in Port Royal to Martha G. Elizabeth, race unspecified; and, almost exactly a year later, another son named John, born to an eighteen-year-old

> Francis [*sic*] Edwards, a 'free mulatto woman', ... on 28th November 1767. Both this John and this Elizabeth are the two youngsters Lindsay referred to as his 'reputed children' in his 1783 will. It had previously been thought—erroneously—that Elizabeth and John had been born in Scotland.[6]

With the exception of Dido, who was born in London, all these children were born in Jamaica.[7] Although Sir John and Mary had no children, no other illegitimate children were born to him after his marriage, suggesting that he settled down into marriage.

Maria Belle, Bella or Bell has variously been described as an African woman, a slave, a former slave and a woman captured from a Spanish ship. How much of that is true? Paula Byrne, in her film-companion book *Belle. The Slave Daughter and the Lord Chief Justice*, writes that 'At some point in his West Naval adventures, Lindsay met a slave woman who was almost certainly named Maria. She would be Dido's mother.'[8] But Sarah Murden and Joanne Major, the meticulous researchers and authors of their important blog *All Things Georgian*, offer much more specific information. Their research shows that in 1761 the *Trent* captured as a prize the *Bien Aimé*, headed for France with a load of sugar, and sailed her into the Downs in May. According to stories told by Mansfield during Dido's lifetime, the now very pregnant Maria was on board the ship, even though Lindsay was not, and they had travelled together before this. Their daughter Dido was born in May, in London, but was not baptized until five years later, with her mother named as Maria Bell and her father unnamed.

Speculation has always suggested that Maria was taken as a prize from a Spanish ship and was an enslaved person when she was 'acquired' by Lindsay, who freed her at some point before 1772,

6 Major, 'Dido Elizabeth Belle'.
7 Major, 'Dido Elizabeth Belle'.
8 Byrne, p. 22.

according to Margo S. Stringfield, who specializes in the history and archaeology of Pensacola, Florida during the two Spanish and one English colonial occupations.[9] She works extensively with the Admirality and Secretariat Papers, Colonial Office Records [Class Five Files], and with other primary source materials associated with British West Florida to research all the ships that Lindsay encountered during this British period of occupation. She points out that some of these ships are noted to be Spanish but sailing under the French flag, so it is quite possible that Maria Belle was taken as contraband from a Spanish ship sailing under a French flag. Maria remained Lindsay's mistress for some time. However, if not at first in London, she well may have been in Port Royal, Jamaica, as were the mistresses of a number of other naval officers, before settling in London for a number of years to give birth and live with Dido, and eventually moving to Pensacola where Lindsay had deeded her a house. Maria Belle was living with Lindsay in Pensacola in 1764–5.[10]

Stringfield further believes that Maria Belle may have been able to communicate in several languages, given the multicultural dynamic of the Atlantic world at that time. While Florida was under British rule for eighteen years (1763–81), the years before and after this period were dominated by the Spanish. On the Gulf Coast of Florida there was also a strong French and Afro-Caribbean influence.

Stringfield has a particular interest in the whole dynamic of West Florida and the Caribbean Basin, where liaisons between British men and women of colour or slaves were common, if not always permanent.[11] Given this, the relationship between Maria Belle and the mothers of Lindsay's other children is not surprising. What is surprising, however, is that, unlike the mothers of his other children, Lindsay brought Maria to London, where their daughter was born and where Maria Belle had the opportunity to be with her daughter for much longer than previously thought. One researcher believes that Dido lived with her mother, possibly for a longer period than was

---

9 John J. Clune and Margo S. Stringfield, *Historic Pensacola* (Gainesville: University Press of Florida, 2009; revised paperback edition, 2017), p. 113.
10 Clune and Stringfield, p. 113.
11 Conversation with Margo Stringfield, 6 October 2018, and email 27 October 2018.

thought earlier, but Stringfield believes that, except for periods during Dido's infancy and early childhood, they did not live together, but did live in close proximity to each other and probably interacted with each other.[12] Records suggest that Maria Bella was in London from 1761 to 1774, except when she lived with Lindsay in Pensacola in 1764–5, and, according to Etienne Daley, who has been researching Dido and her family for years, 'certain paperwork says: Maria Bell, a negro woman formerly of Pensacola but now living in London'.[13]

In 1774 she was back in Pensacola. Stringfield's research on Maria Belle and a town lot she owned began in the 1990s, prior to archaeological investigations on a British colonial town lot. Sir John Lindsay received the lot in 1764 as the British began to design a town plan for the newly acquired colony. He was commander of naval forces in Pensacola from 1764 to 1765 and built a house on the lot. When he returned to England in 1765 he retained ownership of the property until 1773, a year after the famous James Somerset case, in which his uncle Lord Mansfield had ruled that this slave in London could not be returned to West Indian slavery. According to Stringfield, Maria Belle was living in London at the time.

Stringfield and other University of West Florida archaeologists have investigated a number of sites in the colonial community, including areas in the nearby British fort. Artefact recovery in the fort area reflects a masculine, military presence: bottle glass, striking glasses and pipe stems abound. Excavations of a rubbish-filled well and storage pit associated with Maria Belle's ownership of lot six in the Navy Yard produced artefacts that are decidedly different in nature, suggesting a rather genteel life with access to British luxury goods (see below). Stringfield believes that Maria Belle's taste for British wares was formed during the years that she lived in London.

In London

At some point Dido moved into the home of Lord Mansfield, possibly at the same time that her cousin Elizabeth Murray also moved there. Both girls were familiar sights to visitors and friends. Dido came in

---

12 Email with Margo Stringfield, 27 October 2018.
13 Daly email, 25 October 2018.

after dinner to sit comfortably with family and guests, giving rise to one of the only recorded encounters with her by a visitor. Thomas Hutchinson, formerly governor of Massachusetts but now exiled in England, knew Mansfield and visited him several times at Kenwood. He recorded in his diary that Mansfield had told him more than once that Dido was born in England: 'I knew her history before, but my Lord mentioned it again. Sir John Lindsay having taken her mother prisoner in a Spanish vessel, brought her to England, where she was delivered of this girl.'[14] He does not specify when Dido became part of the Mansfield household, but the story is remarkable for two reasons: first, that Mansfield made sure to tell it twice to Hutchinson; and, secondly, that he insisted on letting Hutchinson know that Dido was English born, and therefore free.

There is no reason to disbelieve this account given to Hutchinson by Lord Mansfield, written down after their conversation, even though later descendants of Mansfield believed that Dido had been born at sea. Family memories, especially when passed down over the centuries, are notoriously faulty. Interestingly, however, it was not until the twentieth century that the family knew that the young woman of colour in the lovely double portrait was Dido, and that she and Elizabeth were cousins; a 1904 inventory of property in Kenwood House listed the painting as being of Elizabeth and an unnamed Negro servant.[15] The belief that Dido was a former slave may in fact stem from the early twentieth century.

It is also possible that the assumption that Dido was born a slave partly originated from an American understanding of slavery. In North America and the Caribbean children 'followed the condition of the mother', meaning that if the mother were enslaved, her children were also. However, these rules would not have applied to children born in England (or perhaps even at sea). For Sarah Murden and Joanne Major, Hutchinson's contemporary account overrules the much later, and undocumented, family rumours. Writing on 13 September

14 Sarah Murden, 'Dido Elizabeth Belle Portrait—BBC Fake or Fortune' (blogpost), in *All Things Georgian*, 13 September 2018, https://georgianera. wordpress.com/category/dido-elizabeth-belle/.
15 *Fake or Fortune*, BBC One Series 7, 'A Double Whodunnit', 26 August 2018. https://www.dailymotion.com/video/x6vvmth

2018, shortly after the airing of the *Fake or Fortune* episode, Murden unequivocally states that

> Dido Elizabeth Belle was NOT born into slavery. Whilst her mother had been a slave who was brought to England by Sir John Lindsay, Dido was born in England and not as a slave, but the natural daughter of an aristocrat.[16]

Etienne Daly, who has been researching Dido and her children for years, and has discovered more about Dido and her children in England than perhaps anyone else, concurs, not only noting the accuracy of Murden's research but asserting: 'Not correct saying Dido was a slave—this [is] an Americanism.'[17] However, Paula Byrne repeats the notion that Dido had been born a slave when she writes that 'Dido Elizabeth Belle was an authentic London immigrant',[18] rather than a native-born Englishwoman, and throughout the *Fake or Fortune* episode the hosts unfortunately refer to her as a former slave, without attribution.

This misunderstanding about Dido's freedom may also stem from the fact that Mansfield's will, written in 1782, seemed to confer freedom on Dido. Byrne and others have interpreted it this way, but in fact the wording states that 'I *confirm* to Dido Elizabeth Belle her freedom' [italics mine], which is very different matter from newly bestowing freedom upon her. At a time when black and mixed-race people were in danger of being kidnapped and sold into, or back into, slavery, he wanted it to be clear that she was free, and that the inheritance she would receive was hers alone,[19] especially now that her mother had returned to Florida and Dido had been part of his household and family for some time.

It is not exactly clear when Maria Belle returned to Florida. In the 1990s Stringfield and her colleagues at the University of West Florida discovered the contract in which Sir John Lindsay conveyed a large amount of land to Maria Belle. Lindsay had been stationed in Pensacola for a year in 1764–5, and Maria Belle was with him there.

---

16 Murden, 'Dido Elizabeth Belle Portrait'.
17 Etienne Daly, email to Gretchen H. Gerzina, 16 September 2018.
18 Byrne, p. 103.
19 Byrne's interpretation is on p. 170.

He later initiated the contract in 1773, a year after the Somerset case. According to Stringfield, Maria Belle was living in London at the time, but was 'referred to as a Negro woman of Pensacola' in the contract.

> It recorded conveyance of a piece of property (near today's downtown) for a nominal amount of money, consideration of a peppercorn a year. Also, included in the text was a requirement that Belle build a house. That detail suggested that the original house had probably been destroyed in one of the storms that had hit Pensacola in the previous years.[20]

Stringfield and her team were able to study the excavations of both the nearby original British fort, where the findings were masculine and military, and Maria's house nearby, where they found 'things like elegant decanter stoppers and delicate wine glass fragments', as well as 'ceramics and white salt-glazed stoneware, many associated with tea, that are indicative of a higher-status life-style'.[21] Stringfield believes that Maria Belle's taste was formed during the years that she lived in London.

As impressive as these finds indicate that the house that Maria Belle had built was, it was nothing compared to Kenwood House, where Dido eventually lived. Known by many at the time as 'Caen Wood' or 'Caenwood',[22] the house was purchased in 1754. Born in Scotland, William Murray, the future Lord Mansfield, attended school and university in England, which remained his home. He was a gifted attorney and judge, rising steadily through the ranks to become Lord Chief Justice just two years after purchasing the stately home, which then stood on 112 acres on a hill facing Hampstead Heath. It was to become the weekend retreat for himself and his wife, Elizabeth, and he set about expanding the house, modernizing the landscaping and

20 Sandra Everhart, 'Real Story of "Belle" has Pensacola Connections', interview with Margo S. Stringfield, WUWF Public Radio 88.1, 23 May 2014, http://www.wuwf.org/post/real-story-belle-has-pensacola-connections (accessed 9 November 2019).
21 Everhart, 'Real Story of "Belle"'.
22 Ignatius Sancho refers to it by this name on 9 June 1780, in a letter to John Spink describing the Gordon Riots. Vincent Carretta, ed., *Ignatius Sancho. Letter of the Late Ignatius Sancho, An African* (New York: Penguin Classics, 1998), p. 220.

interior and purchasing more surrounding land. It later became their permanent home.

He and his wife were childless, so willingly took in a niece, Anne Murray, and then two great-nieces, the daughters of his nephews Sir John Lindsay (Dido) and David Murray (Elizabeth). David Murray's first wife, Henrietta Federica von Bünau, had died in 1762. Dido was born on 29 June 1761 and Lady Elizabeth on 17 May 1760. Dido was later baptized in 1766 in St George's Church, Bloomsbury, the area where Lord Mansfield and his wife kept the townhouse they lived in during the week. Once they moved into the Mansfield household, the girls spent weekdays in the Bloomsbury house and weekends in idyllic Kenwood—or Caen Wood—House, with its gorgeous grounds, complete with poultry house, dairy, hothouse and orangery, Venetian paintings, mirrors, china and silver. The girls were educated at home and had the benefit of Kenwood's extensive library. Around August 1780, after the Gordon Riots partially destroyed the contents of the Bloomsbury house, the family moved fully into Kenwood House.[23]

Much has been said about Dido's position in such a household, where she was a mixed-race natural daughter, unlike the well-born Elizabeth. Most commentators note the fact that she had beautiful handwriting, and yet speculate that perhaps she also worked in some way in the poultry house and the dairy. The conjecture by earlier writers, myself included, was that she occupied some sort of middle state between family member and upper servant. We may never know her daily routine, but we know that she was dressed beautifully, in the latest styles, slept in a bedroom hung with chintz and was left money in her great-uncle's will—an amount that he later increased in subsequent codicils. There can be no doubt of his and his wife's deep fondness for her, and his concern about her future, which he hoped an inheritance would secure.

Some of this conjecture about her role in the household arises from a comment from the same Thomas Hutchinson mentioned above, the American who wrote down Lord Mansfield's comments on Dido's birth in England. Frankly shocked by Mansfield's making her part of his family, he noted that, after a dinner at Kenwood, Dido unabashedly and comfortably joined the rest of the family afterwards, arm in arm

---

23 Daly, email 25 October 2018.

with her cousin, for coffee. Unaccustomed to such mixing of the races, he described her as being physically unappealing, with frizzled hair beneath a high cap (a fashion at the time), and 'neither handsome nor genteel', and hinted that perhaps there was a less salubrious reason for Lord Mansfield's fondness for her.[24] His negative attitude could well be the reason Mansfield twice, on different occasions, clarified her background. He no doubt sensed his American guest's aversion to Dido's race. In addition, the circumstance of her birth in England would make it clear to Hutchinson that she had been born free, especially if the former governor repeated the conversation to others.

The Painting

Although long attributed to Johann Zoffany, there are now a number of reasons to suspect that the double portrait was painted by someone else. The most important of these is that in 1779, the year of the painting, Zoffany was not in England long enough to have executed it.[25] Most recent attributions settle upon David Martin, a fellow Scot who had painted the magnificent portrait of Lord Mansfield in his robes and was a protégé of the famous painter Allan Ramsay. Although it is said that Lord Mansfield commissioned the painting, there are no records of it in his accounts, so the artist cannot be confirmed in that way. David Martin is certainly a strong possibility, based on similarities between this and others of his works, but he was also taught by Ramsay, so it is impossible to discount that influence. However, *Fake or Fortune* unambiguously attributes it to Martin. Indeed, in the finale of the programme, a new identifying plate is painted and attached to the portrait, to the great satisfaction of the family.

Murden and Major, along with Etienne Daly, are convinced that Allan Ramsay makes the more likely candidate, partly because of style,

---

24 Peter Orlando Hutchinson, ed., *The Diary and Letters of His Excellency Thomas Hutchinson, Esq.* (London: Sampson Low, Marston, Searle and Rivington, 1886), Vol. 2, pp. 276–7. Quoted in Gerzina, *Black England*, pp. 88–9.
25 Sarah Murden, 'Dido Elizabeth Belle—A New Perspective on Her Portrait' (blogpost), in *All Things Georgian*, 15 May 2018, https://georgianera.wordpress.com/2018/05/15/art-detectives-a-new-perspective-on-the-portrait-of-dido-elizabeth-belle/.

but also because of his closeness to the family. Ramsay was the 'principal painter to the King (George III), and furthermore, was married to Sir John Lindsay's sister, and knew both young women well. He had also painted Dido's father at least once'.[26] Finally, Murden, Major and Daly point out that the relaxed way that the two young women pose for the picture indicates their ease with the artist himself, supporting the suggestion that Allan Ramsay could have been the painter. Could both men have had a hand in the painting? This is a particularly pertinent suggestion, as new evidence has come to light that the painting we now know was added to later by a different artist.[27]

It is interesting that different writers on Dido interpret the painting differently. Byrne sees Dido as rushing along from the hothouse, bearing fresh fruit for the dining table, with Lady Elizabeth touching her arm in order to make her pause. Byrne sees 'the basket of exotic fruit' as pointing 'to the black girl's foreign background … with the ripe fruits suggesting her lusciousness'.[28] James Mulraine, on the other hand, views the scene completely differently:

> It is a remarkable painting. The staging implies that the two girls have been surprised by the arrival of a visitor, the viewer. Lady Elizabeth Murray composes herself according to etiquette, reading, or pretending to read, but from her smile and Dido's barely-suppressed grin it's clear they've been laughing just that moment before. More importantly, Dido has leapt to her feet, but Lady Elizabeth's touch on her arm restrains her, as if she is saying she can sit down again. Dido is dressed in a turban like a black attendant in a painting, but they seem more like sisters.[29]

The painting is indeed remarkable, but how can it be known that Dido was rushing from the hothouse to deliver fruit to the Mansfield dinner table, or has leapt up in surprise from the bench? The Orangery,

26 Murden, https://georgianera.wordpress.com/2018/09/13/dido-elizabeth-belle-her-portrait/.
27 Murden, 'Dido Elizabeth Belle Portrait'.
28 Byrne, p. 6.
29 James Mulraine, 2 May 2014, https://jamesmulraine.com/2014/05/02/709/ (accessed 9 November 2019).

or hothouse, was on the left, and not on the right, the direction from which Mulraine says that she seems to have been moving. Furthermore, as Murden has shown, turbans were high fashion at the time, worn by aristocrats, and Dido's is made of expensive silk, adorned with diamonds and topped with the ostrich feather that had been made so fashionable by Georgiana, duchess of Devonshire, that ostriches were in danger of being driven to extinction.[30] As Murden comments,

> The turban that Dido was wearing was not merely a fashion statement but was a gift to her from her father, Sir John Lindsay, so it was not part of a portrait 'costume' as had been assumed ... Sir John was invested as a Knight of the Bath in an extravagant ceremony in India on 11th March 1771.

Murden and Major find that Dido wearing the turban in her portrait 'seems a lovely gesture' and a 'nod' to her father, in the only known portrait of her. Despite his probable misinterpretation of Dido's clothing, Mulraine agrees that the two women seem to act like sisters. There is no doubt that the two cousins exhibit a closeness and ease that they are willing to display to the painter observing them. Although David Martin was the younger painter, Ramsay was the more familiar to Dido and Elizabeth, lending credence to the possibility that Ramsay began the portrait, but that Martin may later have supplied the finishing touches.

What Happened after Mansfield Died?

Mansfield's will, mentioned above, was written shortly before his death, and was added to several times to increase the amount of Dido's inheritance. She was now nearing thirty, and unmarried. Her cousin Elizabeth, now Elizabeth Finch, was married with two children. Dido's father had perhaps left her and her brother £1000 to share (assuming that she was the Elizabeth and he was the John that he calls his purported children in his will, but this is unlikely). More likely

---

30 Murden, 'The 18th Century Fashion for Turbans' (blogpost), in *All Things Georgian*, 30 January 2018, https://georgianera.wordpress.com/2018/01/30/the-18th-century-fashion-for-turbans/.

is that he knew that Mansfield would provide for her, so he did not leave a separate amount in addition to that. Mansfield's original will gave her an annuity of £100 so that she would have an annual income. He thought further about the sufficiency of this amount, and in the first codicil added a lump sum of £200 'to set out in life'. The second codicil is evidence that he worried about her financial future, for he added a further lump sum of £300.[31] This was enough to set her up in a comfortable independent life, but also to make her a more desirable marriage prospect. These sums represented a substantial amount, but not the great wealth that the film portrays her as having, however. As Byrne puts it, 'Financially, she was better off than many genteel women of her era',[32] if not a great heiress.

But Dido did marry, and have children. Although the film presents her husband as an abolitionist clergyman from England, he was in fact a Frenchman, probably a steward to someone living in London. His name was John Daviniere, or Davinie, or Jean Louis Davinieré. Murden opts for the latter spelling, and the *All Things Georgian* blog gives more details about him than had been discovered earlier. Daviniere was born

> in the town of Ducey in the Normandy region of France and was one of several children born to Charles Davinieré and his wife Madeleine Le Sellier. He was baptised on 16th November 1768, and so was several years Dido's junior.

Dido and Daviniere married on 5 December 1793 'at St George's, Hanover Square, [and] the couple moved into a newly built house, 14, Ranelagh Street North, near St George's Hanover Square'[33] in March 1794.[34] The house seems to have been purchased with Dido's money. They were apparently happily married, and had three sons.

Murden writes that, although no one knows how the two met, 'it seems likely that the Murray or Ramsay family would have been

---

31 Byrne, p. 227.
32 Byrne, p. 228.
33 Murden, 'Dido Elizabeth Belle and John Daviniéré, What Became of Them?' (blogpost), in *All Things Georgian*, https://georgianera.wordpress.com/2018/07/10/dido-elizabeth-belle-and-john-daviniere-what-became-of-them/.
34 Daly email, 6 October 2018.

involved in some way'. One of the witnesses to the marriage was a son of the 6th earl of Coventry, whose portrait Allan Ramsay had painted, and for whom Daviniere may have worked as a steward. The other witness was 'Dido's close friend, Martha Darnell'.[35]

Two of their sons were twins, one of whom died, but the other two, Charles (1795–1873) and William Thomas (1800–1867) survived into adulthood.[36] Dido herself, alas, died on 25 July 1804, and, according to Etienne Daly, was buried in

> St George's Burial Ground, St. George's Field, then on the Uxbridge Road circa 28th/29th July 1804. [Her grave] may still be there even after excavations for apartment flats. Certain areas of the plot were not fully excavated [and] she was buried in the 1st class plot, part of which was never touched in development.[37]

Etienne Daly has made it a mission to discover more about the family, and has done a great job of discovering more about her life in England. He has located the spot on the Kenwood property where the famous painting was probably set, and has also located the graves of her sons Charles and William, and of her grandson, Charles Georges Daviniere, in Kensal Green Cemetery, and is having them restored.[38] Murden and Major discovered that Dido's half-brother John Lindsay, Jr (1767–1820) 'rose to become a Colonel in the Madras Army and amassed a fortune there … he was a quadroon.'[39] His search continues for Dido's grave, as does his search for whatever else he can find out about her life and descendants.

Daviniere, with two sons to raise, later remarried, to Jane Holland (apparently, some years afterwards, they produced two children of their own). They eventually moved back to Ducey, in France, where Daviniere was born.[40] Thus ends the life of Dido Elizabeth Belle. But the afterlife goes on, all sparked by one remarkable painting.

---

35 Murden, 'Dido Elizabeth Belle and John Davinieré'.
36 Murden, 'Dido Elizabeth Belle and John Davinieré'.
37 Daly email, 25 October 2018.
38 'New lease of life given to family graves of "18th century Meghan Markle"', *Brent & Kilburn Times*, 8 December 2017.
39 Daly email, 6 October 2018.
40 Murden, 'Dido Elizabeth Belle and John Davinieré'.

Gretchen H. Gerzina

The Modern Afterlife of Dido Elizabeth Belle

I first saw the portrait at Kenwood House when I was completing my book *Black England*, before it was removed to Scotland. I had selected another image for the cover, but my editor rightly chose this one once I showed it to him. It has remained the cover through its many editions: hardcover, softcover and digital (with the permission of Scone Palace). It is a striking image, and my book is known on both sides of the Atlantic, so I was surprised when another book—a new edition of an eighteenth-century novel—later used it on its cover as well.

The painting of the two lovely young women, even as a copy and a facsimile, strikes viewers similarly. Amma Asante, the director of the film *Belle*, says that 'Everything you see in the film, the vision I have created, comes from the painting.'[41] And yet, as fascinating as the true story is, Asante, like all filmmakers, felt the need to take liberties with the truth. In *Belle*, Dido is left at Kenwood House straight off the boat by her father John Lindsay when she is five, rather than being born in London and having close relations with her mother. In the film, without a mother, Dido must leave it to a black maid to show her how to brush her hair. She inherits a vast sum before the death of a great-uncle, making her even wealthier than her cousin Elizabeth, and despite her race a greater marriage prospect. The racism she encounters from the brother of one suitor could have occurred, but we don't know if she had other offers in real life.

In its dealings with abolitionism, slavery and activists become the centrepiece of an otherwise romantic cinematic tale. Mansfield, who was at the time adjudicating the Somerset case, was presented instead as dealing with the horrific, case of the *Zong*, in which enslaved Africans were thrown overboard by a ship's captain so that insurance could later be claimed for the loss. Mansfield did judge that case as well, but at a much later date. The film offers up Daviniere as an English abolitionist and clergyman (to be fair, for years it was thought that he was a clergyman, rather than a French steward) who educates the relatively innocent Dido to an understanding of the horrors of slavery.

41 Bridget Galton, 'How a Kenwood House Painting Inspired Amma Asante's "Belle"', in *Ham & High*, 12 June 2014.

We do not, in fact, know her thoughts about race, nor what influence her presence in Mansfield's household may have had on his judicial rulings. Everyone in the film, except for the suitor's brother, is, in fact, exceptional: beautiful, high-minded, morally impeccable. Much of this, too, could have been true. But the fact that Dido was unable to find a husband until she was thirty belies both her portrayed wealth and ability to compete in the Georgian marriage market, even with her lofty connections and independent income. Mansfield's repeated codicils seem to acknowledge this difficulty, by making sure she would have enough to survive on. There is no doubt that it makes for a wonderful period costume drama, with its stellar cast and striking sets. In its star, Gugu Mbatha-Raw, *Belle* features a lead character difficult to look away from, and a love story that combines history, drama and attractiveness.

The *Fake or Fortune* episode takes a somewhat different tack. Advertising itself as an artistic 'whodunnit', it hammers away at the unlikeliness of a woman who was born a slave and ended up in a fabulous house and famous family. Their unquestioning insistence on repeatedly referring to Dido as a former slave is meant to heighten their own drama of discovering who the 'real' painter was, and to tie up the ending with a bow, done and dusted, with the Mansfield family delighted to at last know the purported truth. This is all reinforced by the fact that they paired the search to find the painter of Dido's portrait with the search to find the painter of the two black girls, possibly enslaved. A combination of blackness, slavery and gender were used to link the two pictures, each painted in a different century, probably in two different countries, by two different artists, for two different purposes. Nevertheless, the combination of the three proved to be, for television producer and film director, as irresistible as the painting of the lovely Dido herself.

We have not seen the last of Dido, or of women like her. A new video, on women's clothing in eighteenth-century England shows a maid dressing Dido for her portrait with her cousin Elizabeth to demonstrate the many layers that it took to clothe her, from undergarments to the sash and turban that complete her outfit.[42]

42 Getting Dressed in the 18th Century–Dido Elizabeth Belle (1779), https://youtu.be/zLQXaw9GtqY.

In the midst of these ways that history is repeating itself—from the early 'Black Poor' left to beg on London streets, to the Windrush arrivals being made to prove their right to live in Britain—we see the modern story of another beautiful mixed race girl plucked out of history to spark the popular imagination and debate. Yet long before Meghan Markle, the story of Dido Elizabeth Belle challenges us to rethink what we thought we knew about Britain's black past, about women like her, and about their lives in unexpected places.

CHAPTER TEN

Ghostly Presences, Servants and Runaways: Lancaster's Emerging Black Histories and their Memorialization 1687–1865

Alan Rice

How to tell the story of the historic black presence in Britain when there is so little material evidence has been especially problematic in areas beyond the major concentrations of African-descended people brought about by the transatlantic slave trade in London, Liverpool and, to a lesser extent, Bristol. The fourth largest slave port, which was responsible for around 200 voyages and nearly 30,000 Africans transported, was Lancaster and yet, with a tiny contemporary African Caribbean population, it is all too easy for this slavery-infested history to be elided and marginalized. However, Lancaster is in many ways uniquely connected to all the major narratives of the story of slavery from the seventeenth to the nineteenth century; from the West Indian trade through the transatlantic slave trade to the industrial revolution and its growth of cotton factories dependent on colonial slave labour to the fall of King Cotton and its Empire in the calamitous and deadly 'Cotton Famine' of 1861–4.

It is the most recent of these narratives that is the least noticed by both historians and residents, but there is an extant memorial of Lancaster's connection to the American Civil War and its effects on the town. In Williamson Park, Lancaster, is a stone bench, one of three in that area of the city.[1] It is inscribed with 'Rev. T.R. London, 1863'. This act of philanthropy from a metropolitan clergyman to his Northern countrymen, an offer of sleeping amelioration to the vagrant poor, is one of the few signs left of this deadly event, which impacted on the entire Lancashire region. Lancaster was one of twenty-nine towns in the county that handed out extra Poor Relief during 1861–4 after the embargo of cotton by the North in an attempt to destroy the economy of the Confederate South during the American Civil War.

The devastating economic effects on Lancashire cotton mills meant that thousands from all over the world (including the pope and President Lincoln) donated to ameliorate the conditions of workers. Hundreds of thousands of male, female and child labourers were laid off during the horror years of 1862–3 and some were forced into vagrancy, while untold hundreds died as a consequence of poverty-induced famine. Williamson Park's beautiful gardens, walkways and water features were hewn out of the quarry on the edge of town as a result of public works projects designed to keep otherwise idle hands employed. While it was the labour of the ex-cotton workers that created the splendour of the park, the bench is really the only extant memorial of their labour in a park that glories in memorializing the industrialist James Williamson, who was later to build a Taj Mahal-like memorial to his deceased wife at the centre of the park, now known as the Ashton Memorial.

The bench is an amazingly resonant, if simply constructed, intersectional symbol: it highlights class exigencies, through its remembering of the workers; matters related to gender, in that, as Sven Beckert asserts in his seminal study *Empire of Cotton*, 'We tend to recall industrial capitalism as male-dominated, whereas women's labour largely created the empire of cotton';[2] and race, because the Confederate States built an economy where cotton was king on the backs of a slave system that by 1860 had used nearly four million enslaved Africans. There is no plaque on the bench to make these links and an explanatory panel in the permanent exhibition in the Ashton Memorial has a cursory

---

1 When talking about contemporary Lancaster, I refer to it as a city and historically as a town. It was granted city status in 1937, the only town to be conferred in the wake of the coronation of King George VI.
2 Sven Beckert, *Empire of Cotton: A Global History* (New York: Vintage, 2014), p. xviii.

explication which fails to situate the philanthropy in its full context. The tragedy on which the exhibit concentrates is the personal tragedy of James Williamson, Lord Ashton, who was said never to have recovered from the death of his wife, whose monument can still be seen for miles around as it bestrides this highest point in the city.[3]

The warning from history, then, is that we should not be blinded by the light of extravagant memorialization by those in power, for it will often elide darker and so-called minority histories. Majoritarian narratives might be very interested in the death and memorialization in Williamson Park, but a politically astute critique would look beneath the memorial's staged magnificence to find histories that it occludes. Many of these histories are not written down or are lost in obscure documents and must be discovered in the interstices of the archives and beyond. Many of them are being discovered as we speak. Hence, the autobiography of the ex-slave James Johnson makes links between these intersectional histories and exemplifies the vagrants' life that benches such as the Reverend's helped succour. He does not relate getting as far north as Lancaster in his sojourn through the highways and byways of Lancashire and far beyond, but his is an exemplary journey occasioned by the Cotton Famine and I want to share it here as his footsore travels highlight different types of black presence in the region that are only now being unearthed.

His pamphlet, *The Life of the Late James Johnson, Coloured Evangelist: An Escaped Slave from the Southern States of America, 40 Years Resident in Oldham* (1914) was rediscovered in the Oldham archives during the 2007 Manchester Museums' *Revealing Histories*[4] project, which made dynamic connections between slavery and the industrial revolution in the birthplace of that revolution. It details the wandering of Johnson on his arrival in Britain in December 1862 at the height of extreme unemployment and its attendant misery:

> I was worse now than ever—cotton stockings and a pair of slippers
> in bleak December, friendless and homeless, roaming the streets

3 Exhibition panel at Williamson Park Memorial Exhibition (accessed 1 July 2018).

4 *Revealing Histories, Remembering Slavery*, http://revealinghistories.org.uk/home.html (accessed 31 July 2018).

of Liverpool. I walked over to Southport, and finding nothing to do, walked by Ormskirk to St. Helens, on to Warrington, thence to Manchester; again on to Wigan, Huddersfield, Leeds, York, Beverley and Hull, where I took to singing, dancing and rattle-bones, which I found was easier than begging.[5]

James Johnson's torturous wanderings through northern England in December 1862 are unremarkable for a working-class man seeking employment at the height of the Lancashire Cotton Famine, but the linking of this vast region as devastated by economic disaster is key to understanding class as well as global racial realities in this period. For his sojourn was different and, despite the hardship, strangely liberating, for he had played his part in the Civil War that had caused the embargo of cotton which had created these awful conditions. An African American slave escaping to Union lines earlier in 1862, he had withdrawn his enforced labour from the Confederate cause and had then travelled to Britain to ensure his freedom away from a country stained by the 'Peculiar Institution'. Finally settling in Oldham, his brief autobiography was published posthumously in 1914 by his Lancashire-born daughter and lay almost completely unread until its rediscovery during the bicentenary commemorations of the abolition of the slave trade in 2007. Such working-class black voices are rare in Victorian Britain, especially beyond London, but their uncovering is vital to telling the fully nuanced story of working-class and black people in Britain. For Johnson, vagrancy and extreme hunger in Britain did at least have the sweet smell of freedom.

Autobiographical accounts such as Johnson's interrupt lazy narratives of imperial and mercantile glory that are over-reliant on 'great men' theories of history. Through a politicized critique their narratives can play a role in creating more dynamic, radical models of historiography that are urgently needed in even the most conventional of tourist sites. For it is the willingness to work through multiple chronologies and to foreground multiple memorial standpoints that should guide us. Michael Rothberg notes the importance of attending

---

5 James Johnson, *The Life of the Late James Johnson, Coloured Evangelist: An Escaped Slave from the Southern States of America, 40 Years Resident in Oldham, England* (Oldham: W. Galley, 1914), p. 13.

to memory's multiplicities, describing how moving away from essentialism, particularism and competitive victimhood between classes, races and ethnicities can lead to richer and more politically astute interpretations of our complex historical narratives and, I believe, can help work toward a praxis that builds more sustainable local and national narratives. Rothberg describes how:

> It is precisely that convoluted, sometimes historically unjustified, back and forth movement of seemingly distant collective memories in and out of public consciousness that I qualify as memory's multidirectionality. [...] Thinking of memory as multidirectional instead of competitive does not entail dispensing with a notion of the urgency of memory, with its life-and-death stakes. Rather these examples alert us to the need for a form of comparative thinking that, like memory itself, is not afraid to traverse sacrosanct borders of ethnicity or era.[6]

In other words, we should work for a memorial praxis that will never be satisfied with unitary narratives (of any ideological persuasion) and will be attuned to voices that will make for a more inclusive and multiply defined historiography. The warning from history is to be wary always of its hegemonic tendencies and to promote heterogeneous perspectives, especially from those who are currently, and have so often before been, excluded.

The history of the black presence in Lancaster and beyond in the rural north-west shows us the importance of listening to these heterogeneous voices even if they are difficult to find. For the most part it is the Lancaster merchants who have dominated this story, but increasingly, if we look hard enough, we find other records of black residency and occasionally voices or even spectral presences that give clues to a range of black experiences. The story of Lancaster's involvement with slavery begins in the late seventeenth century. In 1687 the first recorded voyage was made from Lancaster to Jamaica, by the fifty-tonne ship *The Lambe*. As Melinda Elder reports, it 'traded for sugar,

---

6 Michael Rothberg, *Multidirectional Memory: Remembering the Holocaust in the Age of Decolonization* (Stanford: Stanford University Press, 2009), p. 17.

cotton and logwood'.[7] This trade gained more impetus when in 1720 the prominent Quaker merchant Robert Lawson built warehouses and quays at Sunderland Point, a few miles downriver, in order to forestall difficulties navigating the Lune River. By 1728 he was bankrupt, but Sunderland Point's importance as a key location for narrating the story of Lancaster's involvement in slavery and its black presence was only just beginning. The first recorded slave voyage to Africa out of Lancaster was that of the *Prince Frederick* in 1736, and Sunderland Point was the site of the first acknowledgement of a black presence connected to the West Indies and to the trade in human beings. According to the *Lonsdale Magazine* of 1822, the African-descended boy Sambo arrived around 1736 from the West Indies in the capacity of a servant to the captain of a ship (to this day unnamed):

> After she had discharged her cargo, he was placed at the inn … with the intention of remaining there on board wages till the vessel was ready to sail; but supposing himself to be deserted by the master, without being able, probably from his ignorance of the language, to ascertain the cause, he fell into a complete state of stupefaction, even to such a degree that he secreted himself in the loft on the brewhouses and stretching himself out at full length on the bare boards refused all sustenance. He continued in this state only a few days, when death terminated the sufferings of poor Samboo. As soon as Samboo's exit was known to the sailors who happened to be there, they excavated him in a grave in a lonely dell in a rabbit warren behind the village, within twenty yards of the sea shore, whither they conveyed his remains without either coffin or bier, being covered only with the clothes in which he died.[8]

Sambo was buried in such a lonely grave because he was not baptized and had to be laid in unconsecrated ground. Like most Africans arriving in Britain as 'servants' (usually slaves), he appeared

7 Melinda Elder, *The Slave Trade and the Economic Development of 18th Century Lancaster* (Keele: Ryburn Press, 1992), p. 22.

8 J.T., 'Samboo's Grave', *Lonsdale Magazine and Kendal Repository*, III: xxix, 31 May 1822, pp. 188–92 at p. 190.

to suffer a profound sense of culture shock, being landed among strangers with whom he could not communicate. There has been much speculation about the cause of his death, ranging from the pragmatic (pneumonia) to the sentimental (profound homesickness). The latter provided the grist for anti-slavery panegyrics such as the Reverend James Watson's 'Sambo's Elergy' (1796), the last three verses of which were eventually appended to a brass plate on a freestone slab at the burial site itself.[9] The tone of the memorial is sentimental in the extreme, praising Sambo as a 'faithful Negro' who had died because of his 'service' to his master. James Watson's interest in the slave grave is not without irony, however, as his brother William Watson was a leading light in the Lancaster slave trade, being 'one of the most committed investors in Lancaster slavers [whose] tenacity was no doubt instrumental in keeping the slave trade alive at Lancaster'.[10]

Watson collected the money for the memorial from visitors to Sunderland Point. These visitors would follow the trail along the terrace of houses to the footpath that starts at the inn and leads across the headland to the rabbit warren where Sambo is buried. In retracing Sambo's journey they and subsequent visitors would be able to see the upstairs room where he had died and his body had been laid out, then follow the passage of Sambo's coffin down the path. Today the trail is unaltered and the inn, now renamed *Upsteps Cottage*, still stands. The repeated pilgrimage over 200 years is in itself a memorial event that works to remember not only this boy's life and death but also the larger issue of slavery.

In 'transforming the physical absence of the lost object into an inner presence',[11] visitors to the site take on the task of inserting the boy into a historical record that would traditionally have reduced him to mere chattel. Sambo's grave and memorialization shows how the actions of ordinary citizens can be just as important as those of official historians

---

9 The final three verses of the poem are reproduced in the author's *Creating Memorials, Building Identities: The Politics of Memory in the Black Atlantic* (Liverpool: Liverpool University Press, 2010), p. 35.
10 Elder, p. 144.
11 Paul Ricoeur, *Memory, History, Forgetting*, trans. Kathleen Bramley and David Pellauer (Chicago: University of Chicago Press, 2004), p. 366.

in effective historical retrieval. A traditional way to mark a pilgrimage to a gravesite is to bring a stone, and Sambo's grave has always been replete with such markers. From at least the 1970s schoolchildren have been encouraged to bring stones painted with scenes and panegyrics to Sambo's memory to enable them to empathize with a boy of around their own age whose life was cruelly foreshortened by the operation of a transatlantic slave trade originated in Lancaster. These stones, with their scenes of seafaring and lost African landscapes, add to the colourful and poignant scene, which creates, in Pierre Nora's words, a *'lieu de mémoire'*, a site of memory, that is deeply affecting.[12] The loneliness of the grave adds to this sense of desolation that visitors seek to make more palatable by inhabiting the grave with objects. In keeping with the gravesite of a child, visitors have also brought small toys, and recently young girls have been tying hair bobbles to the cross at the site, showing their intimate attachment to the story and its importance to them. These mementoes bring the grave alive in ways that help to transform Sambo's status from solitary human chattel to socialized human being, if only in death.

The grave site is such an important marker because it brings a palpable human presence to the narrative of Lancaster's involvement in the trade, but Sambo spent only a few days in Lancaster and we must look elsewhere for records of black men and women who made their lives in the town. The day-book of Henry Tindall, found in a skip in East Lancashire in 2004, is fascinating. A Lancaster merchant, Tindall relates how in 1759 he was charged with looking after two white boys from Barbados accompanied 'by their black man, Oxford'.[13] The boys were William and Edmund Eversley (1752–1823), the sons of a planter, who attended schools at Kellet and Scorton near Lancaster. Edmund was either six or seven when he attended school in Lancashire, but his family's involvement in owning slaves and the plantation economy in Barbados was to continue until the end of slavery, as his son William received £71 17s from the British government in compensation for six

12 Pierre Nora, 'Between Memory and History: *Les Lieux de Mémoire*', in Geneviève Fabre and Robert O'Meally (eds), *History and Memory in African American Culture* (Oxford: Oxford University Press, 1994), pp. 284–300, at p. 289.
13 Henry Tindall Daybook m/s, n.p. (Lancaster Maritime Museum).

enslaved Africans he still owned in the 1830s.[14] Oxford was probably a trusted house slave with family at the plantation, thus ensuring his loyalty and attention to his charges and preventing him from contemplating escape. Tindall acknowledges payments of £2 5s for board and lodgings for Oxford between October and December 1859 and 5s on his return to Barbados on 17 December. This is the last we hear of Oxford, who returns to the plantation after this brief taste of life away from the slavery-infested colonies.

Other black individuals in Lancaster appear as more unambiguously free. Intriguingly, Thomas Brunson, a sailor from Sunderland Point, in 1781 signed his own marriage bond to a Mary Tomlinson, showing that some free blacks had access to rudimentary education. His black writing hand is a rare one, however, and there are very few black individuals recorded in Lancaster in this period. The baptismal records of Lancaster's St Mary's Church reveal several people, for most of whom there is no other record of their existence apart from the ironic fact of their baptism into Christianity. The most copious records are for the period 1777–85, and include

> 12 Sep 1777 John Chance, a black, aged 22 years & upwards in the service of Mr Lindow
> 2 Apr 1778 Frances Elizabeth Johnson, a black woman servt to Mr John Satterthwaite, an adult aged 27 years,
> Lancaster 15 Feb 1779 Thomas Burrow, a black, an adult,
> Lancaster 22 Jan 1783 George John, a negro & adult,
> Lancaster 3 Feb 1783 Isaac Rawlinson, a negro & adult,
> Lancaster 6 Oct 1783 William Dilworth, an adult negro,
> Lancaster 13 Oct 1785 Thomas Etherington, an adult negroe, agd 22 y, Lancaster[15]

The Lindow, Satterthwaite and Rawlinson merchant families are all documented here as having black slave-servants, in keeping with their involvement in the slave trade and West Indian trades in the port

---

14 Legacies of British Slave Ownership database, 'Barbados 618', https://www.ucl.ac.uk/lbs/search/ (accessed 30 July 2018).
15 Anon. *Handlist 69: Sources for Black and Asian History* (Preston: Lancashire Records Office, 2007), p. 7.

town. From these scant details in merchants' daybooks and church records we can document a black presence, but there are few other records of these individuals. Remarkably, however, new information about one of these individuals has emerged recently. It came in the form of an autobiographical narrative from a descendant of Lancaster slave traders. She described a relic from the late eighteenth century, something personal and in its way gruesome. It was a mummified black hand, perfectly preserved and meant for display. It had been a central feature of the domestic scene in a white British family home as late as the 1940s and thereafter was passed down as a legacy. As Eliza Dear explains in her autobiographical pamphlet:

> in prize position over the fireplace, was a black hand. It was dried, the bones were cut neatly and I was told it had belonged to someone's favourite slave. My mother was very proud of this hand. I used to play with it and, as I was often lonely, I used to wish the owner of the hand was there with me.[16]

This narrative is particularly intriguing in a British context precisely because of the openness of the display. By the mid-twentieth century any traces linking slaving families or institutions to their dark pasts were usually obliterated as shameful indices of pasts that were hopefully long forgotten. In this family it seems to exist almost as a trophy placed amid hunting ephemera and, like these indices of wealth and power, exhibiting the heft of the old merchant family. The incidental details from Dear's recollection are chilling. The hand had 'belonged to someone's favourite slave', the implication being that it was perfectly within the rights of the owner to continue their custodianship of the body after its death. Her mother's pride in this frankly grotesque family heirloom is chilling, but not as disturbing as her young only daughter being allowed to use it as a plaything. Dear's mother was 'very proud' of the hand, and her pride, and that of her ancestors that made them believe they had the right to cut off the hand and retain it as a memento, can be understood best in light of Dionne Brand's astute observation of the way slave-owners inhabited the bodies of their slaves:

16 Eliza Dear, *In Celebration of the Human Spirit: A Look at the Slave Trade* (Settle: Lambert's Print and Design, 2000), p. 3.

[They are] the captors who enter the captive's body. Already inhabiting them as extensions of themselves with a curious dissociation which gave them the ability to harm them as well. Slaves became extensions of the slave owners—their arms, legs, the parts of them they wished to harness and use with none of the usual care of their own bodies ... projections of the sensibilities, consciousness, needs, desires and fears of the captors.[17]

For Eliza Dear's mother, then, the hand is not treasured because it remembers a family slave/servant she never knew, but because it represents nostalgia for a lifestyle and power the family once had and exercised through their ownership of human beings. The hand had almost certainly belonged to one of the black individuals recorded in the Lancaster Priory register: Frances Elizabeth Johnson (Fanny), born in St Kitts in the West Indies in 1751 and brought to Lancaster by her owner John Satterthwaite in 1778. He had married Mary (Polly) Rawlins from the Rawlins plantation on St Kitts in 1777 and this marriage had combined two significant Lancaster-connected families who made their money in the slave and West Indian trades and abroad. They had considerable investments in plantations, which had developed from their trading in the Caribbean. Fanny Johnson was a privileged house slave, probably Mary Rawlins's personal maid and hence crucial to her comfort on the journey and once abroad in a new home in England. The Satterthwaite family were originally Quakers, but this had not inhibited their slavery activities and, by the time John entered his father Benjamin's ignoble trade, they had turned Anglican, perhaps in a direct reaction to the Quakers' opposition to the trade. John's letter book discusses the business with the commercial objectivity and indifference to human suffering that scholars of slavery have become used to. In September 1781 he writes to Michael Hethering:

I am concerned in a small guineaman the Sally, Captain Harrison, who [sic] may be expected at St. Kitts pretty soon after this letter may reach you, that if it is agreeable for you to take her up, will

17 Dionne Brand, *A Map to the Door of No Return: Notes to Belonging* (Toronto: Doubleday Canada, 2001), pp. 30–1.

you be so obliging on receipt here of to drop Mr Robinson a line acquainting him what you think a small cargo from about 100 to 150 slaves might fetch at your island.[18]

Such a discourse, common throughout the literature of the business of slavery, enables the black presence to be marginalized and made foreign to the home port of Lancaster. It is a business whose profits returned, but whose bodies, broken and mutilated, remained elsewhere. What the returned public appearance of the hand does is to interrupt such convenient elision, introducing the black flesh on which such profits were made and, of course, the traumatic histories it carries with it. As Cathy Caruth reminds us, 'history, like trauma, is never simply one's own, that history is precisely the way we are implicated in each other's traumas.'[19]

The freight carried by the hand is the traumatic history of the local slave traders themselves and its link to a global history of abuse. Saidiya Hartman describes how 'the *body* of memory—that is the dominated, social collectivity of enslaved Africans and the brutal operation of power on these captive bodies'[20]—is always elided in the master narratives of the powerful, like the letter above, with its bland detailing of commercial operations. However, the severed hand haunts those who promote such wilful amnesia, undermining their desire to reduce the enslavement of human beings to a mere commercial operation of profit and loss. The scattered and spectral records of black presence in a city whose major Georgian buildings and commercial success in the eighteenth century were built on the slave and West Indian trades exemplify the importance of looking between the lines of the written record and indeed of going beyond it to gain an understanding of the ghostly shadow underpinning the city.

The only words we have describing Fanny's life come from her baptismal record, dated April 1778, at the Lancaster Priory church:

18 Quoted in Dear, *In Celebration of the Human Spirit*, p. 9.
19 Cathy Caruth, *Unclaimed Experience: Trauma, Narrative and History* (Baltimore: The Johns Hopkins University Press, 1996), p. 21.
20 Saidiya Hartman, *Scenes of Subjection: Terror, Slavery and Self-Making in Nineteenth Century America* (Oxford: Oxford University Press, 1997), p. 75.

'Frances Elizabeth Johnson, a black woman servt. to Mr John Satter-thwaite, an adult aged 27y.' The mummified hand is left to speak for her presence beyond the parish register. In 1997 Fanny's mummified hand was buried in a special ceremony at the priory church where she was baptized. Dear procured some soil from the Rawlins plantation, a memento of her home island, and it was buried along with the hand in a casket in the Garden of Remembrance alongside the priory church, with the inscription 'F.E.J. 2 April 1778'. This date—her baptismal date—is the only marker we have, apart from the hand, of Fanny's life. Nevertheless, it still seems a strange date to choose as defining her life, being her entrance into and the only record of her in written English history, eliding what went before, her ancestry in Africa and her life in the Caribbean. However, for black people in Britain such ambiguities are a commonplace; they were often treated as goods both in life and death, and their human existence can sometimes be pieced together only through documents written by others. In Johnson's case we have more than documents, but her hand, though enabling more under-standing, is a spectre that is difficult to fully fathom and leaves as many questions as it supplies answers.

More incontrovertible is the fact that masters such as the Satter-thwaites used the profits from plantations in the West Indies and the African slave trade to invest in and help drive the development of the industrial revolution. In Lancaster and its environs we can trace this directly through several individual merchants. I would contend that the ghostly presence of blackness, sensed through these investments with money made off the back of black labour, are vital to unpicking the meaning of race in what Paul Gilroy has called our time of 'post-imperial melancholia'. The period after Lancaster's actual trading in black bodies from Africa is vital to discussing the way in which their contribution has continually been marginalized in contemporary discussions. Paul Gilroy describes how,

> Once the history of empire becomes a source of discomfort, shame and perplexity, its complications and ambiguities were readily set aside. Rather than work through those feelings, that unsettling history was diminished, denied and then if possible actively forgotten. The resulting silence feeds an additional catas-trophe: the error of imagining that postcolonial people are only

unwanted alien intruders without any substantive historical, political or cultural connections to the collective life of their fellow subjects.[21]

Following the money can allow us to show the connections between the wealth invested in the industrial revolution and the way a crucial portion of the money came from the backs of black labour, in order to domesticate those 'alien intruders' and show that they were crucial to the making of Lancashire and Britain, despite denials. The evidence comes through three key individuals, all merchants in the slave trade and West Indies trades: Thomas Hodgson, James Sawrey and Thomas Hinde.

Thomas Hodgson had been a Lancaster slave trader who moved to Liverpool to maximize his trading; however, when it came to investing his profits he returned home, establishing the Low Mill in his native Caton, five miles from Lancaster in 1784. This cotton mill was a crucial and early contribution to the development of industrial Lancaster. The inscription on his commemorative plaque in the nearby local church at Brookhouse eulogizes him thus: 'After passing the early part of his life in foreign climes he was for many years an eminent merchant in Liverpool and founder of the cotton and silk works in this his native place.'[22]

Hodgson's sojourn in 'foreign climes' is a handy euphemism for his tropical investments in human flesh. Another slave trader and merchant whose investments helped promote the development of Lancaster's industrial revolution was James Sawrey, who became a freeman of the town. His trading on all sides of the Triangular Trade is shown by the report in the *Liverpool Advertiser* of his ship the *Sally* being in Sierra Leone on 21 August 1774 with thirty slaves already shipped,[23] and, in 1785, by the West Indian sojourn of his company's ship the ninety-tonne *Fenton*, which brought an entire cargo of mahogany for the Lancaster furniture trade from Jamaica, consisting of 541 planks.[24] Sawrey used

21 Paul Gilroy, *After Empire: Melancholia or Convivial Culture?* (London: Routledge, 2004), p. 98.
22 Elder, p. 188.
23 Elder, p. 59.
24 Elder, p. 99.

the money earned from this trade to buy substantial shares to help fund the Preston–Lancaster Canal, opened in 1797. This waterway was used to transport the coal from inland mines to fuel the nascent Lancaster cotton trade, and seven substantial mills opened close to the canal. As we have seen, these mills were often linked to Lancaster slaving families, but their productivity attracted the attention of mill owners further afield and in 1825 the Greg family, who had established an epoch-defining cotton mill at Quarry Bank, outside Manchester, in 1784, purchased Moor Lane Mill South and were to acquire Moor Lane Mill North in 1846. The Gregs had made their fortune in the West Indies through ownership of the Hillsborough Estate in Dominica and used family connections with the Hodgsons to move into the North Lancashire cotton business, acquiring Low Mill in Caton as well as the two Lancaster mills. The presence of the most important cotton indus-trialist family in Lancaster attests to the desirability of these mills.

The final individual is Thomas Hinde (1720–1799), twice mayor of Lancaster, who was a slave ship captain who became a merchant. 'He sent more ships to West Africa and stayed in the trade longer than anyone else at Lancaster.'[25] He conducted five voyages himself as captain before becoming a merchant and investor in slave trade voyages and in the West Indian trade. Like Hodgson and Sawrey before him, he invested some of the profits from the trade in black bodies into industry, a worsted mill in Dolphinholme. The Hinde family were also involved in the trade and his brother James Hinde, like many, flaunted his wealth by purchasing a black slave-servant. This member of his household has only recently become known to scholars through the University of Glasgow-based project Runaway Slaves in Britain.[26]

On 23 November 1864 this black man, Harry, absconded and moved from anonymity into the pages of the British periodical the *St. James's Chronicle*. It describes the runaway thus:

RUN away from Lancaster, on Friday the 23d Day of November last, a Negro Man named Harry, about twenty Years old, five Feet four Inches high, strong made, and one of his Ears bored; the

---

25 Elder, p. 141.
26 *Runaway Slaves in Britain*, https://www.runaways.gla.ac.uk/ (accessed 31 July 2018).

Colour of his Clothes is unknown, as he absconded in the Night without his Clothes, and is supposed to be gone for London. Whoever secures the said Negro shall be well rewarded, and all Expences paid, upon applying to Mr. James Hinde, Merchant, in Lancaster, or Mr. Smith, Book-keeper, at the Swan-with-two-Necks, Lad-Lane, London.[27]

Harry's decision to make a bolt for freedom to London, nearly 200 miles away, makes sense, as there he would hope to meld into the black population of several thousand, both slave and free, concentrated in the city. What happened to him after his escape is not recorded, but his flight enables an individualized record of his existence to embellish our record of Lancaster black presence. There is only one other specific record of a Lancaster runaway on the database, an anonymous boy who escaped enslavement and whose runaway advert again appeared in the *St. James's Chronicle*:

RUN away from the House of the Rev- Mr. Clarkson, Rector of Heysham, near Lancaster, early in the Morning of Monday the 26th of August last, a Negro Boy, of the Ebo Country, slender made, about five Feet three Inches high, his Left Knee bending inwards, which makes him ha[l]t, a small Lump on his Forehead, with his Country Marks on his Temples; had on, when eloped, a blue Jacket, a grey Waistcoat, and Leather Breeches; he speaks broad Lancashire Dialect.[28]

Thomas Clarkson was the rector of Heysham from 1756 to 1789 and his ownership of an enslaved African highlights that slave-servant ownership in the Lancaster area spread beyond those with West Indian interests. Furthermore, his status as a Church of England clergyman clearly does not proscribe him from ownership of his fellow man, exemplifying the Church's complicity. This is further demonstrated

27 *St. James's Chronicle*, 6 December 1764, *Runaway Slaves in Britain* https://www.runaways.gla.ac.uk/database/display/?rid=340 (accessed 31 July 2018).
28 *St. James's Chronicle*, 10 September 1765, *Runaway Slaves in Britain* https://www.runaways.gla.ac.uk/database/display/?rid=796 (accessed 31 July 2018).

later by the large amounts of compensation the Anglican Church received in the 1830s from the British government for the slaves it owned. This fascinating advertisement details the boy's ethnicity as Ibo and describes distinguishing marks caused by scarification that suggest he was African-born. Having escaped in his servant's clothes, he was distinctive and potentially easily spotted, but in London what might have given him away most was his 'broad Lancashire dialect'. This detail highlights the significant time the boy had spent among Lancashire folk and how he has adapted so much that his English was shaped not by his colonial background but by his Lancaster home. There might have been few black individuals in Lancaster in the 1760s, but already some of them were putting down truly local roots. The recovery of such important lives from the depths of the archives enables new narratives to emerge that deepen our appreciation of the importance of slavery and a black presence to a full understanding of provincial British culture. They show the deep imbrications of slave cultures into British homes and the deep roots of black British culture throughout the polity. A case study such as Lancaster crucially shows that black individuals are constantly being unearthed, creating new narratives that disrupt monocultural myths. As Julie Thorpe says of such discoveries:

> Entering into spaces of displaced lives, we might only discover a name, age and place of imprisonment (enslavement) and encounter only traces of life ... . But these fragments—silent deposits of history—are also an invitation, for those with eyes to see, into the lives of those who having lost ... were able to recreate them ... creating in the process a language of mourning that bequeaths to us in the present an entry into unspeakable pasts.[29]

29 Julie Thorpe, 'Nostalgic Histories of War: Refugees in Austria Hungary 1914–2014', in Alexander Dessingue and Jay Winter (eds), *Beyond Memory: Silence and the Aesthetics of Memory* (New York: Routledge, 2016), pp. 65–77 at p. 74.

CHAPTER ELEVEN

Staging Sancho

Paterson Joseph

I first considered writing a performable story about a black historical personality as an act of defiance in the face of many obstacles, internal and external. My confidence as a writer had never been huge; academic success eluding me till after I left school. The world seemed very unready for whatever garbled mess an under-confident fledgling writer like me might turn out. Especially when—as I heard often in the earliest days of writing *Sancho*—the profession was not wide open to stories about black historical characters.

TV companies I approached later would claim that the 'special' audience needed to make a filmed version of Sancho's life a success were just not large enough to justify spending any money on such a project. For 'special', read black—as if white people just turn off or switch channels when they see that a drama is being led by black performers or has a black personality from history as its chief protagonist. Nonsense; but that had become orthodoxy, until *Black Panther* and its myth-busting billion-dollar worldwide box-office record in 2017. Unhelpfully, theatres were not exactly brimful of plays in monologue form, on the grounds that it is hard to sell a short show with only one actor in it. Obstacles everywhere.

On my side, as an actor, I had a wealth of experience at the National Theatre (NT), on the London fringe circuit, in touring theatre, and with the Royal Shakespeare Company (RSC), among many others. My TV profile was, if not stellar, at least visible. There seemed little or no good reason why I could not command the best classical/historical roles. At the very least, I should be *seen* for them (our jargon for an audition).

Auditions for these on-camera roles were rare, and by no means a given in the—more enlightened—theatre world, either. Offers of leading roles in period TV dramas were, in fact, non-existent. Shakespeare gave me my only chance at this, with a small but good role in Shakespeare's *Henry V* for the BBC Hollow Crown series. But that is the only time in a thirty-year career that 'action' was called with me wearing a costume dating from before 1948.

It was a long-held desire of mine to break this monotoned view of British historical drama, of the British story, *per se*. In fact, for many ethnic minorities in the UK, British history has always been presented as White History to us.

*

The urge to create a period drama with a black protagonist that I could portray led me to choose a somewhat divisive character from the pages of Afro-British history: Charles Ignatius Sancho.

Sancho seemed—on the surface—more appeaser than protester of the slave trade and British hegemony in general. A musician and bon vivant, a royal court denizen, writer, actor and erstwhile valet to the duke of Montagu, Sancho's life encapsulated for me the struggles of many of us who have chosen to engage directly with the dominant culture, in particular in terms of how we negotiate this with dignity and intelligence.

Sancho died in 1780 as a struggling Westminster grocer with seven children and a Jamaican-born wife, Anne. He was neither failure nor 'Uncle Tom'. On the contrary: as the proprietor of a grocer's shop in Charles Street in Westminster, he was eligible to vote, and in 1774 he became the first black man in England to do so.

How, then, to translate this man's eighteenth-century life—born on a slave ship; orphaned at birth; sent at three years old to live in Greenwich with three spinsters; running away from home because he was discouraged from learning to read; found by John, duke of Montagu; secretly educated by him; becoming an actor, musician, writer and grocer after a career in the courts of the Georgian kings— into a seventy-five-minute play that a twenty-first-century audience could empathize with and understand? How to make his words, his personality and very presence reach us today? And, more importantly to me, what would his effect on that audience be? In short, I feared that Sancho's story would simply not be *relevant* to the struggles of Afro-Britons today.

I needn't have worried. Sancho's story—when I eventually completed it—touched the hearts of many diverse communities across the USA. My return in April 2018 to play—among other venues—three weeks at the National Black Theatre under the auspices of the Classical Black Theatre added more fuel to my story. Wilton's Music Hall in the east of London, Britain's oldest surviving music hall, hosted *Sancho—An Act of Remembrance* in its native home—for the first time—in June 2018. The reactions to Sancho himself will be discussed further below; for me, they were the most important aspect of my journey with Charles Ignatius. But before there could be reactions, a play had to be written.

Staging Sancho

> I wrote this play ... because I wanted to be in a costume drama.
>
> (*Sancho—An Act of Remembrance*)

The quotation above is no lie. It is incumbent upon me to state that from the start. The journey to writing this play was pretty shallow. I did, indeed, feel I was built for costume drama. So, I set out to write one I could be in myself. After all, my training at drama school and the early part of my career were aimed in that direction. But my arena of greatest competence was as an actor. How would I fare as a writer? After all, being competent in one part of our art is not a guarantee that you can be a success in another part.

In the end, this was an improvised creation. I had no idea what I was doing until well into the process. I don't want the reader to imagine that they are dealing with a carefully thought-out methodology that could be easily explained here and even more simply used as a blueprint hereafter. Nothing could be further from the truth. But out of chaos came order ... eventually.

For the creative process to be truly spontaneous—a vital component of fine art—it has to run the risk of failure. The closer to that edge one dares go, that edge where it all seems to want to fall apart, the nearer we get to truly great art. There is no formula contained in that statement. It is merely the beginning—the attitude required—to begin the process of finding the art in our Art.

My attitude was set to tentative from the very first time I spoke about such a project in 1999. I was working with the actor Tilda Swinton on a long film shoot. As well as being an outstanding performer and artist, Tilda also has a forensic curiosity about what makes people tick. Her favourite question to tease the deepest secrets out of people is: 'When you're about to breathe your last, what would you ideally want to have left behind?' I wanted to think it through for a moment or two, but almost to my surprise it didn't take long to answer. 'I want to leave behind a play, a film or a novel that reveals the Black British story and leaves a record of the positive contribution made by African people in British history for the next generation.'

Such a grand goal. I had no idea how I was going to go about this then, as I didn't consider myself a writer in any way other than aspirationally. I hadn't written anything of any note up to that point, though I had dabbled in writing since my earliest days as an actor. But something about the intellectual and structural basis of good writing stumped me. I felt like an interloper in a world I had little technical knowledge of. I'd read a little on the subject, but, in the end, I was bored by reading about writing, felt I had read so many plays and screenplays that I had surely metabolized the methodology and shape behind a decent theatre script. Rightly or wrongly then, I decided to write Sancho's story for the stage. However, another little-known component of any artistic endeavour is the incremental chipping away of one's confidence that what one is creating is of value outside the interest of the artist. Would the same thrill at his exceptionality be felt by those coming to the story of Charles Ignatius Sancho for the first time as I had experienced it many years before?

Finding a way to communicate a vision is the starting point of any creative piece of work. Whether one works in abstract or performance art, the method of conveying our ideas is key. For me, as an actor, it seemed clear that if I wanted to get people as excited as I was about Charles Ignatius Sancho's life they needed to meet him. Simple, but how? The answer came to me almost immediately: a monologue.

The purest form of theatre.
One person. An audience. Words.

Having set that as a plan in my mind, it was then a matter of writing the material. His 'voice'—sourced from his prolific letter-writing—came surprisingly swiftly. The disputed Joseph Jekyll early preface to Sancho's letters makes mention of a speech impediment that scuppered Sancho's plans for an acting career, perhaps alongside his friend, and the finest actor of the eighteenth century, David Garrick. What could that impediment be? And how does one comfortably sustain a speech impediment on stage—over seventy-five or so minutes of monologue—an impediment that supposedly prevented a career in acting? Who wants to sit through that?

For now, however, I studied the period syntax, vocabulary and grammar. Read James Boswell on Samuel Johnson. Read Samuel Johnson on anything. *Tristram Shandy*, that great—seminal—comic novel by Charles Ignatius's hero Laurence Sterne was a key find, as Sancho imitates the style of Sterne in his letters, using new-coined words and wordplay to get his points across. And, finally, I read the reams of Sancho's letters that had been originally published in 1782. They have been published in a number of modern editions from 1955, several of these within the last twenty-three years. Armed with this research, and after nearly six years of procrastination, I finally bit the bullet and did what we learnt to do in drama school when we needed to build a character: Hot-Seating.

'Hot-Seating' is the act of speaking for—and as—your character through a series of interrogatory and intimate questions—the kind of questions a psychiatrist or confessor might pose. After mulling over how he would have spoken—his accent, his syntax, his vocabulary—and adding a mild lisp, I simply launched into a monologue in which Sancho is sitting for his 1768 portrait. I started to put pen to paper in 2005. One afternoon, the first ten to fifteen minutes of the play were written—in an inspired burst—at that one sitting.

Once I had decided that an 'Audience with Sancho' would be the set-up, it took only a little imagination to bring me to set the entire first act in Thomas Gainsborough's studio in Bath. Here was a very captive audience. Possibly hostile, but definitely curious. Having learnt that the 1768 portrait of Sancho by Gainsborough took roughly one hundred minutes to complete, it was only a matter of time before the idea that the theatre audience was his 'audience' in the studio became obvious. This would be a performance that would dispense entirely with the famed fourth wall—that imaginary screen between the theatre audience and the performer on stage.

Months of writing ensued. The story and the scope expanded; Mrs Sancho made a risky appearance and the show ran to about ninety-five minutes. Too long for a monologue. The Holy Grail of Monologue Timing is set at a firm seventy-five minutes, dead.

The strange thing about writing in general is how uncollaborative and downright lonely it can be compared with acting. However, theatre writing has the advantage of never remaining in the head of one person for long. Once it is given over to a director, designer and musical director—not to forget costumiers—it transforms into something much greater than the sum of its parts. This was apparent from the very first time I stuck my neck out and began to tell friends and colleagues of my intention to write this play. Writers gave me tips about form, actors gave me insights on staging monologues and musicians gave me atmosphere and tone.

After the stuttering start to my writing *Sancho* in 2005, it wasn't until two more years of research and several acting jobs later that I finally had a draft I was happy to show to folks. But to whom? Always a frightening prospect. Your precious work, in the hands of a perfect stranger to it. We writers are very circumspect about who we first let see our Precious. Which way to go? Tender, loving and largely uncritical friend; or bluff, dismissive no-nonsense truth-sayer?

I chose the most honest, sometimes brutish, critic I knew. Actor, director and writer George Costigan, a very straight-talking Northern Englander. I was stunned to hear him say that it was well-written but was too long and lacked something … climactic? But his biggest negative criticism was levelled at my pet love in the show: history. 'Too much history we don't care anything about, Pat. Too much stuff that clearly only the writer enjoys. And while that's interesting for a bit, it cannot sustain our attention for 75 minutes, let alone the 90 you got here.' George, out.

Luckily, I had other friends who were less harsh about the history bits but more concerned about the length of the piece and sustaining an audience's interest. I began to feel that the two 'problems' were not mutually exclusive. I excised many pages, equivalent to at least twenty minutes of monologue, in the next few months, shedding all references that did not move the story on to the next fact or incident of interest in his life.

In some ways, that first draft—a draft I had the good fortune to present at the National Theatre Studio in 2010—was a little staid and polite. For example, even though Sebastian Born, then the literary manager at the NT and one of the very earliest of readers, urged me to add some tension between Sancho and the audience, I hadn't managed to inject more than a perfunctory nod at this in the following, early section:

A challenge now. Watching us, assessing us. Imitating audience members talking behind their hands.

'But who is this', you wonder? 'Who speaks so boldly to us? Who holds the name of England's sovereign in his mouth as of a right? Who is this ... this ... Negro ... this ... black? Is this a joke?' Ah ... Now, perhaps some among you have not had the privilege in your lives to consort with educated Negroes. It goes hard, but thereby we are enlightened, ladies and gentlemen. A taste of something ... other? For this, you must enter into another world ... a world of hardship and joy, of terror and pleasure; in short, the world of ... Sancho. And when we are done, who between you and I will have learnt the most? Qui sais, sauf Dieu?

My Sanchonettas

Sancho had a long way to go before it reached its present-day form. Charles Ignatius was the first black man to cast a vote in Britain, but 'The Vote' as the play's climax had not occurred to me until I started work on a *Sancho* screenplay after the first theatre shows. I felt it was right to complete most of the stage journey before embarking on a screen version. I wanted them to be separate, as storytelling is different in these two mediums. A quick rule of thumb: stage needs words as a frame of reference, screen needs fewer words and more visual clues. I would go on to find that one lent its own flavour to the other. This transformative stage of the process had already begun in 2010 in many ways, once my collaborators came on board.

I had known Ben Park, my musical director and the arranger of the music in *Sancho*, for three years. I felt confident that he was the right man for the job, and when he presented me with the fruits of his labours—*Sancho*'s sheet music, sourced from the amazing archive at the British Library—I knew we would make a great team. The first time I got my clarinet teacher to play *Sancho's* 'Friendship, Source of Joy', my heart soared. Hearing the man's music for the first time was as important as discovering the portrait. Such a playful composer could never be mawkish or self-indulgent, despite his trials. It was a major stage in creating the character of Charles Ignatius.

My friend, actor, writer and director Elliot Cowan, came on board next. His contribution was vital. Elliot was smart enough to let me largely choreograph my own movements. As I wrote the piece, I was conscious of where I might need to demonstrate Sancho's drinking, for example. Choosing moments that could take the pause it required. Trying to adjust where I raised a glass, and so on. Funnily enough, it was one of the first things to go when we remounted the show some years later. There was simply not enough time for drinking once the play developed into its present form.

To pin Sancho's personality down, I rehearsed how the obesity he suffered from for much of his life affected the way he might think, walk and move about. Our physical being affects our character, after all. Character is the specific way we choose to act and speak. Accent is attitude. Put these together and you have the makings of a rounded personality fit to be seen on stage.

Linda Haysman, my costume designer and friend, gave me the other great key to eighteenth-century deportment and physicality. The clothes we wear naturally affect the way we sit, stand and walk. When you add a thick frock-coat, a bright red plush waistcoat and high-heeled buckled shoes, your way of standing and moving is immediately changed. A grace was needed to pull this off and avoid clumping all over the stage. Sancho's deportment came largely from these costume choices (Figure 11.1).

A drama-school friend, choreographer Jack Murphy, helped with the minuet Sancho dances with a member of the audience. But he did much more than that. After I had read the play aloud at the start of that first rehearsal Jack pointed out the obvious autobiographical aspects of the play. Strange to say, I hadn't noticed this while writing *Sancho*. The fact that Sancho was seen as 'other'; the way he integrated into the world he found himself in; his love of Shakespeare and theatre; and, finally, his worry for future generations and their progress. All this mirrored concerns in my own life.

11.1 The actor Paterson Joseph as Ignatius Sancho.
Photo credit: Robert Day.

This early, rough version of *Sancho—An Act of Remembrance* was so well received that I was invited by the Oxford Playhouse (OP)—in the shape of Michelles Walker and Dickson—to co-produce the play with them in 2011. This connection was made possible largely through the relationship Ben Park had as Artist-in-Residence at the OP.

Our rapid rehearsals, with another kind friend, Ian Flintoff, co-directing, were followed by a short week of performances in the small, but perfectly formed, Burton-Taylor Studio. With its sixty-seat capacity, it would be the smallest house I was ever to play to on the journey with *Sancho* in performance. Being the first venue, it stays in the memory like the moment a parent witnesses their offspring's first, tentative baby-steps: a mixture of relief, fear and pride.

Two years later, when I was in New York with Shakespeare's *Julius Caesar* at the Brooklyn Academy of Music (BAM), Michelle Dickson of the OP asked me to meet with a producer friend of hers who she thought might suit me as a collaborator on *Sancho*. And so I duly met with Tim Smith of Pemberley Productions, a company he'd started shortly before, having spent many years stage-managing and producing shows for Druid Theatre in Galway and the RSC. We both remember very vividly our first conversation at the Algonquin Hotel in New York. It was a meeting that led to the last five years of collaboration and a whole lot of fun. It was Tim who managed to wangle development money from the Arts Council and procure various venues in the States, an invaluable contribution that put *Sancho* on course for the success that followed.

As for the rest of the team, my brilliant co-director Simon Godwin brought along Anna Girvan, our talented and able assistant director. Tim Smith was mainly responsible for gathering most of the rest of my team of 'Sanchonettas'—as Charles Ignatius dubbed his own family. There were my dazzling lighting crew, Lucrecia Briceno and Anshuman Bhatia; trusty Tim Boyd from the OP; and the superb and irreplaceable Pamela Salling as my stage-manager/counsellor. Michael Vale designed a set so simple and yet effective that we have not had to alter a thing since he first presented his Matt Box design. It was a truly eclectic and excellent collection of practitioners.

Performing Sancho

For all our research, those of us interested in bringing Afro-British stories and personalities to public knowledge are limited in our reach. A book may be full of great detail and insights into eighteenth-century life in general, for instance, but cannot hope to physically present one of those personalities to us in a way that allows us to feel we are meeting them in person. Also—importantly—a book is not designed for the communal event of 100 people sitting in one room over seventy-five minutes. This is the remit of theatre and the performing arts; they allow us the opportunity of bringing to life long-dead heroes and villains, watched by an attentive crowd of strangers. A good play can, at its best, give us graphic insight into the ordinary as well as the extraordinary aspects of the life of the Exceptional.

Up until now I haven't written much about the minutiae of my discoveries surrounding Sancho. I thought the best way to rescue the potentially dry retelling of any research adventures was to relate my interactions with audiences in the US and UK. These post-show sessions were invaluable in strengthening my confidence in telling Sancho's story and in broadening the scope of its impact. I later transcribed these recordings I made at the National Black Theatre in Harlem in April 2018. But the questions posed, and the answers given, form the same basic pattern as in all my encounters with audiences for *Sancho* wherever I have performed the play.

The first question and answer session—talkback, in US parlance—was at the Kennedy Center in Washington DC. I have written elsewhere about how moved I was by the thought that Sancho always wanted to travel to America but died before he was able to fulfil that dream. And here I was, with a play about his life, in the shadow of the iconic monuments at the political heart of America's capital. I cried a little, gazing over the Potomac River, and was blessed to see that after our first performance and talkback my producer, Tim Smith, was also moved to tears. Sancho—in the form of my little tribute to his life—had at last made that journey across the Atlantic. And his effect was unexpected and explosive.

*

A compelling moment that is crucial to our understanding of the effect of *Sancho—An Act of Remembrance* on audiences comes at the end of the piece, when Sancho is looking for his property papers. These were vital documents one needed in order to qualify to vote in UK elections. This particular ballot, for the 1780 parliamentary election, featured Charles James Fox—an earlier abolitionist politician—who stood in the Westminster Borough in the year Sancho last voted and in which he died. Yet, bizarrely to me now, I had not had the foresight to include an actual vote in the first drafts. I thought it unnecessary, as folks would surely come to the show already knowing that Sancho was the first Afro-Briton to vote in a parliamentary election.

My co-director Simon Godwin—a brilliant dramaturg as well as an innovative associate director at the NT—insisted on restructuring the second half of *Sancho*. He felt that there was not enough of a dramatic climax to the second section and wondered if there was anything I had left out? The Vote, contained in the draft screenplay, seemed an obvious choice. Once we had plotted it in, it became startling clear that this was the missing ingredient all along. The sweep of the show, leading to such a powerful—and politically hot—ending, gave the first half and build-up to the climax a great deal of confidence and freedom. Sancho's indulgent frivolity and humour could be given full rein, as I now knew the punch that was coming at the end of the play.

During that Kennedy Center performance, when Sancho's desperate search for his papers appears futile, there was a palpable sense of tension in the auditorium. The applause that followed when this tension was released as Sancho voted was powerful and largely unforeseen. I was shamefully ignorant of current American politics, particularly how thinly disguised racist policies adversely affected the African-American electorate. Washington proved to be an education.

In several, largely Republican, states the need for photo ID has caused many in the African-American community to be shut out of the electoral process. This tactic of demanding exceptional and time-consuming effort from the black electorate is deliberate and cynical. This chicanery, dressed-up as a legal requirement, is subject to a major push-back in the Hispanic and African-American communities. Sancho's act of defiance was simply to vote. African-Americans face a shamefully similar challenge to meet the exacting criteria for full enfranchisement.

What follows is an edited transcription from my Q&As at the National Black Theatre in Harlem in April 2018. It shows the ways that the American audiences engaged with Sancho and wanted to better understand his life.

A Q&A in Harlem

I loved this first question, as it revealed that the audience truly cared about what happened to Charles Ignatius. They had taken in and metabolized his concerns. This was rewarding for me as the writer, justifying my confidence that, if people 'met' Sancho, as I had, they would love him, as I had.

Q: Do you know anything about Sancho's descendants?
A: The records for the Sancho family come to an end in 1837, the year Elizabeth 'Betsy', Sancho's third daughter with his West Indian wife, Anne Osborne, died. She would have been 71—quite old for a woman to die in those days, where life-expectancy for either sex was no higher than 41. Her handwriting was legible but not as elegant as either her father's or her younger brother William 'Billy' Osborne's. This suggested to me that care was taken over Sancho's daughters' education, but no money could

likely be found to have them educated privately. Billy may have had some sort of parish education but, again, I have found no records of that. Perhaps they were all home-schooled.

Two years after Sancho died, his letters were collated and published by Joseph Jekyll. There was a rumour that Samuel Johnson was on the verge of writing the biographical preface to the letters. However, a friend left a widow in his care, so that his notoriously tender heart led him to be distracted from completing, or even perhaps starting, any work on it.

The Letters of the Late Ignatius Sancho—an African were published posthumously in 1782, and its list of subscribers— including gentry, artists and the aristocracy—was the longest in publishing history, beating the record previously set by the first edition of *The Spectator*. Sancho's fame was such that the letters were a best-seller and made a lot of money for the Sancho family. In 1802 his son, Billy, finding it impossible to engage a printer to reprint his father's letters, converted the family grocery store into a print works. He had the letters reprinted and, again, that would have helped Sancho's family out enormously.

Anne Osborne died in 1817. Betsy was the last surviving child. Before she died in 1837 she gave the Gainsborough portrait of her father to William Stevenson, a friend of the family. It was sold at auction in the late 1800s, and today we find it in the National Gallery of Canada in Ottawa. I've just called them, and they may allow me to perform the play in front of the actual portrait sometime in the near future.

It's an interesting thing about DNA, and where it goes. Because many very Caucasian-looking people are discovering— now that DNA tests can be done more rapidly—that they have a fair amount of African DNA in their make-up.

One possible cause of this phenomenon is the presence in England of an estimated 15,000–30,000 African people in the eighteenth century. Remember, too, that in the play we go back to third-century Britain and an estimated 40,000 foreign troops arriving in England with their Roman governor Septimius Severus, who originated from Libya. Where are the children from relationships between the ancient Britons and these foreign legionnaires?

With cross-cultural intermarriage quite common among African men in particular in the eighteenth century, within a generation or two the African features of the newly arrived Africans and Afro-Caribbeans would be diminished, soon becoming too subtle to be noted. It would only take a hint of shame at having a slave ancestor to lead to a black ancestor being forgotten within a generation. So, Sancho could well be among us in the UK population and beyond. Our stories are inextricably linked.

Q: It seems really sad that members of the African Diaspora in the UK and US are so ignorant of each other. What can you do about strengthening that link between Diasporic peoples?
A: Not much, I'm only an actor (Cue laughter). But with wonderful people like Ty Jones at the Classical Black Theatre—please support them—I am able to reach a wider audience than just the UK one. I have learnt as much about the African-American experience as you will have learnt about the Afro-British experience. I didn't know our stories were that linked until I came here. And they're linked in a way that I partly find sad.

When I came to the US to do the show for the first time I opened at the Kennedy Center in Washington. I performed in front of about 450 students and a few adults. In the Q&A afterwards four older African-American ladies—in their eighties perhaps—said, 'Son, this is not an old story. This is happening to us today. We need to prove that we're American citizens so that we can vote.' That statement shocked me to the core.

Coincidentally—if you search online for Windrush Generation—that's my parent's generation—who came to the UK in the 1940s, 1950s and 1960s, they're also being disenfranchised in other ways right now. Their papers are also 'missing' ... . So, it's—unfortunately—a present story as well as an old story.

Q: Have you done the show in the UK? Is Sancho very famous in Britain?
A: Unfortunately, I wasn't able to get a London venue at first, which is where I wanted to do it. I've done a few performances at the Oxford Playhouse and at Birmingham Repertory Theatre.

But in June 2018 we head to Wilton's Music Hall in the heart of London's East End; a beautiful old music venue. Variety or Vaudeville acts have performed there since 1859, and it is one of the most beautiful theatres I have ever seen.

Sancho was certainly not widely taught in schools when I was growing up. Up until very recently he was pretty much ignored by most museums and galleries dealing with eighteenth-century London life. This new interest in early Afro-British figures like John Blanke (King Henry VIII's trumpeter), Dido Elizabeth Belle (great-niece of Lord Chief-Justice Mansfield), Olaudah Equiano (African anti-slavery campaigner) and Francis Barber (Samuel Johnson's servant/heir)—has meant that it will only be a matter of time before we get more stories from black British history on our screens and stages.

When I began writing the play there were very few websites one could visit to find good, detailed black British history. Now, we find a plethora of sites and new literature to choose from. Very pleasing.

The questions Sancho's story prompted in the London audience can be summed up in one:

Q: How can we find out more about Charles Ignatius?
A: I found him in Gretchen Gerzina's great book *Black England*. I would highly recommend his letters, published by Penguin, though there are other versions. A few letters and possibly some of Sancho's compositions are thought to still be with the surviving Montagu family. I hope to write a fuller account of his life in the near future and, perhaps, I could persuade the Montagus to let me have those missing artefacts.

It seems to me the more we know about Charles Ignatius Sancho and the Afro-British world of the eighteenth century the more we want to know. Given how much a part-time history sleuth like me could find out, I'm sure someone with more time and resources on their hands will find even more.

Though these are only a fragment of the questions and answers over the course of our tour, I think they show how the audience's curiosity is piqued by this man. I did not take this fact for granted when I started this journey.

Sancho—Homecoming

Back in 2010 many of the theatres that I approached cited the difficulty of selling a short monologue about an obscure figure. They insisted that they loved the work, they loved Sancho's story, but not enough to put their money where their mouth was, with the exception of the earlier-mentioned Michelle Dickson and Michelle Walker at the Oxford Playhouse. I did approach the Kiln Theatre in Kilburn, very local to me in north-west London. They declined, on the grounds that they had recently presented a historical play about a black man who performed Shakespeare ... *Red Velvet*, by Lolita Chakrabarti.

Interestingly, that excellent play—starring the wonderful Adrian Lester—is about Ira Aldridge. American. One hundred years later. If these two stories are similar, it is only in that both men enjoyed theatre and were black. Not 'the same' in my opinion, but these strangely ignorant views are what I've been met with ever since I started on this road. There seemed to be no room—even in very enlightened theatre and TV folks' minds—for more than one story about a historical black character who enjoyed the theatre. The four new biographies of Winston Churchill or the three theatre versions of the life of fictional Jane Eyre—which can be found somewhere in the UK at any season—seem not to bother such commentators.

*

London was going to be a challenge after the success of our Harlem shows. The intimacy of that space, the reactions to the brand-new story, the surprise his accent brought to the audience: all these would perhaps be lost on London's more 'sophisticated' theatre-goers. In fact, Wilton's Music Hall proved to be the best of venues for Sancho's homecoming. The immersive experience was enhanced by the intimacy of a space that is physically larger than most venues I had played on the road, while being acoustically lively and easy on the voice.

Smashing the fourth wall and being able to see, touch and address the folks in the auditorium lent the whole 'Audience with' vibe an added immediacy. At Wilton's the participatory nature of music hall—with its banter, heckling and general sense of entertaining chaos—was a surprisingly positive addition to the play's feel.

I realized something at Wilton's that had not occurred to me in any concrete sense before. *Sancho* is militantly jolly and witty; in some ways, it feels like an act of defiance. Though his people were seen as the lowest of the low in human terms, were oppressed in the West and hunted all along Africa's west coast, he still maintained a sense of freedom—a freedom of expression and artistry. Flipping cultural expectations and societal limitations was Sancho's *modus operandi*. I know that I have been subtly influenced by this in my own life.

In London I met several groups of people who had either been researching Sancho for years or had recently discovered other figures who had a major influence in the Afro-British story. Film and TV production companies began to propose meetings, to chat about a possible filmed version of Sancho's life story, possibly using my play as a blueprint. After a decade of banging my fists on the door of TV production companies and networks, it seemed like they had suddenly realized that the idea of a niche market for such stories had—somehow—evaporated. Perhaps vaporized by the powerful wind of change that is the *Black Panther* phenomenon.

Final Thoughts

Sancho's life lent itself so well to the stage because of his innate theatricality and the colourful life he led. The audiences that came to see the show in Austin, Philadelphia, Pittsburgh, Chicago, New York, Washington, Oxford, Birmingham and London were my teachers along the way. As always, when a rehearsed show is presented in front of strangers to the material a sea-change occurs, and the very nature of the show alters nightly and permanently. Oxford taught me to be clear in speech. A seemingly unemotional but powerful way to convey horrific truths. Washington taught me to look deeper into the links between the African Diasporas; to always relate the past with the present. Harlem taught me that an intimate encounter with Sancho could bring the fruit of a life-long connection to his story. A personal encounter for me, too, as I learnt to communicate with my African-American family.

But most significant of all, so far, to me was the London audiences who taught me that they, too, consider Charles Ignatius Sancho one of their own, and a very Great Briton indeed.

I hope that any screen version inspired by this play will do the job of showing the man in three dimensions, adding a fourth of intense intimacy, a difficult trick at times in the theatre. Regardless of how he gets there, whatever journey takes Charles Ignatius to the screen will be worthy of the man's uniquely challenging, vibrant and extraordinary life.

CHAPTER TWELVE

Julius Soubise in India

Ashley L. Cohen

There is no shortage of heroes in Black British history. The eighteenth century alone boasts a violin virtuoso (George Bridgetower), a Cambridge-educated poet and classicist (Francis Williams), an Arabic translator (Job ben Solomon) and a man of letters and composer (Ignatius Sancho), as well as countless antislavery activists, writers, and public speakers, from Olaudah Equiano to Ottobah Cugoano. Julius Soubise is an uneasy fit in this accomplished cast of characters, his most lasting achievement being his notoriety. While his friend and mentor Sancho was hard at work securing his legacy as the first Afro-Briton to vote in a parliamentary election, Soubise was busy building his reputation as an *enfant terrible* in London's fashionable world. Yet Soubise is nonetheless well worth studying, on many counts. This essay explores just one: as Soubise eventually settled in India, his life represents a rare opportunity to explore the global dimensions of Black British history.

Soubise was born on St Kitts in the mid-1750s to a mother of African descent and a European father. In 1764 he was brought to England and entered the household of the duke and duchess of Queensberry.[1] Although he started life there as an ornamental 'pet' slave, he was eventually raised in the manner of an orphaned ward, occupying the

---

1 This biographical sketch draws from: Henry Charles William Angelo, *Reminiscences of Henry Angelo* (London: H. Colburn, 1830); Angelo, *Angelo's Pic Nic; or, Table Talk* (London: John Ebers, 1834); Lady Mary Coke, *The Letters and Journals of Lady Mary Coke* (Bath: Kingsmead Bookshops, 1970), vol. 1, pp. 194–5.

same position Francis Barber filled in Samuel Johnson's household.[2] Whereas Barber was educated to keep pace with Johnson's bookish pursuits, Soubise was raised like a pseudo-aristocrat. He studied fencing and horsemanship with Domenico Angelo, the European master who instructed England's royal princes (Figure 12.1); and he was painted by Johann Zoffany, a portraitist employed by George III.[3] Styling himself as a 'Black Prince' and living as if aristocratic excess were his birthright, Soubise became a fixture in London's fashionable world in the early 1770s. Britain's first 'black dandy' and a virtual socialite, he frequented the Opera, Pantheon, Ranelagh and Vauxhall.[4] He was also a celebrity. He was immortalized in satirical prints and caricatured onstage by comic legend Samuel Foote (alongside the period's most infamous aristocratic bad boy, Charles James Fox), and his sexual exploits were chronicled in a semi-fictional guide to London's high-end brothels.[5] If devotion to high fashion and luxurious living were Soubise's only foibles it would be easy to celebrate him unabashedly alongside his more staid Afro-British peers. But Soubise's bad reputation was earned: by all accounts he was a womanizer and spendthrift who never paid his debts. For years he was shielded by the duchess, who paid his creditors and tried (without success) to silence a rape allegation. But when his patroness died the only way for Soubise

2 For 'pet' slaves, see Srinivas Aravamudan, *Tropicopolitans: Colonialism and Agency, 1688–1804* (Durham, NC: Duke University Press, 1999), pp. 33–49; David Dabydeen, *Hogarth's Blacks Blacks: Images of Blacks in Eighteenth-Century English Art* (Manchester: Manchester University Press, 1985), pp. 21–34; Peter Fryer, *Black People in the British Empire: An Introduction* (London: Pluto Press, 1988), pp. 21, 25, 73. For Barber see Gretchen H. Gerzina, *Black England: Life before Emancipation* (New Brunswick: Rutgers University Press, 1995), pp. 43–52; Bundock, *The Fortunes*.
3 Ashley L. Cohen, 'Fencing and the Market in Aristocratic Masculinity', in Daniel O'Quinn and Alexis Tadie (eds), *Sporting Cultures, 1650–1850* (Toronto: University of Toronto Press, 2018), pp. 66–90.
4 Monica Miller, *Slaves to Fashion: Black Dandyism and the Styling of Black Diasporic Identity* (Durham, NC: Duke University Press, 2009).
5 I make this argument about Foote's *The Cozeners* (1774) in *The Global Indies: British Imperial Culture, 1756–1815* (New Haven: Yale University Press, 2020); *Nocturnal Revels: or, The History of King's-Place, and other Modern Nunneries* (London: M. Goadby, 1779).

A MUNGO MACARONI.

Publish'd according to Act, by M.Darly, 39 Strand, Sept.r 10.1772.

12.1 Matthew Darly, 'A Mungo Macaroni', 10 September 1772.
A joint caricature of Soubise and the Scottish politician Jeremiah
Dyson, this print is assumed to be a likeness of Soubise. The
image may have been modelled on an illustration from the fencing
manual *L'Ecole des Armes* (London: R. & J. Dodsley, 1763), more
specifically, Plate I, which depicts Soubise's fencing instructor and
employer, Domenico Angelo, in the act of drawing his weapon.
© Trustees of the British Museum (by permission).

to escape prison or worse was to flee. In July 1777 he boarded a ship bound for India, where he remained until his death in 1798.

The location of Soubise's long final act has stymied scholarship on him. Eighteenth-century Black British history has tended to focus on the African slave trade, and thus the Atlantic world. When Soubise exited this region he also exited the geographical framework used by scholars to study him, effectively going off stage. The available archival record is also to blame. In London Soubise was a cause célèbre; his life was well documented. In India the paper trail runs dry: the only glimpses into his life come from a handful of newspaper paragraphs. Given this, it is entirely understandable that scholars have ended Soubise's story with his embarkation for India. However, a new discovery has radically altered the material record. Peter Robb's extensive work on the eighty-volume manuscript diary of Richard Blechynden—an architect and surveyor who lived in Calcutta from the 1780s until the 1820s—has revealed that Blechynden's on-again off-again business partner and friend was none other than Soubise, who appears in the diary dozens of times between 1794 and 1798.[6] In fact, Blechynden's diary contains over 20,000 words about Soubise, illuminating many details of his life in India for the first time. The remainder of this essay explores this exciting new source. First, however, we will fill in the gaps between 1777 and 1794.

When Soubise arrived in India he established himself as a fencing and riding master. Unfortunately, success eluded him. The newspapers that document these years are a chronicle of financial instability. Puff pieces placed by Soubise to advertise new ventures—fencing lessons, horse dressing, a mare for sale—are followed at regular intervals by notices of insolvency. Yet, whether he was imprisoned for debt, hounded by creditors or suffered the sale of his stables at auction, Soubise inevitably bounced back with new ventures. Then, in 1789, he survived a brush with death when a French neighbour took a razor

---

6 Peter Robb, *Sentiment and Self: Richard Blechynden's Calcutta Diaries, 1791–1822* (Delhi: Oxford University Press, 2011); Robb, *Sex and Sensibility: Richard Blechynden's Calcutta Diaries, 1791–1822* (Delhi: Oxford University Press, 2011); Robb, *Useful Friendship: Europeans and Indians in Early Calcutta* (Delhi: Oxford University Press, 2014). I am extremely grateful to Robb for his insightful comments on this essay and for his early guidance in working with the diaries.

to his throat.[7] After recovering, he disappeared from the Calcutta record for three years. Perhaps he travelled to Lucknow to visit the Nawab of Awadh's famed stables.[8] Then, in 1794, he suddenly entered Blechynden's social orbit—and diary—when he married the daughter of Blechynden's friend, William Pawson.

In London Soubise had been a member of what I have elsewhere called 'the sociable service elite': professional men and women who socialized with the aristocracy not as equals in rank or fortune but by dint of their cultural capital, which they used to render peers some service.[9] In this capacity, Soubise brushed shoulders with some of the brightest luminaries of his time—actors such as David Garrick, John Bannister and Thomas Sheridan; playwrights such as Samuel Foote, George Colman the Elder and Richard Brinsley Sheridan; painters such as Joshua Reynolds, Thomas Gainsborough, Benjamin West and George Stubbs; and composers and musicians including Johann Christian Bach and Elizabeth Ann Linley.[10] As Angelo's assistant, Soubise taught fencing to aristocratic and royal pupils, who seem to have generally enjoyed his company.[11] Meanwhile, the Calcutta social milieu Soubise entered after his marriage was a world away from such exalted circles. Pawson, who joined the East India Company in 1765, was the son of a London wine merchant.[12] Although he eventually

---

7 *Calcutta Gazette*, 26 March 1789. He bore a 'large Scar on the left side of the Throat' from this encounter until his death. British Library (BL) Add MS 45606, 245.

8 The horse Soubise sold Blechynden was from Awadh. BL Add MS 45591, 199–202.

9 Cohen, 'Fencing and the Market in Aristocratic Masculinity', p. 74.

10 These men and women were all regular guests at Angelo's Academy, where Soubise worked and lived for several years. Cohen, 'Fencing and the Market in Aristocratic Masculinity', p. 103.

11 Angelo's pupils included Frederick Prince of Wales (the future George IV), who befriended his son Henry and frequented his Academy. Henry indicates that Soubise was popular with Angelo's elite pupils: 'Indeed, so far from what my father had feared, that his [Soubise's] colour and humble birth might have made him repulsive to his high-born pupils, on the contrary, these circumstances seemed to excite a greater interest in his favour. His manners were engaging, and his good nature gained him the affection of every one who came to the house.' Angelo, *Reminiscences of Henry Angelo*, 1:449.

12 *Bengal: Past and Present*, 40: 2, 1930, p. 157.

rose to a position of some note as military paymaster general, he was removed from this office for financial irregularities sometime after 1780, and never fully recovered from this disgrace—it was simply too difficult to thrive in Calcutta outside Company employment, especially during the economic downturn caused by war with the French in the 1790s.[13] In 1791 Blechynden remarked of Pawson, 'his debt is desperate.'[14] Pawson's unpropitious finances were only made worse by his daughter's marriage.

Like her father, Catherine Pawson can be counted as a member of Calcutta 'polite society', even though she was not always altogether 'polite'. Upon making her acquaintance in 1793, Blechynden 'thought she was very forward for a young lady', an opinion later confirmed by a mutual acquaintance, who 'had a long talk with me about Miss Pawson over which it is as well to draw the veil'.[15] The implication is that she was either sexually promiscuous or not particularly protective of her reputation. A newspaper poem published by one of her admirers gives a similar impression, as does her penchant for acting, an activity considered out of bounds for gentlewomen.[16] Although 'respectable' European women were held to looser standards in Calcutta than in England, Blechynden still gives the impression that Miss Pawson was skirting the boundary of respectability. Despite all this, Blechynden was still shocked to learn of her relationship with Soubise. As he records in his diary in April 1794, when a friend 'told me that Soubise the Coffree was to marry Miss Pawson. I stared at this but only said that I had seen so much of human nature that I was *surprised* at nothing—and that *this Country is famous for extraordinary marriages.*'[17] Later he repeated this sentiment to the bride's father, insensitively telling him 'I had heard' about the marriage 'but *scarcely knew how to believe it*'.[18]

---

13 H.E. Busteed, *Echoes from Old Calcutta: Being Chiefly Reminiscences of the Days of Warren Hastings* (Calcutta: Thacker, Spink, 1897), 185; BL Add MS 45592, 21–3; BL Add MS 45590, 195–9.
14 BL Add MS 45581, 112.
15 BL Add MS 45588, 148, 152.
16 Busteed, *Echoes from Old Calcutta*, 185. In 1797 (the year before Soubise's death) she 'played with great applause at the Theatre'. BL Add MS 45603, 233.
17 BL Add MS 45589, 295–6.
18 BL Add MS 45590, 196.

Although Blechynden's disbelief may seem warranted given what we know about racism in the eighteenth century, it is actually somewhat difficult to pinpoint *exactly* what made Soubise's marriage so '*extraordinary*'. After all, interracial matches were relatively common in India, especially among men of Blechynden's milieu, who tended to establish long-term relationships with Indian 'bibis', albeit often outside the legal institution of marriage.[19] Of course, in the case of Soubise's marriage, the racialization of gender was reversed from the conventional model. This might be one source of Blechynden's dismay. Yet, as Pawson was quick to point out, his daughter's marriage would not be unheard of in England: Pawson 'inquired if Black people did not marry white women in England &c. &c. I replied in the affirmative and endeavored all in my power to sooth the old man as the matter is past remedy.'[20] Blechynden's assurances were in fact well-founded, since white women did sometimes marry black men in England.[21] However, such matches were mostly confined to servants and the labouring poor. Although Blechynden and his friends struggled with debt in the 1790s, they nonetheless considered themselves genteel. Blechynden kept a garden residence outside the city where he spent his leisure time hunting in the manner of an English squire. Perhaps he reacted so strongly to Catherine Pawson's marriage because he believed it undermined her class identity and social standing. Soubise's reputation for unscrupulousness also must have had some role to play in Blechynden's response. A chronic debtor and all-around rogue, Soubise hardly promised to make an ideal husband.

Despite the objections of her father's friend, Catherine Pawson was devoted to Soubise. Blechynden often dined with the couple, and it is clear from his descriptions that they were passionately in love. It is a measure of Blechynden's racial prejudice that he found affection between a white woman and black man difficult to countenance.

---

19 Durba Ghosh, *Sex and the Family in Colonial India: The Making of Empire* (Cambridge: Cambridge University Press, 2006). Blechynden coupled with 'Bebee[s]' and a Eurasian woman. Robb argues that 'class and social status often mattered more than race' in guiding Blechynden's treatment of women. Robb, *Sex and Sensibility*, p. 213.
20 BL Add MS 45590, 196–7.
21 Gerzina, *Black England*, pp. 21–2.

After his first evening with them he seemed displeased to find 'Mrs. Soubise's Bosom ornamented with a Portrait of Soubise', and compared the couple to 'Othello and Desdemona', a comparison that echoed Hester Thrale's biting remarks about Francis Barber's marriage to a white woman.[22] In both cases the Shakespearean reference seems to imply that the marital unions were libidinally charged. Indeed, Pawson openly speculated as much, saying 'to someone who was expressing his surprise at his daughter marrying Soubise, that he supposed the Coffree *screwed her up tight*—and that was the reason she preferred him—from which we must understand that he tried if matters would fit before marriage!'[23] Ribaldry aside, the couple's devotion withstood the test of time. Years later, when Soubise was physically decrepit and financially bankrupt, Blechynden asked Pawson

> what could induce her to remain with him? it could not be his Colour—or the Company he brought home with him—we all knew he could not pay her in Money and he appears but a sorry subject to pay it in *Love*—'without a leg to stand on',

to which Pawson replied 'it could only be infatuation and so I think we must allow it'.[24] In the eighteenth century 'infatuation' implied a passion that ran counter to reason and thus rendered one 'utterly foolish'.[25] The implication—that a white woman must be of unsound mind to remain with her black husband through difficult times—is clearly racist. But if Catherine Pawson was a fool in love, so was Soubise. One evening 'during dinner Soubise said "I declare my Wife grows handsomer every day"', adding, after more romantic banter, 'I wish I had a couple of you!'[26] Despite Blechynden's repeated expressions of 'pity' for Pawson and his daughter, reading between the lines of his diary one glimpses a portrait of a couple in love.[27]

22 Gerzina, *Black England*, p. 50; BL Add MS 45591, 91.
23 BL Add MS 45591, 83.
24 BL Add MS 45598, 147.
25 'infatuation, n.', *OED Online*.
26 BL Add MS 45591, 109.
27 BL Add MS 45591, 91. Just after learning of the match he wrote: 'I fear [it] has had an effect upon his [Pawson's] Intellects for he appears to me to be Crazy.' BL Add MS 45590, 197. On another occasion he wrote of a dinner at

In the passages quoted above, Blechynden repeatedly uses the word 'Coffree' to describe Soubise. Originally an Arabic term meaning infidel (*kafir*), *coffree* was used by Europeans in India and the Cape Colony to differentiate Africans from themselves, on the one hand, and from East Indians, on the other. The need for such a label attests to the presence of a significant number of Africans in British India. Some were enslaved, brought to India by Europeans or by Muslim slavers operating in East Africa and the Red Sea.[28] Others were free. Sancho's friend Charles Lincoln was a free black musician from St Kitts who travelled to India with Soubise in search of work.[29] The presence of two West Indians on the same ship bound for the East Indies is a reminder of the density of the global networks laid down by British imperialism.

Blechynden's diary reveals that racial prejudice travelled on these global networks as well. In India Soubise faced racism on account of his African ancestry. Blechynden, for example, was wary of doing business with him because of his race. When Soubise and Pawson approached him about building commercial stabling for them in 1794, Blechynden wrote in his diary, 'I do not wish to have anything to do with Soubise.' This was partly due to Soubise's reputation for insolvency, as '*Creditors* might seize it [the stabling] if known to be his property.'[30] But Blechynden's wariness also sprang from racism. Other Europeans in Calcutta apparently shared his prejudices. In 1795 Blechynden explained why he thought Soubise's stabling did not have more subscribers, despite its superiority to other available options:

Soubise's: 'The Company were 2 black Women 1 Black Man and 1 European. I pity Pawson's daughter yet she deserves it.' BL Add MS 45591, 187.

28 Gwyn Campbell, *The Structure of Slavery in Indian Ocean Africa and Asia* (London: Frank Cass, 2004); Joseph E. Harris, *The African Presence in Asia: Consequences of the East African Slave Trade* (Evanston: Northwestern University Press, 1971); Shihan de Silva Jayasuriya and Jean-Pierre Angenot, *Uncovering the History of Africans in Asia* (Leiden: Brill, 2008); Ronald Segal, *Islam's Black Slaves: The Other Black Diaspora* (New York: Farrar, Strauss and Giroux, 2001), pp. 71–6; Andrea Major, *Slavery, Abolition, and Empire in India, 1772–1843* (Liverpool: Liverpool University Press, 2012).

29 Ignatius Sancho, *Letters of the Late Ignatius Sancho, An African*, ed. Vincent Carretta (New York: Penguin Books, 1998), pp. 28, 148, 205.

30 BL Add MS 45591, 109.

I happened to observe that *perhaps* many persons might give the preference to an European to Soubise—he [Pawson] called it illiberal—I therefore asked him if Soubise were not his Son in law—& he had a Horse to Stand at Livery which would he prefer—Soubise's or Fewell's on the Supposition that both places were equally good—he said *Soubise's!* I then said—we will not speak of Horses & Stables—but suppose that a Europe Shop Keeper and a China Bazar man had Goods of equal quality and the same price to dispose of—to which would he give the Preference? he said the *Bazar-man!* on my staring at him he added under certain Conditions—I replied I presumed those Conditions would be that he had married his daughter he said no—I told him ... Providence has wisely implanted this Partiality in us—for we first prefer our Parents—then we add to them our Brothers & Sisters after them our more distant relatives—next our fellow Associates (or *friends* as the world in general call them)—our fellow Parishioners Our Townsmen—Our Country-men—then other Countries in preference and lastly all the world—and when our Philanthropy was so enlarged—we might then term ourselves Citizen of it—but that that man *lied* who pretended that all men were alike to him—he that did not prefer his parents & kindred was a monster-! x^c x^c—after similar commonplace remarks he said—well 'I wish the Stable was full'—As this was adequate to saying I am of your opinion at the bottom I squeezed his hand and said 'And so do I, with all my Heart.'[31]

Many of the sentiments expressed here were commonplace in the eighteenth century, especially in an international city such as Calcutta, where the presence of English, French, Swiss, Italian, Armenian, Persian, East Asian and African people—as well as Indians from all over the subcontinent—fostered both a degree of cosmopolitanism *and* a preference to stick with one's own community when possible. All that said, it is noteworthy that Blechynden excludes Soubise from the circle of his 'Townsmen' or 'Country-men'. Even though Soubise was raised largely in England, and lived completely in the style of a European,

31 BL Add MS 45592, 153–7.

Blechynden classes him alongside 'a China Bazar man'.[32] The only explanation for this snub is anti-black racism.

It may be counted as a measure of Blechynden's racial antipathy that he never really recognized Soubise's marriage as legally legitimate, which it perhaps was not. After hearing rumours that 'Soubise is not married to Miss Pawson' and that 'Pawson knows they are not married or at least strongly suspects', Blechynden investigated the matter.[33] In 1796, when Soubise's fortunes were at a low point, he counselled Pawson to encourage his daughter to leave her husband, telling him 'they are not married as it had been well cleared up to me by Padre Geovans', a colleague of the priest who purportedly married the couple in a private ceremony.[34] But if Blechynden was unable to accept that Miss Pawson was in fact Mrs Soubise—he wrote in his diary 'I cannot think her his Wife'—this was partly owing to his disinclination to believe that a white woman he clearly found attractive would choose a black man for her husband.[35]

Despite all this, Blechynden did count Soubise as a friend for a brief time. During the four months he spent constructing the stabling Blechynden interacted with Soubise daily. This professional rapport soon led to sociable intercourse. At first Blechynden resisted all friendly overtures. The first time Soubise invited him 'to dine with him' Blechynden 'declined the invitation on pretense of Business' since, as he confided in his diary, 'I do not like to be seen there.'[36] But Blechynden's long-standing friendship with Pawson made it difficult to dodge his son-in-law entirely. At times he attributed his consent to dine with the couple to compulsion: '[Soubise] asked me to dine with him—I fought off as long as I could but all would not do, and Pawson said he would go if I would—and insisted so strongly that I was obliged to comply.'[37] On another occasion, 'Soubise and Pawson both ... tiezed

---

32 Blechynden's mixed-race children were educated as Europeans; and their descendants passed as white. Robb, *Sentiment and Self*, pp. 163–79.

33 BL Add MS 45591, 117–18.

34 The fact that a Portuguese pastor married the couple is one indication of their liminal positioning in polite society. BL Add MS 45598, 145–7; Email exchange with Peter Robb, 19 August 2018.

35 BL Add MS 45591, 127–8.

36 BL Add MS 45591, 97.

37 BL Add MS 45591, 186–7.

me so much to dine with them that I was obliged to Comply', a drama which repeated the following day, when 'Soubise called again and made me go home and eat Oysters with him and Mrs. S.'[38] Eventually, Blechynden dropped this pretence.

This occurred as a result of another man's racism. One day in mid-December Blechynden was dining at Soubise's when the cruelty of a mutual friend, Dr Hare, outraged him:

> Berkely's Children were there also and that beast Hare asked Mrs. S— how would she like to have a Child like one of them! Soubise said 'well that's very pretty, it could not be by *me* at least' when Hare was gone Mrs. S expressed her anger at the speech he had made saying that the Child is not pretty and how was she to have so fair a Child by her husband? Invited her for Xmas day but they are engaged.[39]

Blechynden was content to disparage Soubise's race behind his back, but he evidently considered it beyond the pale of politeness to do so in front of his wife. His friendly overture in the form of an invitation for 'Xmas day' was a sympathetic response to Hare's cruelty.

This was the height of Blechynden's friendship with Mr and Mrs Soubise. Although he appeared to genuinely enjoy the couple's company, Soubise's roguery soon soured the relationship. To begin with, Blechynden was outraged by Soubise's rudeness when the latter failed to show up for a hunting outing at Blechynden's garden residence. Blechynden 'waited till 9 for Soubise' to arrive that morning; and when his guest did not appear he was 'so angry about Soubise that I could not shoot [and] killed only 2 snipe one of which was lost'. When he returned home from the field there was still 'no Soubise, no Servants of his or any excuse suspected he had forgot it'. Just then, his company arrived: 'Mrs. Soubise looked most Charmingly—laid blame on Soubise She wanted to come out at Gun fire and dress here. Presently after Pawson came and Soubise Daughter also we had an excellent dinner and were very funny.'[40]

---

38 BL Add MS 45591, 200, 204.
39 BL Add MS 45591, 236–7.
40 BL Add MS 45591, 253–4. The daughter was from a previous relationship.

The breaches of decorum soon mounted. In late December Blechynden 'lent Soubise a clean shift of Linnen' after a morning spent hunting together at his garden home, and that night he also lent Mrs Soubise 'my Boat cloak to keep her warm' on her way back to the city.[41] The next day he was dismayed to find 'no Boat Cloak or Linnen returned'; and even after his 'Peon got back my Boat Cloak— Shirt—Stockings and Neckcloth' he never recovered his 'Banyan Shirt, or Pocket Handkerchief'.[42] Nor did he ever forget the slight. The final straw came when the Soubises stood up Blechynden for the second time. On a mid-January evening Blechynden received a last-minute 'Chit [note] from Pawson—that Soubise said he could not come out tomorrow [to hunt at Blechynden's garden home]—as he feels a return of the Rheumatism which will prevent his taking the pleasures of the Field'. Blechynden was

> much vexed at this rudeness—I have incurred a good deal of expense and they have had a Week's notice ... Ans^d Pawson that there was no necessity for Mr. Soubise's going out Shooting ... and that I wish they had informed me of the *sudden change* some hours former.[43]

Apparently, Blechynden still expected the family to come for dinner, as they had done on the previous occasion when Soubise missed the hunt. But this time they 'did not come—so we 4 sat down to a dinner fit for 10'.[44] This represented an insult (and waste of resources) that Blechynden would never forget or forgive.

There were other, more serious, reasons for their falling out. As Robb argues, 1790s Calcutta was cash-poor: a dearth of liquid assets rendered Europeans and non-Europeans alike dependent on credit.[45]

She may be the Mary Soubise baptized in Calcutta on 20 June 1785. BL N/1/3 f.60.

41 BL Add MS 45591, 276–7.
42 BL Add MS 45591, 278, 281–2.
43 BL Add MS 45592, 46–7.
44 BL Add MS 45592, 47–8.
45 Peter Robb, 'Credit, Work, and Race: Early Colonialism through a Contemporary European View', *Indian Economic & Social History Review*, 37: 1, 2000, pp. 1–25, at pp. 2–3.

Since most credit was procured privately, social networks were bound by elaborate webs of debt.[46] In this context, Robb argues, 'friendship' had to be 'useful': friends 'helped guarantee loans, affected the award of contracts, shaped the conduct of business, and so on'.[47] It was thus to be expected that, as Soubise's friendship with Blechynden progressed, so too did his appeals for credit. The first request came in October 1794, only a few weeks into their business relationship. While at the stabling, Blechynden received a note from Soubise with

> a request for a loan of 200 Rs. *promising faithfully* I should have it before I could possibly want it for the Building (of which he must be a proper judge!) with a P.S. from her [Mrs. Soubise] that *she* will take care it is returned before wanted.[48]

On this occasion Blechynden would have done well to heed Sancho's warning about Soubise: 'I do strictly caution you against lending him money upon any account, for he has every thing but principle; he will never pay you.'[49] Unfortunately, Blechynden 'could not muster up fortitude enough to refuse them ... there is no refusing a Lady's request.'[50] He never saw the 200 rupees again. The next request came in early December:

> Pawson and Soubise called there [at the stabling] the latter told me he had a very particular favor to beg of me—it proved to be joint bail with the former for him—on my appearing to demur he said the Sum was only 300 Rs. and that P— would give me an Indemnification so I was obliged to comply as also to dine with S—.[51]

This represented a more complex financial favour because, instead of loaning money outright, Blechynden was putting himself on the line should one of Soubise's creditors seek to imprison him for debt. Less than two weeks later Soubise requested another favour of this sort:

46 Robb, 'Credit, Work, and Race', p. 4.
47 Robb, *Useful Friendship*, p. xi.
48 BL Add MS 45591, 123.
49 Sancho, *Letters of the Late Ignatius Sancho*, p. 28.
50 BL Add MS 45591, 123.
51 BL Add MS 45591, 217.

'Soubise wrote me to be one of his securities to the Asiatic Society for 5000 Rs.'[52] This time Blechynden summoned the wherewithal to refuse:

> told him I have already taken up the same sum and therefore the Society will not allow me to be security for any body. This is not true but I had no other come off and to agree to this proposal would be only adding to the ruin of myself and Children.[53]

As we shall see, Soubise's 'ruin' was a cause for worry too.

The straw that broke the back of their friendship came when Blechynden learned that Soubise had used his name to obtain credit without his permission. In a society that depended on private credit underwritten by nothing more than personal honour, this was a serious matter. The next time Blechynden saw Pawson, he records, 'I rated him about his making use of a person's name in money matters without his Consent.'[54] Pawson blamed his son-in-law. Apparently, Soubise remained unmoved by the reprimand, since two days later he made another request:

> Soubise said Oh! Oh! you must go to Swinhoe's to sign a Bond—I enquired about what? he told me—answ^d. that he did not speak in the style of one requesting a favor but like one who had waited on an Att. at my request ... adding a Jobation about making use of any man's name in Money matters without his Consent. He laid the blame on Pawson.[55]

Although Blechynden refused to lend Soubise any more money after this incident, he was already too entangled in his financial affairs to withdraw entirely. In addition to the transactions described above, Blechynden had also *de facto* advanced Soubise several thousand rupees for the stabling, which was not entirely paid for upfront.[56] When

---

52 BL Add MS 45591, 241–2.
53 BL Add MS 45591, 243–4.
54 BL Add MS 45591, 265.
55 BL Add MS 45591, 272–3.
56 Blechynden charged 15,000 rupees for the stabling, took 5,000 down and another 5,000 in credit from a mutual associate. BL Add MS 45591, 106–9.

a mutual friend who was also owed money by Soubise threatened to take 'an Assignment out of the Bail Bond' that Blechynden had signed (and never in fact been indemnified for), Blechynden had few options at his disposal. At this juncture, his response bears out Robb's argument that race was an important factor in a credit economy that ran on personal reputation.[57] For Blechynden, the choice was between losing money and losing face by revealing himself to be a creditor of Soubise:

> rather than have my name bandeed about in a Court of Justice with Soubise's or be looked upon as his friend or Patron, I would much rather pay the money at once and (as my Circumstances are very narrow indeed) arrest Soubise instantly for the money and the 200 he owes me already—but as this would naturally make a difference between Pawson and myself which I wished to avoid.[58]

In the end, Blechynden's regard for Pawson prevented him from sending Soubise to prison for debt, but his days of friendly sociability with the latter were over. Needless to say, he never received repayment for any of the money Soubise owed him.

After their friendship cooled in 1795 Soubise no longer featured prominently in Blechynden's diary. The final three years of Soubise's life were a downward spiral. The stabling proved unprofitable and by 1795 he was already in search of new revenue streams. To Blechynden's dismay, Pawson considered purchasing the 'old Harmonic' (a multi-function tavern) to set Soubise up as an auctioneer. Blechynden exhorted his friend to give up the scheme, recording in his diary a recent conversation with another mutual friend of Pawson's, who was also dismayed: 'how then could Soubise prosper without money—without Interest—without friends—and without a particle of public confidence—and concluded by observing that had he studied how to ruin a man of fortune he could not have devised a better mode than setting him an Auctioneer'. Indeed, when Soubise had tried a horse auction in 1794 it was an unambiguous flop. Despite this 'glaring fact',

---

57 Robb, 'Credit, Work, and Race'.
58 BL Add MS 45592, 50–3.

Blechynden feared 'I talked to the Wind—all his Geese are Swans', as 'he is Bent upon his Scheme and I may add his *ruin* and there is no remedy'.[59] The doomed 'Scheme' was given up in favour of other, equally ill-conceived, ventures. Fine horses were luxury commodities in India and, given Soubise's history, it is only natural that he was drawn to the horse trade.[60] But, as he learned, horses were also risky business. In August 1796 he spent 5,000 rupees of Pawson's borrowed money on horses from the famed stables of Saadat Ali Khan (the soon-to-be Nawab of Awadh), ultimately losing 3,500 rupees in the venture.[61] In the same month he was imprisoned for shortchanging a customer on the sale of a horse in another complicated credit transaction.[62] Shortly thereafter Pawson tried to interest Blechynden in another 'Scheme' for a 'lottery'; it never got off the ground.[63] In 1793 Blechynden had worried that Soubise would eventually 'drain every Rupee from the old Man [Pawson]'.[64] Now his prediction was coming true.

In 1795 Soubise took on a new business partner at the stables: the Chevalier de l'Etang, Virginia Woolf's great-great-grandfather and a rumoured lover of Marie Antoinette, who was waiting out the French Revolution in India.[65] Unfortunately, Soubise's new partner didn't hesitate to have him imprisoned for his debts. Blechynden was

59 BL Add MS 45594, 157–61.

60 Jos Gommans, 'The Horse Trade in Eighteenth-Century South Asia', *Journal of the Economic and Social History of the Orient*, 37: 3, 1994, pp. 228–50; Monica Meadows, 'The Horse: Conspicuous Consumption of Embodied Masculinity in South Asia, 1600–1850', dissertation, University of Washington Department of History, 2013.

61 BL Add MS 45598, 145–7. The stables of the Awadhi court were some of the largest and best on the Indian subcontinent. In 1813–14 Soubise's one-time business partner, the Chevalier de l'Etang, was employed by the Nawab. Gommans, 'The Horse Trade in Eighteenth-Century South Asia', p. 245; BL IOR/F/4/508/12262.

62 BL Add MS 45594, 120–1.

63 BL Add MS 45594, 145.

64 BL Add MS 45591, 178. In 1795 another mutual friend declared himself 'heartily wearied with Pawson's being the Dupe of Soubise and that they are troubled with little frivolous Bills of 3 and 4 Rupees to pay on his account'. BL Add MS 45593, 49.

65 See n. 61 above. BL Add MS 45597, 54–5; Hermione Lee, *Virginia Woolf* (New York: Alfred K. Knopf, 1997), p. 88.

disgusted by the inhumanity of 'Deletang' (as he called him), and, just as he had done when faced with Hare's cruelty, he sided with Soubise. When de l'Etang resisted sending Soubise his half of the stables' profits in prison, Blechynden exclaimed 'how is the poor Devil to live! a Jail is misery enough without adding Starvation to it!'[66] A few days later he refused to help him correct a letter to Soubise, writing

> I am sick of this trouble and more so at the roughness of his treatment of that unfortunate man. That Soubise is an extravagant fellow is very certain—but Deletang should remember that he has *persuaded* him already—and need not overwhelm him with rough usage whilst in duranee [jail].[67]

Soubise's health took a turn for the worse around this time. In 1796 he was so crippled by rheumatism that he could not walk up stairs.[68] The next year, he was 'a perfect *Caricatura*—his legs and thighs entirely wasted so that another leg might be slipped behind his into the Boot'.[69] On all fronts, he was in decline.

Then, suddenly, his luck changed. In May 1798 a new business partner, 'Nilmoney Holdar' (Nilmani Haldar), a wealthy Indian entrepreneur and developer, began building a Riding House for him.[70] The venture was, however, tragically short-lived. On 25 August Soubise was riding (and presumably training) 'a Gray Arab belonging to Joseph Thomas Brown' when 'the Horse stumbled and fell with him'.[71] Blechynden learned of the accident almost immediately:

> Mr. Boileau passed in his Buggy and Stopped—he called Carver and told him that Soubise was just thrown from a Horse and lay in the Road with his Skull fractured—I immediately mounted my Horse and rode to the place—but found he was already

66 BL Add MS 45600, 220–1.
67 BL Add MS 45600, 227–8.
68 BL Add MS 45595, 153.
69 BL Add MS 45603, 24.
70 BL Add MS 45603, 167. Blechynden served as Haldar's agent for a time; and Haldar was 'a banian [trading broker] to Sir Henry Russell, the judge'. Robb, *Useful Friendship*, pp. 42, 160.
71 BL Add Ms 45606, 247.

taken into the Manége [*sic*], thither I went and found him in the Gallery laying on a Mat—the rolled up part of which served as a pillow he perspired profusely—his head was slightly cut behind—but his Skull did not feel fractured—he opened his eyes now and then—and once turned him-self with wonderful facility from his left to his right side, which induced Deletang who was standing near him to say he was coming to—and that his hurt was nothing—but as I saw blood ooze out of his right ear, I think the blow is not only very dangerous but most probably *mortal*— as it shews some of the Vessels of the Brain are ruptured and till this blood lodging on it is removed either by Trepanning or otherwise he certainly will not come to himself.[72]

Blechynden demanded Soubise's skull be trepanned, but to no avail. Unfortunately, his prognosis proved correct: 'Pawson and Mrs. Soubise each went to the Hospital and remained with him till he died' the next day from hemorrhaging in his brain.[73] He was forty-four years old. In the aftermath of his death, Soubise's father-in-law and widow were left in straightened circumstances. They tried to raise money through a horse auction, but were forced to move into barrack housing together.[74]

Blechynden's final reflections are generous and provide a fitting end to Soubise's story:

I rode home—very melancholy for I strongly suspect that this blow is fatal and though Master Soubise is a mauvais sujet—he is clever in his profession—and I think a Carreer [*sic*] was at length opened to him of getting out of his difficulties in short we can 'better spare a better man'.[75]

72 BL Add Ms 45606, 244–5.
73 BL Add Ms 45606, 301.
74 BL Add Ms 45606, 313–14, 234.
75 BL Add Ms 45606, 248.

CHAPTER THIRTEEN

The Gravity of Mary Prince's *History*

Sue Thomas

In February 1831 *The History of Mary Prince, a West Indian Slave, Related by Herself. With a Supplement by the Editor. To Which Is Added the Narrative of Asa-asa, a Captured African*, was published by Thomas Pringle, the secretary of the Anti-Slavery Society, on his own undertaking. A new parliamentary session during which the unconditional abolition of slavery was scheduled to be debated was about to open. Prince and Asa-Asa were working as servants in the homes of Pringle and George Stephen respectively.[1] Stephen, who in 1831, with Joseph Sturge, founded the Agency Committee of the Anti-Slavery Society to press for unconditional abolition, outlines the 'anti-slavery creed' of the early 1830s: 'to uphold slavery was a crime before God, and … every Christian was called upon to aid its suppression'.[2] 'I will say the truth to English people who may read this history', Prince affirms in the peroration of her narrative. 'All slaves want to be free— to be free is very sweet. … I have been a slave myself—I know what slaves feel—I can tell by myself what other slaves feel, and by what they have told me.' Her experience of slavery is both singular and representative, and she urges 'English people' 'to never leave off to pray God, and call loud to the great King of England, till all the blacks be

---

1 On Asa-asa's life see Sue Thomas, 'New Light on Louis Asa-Asa and the Publication of His Slave Narrative', *Notes and Queries*, 64: 4, 2017, pp. 604–7.
2 Sir George Stephen, *A Memoir of the Late James Stephen* (Melbourne, 1875), p. 69.

given free, and slavery done up for evermore'.[3] Prince's slave narrative, edited by Pringle, ran to three editions within the year; a planned fourth edition was abandoned after Prince's owner in Antigua, John Adams Wood Jr, sued Pringle for libel in early 1832.[4] It was hailed in 1831 as an exposé of 'the effects of certain species of taskwork, and the mode of tasking, on human health, happiness, and longevity', as telling at the scale of a life as the pioneering work of Charles Turner Thackrah on occupational health in Leeds, and being 'as absorbingly interesting in its way as Caleb Williams'.[5]

Contemporary editions of *The History of Mary Prince*, appearing from 1987 onwards, have brought Prince's narrative to renewed historical attention and to literary critical consideration. It has also inspired contemporary creative writers, artists and musicians, and scenes from Prince's text have been curated as part of new British museum exhibitions commemorating slavery.[6] In 2012 Prince, who was born in Bermuda in 1787 or 1788, was declared a Bermuda National Hero. Fred D'Aguiar writes that in the 1830s

> Britain needs Mary Prince because she represents its flickering hope to transform itself into a civilised nation founded on Christian values. ... She returns an emotional intelligence to the centre of a legislative malaise.
>
> Mary Prince's narrative retains that moral charge ... It continues to be crucial to Old and New World societies because

3 Mary Prince, *The History of Mary Prince, a West Indian Slave*, ed. Sara Salih (London: Penguin, 2004), p. 38.

4 The scale of each of the three editions is not known.

5 'Monthly Literary Gazette', *The Englishman's Magazine*, April 1831, p. 127. Thackrah's *The Effects of the Principal Arts, Trades, and Professions, and of the Civic States, and Habits of Living, on Health and Longevity: With a Particular Reference to the Trades and Manufactures of Leeds, and Suggestions for the Removal of Many of the Agents which Produce Disease, and Shorten the Duration of Life* was reviewed in the same article. Caleb Williams is the protagonist of William Godwin's *Things as They Are; or, The Adventures of Caleb Williams* (1794).

6 The scene of Prince's mother preparing her children for sale and the auction have been recorded as part of exhibitions at the British Empire and Commonwealth Museum for the 2007 bicentenary of the British abolition of its slave trade and the International Slavery Museum in Liverpool.

of its moral imperative: slavery then and how to commemorate it now form a twin axis of moral gravity.[7]

The narrative and its republication anticipate regeneration of what David Scott terms '*counter*-memory: the moral idiom and semiotic registers of remembering against the grain of the history of New World black deracination, subjection and exclusion'.[8] In her Preface to the 1987 Pandora edition Ziggi Alexander hails the recovery of *The History of Mary Prince* as heightening 'awareness' of and legitimizing 'the significance of black British history', and validating both its 'black female perspective' and its reclamation for the 'black community'.[9] She anticipates that the valorization of Prince's agency might supplement 'the pervasive notion of European benevolence and Christian sacrifice in the interests of African liberation',[10] what Barnor Hesse terms '*abolitionist memory*', 'the heroic consecration of white liberators ... as defining the cognitive limit on the political memory of slavery'.[11]

Since the late 1990s much literary critical energy has focused on the mediation of Prince's voice at the 'crowded' 1831 'writing scene'.[12] The pamphlet is 'not a straightforward autobiography, but a collection of texts', Sara Salih reminds readers. 'Prince's story is mediated to us via the pen of Susanna Strickland', later Moodie, the amanuensis, 'a friend of Thomas Pringle's, and the text itself is bolstered by an editorial supplement and appendices, an apparatus almost equal to the narrative in length that is designed to validate Prince's testimony'.[13] By 2000, *The History of Mary Prince* was, Salih notes, 'a staple component of

---

7 Fred D'Aguiar, 'Mary Prince', http://www.penguin.co.uk/shared/WebDisplay/ 1,,49152_1_0,00.html?cs=10 (accessed 26 November 2003).

8 David Scott, 'Introduction: On the Archaeologies of Black Memory', *Anthurium: A Caribbean Studies Journal*, 6: 1, 2008, para. 1.

9 Ziggy Alexander, 'Preface', in Moira Ferguson (ed.), *The History of Mary Prince* (London: Pandora, 1987), pp. xiii, xii.

10 Alexander, 'Preface', p. x.

11 Barnor Hesse, 'Forgotten Like a Bad Dream: Atlantic Slavery and the Ethics of Postcolonial Memory', in David Theo Goldberg and Ato Quayson (eds), *Relocating Postcolonialism* (Oxford: Blackwell, 2002), p. 155.

12 Gillian Whitlock, *The Intimate Empire: Reading Women's Autobiography* (London: Cassell, 2000), p. 13.

13 Sara Salih, 'Introduction', in Prince, *History*, p. xiii.

anthologies of early black writing, slave narratives, black Atlantic writing, and black women's writing'.[14] At stake in studies of the mediation of 'slave voice' in *The History of Mary Prince* is the reading of authorial identity that grounds such canon-formation. A.M. Rauwerda, for instance, states:

> there is reason to believe that neither the narrating voice nor Prince's narrative are actually hers, and that the agency ascribed to her in this narrative may be more representative of the agendas of external creators of the text than of Prince herself.[15]

Such studies bring to the fore 'constellations and representations of power'[16] that constitute 'the conditions that attend the production of the subaltern's speech'.[17] In this essay I turn, rather, to more recent historical research on the archives within which *The History of Mary Prince* might be located and to some salient creative engagements with the text to consider how they do and might qualify and reshape the '*institution of memory* and an *idiom of remembering*'[18] around the text. The projects reframe Prince's life, her narrative and its reception, and have the capacity to deepen and complicate our understandings of them.

14 Sara Salih, '*The History of Mary Prince*, the Black Subject, and the Black Canon', in Brycchan Carey, Markman Ellis and Sara Salih (eds), *Discourses of Slavery and Abolition: Britain and Its Colonies, 1760–1838* (Basingstoke: Palgrave Macmillan and the Institute of English Studies, University of London, 2004), p. 126.

15 A.M. Rauwerda, 'Naming, Agency, and a "Tissue of Falsehoods" in *The History of Mary Prince*', *Victorian Literature and Culture*, 29: 2, 2001, p. 397.

16 Nicole N. Aljoe, 'Testimonies of the Enslaved in Caribbean Literary History', in Nicole N. Aljoe, Brycchan Carey and Thomas W. Krise (eds), *Literary Histories of the Early Anglophone Caribbean: Islands in the Stream* (New York: Palgrave Macmillan, 2018), p. 110.

17 Abdul JanMohamed, 'Between Speaking and Dying: Some Imperatives in the Emergence of the Subaltern in the Context of U.S. Slavery', in Rosalind Morris (ed.), *Can the Subaltern Speak? Reflections on the History of an Idea* (New York: Columbia University Press, 2009), p. 140.

18 Scott, 'Introduction', para. 3.

238

Hauntings

Literary historical, historical and creative scholarship on Prince's *History* has been haunted by the editing and framing of what was 'taken down from Mary's lips',[19] and the questions of authenticity around agency and represented experience, the questions of presence and absence, they raise. Salih's recommendation that scholars research salient 'documents that did *not* originally appear' in *The History of Mary Prince*[20] is taken up, as my first instance, in Maddison-MacFadyen's archival methodology in 'Reclaiming Histories of Enslavement in the Maritime Atlantic and a Curriculum: *The History of Mary Prince*':[21]

> [l]ocating and investigating documents pertaining to her five named owners, to their businesses and vessels, to those of their family members and other named individuals, plus legal documents pertaining to court cases and rulings, letters, *Slave Registers of Former British Overseas Territories*, minutes from abolitionists' meetings and remnants of human-built structures associated with Prince's enslavement.

Her project on Prince, as published to date, is largely organized around 'resolving the issues of exaggeration and/or fabrication' in Prince's narrative raised by the court decision in the libel case Wood v. Pringle, heard in London in March 1833,[22] though she has not unpacked the nuanced detail of the suit or the finding, or weighed the *Times* report of the court proceedings against the other available account in the *Christian Advocate*, topics to which I turn later in this essay. Haunted by the 'transformative' reach of Prince's narrative in her experience and understanding of place,[23] Maddison-MacFadyen extends Moira Ferguson's research into Prince's life in Bermuda and follows Prince's

19 Thomas Pringle, 'Preface', in Prince, *History*, p. 3.
20 Salih, '*The History of Mary Prince*', p. 124.
21 PhD, Memorial University of Newfoundland, 2017.
22 Margôt Maddison-MacFadyen, 'Mary Prince, Grand Turk, and Antigua', *Slavery & Abolition*, 34: 4, 2013, p. 655.
23 Margôt Maddison-McFadyen, 'This White Woman Has Journeyed Far: Serendipity, Counter-Stories, Hauntings, and Ekphrasis as a Type of Poetic Inquiry', *Morning Watch: Educational and Social Analysis*, 40: 1–2, 2012, p. 1.

footsteps in Grand Turk Island, Antigua and England. Her research shows that Prince was traded among an extended family network with business interests straddling Bermuda, Grand Turk Island and Antigua: Charles Myners; Captain and Sarah Williams; Captain John and Mary Spencer Ingham (the I—s, first identified by Ferguson);[24] Robert Darrell (Mr D—, identified by Maddison-MacFadyen);[25] and John and Margaret Wood.

Maddison-MacFadyen works to reframe archival materials of plantation slavery. Simon Gikandi notes that

> slave masters turned to writing as a will to power; record keeping, and the archiving gesture, was a form of violent control; the archive was an attestation to the authority of natural history, the key to the ideology of white power. Here, in the archive, the African could be reduced to the world of nature and the prehuman.[26]

Prince vehemently rejects such reduction of bondspeople to the level of animals in the *History*, to which there is a link on Maddison-MacFadyen's Mary Prince website.[27] Maddison-MacFadyen has curated images of many historical records and archival and recent photographs of places associated with Prince's owners on her website, which is pitched to general readers and viewers. Her children's story *Mary: A Story of Young Mary Prince* (2017) also includes images. The framing of contemporary photographs from Bermuda and Grand Turk Island there and on the website, in particular, acts as "'guerilla memorialisation'" of Prince, showing how 'national stor[ies]' and material wealth are underpinned or haunted by foundational histories of human enslavement and cruel working conditions.[28]

24 Moira Ferguson, 'Introduction', *The History of Mary Prince: A West Indian Slave. Related by Herself*, rev. edn (Ann Arbor: University of Michigan Press, 1997).
25 Margôt Maddison-MacFadyen, 'Toiling in the Salt Ponds', *Times of the Islands*, Fall 2008 (accessed 23 July 2017).
26 Simon Gikandi, 'Rethinking the Archive of Enslavement', *Early American Literature*, 50: 1, 2015, p. 92.
27 https://www.maryprince.org.
28 Rice, *Creating Memorials, Building Identities*, p. 15.

Maddison-MacFadyen's *Mary* draws into sharp focus issues around the treatment of 'the emotional and political fabric'[29] of Prince's narrative, issues germane, too, to other creative engagements with it. Drawing on *The History of Mary Prince*, her research and her experience as a schoolteacher, Maddison-MacFadyen imagines from a third-person point of view Prince's early life in Bermuda. In 'translat[ing]' Prince's account of childhood 'into the idioms and interests of a different epoch' and of the intended child readership,[30] yet 'hop[ing] to have kept the gravity of Mary's situation',[31] she both introduces new narrative layers—her character's sensibility in relation to the natural world, play with dolls with her owner's daughter Betsey and the shared texture of their everyday lives, for instance—and censors 'many of the reprehensible actions' of the Inghams, most notably their part in the agonizing death of bondswoman Hetty, whom Prince calls 'Aunt'.[32] The additions invite reader identification with the character of Mary through sentimentalization of Prince's account of the 'home and family life … subsequently broken through her sale and that of her sisters' that Joan Anim-Addo presciently identifies as part of Prince's 'personalisation project',[33] a political counter-discourse to the reduction of bondspeople 'to the world of nature and the prehuman'. The Inghams bought Mary at the slave sale that separated her from her grieving mother and siblings. The pregnant Hetty was whipped viciously after a cow she tied to a stake 'got loose'. She suffered a difficult miscarriage and was then subjected to further floggings by the Inghams. Of her witness of Hetty's death, Prince records: 'it filled me with horror. I could not bear to think about it; yet it was always present to my mind for many a day.'[34] '[A]nti-racist campaigner' Mark Nash, a Bermudan descendent of the Inghams, comments: 'I didn't know how to contemplate that someone in my family history could beat someone to death with impunity, as described in Mary's book … I felt guilt and shame. Took a

29 Hesse, 'Forgotten Like a Bad Dream', p. 146.
30 Whitlock, *The Intimate Empire*, p. 29.
31 Margôt Maddison-MacFadyen, *Mary: A Story of Young Mary Prince* (n.p.: Sisters Publishing, 2017), p. 8.
32 Prince, *History*, p. 15.
33 Joan Anim-Addo, *Touching the Body: History, Language and African-Caribbean Women's Writing* (London: Mango, 2007), p. 120.
34 Prince, *History*, pp. 15–16.

while to accept.' '[T]o honour a heroine in the struggle for the abolition of slavery', Nash in 2011 contributed towards the cost of restoring the blue plaque for Prince in London originally unveiled in 2007.[35] As a reader of Prince's *History*, Nash recognizes the moral gravity of Prince's interpellation of slaveowners as 'shame'.[36] In her critical study *Touching the Body*, Joan Anim-Addo highlights in relation to Hetty the importance of '[s]ubstitute kinship, a feature of resistance adopted in slavery'.[37] In *Haunted by History: Poetry* she eulogizes Hetty in 'Aunt Hetty—Other Mother', written in the first-person voice of Prince.[38] Anim-Addo deepens understanding of Prince and Hetty's relationship and Prince's trauma over her death by drawing out the ways in which Hetty fostered Prince after her separation from her mother, fulfilling the customary role of African diasporic other-mother through an 'ethic of care so critical to the survival and well-being' of the 'enslaved community'.[39]

In the video and sound installation *Black Mary; or Molly, 'Princess of Wales'* (2016), an experimental opera, Joscelyn Gardner represents the character Mary's place within landscape conventions and uses a doll in more sophisticated ways than Maddison-MacFadyen for an adult audience. The installation is one of a number of projects by Gardner that aim to restore the ghostly 'voices/images/traces of the women' marginalized in 'patriarchal or colonial versions of history', 'address[ing] the repression and disassociation that operate in relation to the subject of slavery and white culpability'.[40] The composer and

35 Hugh Muir, 'Hideously diverse Britain: His ancestor was a slaver. Now he's saying sorry', *Guardian*, 13 July 2011, https:www.theguardian.com/uk/2011/jul/12/hideously-diverse-britain. The blue plaque was an initiative of the Nubian Jak Community Trust.
36 Prince, *History*, pp. 24, 37.
37 Anim-Addo, *Touching the Body*, p. 122.
38 Joan Anim-Addo, *Haunted by History: Poetry* (London: Mango, 1998), p. 35.
39 Stanlie M. James, 'Mothering: A Possible Black Link to Social Transformation?' in Stanley M. James and Abena P.A. Busia (eds), *Theorizing Black Feminisms: The Visionary Pragmatism of Black Women* (London: Routledge, 1993), pp. 47–8.
40 Joscelyn Gardner, 'Artist Statement', in National Gallery of Jamaica, *We Have Met Before: Graham Fagen, Joscelyn Gardner, Leasho Johnson and Ingrid Pollard* (Kingston, Jamaica: National Gallery of Jamaica, 2017), p. 22.

musical director Stefan Walcott comments that in *Black Mary* he worked to authenticate the accompaniment

> around the perfect 5th and tri-tone intervals. The 5th suggests openness while the tri-tone is the most important interval of the Blues. I was therefore sonically representing the hope of Mary as well as the constant sadness and strength of the blues.[41]

The title of the installation draws together three names by which Prince was known.[42] Gardner has uploaded on her artist website the scene in which her character Mary describes through voiceover and song being owned by the Inghams and witnessing the treatment of Hetty.[43] Mary carries a black doll and acts out the whipping of Hetty on it, reliving the haunting viscerality of her witness. Gardner's set invokes period toy theatre conventions to highlight the performative dimensions of Prince's narrative in its day and in our contemporary moment, and to draw out the constructedness of our awareness of history and the ways in which approaches to genre and authenticity shape the reception of the literary and creative artefact. In the installation the character Mary's telling of her experiences is interrupted by historical figures from the 1830s and contemporary voices 'confirm[ing] or challeng[ing]' her narrative. Gardner explains: 'The conflicting viewpoints serve to problematize the legacy of slavery in Bermuda (and the wider region) and point to the construction of both (white and black) Creole identity as Other.'[44]

The portraits of a slaveowning family in a stylized landscape are based on a '1760 "conversation piece" painting'. The vegetation

---

41 Quoted in Bermuda National Gallery, *Joscelyn Gardner Staging Mary Prince: In Her Own Words* (Hamilton, Bermuda: Bermuda National Gallery, 2016), p. [4].

42 Strickland calls her 'black Mary'; the Woods call her 'Molly'; and the Anglican minister Rev. James Curtin derisorily inscribes her spelling book 'Mary, Princess of Wales'. Susanna Moodie, letter to James Bird, 9 April 1831, Susanna Moodie Collection, National Archives of Canada, http://www.collections canada.gc.ca/moodie-traill/027013–119.01-f.php?rec_id_nbr=3&anchor =027013–3000-f.html (accessed 21 June 2010); Prince, *History*, pp. 43, 29.

43 joscelyngardner.org (accessed 9 August 2018).

44 Bermuda National Gallery, *Joscelyn Gardner*, p. [3].

camouflages instruments of torture. The adult slaveowners hold whips on their laps.[45] The theatre curtain and the sky on the horizon are printed with text from *The History of Mary Prince*; the foliage of the cedar trees is composed of strips of text from the *History*, visually echoing William Blake's representation of the tattered clothing that covers the loins of a whipped bondswoman whose hands are tied to a tree branch in *Flagellation of a Female Samboe Slave* (1796), an illustration for John Gabriel Stedman's *Narrative, of Five Year's Expedition, Against the Revolted Slave of Suriname*. The allusion evokes the lacerated bodies of bondspeople that are a foundation of Prince's determination to tell her story for publication and suggests that Prince's text covers the violations of her sexual modesty by her owners.

Salt and Sugar

Prince's account of her gruesome working conditions on Grand Turk Island has recently drawn renewed attention to the lucrative salt industry there and the extensive business and trade links between Bermuda and Grand Turk Island; Michele Speitz has argued, indeed, that salt, as mineral and tears, 'is the linguistic linchpin of Prince's narrative'.[46] In around 1802, Captain Ingham despatched Prince to Grand Turk Island—'Cruel, horrible place!' she insists—where a new owner Robert Darrell (1755–1821), living there with his wife and children, put her to work raking salt in the salt ponds. There was a residency requirement for slaveowners;[47] in 1767 local regulation limited the number of slaves who could be assigned work in the 'Pans or Ponds' to six for each resident 'freeholder'.[48] In around 1812

---

45 Bermuda National Gallery, *Joscelyn Gardner*, pp. [2–3].

46 Michele Speitz, 'Blood Sugar and Salt Licks: Corroding Bodies and Preserving Nations in *The History of Mary Prince, a West Indian Slave, Related by Herself*', in Paul Youngquist and Frances Botkin (eds), *Circulations: Romanticism and the Black Atlantic: A Romantic Circles Praxis Volume*, October 2011, para. 3, http://www.romantic-circles.org/praxis/circulations/HTML/praxis.2011.speitz.html (accessed 17 December 2019).

47 Cynthia M. Kennedy, 'The Other White Gold: Salt, Slaves, the Turks and Caicos Islands, and British Colonialism', *Historian*, 69: 2, 2007, p. 225.

48 Kennedy, 'The Other White Gold', pp. 221, 225.

Robert Darrell handed over his business interests on Grand Turk to his son Richard (1790–1853)—'Master Dickey', as Prince calls him.[49] At that time Robert Darrell, family members and Prince returned to Bermuda. In 2007 historian Cynthia M. Kennedy draws extensively on Prince as a documenter of the excruciating labour regime in the salt ponds. Prince comments that 'Mr D— … received a certain sum for every slave that worked upon his premises, whether they were young or old.'[50] Kennedy's research would suggest that Prince is referring to 'a form of self-government' in the Turks Islands instituted in 1744

> known as the Head Rights System … All British subjects present … on 10 February each year were allotted a share of the salt ponds for that season. Slave owners received their slaves' shares. Parents received portions of a share for their children, depending on the height of each child. One third of the ponds was reserved as a contribution to public revenue.[51]

Prince's narrative, Speitz demonstrates, 'records how lethal amounts of salt seep through the skin, forging a visceral, literal, and grotesque union between salt, the commodified substance, and the slave, the commodified worker'.[52] In the 1780s and 1790s, in particular, anti-slavery activism focused on a British consumer boycott of sugar produced by slave labour. The campaign invoked a '"blood sugar" topos' which equated the luxury use of sugar as a sweetener with consumption of 'the blood of slaves'.[53] Salt, though, was a food and food preservation staple and the industry's demand for forced labour was small by comparison with the Caribbean sugar industry.

49 Maddison-MacFadyen, 'Mary Prince, Grand Turk and Antigua', p. 656.
50 Prince, *History*, p. 19.
51 Kennedy, 'The Other White Gold', p. 221.
52 Speitz, 'Blood Sugar and Salt Licks', para. 3.
53 Timothy Morton, 'Blood Sugar', in Tim Fulford and Peter J. Kitson (eds) *Romanticism and Colonialism: Writing and Empire, 1780–1830* (Cambridge: Cambridge University Press, 1998), pp. 87–8.

Reading Antiguan Christianity

Living in St John's, Antigua as a slave of the Woods, Prince converted to Moravianism in around 1822. While she was a servant of the Pringles, Margaret Pringle instructed her in religion and literacy, and her religious instructors were their neighbour Rev. Young and Rev. Mortimer, an Anglican. In July 1832 Prince applied to join the Fetter Lane Moravian congregation in London. This was a month after the Pringles started paying her a weekly allowance of 10 to 12s a week while she was 'out of place', probably as a result of deteriorating health.[54] Christianity, Roxann Wheeler points out, has become 'a dense transfer point—a repository of qualities available for diversion into British national character and whiteness'.[55] The handling of Prince's conversion in critical appreciations of the *History* illustrates such too-easy diversion and blindness to the cultural syncretism of the practice of evangelical religion and community in the Caribbean. Denominational differences among Christians and among evangelical faiths are collapsed. Jenny Sharpe, for instance, argues that for 'Victorian' readers in 1831 [*sic*], 'slave testimony ... was obliged to privilege the Christianized, morally upright, and obedient worker over the Africanized, ungovernable, and troublesome slave. Its teleological narrative necessarily placed the slave on a path toward Christianity and freedom.' She asks, 'How does the moral agency favored by British abolitionists act in the place of other kinds of practices?'[56] Ferguson inaccurately identifies Pringle and Strickland as 'Methodists'.[57] Pringle was Presbyterian, and by 1831 Strickland, brought up Anglican, had converted to Congregationalism. 'Victorian' and 'Methodist' here are stereotypes of the sexual prude.[58]

54 *Times* (London), 1 March 1833, p. 6; *Christian Advocate*, 4 March 1833, pp. 68–9.
55 Roxann Wheeler, *The Complexion of Race: Categories of Difference in Eighteenth-century British Culture* (Philadelphia: University of Pennsylvania Press, 2000), p. 15.
56 Jenny Sharpe, *Ghosts of Slavery: A Literary Archaeology of Black Women's Lives* (Minneapolis: University of Minnesota Press, 2003), p. xxiv.
57 Ferguson, 'Introduction', in Prince, *The History of Mary Prince, a West Indian Slave, Related by Herself*, p. 11.
58 On their broader practices in relation to slave testimony see Sue Thomas,

246

Antigua was the site of highly successful Methodist and Moravian missions. In 1823, of an enslaved population of 31,064, reportedly 18,800 were Christianized, 550 attending Anglican services, 6,650 attending Wesleyan Methodist services and 11,680 attending Moravian (United Brethren) services.[59] The Methodist community was overwhelmingly non-white (99.4 per cent in 1804);[60] the Moravians did not proselytize in the white community. The Moravian congregation in St John's reportedly comprised 5,000 enslaved people and 1,500 free black and coloured members.[61] Sylvia R. Frey and Betty Wood, who have researched the evangelical revival among African diasporic peoples in the American south and the West Indies in the eighteenth and early nineteenth centuries, attribute its reach and success to the creolization of practices of worship and practices of community 'wherein African peoples could develop a sense of belonging and assert a cultural presence in the larger society'.[62] In the Caribbean, Moravian community was organized around 'Negro-assistants' (called godfathers and godmothers), vital to 'a lattice of spiritual mentors and fictive kin who helped incorporate Africans into the evangelical family', 'rebuild[ing] kin connections' for 'people whose intricate tendrils of kinship had been ripped apart by the slave trade'.[63] The telling of lives in various genres, written and oral, was crucial to the formation of Moravian and Methodist communities. Speaking at meetings and love

Telling West Indian Lives: Life Narrative and the Reform of Plantation Slavery Cultures 1804–1834 (New York: Palgrave Macmillan, 2014), pp. 139–52.

59 Sir Benjamin d'Urban, letter to Earl Bathurst, 12 March 1824, The National Archives (TNA), CO 7/10/183.

60 The calculation is based on local figures quoted in Thomas Coke, *A History of the West Indies, Containing the Natural, Civil and Ecclesiastical History of Each Island*, 3 vols (Liverpool: Nuttall, Fisher, and Dixon, 1808–11), vol. 2, p. 456.

61 D'Urban, letter to Earl Bathurst. The calculation of 1,500 free coloured and black congregation members is based on comparison with a figure given by G. Oliver Maynard, *A History of the Moravian Church, Eastern West Indies Province* (n.p.: n.p., 1968), p. 41.

62 Sylvia R. Frey and Betty Wood, *Come Shouting to Zion; African American Protestantism in the American South and British Caribbean to 1830* (Chapel Hill: University of North Carolina Press, 1998), p. 118.

63 Jon Sensbach, *Rebecca's Revival: Creating Black Christianity in the Atlantic World* (Cambridge, MA: Harvard University Press, 2005), p. 93.

feasts (communal thanksgivings), participation in 'speakings' (one-on-one counsellings with spiritual advisers) and the *Lebenslauf* or life course were the Moravian genres of life narrative, genres with which Strickland and Pringle were not familiar. As I have shown in *Telling West Indian Lives: Life Narrative and the Reform of Plantation Slavery Cultures, 1804–1834*, Prince alludes to Moravian doctrine and hymns in the account of her conversion in her *History* and follows some of the standard protocols of the *Lebenslauf. Lebensläufe* would be read at Moravian funerals and meetings; they were part of her Moravian soundscape. There was a global distribution network for exemplary *Lebensläufe*.[64]

Prince's *History*, though, does not display the quietism expected of devout Moravians. Quietism, which has a distinctive vocabulary, is a 'whole ethos of self-yielding, self-abasing resignation to the will of God and the will of the community'.[65] For Moravians enslavement could be part of God's dispensation; in 1819 the Antiguan mission owned nine slaves.[66] Such resignation, Prince acknowledges, is 'a hard and heavy task'.[67] She is adamant in her peroration that 'the condition of the slave is not one of grace, but of being "disgraced and thought no more of than beasts" by shameless slaveowners'.[68] Prince's application to join the Fetter Lane congregation was turned down by the Elders Meeting of 21 July 1832 on the grounds of 'character & circumstances'. The minutes refer to her failure to return 'to her Master', being 'under the patronage of Mr Pringle of the Anti-slavery Society', and her 'immoral conduct' in Antigua, for which she was 'suspended or excluded'.[69] Pro-slavery advocate James McQueen had made much of her alleged sexual history in articles in the *Glasgow Courier* and *Blackwood's Magazine*, the first

---

64 Thomas, *Telling West Indian Lives*, see especially pp. 121–35.

65 D. Bruce Hindmarsh, *The Evangelical Conversion Narrative: Spiritual Autobiography in Early Modern England* (Oxford: Oxford University Press, 2005), p. 175.

66 *Slave Registers of Former British Colonial Dependencies 1812–1834* (Provo, UT: ancestry.com, 2007).

67 Prince, *History*, p. 37.

68 Thomas, *Telling West Indian Lives*, p. 132.

69 Fetter Lane Congregation Records C/36/10/20, Elders Conference Minutes, Vol. 19, 13 September 1828–31 December 1837, quoted in Sue Thomas, 'New Information on Mary Prince in London', *Notes and Queries*, 58: 1, 2011, p. 83.

of which, 'The Anti-Slavery Society and the West-Indian Colonists', was reprinted in the Caribbean.[70] The want of quietism, as much as the allegations, would have told against her character for Moravians; her financial circumstances would also have affected the decision not to readmit her.

Legally Prince could not be cross-examined by the defence in Pringle v. Cadell, as Cadell's plea was changed so close to the hearing date.[71] In giving evidence in Wood v. Pringle, as tendentiously reported in the *Times*, Prince refers to relationships with Captain Abbott and 'a free man of the name of Oyskman' prior to her marriage to Daniel James, 'a carpenter, a cooper, and a violin-player' in about 1825. The account states that, while she told Strickland about the relationships, '[t]hese statements were not in the narrative published by the defendant'.[72] Her 'connexion' with Abbott is mentioned in a letter by Joseph Phillips and in a footnote by Pringle in the Supplement to the *History*.[73] The report of the case in the *Christian Advocate* noted that 'no evidence' of 'immorality' was put to the jury.[74] The case was heard over seventeen hours 'without interruption', yet the proceedings reported in the *Times* would take less than an hour; the material has been 'harshly and misleadingly edited' and compressed for publication. The report 'omits the terms of judgment in relation to costs, leaves legal questions opaque, and contains errors' and historical inaccuracy (about Abbott).[75] In court Pringle was not advised to submit to judgement of libel on all counts crafted by the prosecution. He was ordered to pay the relatively small sum of £25 in damages, but not Wood's legal costs, estimated to be about £250, which were eventually met through local subscription in Antigua.[76] The chronology of the

---

70 See Thomas, *Telling West Indian Lives*, pp. 155, 158. McQueen's July 1831 *Glasgow Courier* article 'The Anti-Slavery Society and the West-India Colonists' was reprinted in the *Bermuda Royal Gazette* (see Appendix 9, Ferguson, ed. *History of Mary Prince*, pp. 152–7) and the *Grenada Free Press, and Weekly Gazette*, 7 September 1831, p. 7.
71 Thomas, *Telling West Indian Lives*, p. 159.
72 'Appendix Three', Prince, *History*, pp. 102–3.
73 Pringle, 'Supplement', in Prince, *History*, pp. 51, 57.
74 *Christian Advocate*, 4 March 1833, p. 68.
75 Thomas, *Telling West Indian Lives*, p. 137.
76 See Thomas, *Telling West Indian Lives*, p. 163.

relationship between Prince and Abbott, as reported in the *Times*, is that they were lovers about 'seven years' before she married James in around 1825 and that '[s]he parted from' him 'on his killing a man on board one of the plaintiff's vessels'.[77] In 1827 Abbott was convicted in the Court of Vice-Admiralty in St Kitts of the manslaughter at sea of carpenter Samuel Frogman and received a jail sentence of six months.[78] He had been arrested at Crab Island (Vieques), Puerto Rico, by Spanish authorities. Prince's account of her dealings with Moravians during the relationship does not place it in the late 1810s. Generally, the accuracy of the *Times* report has been taken at face value by scholars. In 1833 it was repackaged and re-edited for 'colonial readers', a euphemism for colonial upholders of slavery, 'whom it must naturally interest in the warmest nature' under the headline 'Negro Slavery', suggesting that this was what was on trial.[79]

In a finely grained contextual study Jenny Sharpe suggests that the *History* was censored by Pringle and Strickland to produce Prince as a 'decent Christian woman', 'a projection of the kind of slave women Prince's antislavery readers wanted to see'. She reads Prince's relationships with Adam White, a Mr Burchell, both mentioned in the *History*, Oyskman and Abbott as 'signs of a slave woman's manipulation of her sexual availability to her own advantage', 'likely' negotiation of service as a 'concubine in exchange for her purchase price'.[80] In Sharpe's framework Prince's Moravian marriage to James, by contrast, accords with an anti-slavery teleology of freedom through Christianization. Though non-Anglican marriages were not recognized in Antiguan law before 1844, Prince's marriage to James imposed, by the terms of Antigua's 1798 Amelioration Acts, 'financial obligations on the Woods'—rewards for a stable relationship and the births of children—'and provided some protections for Prince, including the criminalization of rape of her by white men'.[81] Mindie Lazarus-Black places the Acts as part of the emergence and rise of a more 'legalistic

---

77 'Appendix Three', *History*, ed. Salih, pp. 102–3.
78 See Thomas, *Telling West Indian Lives*, p. 208.
79 'Negro Slavery', *Port of Spain Gazette*, 7 May 1833, [3], reproduced under exchange commons practice as '*From the United Kingdom, March 3*'.
80 Sharpe, *Ghosts of Slavery*, pp. 121, 134, xviii, 138.
81 Thomas, *Telling West Indian Lives*, p. 134.

kinship order' in Antigua and Barbuda in the late eighteenth and early nineteenth centuries.[82] The institution of concubinage in Antigua was highly politicized during Prince's enslavement there through the work of the Female Refuge Society, instigated and conducted by Anne Hart Gilbert (1768–1834), and the sister Distressed Females' Friend Society. Gilbert, the earliest known published African-Caribbean woman writer, was a free coloured Methodist, her public roles demonstrating 'a creolization of the African diasporic practice of othermothering and biblical models of female excellence'.[83] The charities, addressing what Gilbert represents as the blighting miasma of late plantation slavery culture, campaigned around the economic vulnerability of the families of women in concubinage relationships in a colony where such arrangements were generally short-lived and parochial relief did not extend to non-white people. At the request of mothers, the charities provided foster care for and occupational training of impoverished female children. Gilbert modelled a Creole vision of a Caribbean future around the 'cultural and moral improvement of an "independent peasantry"', a vision shared 'among enslaved and freed people in Caribbean plantocracies'.[84]

Connective

The archives within which Prince might be read and remembered are dispersed and fragmentary. The scholars, writers, artists and musicians the import of whose work I have highlighted have engaged in forms of connective research and reading, valuing what Whitlock describes as 'supplementation rather than completion, ... complexity rather than closure, ... the making of truth rather than its revelation'. She advocates

82 Mindie Lazarus-Black, *Legitimate Acts and Illegal Encounters: Law and Society in Antigua and Barbuda* (Washington, DC: Smithsonian Institution Press, 1994), p. 85.
83 Sue Thomas, 'Affective Dynamics of Colonial Reform and Modernisation in Antigua, 1816–1835', *Feminist Review*, 104, 2013, p. 25. Thomas discusses her work at length in *Telling West Indian Lives*, drawing on discovery of a far richer range of primary sources than those available to Moira Ferguson for the edited collection *The Hart Sisters: Early African Caribbean Writers, Evangelicals, and Radicals* (Lincoln, NE: University of Nebraska Press, 1993).
84 Thomas, 'Affective Dynamics', p. 25.

the 'connected reading' of autobiographies shaped by empire and its 'debris'.[85] My choice of the word 'connective' highlights the agency and innovation of archival researchers as readers and their continuing role in identifying and opening out fresh archives and contexts and more complex idioms of remembering around Prince. Cumulatively, the scholarship and creative practice discussed in this essay reframe the history of slave sale of Prince and her labour; the places of other-mothering and creolized religious practice and community in worlding her life; the limiting binary African/Christian; the conditions and reach of Prince's relation of her narrative; the generic protocols through which it may be read; and newspaper reportage of her evidence in Pringle v. Cadell and Wood v. Pringle. They propose forms of guerrilla memorialization of the legacies of Prince's labour under plantation slavery in our present. They open prospects of re-visions of Prince: 'act[s] of looking back, of seeing with fresh eyes, of entering an old' or familiar 'text from ... new critical direction[s]'.[86]

85 Whitlock, *The Intimate Empire*, p. 204.
86 Adrienne Rich, 'When We Dead Awaken: Writing as Re-Vision', *College English*, 34: 1, 1972, p. 18.

CHAPTER FOURTEEN

Nathaniel Wells: The Making of a Black Country Gentleman

Anne Rainsbury

Nathaniel Wells enjoyed an unusual position amongst the black population of Britain in the first half of the nineteenth century. He was not a servant or enslaved, but a wealthy, educated man of property and standing. He also had a household of his own servants and, moreover, owned enslaved African and Caribbean men, women and children on his sugar plantations on St Kitts. This extraordinary situation was not of his own making. Nathaniel owed everything to his father, William Wells. So, Nathaniel's story must begin with his father's.

William came from an old and distinguished Cardiff family, numbering aldermen and bailiffs of the city among them. His father the Rev. Nathaniel Wells was the first master appointed in 1719 to teach poor boys and girls at the charity school endowed by his kinsman, Craddock Wells.[1] He was also chaplain to Lord Mansell,

Nathaniel Wells was first researched by John A.H. Evans and published in an article 'Nathaniel Wells of Piercefield and St Kitts: From Slave to Sheriff' in the *Monmouthshire Antiquary*, Vol. XVIII, 2002; further discoveries were made by the present author for an exhibition at Chepstow Museum in 2003–4. She has since continued her research both in St Kitts and the UK and is indebted to John Evans for his continued support and to Victoria Borg O'Flaherty, Director of the National Archives St Kitts & Nevis, and also to members of the Wells family around the world.

1 Will Craddock Wells, 5 December 1710; 'Craddock Wells Charity' in Appendix to First Report of the Commissioners appointed to inquire into the Municipal Corporations in England & Wales, Part 1 (30 March 1835).

rector of St Andrew's Glamorgan and of Ilston in the 1730s, and in 1756 rector of Leckwith,[2] Glamorgan, near Cardiff. He was a Methodist sympathizer and invited Charles Wesley to Cardiff in 1740.[3] After the death of his first wife he had been forced to marry his servant when she became pregnant with his child.[4]

William was one of four sons from his father's first marriage who survived to adulthood. Two brothers, Robert and Craddock, married two sisters, Judith and Rebecca, daughters of the late Rev. John Burman, vicar of Newington in Kent, and both settled there in the late 1740s.[5] The Rev. Robert Wells was appointed rector of Ilston in 1748, succeeding his father, but it was only when he became rector of Penmaen nearby in Glamorganshire, in 1757,[6] that he returned to Wales. Craddock died young and only one of his four children survived infancy, a son named Burman.[7]

It has been thought that William and his brother Nathaniel went to St Kitts together in the late 1740s. But Nathaniel's career path was not so straightforward. In 1747, aged fifteen, he was apprenticed to Benjamin Lancaster, coach-maker in London.[8] He would have lived as well as worked with him in Theobald's Row, Holborn, so, perhaps unsurprisingly, Nathaniel married his master's eldest daughter Phebe Lancaster in

2 J. Venn and J.A. Venn, *Alumni Cantabrigienses*, Part 1, Vol. 4 (Cambridge: Cambridge University Press, 1927), p. 363.

3 A.H. Williams, 'The Leaders of English and Welsh Methodism 1738–91', *Bathafarn*, 16, 1961, p. 31.

4 R.T.W. Denning, ed., *The Diary of William Thomas 1762–1795 of Michaelston-super-Ely near St Fagans, Glamorgan* (Cardiff: South Wales Record Society and South Glamorgan County Council Libraries & Arts Dept., 1995), 15 November 1767.

5 Between 1745 and 1756 Rev. Robert and Judith Wells baptized six children and buried four; marriage of Craddock Wells and Rebekah Burman on 9 March 1747; between 1751 and 1760 four children, three buried; 'The Poll for Knights of the Shire to represent the County of Kent', 1754.

6 Newspaper reports refer to 'Rev Mr Robert Wells of Newington Kent': *Public Advertiser*, 8 February 1757.

7 Burman was baptized on 9 August 1752, apprenticed to Linen Draper in 1767, was declared bankrupt ten years later, and was remembered in wills of uncles William and Nathaniel, and Nathaniel's widow.

8 Indenture of Apprenticeship 1 July 1747 London Metropolitan Archives (LMA); Ref no.: COL/CHD/FR/02/0818–0-825.

1755,[9] just a year after completing his apprenticeship. At the end of 1756 he took on his own apprentice, and another in the following year.[10] By the terms of their apprenticeship he would still have been a coachmaker until 1764, but by the end of that year he was in St Kitts. William had probably been in St Kitts since the late 1740s, following in the footsteps of his namesake, probably his uncle, another William Wells.

St Kitts was a latecomer to large-scale sugar plantations but was on the ascendant by the mid-eighteenth century. With increased sugar production went a growing enslaved black population. From 1720 to 1780, the island's period of greatest prosperity, the number of enslaved people trebled from 7,321 in 1720 to 23,462 in 1774, while the number of whites was never more than 4,000 in that time and decreased to 1,900 in 1774.

In May 1753 William, now established as a merchant in the island's capital Basseterre, married Elizabeth Taylor, a wealthy widow aged thirty-six, thirteen years his senior and with five children, ranging from two to seventeen years old.[11] In 1754 William and Elizabeth had a son, William Fenton Wells, who died aged four; their daughter Anstance lived for just nine months, and Elizabeth followed her to the grave a month later, in June 1759.[12] William's marriage brought him wealth that helped him to accrue more: one of the ways he made money was by mortgaging the estates of struggling plantation owners at 8 per cent interest, as well as buying and selling property—not just land, but enslaved men, women and children.

William certainly made financial provision for his step-children,[13] but he had begun to have children of his own. He didn't remarry, but

9 St George Bloomsbury, 2 September 1755 LMA; Ref no.: P82/GEO1/015.

10 The National Archives (TNA) IR 1/21 p. 25 Friday 31 December 1756, Will Martin; p. 80, 6 August 1757 John Neighbour.

11 Date of marriage from Wells family bible. First marriage to Nicholas Taylor 1734 Elizabeth née Fenton described as heiress in Vere Langford Oliver, *The Monumental Inscriptions of the British West Indies* (Dorchester: Friary Press, 1927), p. 129.

12 Surviving tombstone, St George's Basseterre, St Kitts.

13 John Baker with William Wells, George Taylor the eldest and Alexander Douglas, George's brother-in-law, about 'assignment of mortgages and bonds for payment for 2 younger Mr Taylors' fortunes', 25 and 28 January 1767: *The Diary of John Baker, Barrister of the Middle Temple, Solicitor-General of the*

fathered children by his enslaved women. William's brother Nathaniel met the first child on St Kitts. When he made his will in February 1766, back home at Great James Street, Holborn, he named 'Betsey', whose mother was a 'negro woman' called Perrin, among bequests to nephews and nieces.[14] Nathaniel was back on the island by May that year, but by the 1780s re-established himself in London as a West Indies merchant.[15] When William made a return trip to Wales in 1767 the church bells were rung in Cardiff. He had been 'abroad this 18 years or more in St Christopher Island and elsewhere, and now as the report runs, worth £60,000'.[16]

William had already acquired the 216-acre plantation called Vambells in 1765, along with adjacent estates, making a total of 402 acres, and its 144 enslaved. He added another ninety-six acres to the estate in 1767. This was the largest of the three plantations he finally owned. In the devastating hurricane of 31 August 1772 the recorded damage to Vambells itemized

> An elegant new dwelling house torn to atoms; two boiling and two curing houses, kitchen, mule pen, necessary, stable and every out building except the still house, destroyed; eight cattle killed by the severity of the gale; five mules killed, supposed by the roof of the kitchen; and all the negro houses blown away. The crop will suffer at least 100 hhds. [hogsheads of sugar]. Mr Wells was in great danger, being in when the whole roof was carried bodily away with one gust of wind ... .[17]

The perils of natural disasters—earthquakes and floods were also hazards on St Kitts—and diseases, such as epidemics of smallpox, malaria, yellow fever and dysentery, together with more insidious threats, such as rebellion by the enslaved population, or even

Leeward Islands: Being Extracts Therefrom (London: Hutchinson & Co., 1931), p. 187.

14 Nathaniel Wells TNA PROB 11/1218/77.

15 Nathaniel Wells, Merchant 62 Hatton Garden—'London Directories & London Land Tax Records 1781–4', at 2 Great James Street, Bedford Row 1786–92.

16 Denning, 10 October 1767.

17 Published St Christopher (1772).

poisoning by their own servants, made life precarious. Unsurprisingly, most British plantation owners aspired to retirement in their homeland once their fortunes were made and they could afford suitable properties to live in grand style back in Britain. Until the mid-eighteenth century, non-resident plantation owners were uncommon on St Kitts, but from then more proprietors became absentee landlords, leaving attorneys to control their estates and salaried managers assisted by overseers to run the plantations. However, the quality, ability and experience of the latter could often run estates, and their owners, to ruin.

William chose to remain on St Kitts, managing his estates and profitably protecting his interests, including his offspring. In an unusual act, he had three of his natural children baptized into the Christian faith, at the same time publicly acknowledging them to be his: William, 'Mulatto son of the Honorable[18] William Wells', born March 1775; Grace, born 2 January 1777; and Nathaniel, born 10 September 1779, were baptized together at the church at Trinity, Palmetto Point, on 3 March 1783. The uncertainty of the times possibly spurred William to secure their status. The French had taken the island in February 1782, after besieging and systematically bombarding the fort on Brimstone Hill for three weeks, and Vambells lay close by in its shadow.

Altogether, six mixed-race children fathered by William Wells can be identified. Most of the information about them and their mothers comes from his will.[19] Significantly, William's first thoughts were for his enslaved women. It was only with his death that they would attain freedom, but they would also gain financial security. His 'house negro women', Hannah and Juggy, each received an annuity of £60; Cotto and Kate received £20 each; and Hannah was also given 'her negro woman Present and all her children'. William's mulatto woman Sue Hall[20]

18 Honorable William Wells appointed to Council of St Kitts 1771 TNA PC1/60/9; Oliver, *Caribbeana*, Vol. 6, p. 54 for parish registers Trinity, Palmetto Point.
19 William Wells' will TNA PROB 11/1253/24; St Christopher Register, National Archives St Kitts & Nevis (SCR) Series 3 Book E no. 12785.
20 Sue Hall in SCR Series 3 Book E no. 12785 William Wells's will, but Sue Wells in TNA PROB 11/1253.

was granted freedom and £20 annuity, as were his mulatto man Simon, his houseboy Fill and his two drivers,[21] Christian and Caesar. Three daughters, all by different mothers—Elizabeth by Perrin, Ann by Sue Hall and Mary Ann by Sarah—received thousands of pounds as lump sums together with substantial annuities, which would make them wealthy women. William Wells did not consider it necessary to officially free his children or to spell out their status. Close family in Britain and St Kitts received large amounts,[22] but the remainder of his estate he gave to 'my Natural and Dear Son Nathaniel Wells whose mother is my woman Juggy' to inherit when he came of age. Without a legitimate child, Nathaniel, the only surviving son, was named his heir. William estimated this inheritance, consisting of his three plantations, money due to him with interest and money he had in stock, to be worth at least £120,000.

By the time of the will's writing, 10 July 1789, Nathaniel was in England 'for his education and at School at Newington near London' under the care of his uncle Nathaniel Wells. Nathaniel had arrived in London six months earlier. In the only known personal document, a letter addressed to his father on St Christopher, dated 9 January, the nine-year-old Nathaniel writes in beautiful copperplate handwriting a few lines to let him know that he is well and now at his uncle's and would be going to school on Monday next. He asked his father to order him a Watch, and signs as his 'Dutiful Son'. Wells recommended his 'dear son Nathaniel' to the particular care of the executors, asking them to pay attention to Nathaniel's education; when he was fit and qualified, they should send him to Oxford University. If Nathaniel died before he came of age, William's estate would be divided equally between his two brothers and their heirs. By then, William and Grace, baptized with Nathaniel, had presumably died.[23] Elizabeth Wells, a free mulatto living in Basseterre, appears in later records buying and selling property, including enslaved people, but also freeing them.

---

21 Drivers controlled and organized the gangs of enslaved people on plantations.
22 William's brothers Rev. Robert and Nathaniel Wells, £5000; £5,000 as an afterthought to 'son-in-law' (step-son) John Taylor of Nevis. Annuities to half-brother and deceased brother's son.
23 No burial records found.

Mary Ann disappears, but Ann Wells comes to Britain and her fortunes are intertwined with Nathaniel's.

The voyage and arrival in the heart of London to live in the elegant 1720s terrace at Great James Street in Holborn must have been extraordinary for young Nathaniel. It was usual for rich planters to send their children, even mixed-race sons, back to Britain for their education. Living with an uncle who had personally experienced and understood his life on St Kitts must have been some comfort, but lasted only three years, as the senior Nathaniel Wells died in April 1792.[24] Nathaniel and Phebe had had no children, and whether Phebe continued to look after Nathaniel is still impossible to say—there are some 'lost years' where their whereabouts are unknown.[25] Despite William Wells's expressed desire, his son did not go to Oxford University. How and where he completed his education or spent his teenage years are tantalizing to imagine.

William Wells died of 'dropsy' in 1794.[26] Nathaniel's guardianship now rested with his surviving uncle Robert Wells and the three executors on St Kitts who were all still alive until 1800.[27] The Rev. Robert now stood to inherit everything should Nathaniel fail to reach the age of twenty-one.

On 10 September 1800 Nathaniel came of age and should have come into his inheritance. However, he now found that his uncle Robert was contesting William's will. Despite having proved the will and taken his legacy of £5,000, Robert now set up a claim to the plantations and estates, alleging that the will was 'not well and duly executed'.[28] He then proposed that he would release all claims in exchange for £10,000. Nathaniel, 'to avoid all trouble, contention and expense', accepted the proposal and the matter was finally settled on 10 February 1801. All William Wells's estates, three plantations—Vambells, Point Estate and The French Ground or Fahies—and a property in Sandy Point on

24 'Died at home', in *Lloyd's Evening Post*. Buried Warlingham, Surrey, 27 April (parish registers).
25 In 1797–8 Nathaniel was at 24 Gloucester Place, Marylebone and Phebe in Theale near Reading, where her sister lived (land tax).
26 He was buried at St Thomas Middle Island, despite his request in his will to be buried with his wife and children at Basseterre.
27 His friend Henry Berkeley, John Julius and Dr Adam Sprott.
28 SCR Series 3 Book L Nos 14004 & 14005, Wells to Wells.

St Kitts, including all the buildings, plantation equipment, the negroes and slaves, the livestock and the sugar canes, woods and water, all now belonged to the twenty-one-year-old Nathaniel Wells. Nathaniel had not hesitated to take control of his inheritance. On 16 October 1800 he appointed William Stephens and Jedediah Kerie of St Christopher's attorneys[29] to manage his plantations, just as if he was any absentee owner, which meant that they would have managers and overseers. His fortunes, and the fortunes of his enslaved people, would depend on them.

In the autumn of 1800 Nathaniel was living at 61 Pall Mall,[30] a street of grand houses and shops. Now very rich, the young Nathaniel lost no time in finding himself a wife. On 9 June 1801 he married pretty twenty-year-old Harriet Este in the fashionable church of St George's, Hanover Square, with the consent of her father, the Rev. Charles Este.[31] He was a colourful character, one of the king's reading chaplains at Whitehall and preacher at the Percy Chapel, St Pancras,[32] who also wrote theatre reviews, had a half share in a newspaper, *The World*, and knew most of the eminent actors of the day.[33] He was a good friend of the portrait painter Sir William Beechey, whose painting of Harriet survives.[34] At Harriet and Nathaniel's wedding the witnesses included Samuel Boddington. The Boddingtons were extremely wealthy West India merchants. The previous day, Nathaniel, Harriet, Charles Este and Samuel Boddington and partners had agreed a very favourable marriage settlement for Harriet: £15,000 of 4 per cent bank annuities in the event of Nathaniel's death.[35] For Nathaniel it was the beginning

---

29 SCR Series 3 Book N no. 14577 Wells to Stephens. Dr William Stephen, brother of James Stephen.

30 11 October 1800 Sun Insurance Policy: LMA, CLC/B/192/F/001/ MS11936/419/706863.

31 LMA DL/T/089/001.

32 Charles Este, *My Own Life* (London: Printed for T. and J. Egerton, at the Military Library, Whitehall, 1787).

33 John Taylor, *Records of My Life*, Vol. 2 (London: Edward Bull, Holles Street, 1832), Chap. 21.

34 Portrait 93.5 × 57 inches, sold by Charles Augustus Este Wells (grandson of Nathaniel and Harriet) c.1914. Sold at Christies New York in 1979 to a private collector in the USA.

35 Gwent Archives (GA) D412/43.

of a tortuous financial entanglement with the Boddingtons that lasted for the rest of his life and beyond.

In October 1801 Nathaniel made the first of just four manumissions; six months later he freed three others, two of them his cousins, his mother's nephew and niece.[36] It seems he was in touch with his mother, as he must have been instrumental in buying a property in College Street, Basseterre, for £1,200 in December, although the deed of sale cites the purchaser as his mother, Joardine Wells, 'commonly called or known by the name of Juggy Wells's spinster'.[37] Joardine Wells made her will in 1802, leaving not just her house but her own two 'Negro slaves', Venus and Cuffy, to her sister's children (including Nathaniel's recently freed cousins) and grandchildren. Joardine's sister, Catherine Wells, also had her own chamber in the house. In the unlikely event that all her sister's family were to die, Nathaniel and his heirs would inherit. In 1806 she added her 'son Nathaniel Wells of the Kingdom of Great Britain Esquire' as one of her executors.[38] So Joardine, herself a freed black house servant, was the owner of two black enslaved people, probably now her house servants. It was not unusual for 'free blacks and coloureds' to own enslaved people if they could afford to; it was a sign of status, reinforcing their own position as free people in a society constructed on slavery. But Joardine did not promise Venus and Cuffy freedom after her death, but bequeathed them and any issue, just like the rest of her property. She died in 1811, almost certainly never having seen her son again.[39]

The newly wed Nathaniel and Harriet removed to Bath. Perhaps it was then that they visited Piercefield, as it was fashionable to do. The Piercefield Walks were one of the 'must see' sights of the Wye Valley, and visitors ventured across the Severn from the spas at Bath and

36 SCR Series 3 Book L no. 14049 20 October 1801 'negro woman Big Sarah'; 15 April 1802 no. 14288 'negro man' Tom; no. 14210 'mulatto man' Billy Bowrey; no. 14211 'mulatto woman' Peggy Bowrey. Latter two children of Catherine Wells.

37 SCR Series 3 Book L nos 14105 & 14106 15/16 December 1801 Mardenborough to Wells.

38 SCR Series 3 Book Q no. 15381 5 December 1802 Will & 15382 Codicil.

39 Nathaniel seems never to have returned. Rev. Charles Este made two journeys to St Kitts to conduct business on Nathaniel's behalf. Taylor, *Records of My Life* on Charles Este.

Bristol. Piercefield's fame and attraction to the 'tourists' of the day were the winding walks along the edge of the Wye valley with a series of viewpoints opening on to sublime and beautiful vistas of the dramatic meandering river valley below. These had been laid out by Valentine Morris in the early 1750s: he used his 'Art and Taste',[40] as well as vast sums of inherited wealth from sugar plantations he owned in Antigua, to enhance and reveal the wonders of the natural landscape and to entertain visitors with an extravagance that became legendary.

The then-current owner, Lt Col. Mark Wood, opened not just the walks for two days a week but also his splendid newly finished mansion, which 'scarcely yields to any house in this kingdom in taste and splendour'.[41] Entirely remodelled and enlarged by John Soane in the early 1790s, Wood had completed and embellished it using the architect Joseph Bonomi to add wings and pavilions ornamented with reliefs and statues, and lavish interiors, with painted fireplaces and furniture to match, and Gobelin tapestries that once belonged to Louis XVI illustrating the natural history of Africa.

According to Wells family tradition, Nathaniel

> was dining at Piercefield with the then owner and was so attracted to the place that he offered to buy it. The deal was settled at the dining table whereupon the host changed places with his guest, who as the new owner, offered him a glass of port to celebrate the transfer.[42]

Wood sold Piercefield and its extensive estates for £90,000, a substantial part of Nathaniel's fortune.[43]

Nathaniel needed to purchase a property, as all those that he had inherited were in St Kitts, but his choice of Piercefield is interesting

---

40 'Art and Taste' are words that appear in a lot of commentary at the time. The term was laden with specific meanings in that period, and the two words have a particular connotation in eighteenth-century dialogue about landscape and garden design especially.

41 William Coxe, *An Historical Tour in Monmouthshire* (London: T. Cadell, Jr., 1801).

42 Guy Hemsley Wells, 'A Family History' (unpublished).

43 Sale Piercefield 28 and 29 July 1802 GA D412/44–45/46/47, Nathaniel at Baker St, Portman Square.

14.1 'Piercefield, Seat of Nathaniel Wells Esq.'
Aquatint after a drawing by FWL Stockdale published in No 30
of R. Ackermann's Repository of Arts etc., 1 June 1825, from the
collections of Chepstow Museum, Monmouthshire Museums.

(Figure 14.1). For this was no country retreat; as John Byng had observed in 1787, 'it is a very fine thing to see, but not a desirable place to inhabit ... it is not a station of retirement, or for a man of small fortune; being forever on an exhibition, and in a glare; and so famed, that an owner, and his servants become shewmen.'[44] As Piercefield's owner, Nathaniel could not fail to be mentioned in the many diaries of visitors and guidebooks that were written, yet surprisingly few mention his colour and origins. One who does is Joseph Farington, landscape artist and diarist, who wrote on 24 April 1803: 'Piercefield near Chepstow ... sold to Mr Wells, a West Indian of large fortune, a man of very gentlemanly manners, but so much a man of colour as to be little removed from a Negro'—one of the only physical descriptions of Nathaniel.[45]

44 John Byng (later 5th Viscount Torrington), *The Torrington Diaries, Containing the Tours Through England & Wales of Between the Years 1781 & 1794* (reprinted London, Eyre & Spottiswoode, 1934–8).
45 Kenneth Garlick and Angus Macintyre, eds, *The Diary of Joseph Farington,*

When Farington visited Piercefield later that year he wrote that 'the woman who has the care of the gate told me that Mr Wells is very exact about admission to see the grounds'.

> Every person who goes for that purpose is required [to write] his or her name and the book is carried to him every Saturday night, from which he transcribes all the names into a book which he keeps in his own possession. He does not refuse application for admission on other days than Tuesdays or Fridays, but should a person be seen in the grounds without leave, he would himself go to the gate and express himself angrily to her.

The woman also 'spoke most highly of the charitable and good disposition of Mr & Mrs Wells and of Miss Wells, his sister. Mr Wells is a Creole of a very deep Colour but Miss Wells is fair.'[46]

Miss Wells was Ann, daughter of the mulatto Sue Hall, Nathaniel's half-sister, who had come of age on 28 April that year. Soon after she made a legal declaration acknowledging receipt of her inheritance (£3,500) and the arrears of her annuity (£1,200 less sums paid for her education and maintenance) making her a wealthy woman in her own right. The document details the investments that Nathaniel had made and transferred to her.[47]

Ownership of a major estate in Monmouthshire brought Nathaniel opportunities as well as obligations to hold positions in society. He was able to lead a life in Britain that would have been impossible in St Kitts. 'Free coloureds' still had limited rights there; they

April 1803–December 1804, Vol. VI (New Haven: Yale University Press, 1979).
46 Evelyn Newby, *The Diary of Joseph Farington*, Index, Appendix, The Wye Tour, Tuesday 20 September 1803 (New Haven: Yale University Press, 1998).
47 SCR Series 3 Book M No. 14522 Ann Wells to Nathaniel Wells release. Subsequently Ann remained in Britain, but still had 'property' on St Kitts—enslaved people that she freed: 1816 Lucinda Wells and her children; 1825 Elizabeth Berkeley, mulatto, whom Ann had purchased from Nathaniel but because she had not been 'regularly conveyed' the manumission was made by them both. In 1826 Ann married the widowed Wesleyan minister William Henshaw; in his retirement they lived in North Wales. He died in 1841, she in 1842.

had no political rights or proper place in society, and were treated with contempt even by the Church. They were denied the vote and excluded from magistracies, any public office and even from juries— all things that Nathaniel attained in Britain.[48] There he would have been seen as a threat to the system by the white plantocracy, yet ironically in Britain the same class appeared to accept him, and he was able to play a prominent part in public life. In Monmouthshire, with the resumption of war with France and renewed threat of invasion in May 1803, Nathaniel Wells was one of twelve deputy lieutenants commissioned by the lord lieutenant, the duke of Beaufort, on 30 May.[49] In 1804 he was appointed churchwarden at St Arvans, a post he held for forty years.[50] He was appointed a justice of the peace in 1806.[51] Nathaniel, described as 'worthy' and 'respected', seems to have happily taken roles that put him in the limelight. In November 1817 he was one of three nominees for high sheriff of Monmouthshire, and on 24 January 1818 at the court at Brighton his Royal Highness the Prince Regent in Council appointed the sheriffs for the year, and Nathaniel Wells became, it seems, Britain's first black sheriff.[52] In 1820 he was appointed lieutenant of the Chepstow Troop of the Loyal Monmouthshire Yeomanry Cavalry (probably Britain's first black yeomanry officer), and two years later saw military action when there were serious riots in the Monmouthshire coal mining districts.[53]

In December 1803 Nathaniel and Harriet's first child, a son, was baptized William Meyrick. Phebe Wells was his godmother[54] and left him money in her will. Nine other children followed in quick succession and, although accepted as an important member of the

48 Edward L. Cox, *Free Coloureds in the Slave Societies of St Kitts and Grenada, 1763–1833* (Knoxville: University of Tennessee, 1984).
49 *The London Gazette*, 19–23 July 1803.
50 St Arvans parish records GA D/Pa.2.21.
51 TNA C.202/194/8 Appointment as JP.
52 'Nominations for Sheriff', *London Gazette*, 15 November 1817; 'Appointment', *London Gazette*, 27 January 1818; TNA C.202/206 1A.
53 W.H. Wyndham Quin, 'The Yeomanry Cavalry of Gloucestershire & Monmouth, Cheltenham 1898', in *Hereford Journal*, 21 June 1820 commission; *Hereford Journal*, 8 May 1822 Monmouthshire riots; *London Gazette*, 8 April 1823 resignation 7 August 1822.
54 TNA PROB 11/1547/60 Phebe Wells's will, £100.

community, the colour of his children was noted. According to a Miss Lee, who took a house at St Arvans in 1807, when Nathaniel had just three children 'the daughter is as fair as her mother, but the eldest son Brown and the 2nd son Dark like his father'.[55]

Making provision for his wife and growing family in the event of his death was a growing concern for Nathaniel. In 1804 Nathaniel agreed with Boddington & partners the lease of Vambells after his death to provide £600 a year for Harriet, and in 1807 came to a further agreement with Boddington to provide £10,000 for each of his children after his death, with the Piercefield estate as collateral.[56] By this time, however, Nathaniel seems to have been in financial difficulty. He borrowed from his sister Ann in 1807 over £7,000 of annuities, committing to repay her within a year. He failed to do so and renegotiated the loan, agreeing to pay her back at the rate of £1,000 a year. This turned into a lifelong saga. Ann gave the due twelve months' notice, requesting repayments to begin in 1819.[57] Nathaniel did not make the first repayment until 1839 and had not finished repaying it when she died in 1842.[58] Her husband bequeathed the outstanding monies to his children when he died in 1841.[59]

Despite his financial worries, his lifestyle at that time reveals gracious living and associated extravagance. There are glimpses of the young Nathaniel and Harriet at, for instance, the annual Hunt Ball at Chepstow in October 1807, when over 100 people sat down to a supper 'provided by the members of the Hunt. Pines and grapes were liberally supplied by the hospitable owner of Piercefield.' Special notice is made not of Nathaniel, but of 'his lovely and interesting Lady'.[60] The following March a report from Bath notes that 'Splendid Balls have been given ... by Mrs Wells, of Somerset

55 Kathryn Cave, ed., *The Diary of Joseph Farington* (July 1806–December 1807), Vol. VIII (New Haven: Yale University Press, 1982), entry 4 April 1807.
56 SCR Series 3 Book N Nos 14717 & 14718/13 & 14 September 1804 Wells to Boddington and others; GA D412/54 31 July 1807 Wells to Boddington and others.
57 Coinciding with Nathaniel's first attempt to sell Piercefield, possibly prompted by knowledge of his intention.
58 TNA PROB 11/1964 Ann Henshaw's will 1 April 1842.
59 TNA PROB 11/1947 William Henshaw's will 13 February 1841.
60 *The Cambrian*, 17 October 1807.

Place—the latter entertainment was most sumptuous—the wines rare and excellent, and pine-apples procured for the occasion from their seat at Piercefield'.[61] Hester Lynch Piozzi, the friend of Samuel Johnson, remarked of Harriet, eventually mother of ten mixed-race children, that 'I do half expect being detained a Day by pretty Mrs Wells of Piercefield',[62] despite having written with distaste a decade before of the infiltration of polite society by mixed-race immigrants in London.[63]

The purchase of Piercefield proved unwise, for along with its obvious showiness were hidden problems revealed in the sale particulars when the 'celebrated estate' was advertised for auction in London in 1819. Nathaniel had discovered dry rot: 'infinite pains have been taken, and it is believed, successfully, to eradicate this evil from the Premises.'[64] But Piercefield did not sell, and then real tragedy struck when Harriet died on 23 August 1820. She was not yet forty, left five girls and five boys, aged four to sixteen, and was still 'in the prime of youth and beauty ... one of the most beautiful and amiable women'.[65] From then on Nathaniel seems to have an uneasy relationship with Piercefield itself, repeatedly trying to sell, but still returning to the house to live intermittently right up to the year before his death. In May 1821 he tried letting it for three years, presumably unsuccessfully, as he was still active in Monmouthshire. Despite his financial difficulties, from 1821 Nathaniel contributed to repairs to St Arvans church and to its enlargement, including a new tower and entrances.[66]

At the end of 1822 the family received another blow, with the death at Piercefield of Nathaniel's youngest son, Henry Llewellin, aged twelve,

61 *The Morning Chronicle*, 15 March 1808.

62 Edward A. Bloom and Lillian D. Bloom, Hester Piozzi to Alexander Leak, Wednesday 23 June 1813, in *The Piozzi Letters: Correspondence of Hester Lynch Piozzi 1784–1821*, Vol. 5 1811–1816 (London and Newark: University of Delaware Press, 1999), p. 204.

63 Oswald G. Knapp, ed., Hester Piozzi to Penelope Pennington, 19 June 1802, in *The Intimate Letters of Hester Piozzi and Penelope Pennington 1788–1821* (London: John Lane, 1914), pp. 243–4.

64 Sale Particulars: 13 July 1819 by Mr Wakefield at Garraway's Coffee House 'Change Alley, *Cornhill*, London (Chepstow Museum).

65 Taylor, Vol. 2, Chap. 21 on Rev. Charles Este, p. 299.

66 24 July 1823, vote of thanks St Arvans parish records GA D/Pa.2.21.

and the following April his eldest son, William Meyrick, died after a long and painful illness. Harriet had been spared the anguish of seeing her children die, but Nathaniel would live to see seven of their ten children predecease him.

Amid these tragedies, Nathaniel married again. His second wife was Esther Owen, daughter of the late Rev. John Owen, rector of Paglesham, Essex, formerly curate of Fulham, and principal secretary to the British & Foreign Bible Society. William Wilberforce and members of the Clapham Sect were prime movers in the formation of the Society. In 1820 the Rev. John Owen's elder daughter Mary Frances had married William Wilberforce Jr.[67] They both attended Nathaniel and Esther's wedding, conducted by her brother the Rev. Henry Owen, on 31 January 1823, at St George's Hanover Square—where Nathaniel had married Harriet over twenty years earlier.[68] Nathaniel's relatives, the Bayfords,[69] had probably introduced him into the orbit of the Owen family and thereby into the sphere of the Wilberforce family. William Wilberforce's brother-in-law James Stephen, the abolitionist attorney who had practised on St Kitts and been a friend of William Wells, was aware of him but wary of contact.[70]

Esther was just nineteen years old, only a few months older than Nathaniel's eldest child, and within a year she began producing children herself, and would bear thirteen, ten girls and three boys, although five died as infants, and once again seven would predecease Nathaniel.

At the end of 1823 Nathaniel began the process of divesting himself of plantations in St Kitts. Perhaps Esther, with her family associations, had some influence here. It was the year that a new abolitionist campaign began to gather force, with the establishment of The Society for the Mitigation and Gradual Abolition of Slavery (its first meeting was on their wedding day, and William Wilberforce Jr was on the

---

67 *Caledonian Mercury*, 27 January 1820.
68 LMA DL/T/089/018 Marriage.
69 John Bayford was an admiring parishioner of Rev. John Owen in Fulham.
70 'the reason of our being strangers to each other … . It has been on my part, and probably on his, because I have been proscribed as a public enemy to the sugar colonies.' From James Stephen, *The Slavery of the British West India Colonies Delineated*, Vol. 2 (London: J. Butterworth and Son, 1830), Appendix no. 4.

committee). Or perhaps the decision was purely financial, there being a need to liquidate assets, especially as Piercefield had not sold. Profits from plantations were waning. Emancipation was anticipated by enslaved and owners alike. Without cheap labour there would not be the profit in sugar, and sugar cane now had a rival in sugar beet, which grew in temperate Europe.

Other motivations possibly prompted the sales at this point. While Nathaniel's plantations were initially run by managers, on 1 August 1812 two of them were leased out: Vambells to Michael O'Loughlin and Fahies & Ortons to Terence Comerford for a term of fourteen years. Leased together with the land, buildings and livestock were the enslaved people, the most valuable 'asset' of a plantation. After the abolition of the slave trade many colonies started registers to record the 'legally owned' enslaved against their owners' names. On St Kitts the original return was compiled in 1817, and showed that Nathaniel owned 266 enslaved people on his three plantations, all by then leased out.[71]

From the registers, if not through his attorneys, Nathaniel must have been aware that there were serious problems for his enslaved people on Fahies & Ortons. But the full horror of their treatment between 1815 and 1819 became the subject of a 'case history' in an abolitionist work, published in 1830, by none other than James Stephen.[72] It tells of cruelty and an almost flagrant disregard of the 'Amelioration Laws',[73] all resulting in a 'deathful progress' for the enslaved. At the start of the lease there were 140. Three years later, in 1815, there were only 108, and by 1819 only eighty-six were left. Fifty-four lives were lost, and no births recorded, making the real death toll even higher. Moreover, because the lease stipulated that there should be the same number and value of enslaved at the end of the term, there had even been purchases. An inventory taken in

---

71 St Christopher Register of Slaves 1817, Original Return.

72 Stephen, *The Slavery of the British West India Colonies Delineated*, Vol. 2, Appendix no. 4. Account of the treatment of the slaves on two united estates called Fahie's and Orton's in the Island of St Christopher and the fatal effects that followed.

73 'Amelioration Act', Leeward Islands 1799, minimum standards for humane treatment of enslaved.

1824, a year after Comerford's death, showed that only sixty of the original 140 enslaved people survived. Although he must have known the statistics, Nathaniel would not have been aware of the detail that James Stephen revealed. He had access to, and published extracts from, a journal partly kept by Comerford, partly by a manager in his absence, which had been retrieved by one of Wells's attorneys and passed on to James Stephen.[74]

There is no record of how Nathaniel responded to this information, or whether, having married into an abolitionist family, he felt personally implicated.[75] The route he took was to sell the estates. In 1824 he sold his 120-acre plantation at Trinity, Palmetto Point, with sixty enslaved people, for £3,500,[76] and in 1825 he sold Vambells, with 120 enslaved people, for just £5,000.[77] Nathaniel still owned Fahies & Ortons by the time of the abolition of slavery, and so received compensation of £1,400 9s 7d for eighty-six enslaved people.[78] He would sell the estate in 1836 for £2,500. Through either sale or compensation, Nathaniel, a mixed-race man, profited from these transactions, and the ownership and labour of enslaved people had been fundamental to his fortunes—facts that are central to his story but the most problematic, certainly for modern readers.

Whatever Esther's influence on Nathaniel, the marriage brought another potent force to bear on the Wells family, which had long-term repercussions for Nathaniel's children, grandchildren and great grand-children. The Catholic Apostolic Church, established in the early 1830s to prepare the world for the imminent Second Coming of Christ,

---

74 December 1823, appointed Sidney Stephen, barrister, and William McMahon, merchant, as attorneys on St Kitts with instructions to sell his estates. Sidney Stephen was a nephew of James Stephen.

75 Even James Stephen did not reproach Nathaniel, rather excusing him: 'He was educated in England, ... He probably, therefore, thought he was dealing with his property in no objectionable way, or even in the best way for the slaves of an absent master, when he was placing it in the hands of the lessees; and certainly could not anticipate such truly calamitous results.'

76 SCR Series 4 Book C Nos 17589/17590 11/12 October 1824 Wells to Henry Boon, Merchant St Kitts.

77 SCR Series 4 Book C Nos 17695/17696 30/31 May 1825 Wells to John Benjamin Waterson Esq, St Kitts.

78 T71/879 St Kitts 685 13 February 1837.

included the Bayfords, Esther's brother Henry Owen and three of the Wells children among its early adherents and ministers and brought some of them to settle in Albury, Surrey, the nerve centre of the Church; its evangelical work would eventually take one grandchild to Australia. Intermarriage between the three families strengthened and spread the spiritual bond.

While some of Nathaniel and Harriet's children were marrying and having children of their own,[79] Nathaniel and Esther were bringing up a second family.[80] Nathaniel's attempts to sell Piercefield continued, but two probable sales fell through. In 1833 Nathaniel and his growing family moved out of Piercefield House into another on the estate, Oak Grove, a more modest house which it is likely that Nathaniel had built.[81] At the same time he tried another public sale of Piercefield, employing the successful London auctioneer George Robins, famed for florid language, who advertised extensively 'to the monied world' that he was selling the 'Finest Property in Monmouthshire'.[82] Still it failed to sell, and instead the house was let.[83]

Nathaniel now seemed to look at other ways of realizing income from the estate. In 1833 he had plans drawn up by Bristol architects for twenty-five villas, with their own entrance road and lodge, at the Chepstow edge of his estate. But nothing came of this proposed housing development.[84] Then in 1834 Nathaniel's name heads the list

79 Of their ten children, six married: Harriet Claxton Wells married Rev. Frederick Cuthbert Beresford Earle (three children); Nathaniel Armstrong Wells married Georgiana Lucy Price (one child); Rev. Charles Rush Wells married Vincentia Money Chatfield (no issue); Rev. John Tighe Wells married Ellen Margaret Bayford (twelve children); Henrietta Maria Wells married James Bryan (no issue); Grace Emily Georgiana married George Watkins (three children).

80 No children from this second marriage married or produced children. Five spinster sisters lived with their widowed mother in Brighton.

81 Baptism records, Oak Cottage/Oak Grove 1833–4. Described as new-built residence in 1839 sale.

82 From February 1833, in many newspapers' sale notices, e.g. *Cheltenham Chronicle*, 16 May 1833.

83 Sale result (67,000 guineas) *Bristol Mercury*, 29 June 1833; notice of new auction in September, not of the whole estate: *The Derby Mercury*, 14 August 1833; withdrawal notice same issue.

84 Architect's plan GA.

of a committee of subscribers to build an observatory on the top of the Windcliff, the original 'highpoint' of the Piercefield Walks, but the scheme presumably failed to find sufficient financial support.[85] Giving up, Nathaniel and his large family moved back into Piercefield House and sold the Oak Grove estate in July 1839, advertised along with some sixty lots as the first portion of the Piercefield estate.[86] Several years later, in 1845, Nathaniel got caught up in 'railway mania' and appears as one of the provisional committee and later as a director of the Bristol and Liverpool Junction Railway. However, this bold scheme, and another spin-off from it that would have utilized a proposed bridge over the river Severn, The London, Bristol and South Wales Direct Railway, came to nothing.[87]

Throughout the 1830s Nathaniel remained active locally, especially as a magistrate, and he was also on the committee of the Chepstow Hunt. But in the 1840s his health declined. The newspaper[88] announced with pleasure on 13 February 1841 the convalescence of Nathaniel Wells, 'whose health has latterly been in a precarious state'. But in May 1844 Nathaniel left the neighbourhood, 'on a tour, for the benefit of his health', and Piercefield was let again.[89] One might have expected Nathaniel to go abroad, but a trail of birth and death finds him in his favourite resort Bath, in London and back to the south-west at Clevedon.[90]

In May 1849 Nathaniel was back: 'the worthy gentleman and family are in good health and their return to the neighbourhood was warmly greeted by the inhabitants of Chepstow and St. Arvans' with the ringing of bells.[91] He was at Piercefield when the 1851 census was taken, together with Esther, their five daughters and the last of

85 *Monmouthshire Merlin*, 9 August 1834; lithograph architect's drawing (Chepstow Museum).

86 Sale at Chepstow 10 and 11 July, e.g. *Hereford Journal*, 19 June 1839.

87 *The Times*, 16 June 1845; *Morning Chronicle*, 6 October 1845.

88 *The Monmouthshire Beacon*, 13 February 1841.

89 *Monmouthshire Merlin*, 25 May 1844.

90 His daughter Delia Frances died in Bath in May 1845; his last child, Angela Helen, was born in London in February 1846 and died at Clevedon in June 1847.

91 *Hereford Journal*, 16 May 1849; *Monmouthshire Beacon*, 12 May 1849. *Monmouthshire Merlin* reported the ringing of bells.

his unmarried daughters from his first marriage, Caroline Angelina. But sadly she too died, just after her thirty-sixth birthday, and only nine days before Nathaniel, aged seventy-two, on 13 May 1852. Both of them died at 9 Park Street, a relatively modest house in Bath, the city that Nathaniel returned to so many times, and were buried in Walcot parish. Notices, but remarkably no obituaries, appeared in the papers. Nathaniel, 'magistrate and deputy lieutenant of the county of Monmouth' and his second wife Esther, who survived him by nearly twenty years, are commemorated on a plaque in the chancel of St Arvans parish church.

Nathaniel had made his will in June 1842 not long after the death of his half-sister Ann. He left a tangled web of financial commitments to resolve, with debts still to be paid to his sister's heirs, the £10,000 for each of his children or their heirs, his wife's settlement and the mortgages to Boddingtons and associates that had been added to over the years. Piercefield now really had to be sold to satisfy the legacies and debts; he even authorized the demolition of the house and outbuildings if it made it easier to sell the estate, with the sale of all the building materials as well as the timber from the woods.[92] Fortunately the house survived this, although now it stands as a fragile ruin, its fame eclipsed by the Chepstow Racecourse built in its parkland, the property used today for music festivals, events and country walks.

The story of Nathaniel Wells, a man of colour who inherited great wealth, serves to shed light on Britain's black past. Without knowing stories like his, it is simple to imagine a time of polarized biographies and histories: either the slave narratives, such as those of Ottobah Cugoano and Mary Prince, which call attention to atrocities of slavery and the slave trade, or the more complicated lives of Olaudah Equiano, who fought for abolition, or Ignatius Sancho, who gives a more complex view of the possibilities of black lives during a time of slavery. Wells, however, belongs on both sides. He was born and spent his early childhood with a mother who was still enslaved on a plantation in the West Indies, but he went on to willingly profit from slavery. He seems to have forgotten or not to have completely understood—or perhaps wilfully ignored—the atrocities that went along with that. He came into his inheritance as a young man and his father's money bought

---

92 TNA PROB 11/2157 Nathaniel Wells's will.

him a place in British society as a gentleman and landowner of one of the most famous and beautiful estates in the country. But he patently lacked his father's business acumen with property and money. That he was chosen, and that he could chose, to hold positions of power and status belies the explicit racism that we have come to expect for people of colour in his time, but perhaps this very acceptance put him on what we would see as the wrong side of a moral issue.

Most interestingly, his racial background was for many years lost to local history,[93] so that the owner of Piercefield for fifty years was a wealthy West Indies merchant. But it had also been erased over the years by his descendants, many living in Australia today. With no surviving portraits of Wells or even identifiable pictures of his children, their only knowledge gleaned from his accomplishments and titles and some scant family stories, they assumed that he was a legitimate, distinguished white ancestor, and took great pride in him and Piercefield, their ancestral home. The recent discovery that this ancestor was, instead, a man of colour and the son of a black woman has mostly been met with the same keen interest and fascination that his story generally ignites.

93 John A.H. Evans 'Nathaniel Wells of Piercefield and St Kitts: From Slave to Sheriff', *Monmouthshire Antiquary*, Vol. XVIII, 2002.

CHAPTER FIFTEEN

Ira Aldridge in the North of England: Provincial Theatre and the Politics of Abolition

Theresa Saxon

African American actor Ira Aldridge was the first black performer that we know played Othello on English stages (Figure 15.1).[1] From 1825 to his death in 1867, Aldridge performed throughout England, Scotland and Ireland and travelled across Europe, touring widely in Russia and Poland. Over the course of his forty-year theatre career, Aldridge succeeded in negotiating a series of complex political landscapes that circulated around his personal and professional life, significant because his performances as a black actor and as an actor playing black characters were directly entangled with the coterminous history of racialized debates about slavery and abolition in the Caribbean and

---

1 Research has been conducted into the possibility that Ignatius Sancho may have performed the role of Othello in 1760 (notably Errol Hill in *Shakespeare in Sable: A History of Black Shakespearean Actors* (Amherst, MA: University of Massachusetts Press, 1984). However, no supporting evidence has as yet been uncovered and recent publications have argued that it is unlikely that performances of *Othello* featuring Sancho took place. See Brycchan Carey, '"The extraordinary Negro": Ignatius Sancho, Joseph Jekyll, and the Problem of Biography', *British Journal for Eighteenth-Century Studies*, 26, 2003, pp. 1–14, also Felicity A. Nussbaum, 'The Theatre of Empire: Racial Counterfeit, Racial Realism', in Kathleen Wilson (ed.), *A New Imperial History: Culture, Identity, Modernity in Britain and the Empire, 1660–1840* (Cambridge: Cambridge University Press, 2004), pp. 71–90.

15.1 Ira Aldridge as Othello, after James Northcote, c.1826.
Image courtesy of Manchester Art Gallery.

United States of America. Such debates were particularly relevant to three towns in England's North West—Manchester, Liverpool and Lancaster—all directly connected to the material wealth of and ideological campaigning around slavery and abolition. Additionally, and pertinent to this essay, all three towns were also part of a cultural movement in provincial theatre, as regional centres determined to acquire rights of royal patent privilege to produce spoken drama, a privilege that had been granted only in London and only to the Theatres Royal of Drury Lane and Covent Garden. I argue, therefore, that Aldridge's performances in Manchester, Liverpool and Lancaster, and the responses to them, speak to the confluence of abolitionist politics and theatre.

I focus on Manchester, Liverpool and Lancaster as locations overtly and specifically associated with the economic and cultural materiality of, as well political dispute about, the transatlantic slave trade, slavery and abolition. I explore also the influence of religious ideologies and cultural attitudes on regional politics and theatrical aesthetics. This is particularly relevant to investigations of theatre and race, given the anti-theatre stance espoused by Evangelical abolitionists, notably William Wilberforce. Such enquiries into the role of theatre in regional politics and culture reveal splits and schisms over Britain's involvement in the slave trade and enslavement, illuminating the cross-currents of a significant national debate and articulating a fuller and richer understanding of the history and legacy of Ira Aldridge.

Bernth Lindfors's encyclopaedic four-volume biography of Ira Aldridge provides chronology and theatrical geography, extending the seminal work undertaken by Mildred Stock and Herbert Marshall in their 1958 book *Ira Aldridge: The Negro Tragedian*. Building on this body of largely biographical work, this article explores regional accounts of Aldridge, examining the relationship between politics and theatre in the early decades of the nineteenth century. I focus here on the period that begins with Aldridge's arrival in England and his early performances of 1825 and extends to the time of his performance at the Theatre Royal, Covent Garden, in London on 10 April 1833, as these dates are crucial to discussions shaped in Britain, culturally and politically, about the ending of enslavement in the Caribbean colonies. As Paul Gilroy has argued in his analysis of black activists in Britain, Robert Wedderburn, Olaudah Equiano, William Davidson and William

Cuffay, 'the discourse and imagery of race appears at the core rather than at the fringes of British Political life.'[2] The theatre work of Ira Aldridge, not mentioned by Gilroy in *The Black Atlantic*, was likewise at the core of Britain's political atmosphere in the nineteenth century.

Despite Aldridge's appearance as Othello on 10 April 1833 at the Covent Garden theatre (one of the two theatres operating under royal patent and therefore, at that time, permitted to stage spoken drama in London) attracting vituperative press reaction and the pulling of the play, he established himself as a professional with commercial and artistic viability in regional theatres of Britain, some of which also held those royal patents crucial to the staging of spoken drama. This circuit of regional patent theatres included Manchester, Liverpool and Lancaster, all deeply entangled in national debates about the slave trade, slavery and abolition throughout Aldridge's performance career in Britain. But, apart from Ruth Cowhig's important account of Aldridge in Manchester, little work has been undertaken to examine the specificities of reaction in areas closely associated with the complex economic, political, cultural and moral landscape of enslavement and abolition.[3]

Reports of Aldridge's career in the provinces are important, illuminating regional attitudes towards racial identities and racializing structures in the context of this period of national and transatlantic debate about enslavement. In this way, regional responses about Aldridge's performances act as what Robin Bernstein describes as 'scriptive things', which 'like a play-script, broadly structures a performance while simultaneously allowing for resistance and unleashing original, live variations that may not be individually predictable'.[4] Bernstein developed her theory of 'scriptive things' from engagement with unidentified newspaper clippings held in an archive at Yale. Press reviews operate as, Bernstein argues, 'heuristic tool(s) for dealing with incomplete evidence'.[5] The range of press reports and commentaries

---

2 Paul Gilroy, *The Black Atlantic: Modernity and Double Consciousness* (Cambridge, MA: Harvard University Press, 1993), p. 7.
3 Ruth M. Cowhig, 'Ira Aldridge in Manchester', *Theatre Research International*, 11: 3, 1986, pp. 239–46.
4 Robin Bernstein, 'Dances with things: Material culture and the performance of race', *Social Text*, 27: 4, 2009, pp. 67–94 at pp. 68–9.
5 Bernstein, p. 76.

on Aldridge's performances also act as an archive of 'scriptive things'. With these tools, we are equipped to make 'responsible, limited inferences about the past' by focusing on the 'how' rather than the 'why' of the 'scriptive thing'.[6] Bernstein points out that moving debate in this way helpfully locates critics within an analytical scenario where we are concerned with an enriched exploration of 'how did this text produce historically located meanings?'[7] Such analyses should not, as Bernstein asserts, deny agency for the subject but recognize the politicizing agendas of 'how' subjectivity emerges/is produced/is reified. In the case of Ira Aldridge, I explore how his subjectivity came to be constructed through repeated rescriptions in performance reviews within particular sets of conflicting racial meanings.[8]

Theatre's role in the political machinery of Britain should not be overlooked, particularly in terms of its dramatization and collocation of arguments over the slave trade and abolition of slavery in the Caribbean colonies. Theatre was one of the three rods, alongside the Church and the press, that acted as a conduit for what General Gascoyne, Liverpool MP, described as the 'public clamour', gathering together groups that were vocal in favour of abolition.[9] However, the Church and the theatre were frequently at odds with each other. Moreover, abolitionism as a movement was directly associated with the anti-theatre convert to evangelism, William Wilberforce. Nevertheless, although there is no space to discuss it here, Wilberforce, like Thomas Clarkson, would incorporate the performative power of theatre in his talks on the subject of abolition.

Ira Aldridge's arrival in Britain in the 1820s was coterminous with a revival of debates about enslavement and abolition within the British colonies. The abolition of the slave trade itself, which passed into law in 1807, had not subsequently made significant movement towards the enfranchisement of those already enslaved on British plantations. By

---

6 Bernstein, p. 76.

7 Bernstein, p. 77.

8 Bernstein, p. 76.

9 Hansard, 1st ser., viii (15 December 1806–4 March 1807), cols 718–19), cited in Seymour Drescher, 'Whose Abolition? Popular Pressure and the Ending of the British Slave Trade', *Past & Present*, 143, 1994, pp. 136–66 at p. 143.

1825, however, a reinvigoration of abolition societies had developed into overt political advocacy. Significantly, in 1823, a rebellion in Demerara had led to the execution of several hundred enslaved people and, in the same year, The Society for the Mitigation and Gradual Abolition of Slavery throughout the British Dominions was established to provide a framework for local anti-slavery movements. Throughout the 1820s members of this organization repeatedly petitioned parliament for an abolition bill, and their endeavours would eventually lead to the 1833 Abolition Act. This was, of course, the same year as Aldridge's fateful performance at the Covent Garden theatre.

The Covent Garden performances, which have been central to many discussions of Aldridge, feature as the main subject matter of Lolita Chakrabarti's Aldridge-inspired play, *Red Velvet*, first performed in 2012. The play begins in 1867 with Aldridge being interviewed by a young journalist and talking of his reputation as 'the highest paid actor in Russia'. The journalist, however, is more interested in probing his long-past experiences at the Covent Garden theatre. Despite Aldridge's claim that he looks to the 'future' and not to the past, the play shifts the action back to April 1833, to the time that Aldridge was invited to perform as Othello at the Theatre Royal, Covent Garden.

By the end of *Red Velvet* we have revisited the racist commentary that greeted Aldridge's two nights in the role. Starkly, in the penultimate scene, Pierre Laporte, the Theatre Royal manager who had requested Aldridge's services, explains that his final performance had been cancelled, leaving Aldridge speechless on stage, silenced figuratively and literally by the racist attitudes of the London press. The historical events that feature in Chakrabarti's drama have been often recounted. Aldridge's opening-night performance at Covent Garden was rather thinly attended and the second all but empty. Aldridge had been scheduled to appear for a third performance, though not in *Othello*, but that show was pulled. Bernth Lindfors has extensively explored the reporting of Aldridge's performances here, summarizing: 'most commentators were of the opinion that Aldridge had not been wholly successful in portraying Othello but that he had given evidence of a surprising and very promising talent that could be developed further.'[10]

---

10 Bernth Lindfors, *Ira Aldridge: The Early Years, 1807–1833* (Rochester, NY: University of Rochester Press, 2011), p. 266.

Without comment or critique, Lindfors cites the *Age*'s account as a concordance of attitudes generally expressed in these reviews: that 'for a man of colour it was a very clever piece of acting.'[11]

Lindfors documents several even more vicious accounts of Aldridge's performances, notably one in *The Times* that complained 'we could not perceive any fitness which Mr. Aldridge possessed for the assumption of one of the finest parts that was ever imagined by Shakespeare, except, indeed, that he could play it in his own native hue.'[12] The article drew on incipient racial slurs to claim that Aldridge's accent was 'unpleasantly, and we would say, vulgarly, foreign: his manner, generally, drawling and unimpressive'.[13] But Lindfors also highlights a lengthy account in *National Omnibus; and General Advertiser*, whose critic challenged the racist reviews of other London papers, particularly *The Times*. The *National Omnibus* was one of the 'staunchest defenders' of Aldridge, according to Lindfors, and the reviewer of his appearances at Covent Garden requested that the '*leading* journal' (that is, *The Times*), would 'remove the stain from the national character' by supporting 'Mr. Aldridge in the performance of the limited numbers of characters to which the colour of his skin restricts him'.[14] Whether the *National Omnibus* reviewer concurred with ideological premises that imposed 'colour of skin' as necessarily restrictive or was decrying the fact that such ideological, externally imposed restrictions materially impeded Aldridge is not clear. But it is evident that this 'staunchest defender' of Aldridge tabulated his performances in a register of race.

The unstable critical reception we see here symbolizes a dilemma that Aldridge would repeatedly face in his theatrical career. He was repeatedly situated within a series of interpretations by critics whose envisioning of identities reproduced the constructedness of white British narratives and pseudoscientific interpretations of race, which were, throughout the nineteenth century, conflicted and contradictory. Whether critics positioned his performances as awful or astonishing,

---

11 *Nottingham and Newark Mercury*, 10 November 1827, p. 3, cited in Lindfors, p. 263.
12 *The Times*, 11 April 1833, p. 3.
13 *The Times*, 11 April 1833, p. 3.
14 *National Omnibus; and General Advertiser*, 26 April 1833, n.p., cited in Lindfors, p. 2.

whether they defended or despised, their opinions were assembled from a matrix of racial particularisms.

Reviews from Aldridge's first appearances in London were likewise caught up in the rhetoric of racialization. Aldridge had, on his arrival in England from America, headed directly to London. By October 1825 he had found engagements at the Royalty Theatre, appearing for two nights in *Othello*, then in an adaptation of Thomas Southerne's *Oroonoko*, titled *The Slave*, followed by smaller roles in a variety of melodramas featuring characters of colour. Then Aldridge took up employment with the Royal Coburg Theatre, his initial appearance as *Oroonoko* being lined up for particular attention in the press as a result of an early review titled: 'A Negro Roscius!' by *The Times*, which was the most repellent and also the most reprinted account of his time in the capital. This reviewer averred that:

> At the Coburg Theatre last night, a native of Africa enacted the part of Oroonoko so much to the satisfaction of the audience that he kept them in a continual roar of laughter, which was increased ten-fold when he stabbed his wife and twenty-fold when he stabbed himself.[15]

Significantly, Aldridge was employed in London theatres specifically to play in a variety of melodramas and farces that included characters of race, who were almost always enslaved. These characters were either noble heroes, saving their white master/mistress from evil—directly taken from the stock of what Hazel Waters has described as an 'archetype of the noble black [...] drawn straight from the literature of the abolitionist movement'—or emblematic of 'black villainy'.[16] Therefore, the roles allocated to Aldridge operated somewhere among well-established types, although he would subsequently add comic characters to his repertoire. Firstly, there were noble slaves whose actions resulted in the sanctity of white, middle-class Christian values, such as African princes sold into slavery, like Thomas Southerne's

15 *The Times*, 11 October 1825, p. 2.
16 Hazel Waters, *Racism on the Victorian Stage: Representations of Slavery and the Black Character* (Cambridge: Cambridge University Press, 2007), p. 82.

dramatic version of Aphra Behn's *Oroonoko*, whose suffering was tragic because he was socially elite; and secondly there were predetermined emblems of slave rebellions, associated in the public imaginary with the reported brutality enacted by black leaders of revolutions in Barbados, Haiti and Demerara.

To what extent Aldridge was actively involved in discussions about the parts that he played at the Coburg and Royalty theatres is unclear. Aldridge, as a company player, would not have had been in a position to make significant choices about which roles he played at this time— but what he did with those roles was within his purview to influence by means of his performance techniques. Evidence from later performances suggests that he may have been, at this early stage of his career, developing a particular set of performative signifiers that would become a feature of his theatrical repertoire. Notably, one early report of one of his performances as Othello suggested that Aldridge should pay 'stricter attention to the text of the author and to the general substance of the scene', which Lindfors has interpreted as meaning that Aldridge did not know the lines. But we know from later reporting that Aldridge frequently changed the 'text of the author' and the 'substance of the scene' to suit his own, mostly unacknowledged, purposes. It is as likely that Aldridge's lack of adherence to the 'text' of *Othello* here was an early instance of his assertion of agency on stage.[17]

I am not suggesting here that Aldridge would have had prior knowledge of all the roles he played during his residences at the Royalty and Coburg theatres. But it is likely that he would have had familiarity with *Othello*, at the very least. Though stage managers frequently would change the text of Shakespeare's plays (the concept of an authentic Shakespeare text is vexed anyway), the 'substance of the scene' would not have been an alien one. Aldridge had been educated at one of the African Free Schools in New York, and his classmates included, as Lindfors notes, the very successful James McCune Smith, first African American doctor with a medical degree, and Episcopalian minister Alexander Crummell, first black graduate of Cambridge University.[18]

---

17 Early nineteenth-century acting styles on patent stages were generally expected to be stylized and declamatory.
18 Lindfors, p. 24.

Moreover, in New York, as has been well established, he was involved with William Alexander Brown's African Grove and African Theatre seasons, which ran sporadically from June 1821. In New York, however, the African Grove Company was subjected to repeated attacks from white theatre managers and press, survived a major riot in 1822 and finally shut down in January 1824. So, Aldridge had experienced an apprenticeship with a theatre group that had not only performed Shakespearean drama but had been subjected to abuse for doing so. That Aldridge arrived in Britain with a good working knowledge of *Othello* thus seems very likely. It cannot be assumed that if Aldridge deviated from an 'author's text' or interpreted a scene differently it was because he was unfamiliar with the play.

Aldridge's early appearances in London, though lasting until the end of November, came to an end on 26 November 1825 and the actor joined the ranks of peripatetic players who toured the country. Immediately prior to embarking on regional tours, a significant change was made to Aldridge's publicity material. Rather than being billed as an 'American Tragedian', or the 'African Tragedian', or a 'Gentleman of Color', he became the 'African Roscius' across his regional tours. Several actors and actresses in this period publicized themselves as 'Roscius'. At the time of Aldridge's early shows, young Master Grossmith was billed as the 'infant Roscius' and Master Betty was the 'Young Roscius'. The original of the title was, however, Roman performer Quintus Roscius (1 BC), who was enslaved when he was first put to work on stage. One of the racist reviews from *The Times* in London, cited earlier in this article, had used the title 'African Roscius' as an insult and Lindfors speculates that, in adopting the moniker, Aldridge was displaying a 'playful sense of irony', and also possibly marketing his own act on the back of comedian Charles Mathew's famous show *A Trip to America*.[19] This show featured an African American tragedian reciting (badly) from Shakespeare's plays and singing 'Opossum Up a Gum Tree', a song associated in the popular imagination with slaves from American plantations. This grotesque burlesque was performed regularly in Britain between 1822 and 1835 and press reviewers frequently made a link between Mathews's racist skit and Aldridge's performances.

19 Lindfors, p. 85.

However, in assuming the title 'African Roscius', Aldridge also demonstrated his awareness that the press would respond to his race as a primary consideration and his origins would likewise come under scrutiny. Recognizing that his performances had been co-opted for a variety of political aims and appropriated to serve the claims of both pro- and anti-slavery forces, he took steps to secure a degree of autonomy and frame a position for himself as a performer. Thus when Aldridge actually began to perform 'Opossum up a Gum Tree' himself, a main feature of his repertoire in regional touring, he was reappropriating, in ironic formation, the image of the black tragedian.[20]

On tour, now billed as the African Roscius, Aldridge could witness for himself the disparate range of responses to debates about slavery across regional centres in England, particularly in those centres that had worked towards the establishment of a royal patent theatre house. In the late eighteenth century a circuit of regional licensed patent theatres had emerged in Britain, spanning from Edinburgh (the first outside London to be granted the status of Theatre Royal, in 1767, the theatre being erected the following year), to Norwich in the east, Liverpool, Manchester, Hull and Newcastle in the north of England and Bath and Brighton in the south.

The granting of royal patents and temporary rights of patent permission to provincial theatres to enable spoken production was, as Joan Baker contends, a product of the same ideological campaign that resulted in William Wilberforce's Proclamation Society (established in 1787), which was dedicated to the control of perceived 'immorality' in Britain. Nevertheless, William Wilberforce's political drive in his work for the Proclamation Society, however so related to the establishment of provincial theatre, most certainly was not set out to achieve that goal. Wilberforce's Evangelism was specifically anti-theatre, and he decried theatre for his own class as one of a set of dissipations that would lead to 'shapeless idleness'.[21] The Proclamation Society was shaped to

---

20 Similarly, after T.D. Rice came to Britain and gave his performance of 'Jump Jim Crow' in 1836, Aldridge began to include a version of the song in his own repertoire.

21 William Wilberforce, *A Practical View of the Prevailing Religious System of Professed Christians: In the Higher and Middle Classes in this Country, Contrasted with Real Christianity* (London, T. Cadell, 1829), p. 134.

control class boundaries, to police middle-class as well as working-class behaviours and to ensure that his middle-class evangelicals maintained hegemony in matters local, national and international. The Society was invested in controlling and curtailing any rights for working-class groups, and support for the abolition of enslavement certainly did not extend to a wider programme of reform within Britain.

But in British industrial cities, notably Manchester, abolition was embraced alongside a movement towards political reform in the 1820s, running exactly counter to the Proclamation Society's belief in controlling working-class agitation through laws to curtail their enfranchisement. Manchester's anti-slavery committee was the first to petition for a bill to abolish the slave trade in 1787. Seymour Drescher calculates that the petition, signed by nearly 11,000 Mancunians, represented 20 per cent of the town's population and almost two-thirds of its adult men.[22] Drescher also points out that Manchester abolitionists bought adverts in other northern provincial papers to garner support for the cause, and was thus formative in establishing the national campaign in the 1820s.

In 1827 Ira Aldridge arrived in Manchester at a time when its citizens were deeply receptive to the abolition of slavery in both the Caribbean and the United States of America, as well as to class reform on the domestic front. Additionally, Manchester was one of the first cities in Britain to apply for and be granted a royal patent to perform Shakespeare and other dramas authorized by the office of the Lord Chamberlain. The officially licensed Theatre Royal in Manchester staged its first performance in 1775; the building moved location on several occasions, but royal patent was very much in place when Aldridge arrived in 1827.[23]

Manchester's Theatre Royal was, therefore, the first royal patent theatre in Britain to open its doors to Aldridge. He opened on Saturday 17 February 1827 as Gambia in *The Slave*. Then, on his second night, he appeared as *Othello*. *Wheeler's Manchester Chronicle* noted that 'this evening the African Roscius makes his second appearance in

---

22 Seymour Drescher, *Capitalism and Antislavery: British Mobilization in Comparative Perspective* (Oxford: Oxford University Press, 1987), p. 70.
23 *Manchester Mercury*, 3 October 1775, p. 4, announced: 'we are authorised to acquaint the public that the Manchester Theatre Royal will open its doors on 9 October 1775'.

the very difficult character to personate Othello. His reception on Saturday last was favourable (as Gambia), and he obtained considerable applause in the declamatory scenes.'[24] This review is especially useful as it completely contradicts *The Times*' earlier account of Aldridge at the Coburg Theatre, London, in which it was claimed that, 'owing to the shape of his lips, it is utterly impossible for him to pronounce English in such a manner as to satisfy even the unfastidious ears of the gallery.'[25] In Manchester, Aldridge's skill in the declamatory arts was recognized and highlighted.

Aldridge performed regularly over a two-week period in Manchester. On his final night at Manchester's Theatre Royal the *Manchester Gazette* summarized the significance of Aldridge's work so far for this theatre: 'He performed in a manner which practically contradicts the argument of the advocates of slavery, that the sable race are deficient in intellect.'[26] Significantly, the critic here directly challenged the pseudo-scientific ideology of racial superiority/inferiority, which was one of the main arguments in support of enslavement. Whereas, in London, the body of the black performer was arrogated in the service of pro-slavery racist rhetoric, in Manchester Aldridge was discussed as a performer of skill and intellect, and thus as a body of evidence to prove all that was wrong with slavery.

Though Aldridge was not exposed to pro-slavery press in Manchester as he had been in London, he was, nevertheless, subjected to the racist ideology of abolitionist rhetoric. Prior to Aldridge's arrival, the *Manchester Courier* had written an appeal to audiences to 'show their liberality to this descendant of the suffering sons of Africa'.[27] That Aldridge was located as a 'suffering son of Africa' chimes with the rhetoric of abolitionism, exemplified in the marketing of the image of the suffering slave, most notoriously in the much earlier Josiah Wedgewood mass-produced medallion bearing the caption, 'Am I not a Man and a Brother?'[28] Demonstrations of support for enslaved

24 *Wheeler's Manchester Chronicle*, 17 February 1827, p. 4.
25 *The Times*, 11 October 1825, p. 2.
26 *Manchester Gazette*, 24 February 1827, p. 3.
27 *Manchester Courier*, 24 February 1827, p. 3.
28 Marcus Wood, *Slavery, Empathy and Pornography* (Oxford: Oxford University Press, 2002), p. 300.

figures visually swathed in suffering had remained paramount for abolitionist propaganda and some of the characters that Aldridge performed, such as Oroonoko and Gambia, written as sufferers by white playwrights, chimed with such images. In America, Aldridge had not been enslaved, though he had encountered the violence of racism. Yet the *Courier*'s abolitionist stance in this review relied on reifying Aldridge as the embodiment of the enslaved figure as passive sufferer.

This *Courier* commentary in support of Aldridge also reproduced abolition's essentializing racial identities, stating that the actor, in playing 'those characters for which his complexion and accent are peculiarly adapted, approaches nearer to nature than any European actor that we ever saw'.[29] Othello and Gambia were appropriate roles for a black actor, because both characters were scripted as black, even though the playwrights staging such configurations of blackness were white British. The *Courier*'s support for Aldridge, therefore, illuminates Manchester's ties with abolitionism and also the problems with abolitionist rhetorical strategies.

Unlike Manchester's, Liverpool's association with the slave trade is well established and had a direct impact on its theatre culture. In 1808 dramatist Elizabeth Inchbald noted that Thomas Southerne's *Oroonoko*, one of Aldridge's most frequently performed roles, 'is never acted in Liverpool, for the very reason why it ought to be acted there oftener than at any other place—The merchants of that great city acquire their riches by the slave trade.'[30] Nearly twenty years later, in October 1827, Aldridge appeared at the Theatre Royal in Liverpool and the notice in *Gore's Liverpool General Advertiser* stated that he would play *The Slave* for two nights.[31] There is no announcement for the second night and no reports on either show. Liverpool is not unusual in this; throughout Aldridge's career there were performances that attracted little or no media attention. But it is significant that the play advertised, *The Slave*, which covered subject matter very

---

29 *Manchester Courier*, 24 February 1827, p. 2.
30 Mrs Elizabeth Inchbald, *The British Theatre, Or, A Collection of Plays, Which Are Acted At the Theatres Royal, Drury Lane, Covent Garden, And Haymarket*, Vol. 7 (London: Longman, Hurst, Rees, and Orme, 1808), p. 4.
31 *Gore's Liverpool General Advertiser*, 11 October 1827, p. 1.

similar to *Oroonoko*, might have been too provocative to be reported in a region so closely associated with slavery.

Moreover, despite the fact that so many plays were dramatizing romanticized versions of racial hierarchies in slavery and the slave trade were in general circulation across Britain at this time, and were regularly performed in larger theatre centres, Liverpool's theatre seem to have closed itself down to such shows, apart from an announcement, in 1817, for a performance of *The Slave* at the Liverpool Concert Hall.[32] But, as with the performances scheduled in Liverpool for Aldridge, no reviews of this performance can be found. Interestingly, this was not seen in Lancaster or Bristol, centres also associated with the slave trade. From these locations, as was the case in Manchester, come quite detailed reviews of Ira Aldridge's performances in this early part of his career.

By the time of Aldridge's 1827 performance in Liverpool an active abolitionist group existed, set up in 1822. The year 1827 also saw the formation of the Ladies Society of Liverpool. Nevertheless, as Sanderson points out, Liverpool's commitment to abolition was marginal, even though it had elected the abolitionist William Roscoe in 1807:

> Liverpool spearheaded the parliamentary resistance to abolition, sending at least 64 petitions to the Commons or the Lords (as compared to 14 from the London merchants and 12 from Bristol Corporation and merchants). Her representatives in parliament were the most persistent advocates of the trade.[33]

Liverpool in 1827 was a difficult place to stage dramas about enslaved Africans, and the absence of commentary on Aldridge in *The Slave* speaks significantly to the cultural atmosphere and political economy of the region. Perhaps, then, it is no surprise that Liverpool remained peripheral as a performance venue of choice for Ira Aldridge throughout his career.

Aldridge's 1827 performances were reported in the *Lancaster Gazette*, which noted that the 'spirited manager' of the Lancaster

32 *The Liverpool Mercury*, 31 January 1817, n.p.
33 F.E. Sanderson, 'The Liverpool Abolitionists', in R.T. Anstey and P.E.H. Hair (eds), *Liverpool, the African Slave Trade, and Abolition* (Bristol, 1976), pp. 196–238 at p. 196.

Theatre Royal had engaged Aldridge for the 'ensuing week'.[34] This review of Aldridge was short but enthusiastic, describing the actor as 'this complete master of the histrionic arts'.[35] On his return to Lancaster in 1832, Aldridge's performances were reviewed in far more detail and in very specific terms in the *Lancaster Herald*:

> In again expressing the delight we have experienced from the performances of the African Roscius, we do it sincerely. At first, we rather fancied that the novelty might have given rise to a great portion of the feeling which we experienced; indeed, we have more than once been asked if such were not the case; but we now say, as we have invariably answered, that we admire him for his acting, and his conception of the characters which he has filled, when we were present. Yet, we must allow that, identified as he is, by birth, with the beings he personates, he perhaps makes a deeper impression than another performer would. The latter might arouse our sympathies for the while he was before us, but the African Roscius makes an impression of a much longer and more powerful continuance. We feel as though he were the advocate, the representative of a nation, pleading its cause from the heart, and we think of him and that nation, when the dazzling light [...] of theatrical machinery, have passed away,—when we are alone to think, to reflect.[36]

This review is worth citing at length, as it sheds some light on Lancaster's own role in the history of the slave trade.

Lancaster's active participation in the slave trade has been foregrounded in recent years, with Melinda Elder's 1992 publication *The Slave Trade and the Economic Development of Eighteenth-Century Lancaster* providing the primary resources for subsequent studies, notably a chapter in Alan Rice's 2010 book *Creating Memorials, Building Identities: The Politics of Memory in the Black Atlantic*. Much earlier, however, Lancaster's association with the slave trade had haunted Charles Dickens's short tale 'The Lazy Tour of Two Idle

34 *Lancaster Gazette*, 29 September 1827, p. 2.
35 *Lancaster Gazette*, 29 September 1827, p. 2.
36 *Lancaster Herald*, 15 September 1832, p. 285, cited in Lindfors, p. 228.

Apprentices', first published in 1857, which dramatized Lancaster's slave-trade troubled conscience in gothic terms:

> The stones of Lancaster do sometimes whisper, even yet, of rich men passed away—upon whose great prosperity some of these old doorways frowned sullen in the brightest weather—that their slave-gain turned to curses, as the Arabian Wizard's money turned to leaves, and that no good ever came of it, even unto the third and fourth generations, until it was wasted and gone.[37]

With this 'cursed' wealth dispersed across the generations of lucrative inheritance and economic stability, there was also a concerted effort in Lancaster to silence its history of culpability. As Rice argues, Lancaster relied on recounting tales of its slave merchants as 'mere gentleman amateurs' in the trade.[38]

Although there were some Quaker movements agitating for abolition in Lancaster, their voices were almost unheard in the political wrangling over slavery. The *Herald*'s review of Aldridge's two weeks of performances at the Theatre Royal in Lancaster, therefore, subtly exposes the town's own haunted guilt, directing audiences in the region to 'think, to reflect'. In Lancaster, atonement for culpability in the slave trade was (and is) required.

The very public debate over slavery and abolition complicated Aldridge's assertion of agency as a performer but also brought visibility for his work, and he directly engaged in the debate in his performances. By January 1833 he had developed a farewell address for his performances, cited in full by Lindfors and printed in several press publications. The address is a significant and direct criticism of slavery, featuring, tellingly, the lines: 'soon the white man comes, allured by gain/o'er his (the African) free limbs fling slavery's galling chain'.[39]

In August 1833 the Slavery Abolition Act was granted royal assent and declared the gradual abolition of slavery in British colonies. But throughout the years of Aldridge's performances in the lead-up to

---

37 Charles Dickens, 'The Lazy Tour of Two Idle Apprentices', *Household Words*, XVI: LVIII, December 1857, pp. 313–432 at p. 320.
38 Rice, *Creating Memorials, Building Identities*, p. 33.
39 Cited in Lindfors, p. 231.

this most crucial of political milestones for the abolition societies there seems to have been no direct association between Aldridge and key abolitionists. Even in Manchester, whose middle-class elite were dominantly abolitionist, no evidence has been uncovered, as yet, to suggest a collaboration with this black performer in their midst.

William Wilberforce, as has been pointed out, was theologically antithetical to theatre. Nevertheless, Lolita Chakrabarti speculated in *Red Velvet* on relations between him, his main ally Thomas Clarkson and Aldridge. Scene 4 imagines Aldridge and his wife Margaret discussing seeing abolitionist Thomas Clarkson in the audience for Aldridge's Covent Garden performance.

> Margaret: First time I've seen him smile.
> Ira: It's a tense time for him.
> Margaret: ... we met him with the Wilberforces didn't we? He did say William's not well at all. We should send him something.[40]

In the twenty-first century it was hard to resist an imaginary meeting between the black actor and the famous abolitionist. Evidence of collaboration may be available and further research in this field could reveal additional archival resources, further 'scriptive things', to help us with this enquiry.[41]

One intriguing mention of support for Aldridge from an abolitionist appears in an essay by his former schoolmate and long-time friend James McCune Smith, who had studied medicine in Glasgow and was very much a part of the abolition movements in that region. McCune Smith recounted that 'the good people of Glasgow were "down upon" two institutions—Popery and the theatre.'[42] The 'anti-slavery men of Glasgow', Smith continued, who 'were for the most part rigid dissenters,

---

40 Lolita Chakrabarti, *Red Velvet* (London: Bloomsbury Methuen Drama, 2012), p. 61.
41 I am currently undertaking research into Ira Aldridge in the context of other African American travellers in the transatlantic, particularly Frederick Douglass and William Wells Brown.
42 James McCune Smith, 'Ira Aldridge' (1860), in Bernth Lindfors (ed.), *Ira Aldridge: The African Roscius* (Rochester, NY: University of Rochester Press, 2007), pp. 39–47 at p. 42.

entertained this prejudice in the highest degree'.[43] But, according to Smith, the power of Aldridge's performances won the admiration of John Murray, then the secretary of the Glasgow Emancipation Society, whose anti-theatre views were profound and deep-rooted. Murray's attendance at the Glasgow Royal to see Aldridge was his 'one and only visit to a theatre'.[44] McCune Smith's tale indicates the power of Aldridge's performances to support the abolition cause.

Tellingly, in all the years of its publication, *The Anti-Slavery Reporter*, which was the mouthpiece of the British and Foreign Anti-Slavery Society and regularly employed theatrical metaphor within their depictions of the colonial horrors, made no mention of Aldridge. Perhaps Aldridge's performance career, which was rich in interpretations of black characters with agency who challenged the racial preconceptions of his audience and critics, made him too independent of their work in promoting the image of the 'suffering slave'. Ultimately, Aldridge took on the battle against enslavement himself, by offering a different perspective to the abolition movement, performing in unregulated theatres as well as patent houses and speaking openly to a wide, diverse audience, not all of whom would be sympathetic to his presence on a public stage, let alone to his presence as a black performer of cultural and political substance.

43 McCune Smith, p. 42.
44 McCune Smith, p. 42.

CHAPTER SIXTEEN

'Fermentation will be universal': Intersections of Race and Class in Robert Wedderburn's Black Atlantic Discourse of Transatlantic Revolution

Raphael Hoermann

Born in Jamaica probably in 1762 as the mixed-race son of the Scottish–Jamaican slaveholder James Wedderburn and an enslaved black woman named Rosanna, Robert Wedderburn's life and anti-slavery and anti-capitalist activism were inextricably linked to the transatlantic slave economy. As he insists in the opening sentence of a narrative of his early life in Jamaica: 'To my unfortunate origin I must attribute all my misery and misfortunes.'[1] This verdict seems justified, as throughout his life Wedderburn not only struggled with often extreme poverty but was also hounded by the authorities for his radical politics. This was compounded by racism, as most virulently expressed in contemporary caricatures of him. His origins as a mixed-race free black, son of a slaveholder and a slave, place him at the heart of the transatlantic slave economy. Wedderburn claims to have never been enslaved, as his pregnant mother had reached a bargain with his father 'that the child which she then bore should

---

1 Robert Wedderburn, *The Horrors of Slavery and other Writings*, ed. Iain McCalman (Princeton/Kingston, Jamaica: Marcus Wiener/Ian Randle, 1991), p. 44.

be FREE from the moment of its birth', as he explains.[2] Yet, as his writings and speeches attest, despite his free status he was both conditioned by and acutely attuned to the terrors of the totalitarian regime of plantation slavery.

Moreover, his transatlantic migration to London and his later radicalization by followers of the British agrarian socialist Thomas Spence (1750–1814) turned him into a seminal figure of the transatlantic network of diasporan African figures, which Paul Gilroy has pithily termed 'the black Atlantic':

> The history of the black Atlantic [...], continually crisscrossed by the movements of black people—not only as commodities but engaged in various struggles towards emancipation, autonomy, and citizenship—provides a means to reexamine the problems of nationality, location, identity, and historical memory. [...] These traditions have supported countercultures of modernity that touched the workers' movement but are not reducible to it. They supplied important foundations on which it could build.[3]

As I will demonstrate, Robert Wedderburn is intrinsically linked with transatlantic emancipation struggles, slave and working-class, while he cannot be reduced to either a mere abolitionist or a working-class agitator. Paradigmatically, Wedderburn illustrates Gilroy's contention that black Atlantic 'countercultures of modernities' show affinities to working-class movements in their opposition to global capitalism but, in their engagement with race, also transcend it. Wedderburn was intimately linked to the British working-class movement, yet with his black Atlantic perspective he never lost track of the centrality of slavery to the transatlantic capitalist economy, linking class closely to race. In a pamphlet, a journal and speeches he forged a novel black Atlantic discourse of slave revolution that interlaced agitation for slave revolution with stirring-up of working-class revolution in a creolized

---

2 Wedderburn, p. 48. Recent scholarship suggests that Wedderburn was enslaved until the age of two. See Ryan Hanley, *Beyond Slavery and Abolition: Black British Writing, c. 1770–1830* (Cambridge: Cambridge University Press, 2019), p. 204.
3 Gilroy, *The Black Atlantic*, p. 16.

language that 'attempts to bend the King's English to his oral mode and distinctive vernacular dialect'.[4]

Despite forging such an avant-garde revolutionary discourse, interlinking the struggles against class and race exploitation, he continues to feature as an obscure figure on the fringes of both the abolition and working-class movements in Britain. To some extent, he remains one of Michel Foucault's 'infamous men', whose obscure lives have been illuminated solely by 'an encounter with power' and the ensuing official records:[5] in Wedderburn's case, Home Office spy reports and court documents. Hegemonic scholarship on both abolition and working-class radicalism has largely ignored him. Even in a recent history of transatlantic abolition that purposely sets out to highlight black agency in the overthrow of slavery, he is assigned a mere half-page cameo in a hefty 768-page book.[6] This chapter intends to account for Wedderburn's marginalization by highlighting the explosive, avant-garde and provocative nature of his black Atlantic radical rhetoric. As I will suggest, the constant deliberate slippage between race and class and his call for violent transatlantic revolution might have contributed to his silencing.

'If you wrong [the slaves], will they not revenge?' Wedderburn's Radical Abolitionism

The emphasis on revolutionary self-emancipation is the hallmark of Wedderburn's radical abolitionism, which marries a call for a revolutionary overthrow of slavery with a proto-communist insistence on communal land ownership. As he urges the slaves in his journal *The Axe Laid to the Root* (1817): 'Above all, mind and keep possession of the land you now possess as slaves; for without that, freedom is not worth possessing.' His firebrand tirades against slavery achieved

---

4 Alan J. Rice, *Radical Narratives of the Black Atlantic* (London, New York: Continuum, 2003), p. 12.

5 Michel Foucault, 'The Life of Infamous Men', in M. Foucault, *Power, Truth, Strategy*, ed. Meaghan Morris and Paul Patton (Sydney: Feral Publications, 1979), p. 79.

6 Manisha Sinha, *The Slave's Cause: A History of Abolition* (New Haven: Yale University Press, 2016), pp. 197–8.

some notoriety, even among the highest echelons of British aboli-tionism, during his lifetime. When he was imprisoned in Dorchester gaol (1820–2), convicted of blasphemy, he seems to have received a surprising visitor: none other than the 'saint' of British abolitionism and evangelical Christian Tory MP William Wilberforce took the trouble to visit the inveterate disrespectable black radical in prison. However, Wilberforce's attempt to convert Wedderburn to evangelical Christianity and moderate abolitionism seems to have failed. Although Wedderburn dedicates his autobiographical abolitionist pamphlet *The Horrors of Slavery* (1824) to 'W. Wilberforce, MP' he immediately undercuts his praise of Wilberforce as one of 'the glorious benefactors of the human race'.[7] For the black working-class ex-convict not merely ironically thanks Wilberforce for the two expensive religious 'books beautifully bound in calf' (44) that Wilberforce bestowed on to him, but, employing money-lending imagery that emphasizes their socio-economic disparity, he further reasserts that he has not changed his radical political stance. Thanking Wilberforce for his 'advice for which he is still [Wedderburn's] debtor' (44), he distances himself from neither the blasphemies he was convicted of nor his revolutionary agitation by invoking an absolute right to freedom of speech: 'imprisonment has but confirmed that I was right' in 'daring to express my sentiments as a free man', he declares in *The Horrors of Slavery*.[8]

Symptomatic of Wedderburn's refusal to be neatly pigeon-holed, this self-published abolitionist pamphlet breaks the mould of aboli-tionist literature from the onset. It was sold by the radical publishers/ booksellers Thomas Davidson and Richard Carlile, who had been imprisoned in Dorchester gaol at the same time as Wedderburn, and contains a loose autobiographical narrative, followed by an epistolary spat with Wedderburn's white half-brother. Crucially, it combines a withering attack on the inequities of the plantocracy and their place as respectable members of the British establishment with a call for a violent overthrow of slavery. This departure from hegemonic aboli-tionism is already signalled at its opening, as it recalls and at the same time subverts the conventions of the slave narrative. Riffing on the title of the most successful British slave narrative, *The Interesting Narrative*

7 Wedderburn, pp. 43–4.
8 Wedderburn, p. 44.

of the Life of Olaudah Equiano (1789), Wedderburn frustrates his reader with a decisive anti-climax: 'The events of my life have been few and uninteresting.'[9]

Crucially, he viewed transatlantic slavery as part of a global capitalist system of exploitation built on race, class and gender oppression. While the nexus of race and class oppression dominates his work, he occasionally also indicts gender oppression. In *The Horrors of Slavery* he details the sexual abuse of his mother at the hands of his father and the flogging of his grandmother by her owner, whom she had raised. Moreover, in his trademark blasphemous satiric style, he draws on these examples to indict slavery as a system that turns black female bodies into commodities. As he implies, chattel slavery has institutionalized the sexual abuse of the female slaves, which in turn increases the 'personal property' of the slaveholder through the fathering of slave children: 'an acquisition, which might one day fetch something in the market, like a horse or a pig at Smithfield Market in London'.[10]

Wedderburn relentlessly attacks his abusive slaveholder father as a representative of his class. Constructing a blasphemous, anti-climactic, mock-heroic parallel between him and biblical kings, patriarchs and a cockerel on a dung-heap, Wedderburn describes him as a posturing sexual predator with the intellectual faculties of a chicken:

> My father's house was full of female slaves, all objects of his lusts;
> amongst whom he strutted like Solomon in his grand seraglio,
> or like a bantam cock upon his own dunghill. My good father's
> slaves did increase and multiply, like Jacob's kine; and he culti-
> vated those talents well which God had granted so amply.[11]

Denouncing the patrilineal white Scottish slaveholder branch of his family, including fighting an epistolary feud with his probable white half-brother, A. Colville, in the pages of the very same pamphlet, Wedderburn identifies with the matrilineal African line. Brought up by his maternal grandmother 'Talkee Amy', an enslaved market and

9 Wedderburn, p. 44.
10 Wedderburn, p. 46.
11 Wedderburn, p. 47.

medicine woman with strong links to syncretic African-Caribbean religions such as *obeah*, Wedderburn claims to have inherited his rebellious nature from his mother. He shares with her 'the same desire to see justice overtake the oppressors of my countrymen—and the same determination to lose no stone unturned, to accomplish so desirable an object'.[12]

Wedderburn's abolitionism is revolutionary as it is based on retributive justice. At the same time it has a Black Atlantic trajectory beyond the Caribbean colonies. By 'his oppressed countrymen', Wedderburn seems to refer to enslaved Africans throughout the Atlantic world. At the same time he is addressing the British working classes, toiling under emerging industrial capitalism, their conditions exacerbated by a series of socially highly repressive Tory governments. As Alan Rice elucidates, Wedderburn mounts a 'radical critique of capitalism throughout the British Empire' that interlinks the 'two horrors of wage and chattel slavery'.[13]

For Wedderburn, revenge forms a key revolutionary lever. In his pamphlet he asserts the right of slaves to revenge by riffing on Shylock's famous speech in Shakespeare's *The Merchant of Venice* (1598), in which he not only counters the anti-Semitic demonization of Jews by asserting their humanity but also asserts their right to execute 'revenge' on the Christians for the 'wrong' committed against them (III.1, ll. 65–6). Replacing 'Jew' with 'slave', Wedderburn asks: 'Hath not a slave feelings? If you starve them, will they not die? If you wrong them, will they not revenge?'[14] Subversively, Wedderburn undermines the abolitionist rhetoric of sympathy, which turns the shackled passive slave into an object of white pity, perhaps most succinctly expressed in the iconic abolitionist emblem of the shackled slave pleading with the white viewer: 'Am I not a man and a brother?' As Marcus Wood asserts, this image erases black agency, instead positing 'the black as a blank page for white guilt'.[15] With Wedderburn the slave's emotions,

---

12 Wedderburn p. 48.

13 Rice, *Radical Narratives*, p. 9.

14 Wedderburn, pp. 47–8.

15 Marcus Wood, *Blind Memory: Visual Representation of Slavery in England and America, 1780–1865* (Manchester: Manchester University Press, 2000), p. 23.

not the white observer's guilt-induced sympathy, becomes the focus, as he is assigned 'feelings'. Unlike the meek gratitude to the white liberator that mainstream abolitionism projected onto the slave, Wedderburn's slaves thirst for revenge on their white oppressors.

'The Fate of St. Domingo Awaits You': Wedderburn's Discursive Merger of Slave- and Working-class Revolution

Wedderburn's exhortation to revenge is not limited to *The Horrors of Slavery*. Some of the most powerful passages that cast it as the driving force of a transatlantic revolution can be found in his short-lived journal with the formidable title *The Axe Laid to The Root or A Fatal Blow to Oppressors, Being an Address to the Planters and Negroes of Jamaica* (1817).

As the plural 'oppressors' indicates, Wedderburn is attacking not merely the Jamaican slaveholders but also English capitalists and the repressive British government who support them. This becomes even more obvious in a later speech (9 August 1819) delivered in his hayloft 'chapel', in which he gave political sermons as a licensed Unitarian minister: often it has been the same capitalists who are involved both in slavery and the exploitation of British proletarians. Significantly, he terms the proletarians 'slaves' here. Alluding to the practice of a candidate buying the small number of electors in a 'rotten borough' to bribe his way into parliament, Wedderburn insists in front of his presumably working-class audience that it is this double gain, through the slave economy and industrial capitalism, that forms the foundation of the repressive British state. Albeit transmitted in the garbled language of the Home Office spy Sidney Bryant, we find an anti-colonial critique of how the slave trade, with its deliberate provocation of military conflicts in Africa to increase the number of captives, has been the engine for Britain's industrial take-off:

Wedderbourne [*sic*]—rose—Government was necessitated to send men in arms to West Indies or Africa which produced commotion. They would employ blacks to go and steal females— they would put them in sacks and would be murdered if they made an alarm Vessels would be in readiness and they would fly off with them This was done by Parliament men—who done it for gain—the same as they employed them in their Cotton factories to make Slaves of them to become possessed of money to bring them into Parliament.[16]

By spinning a fiction that the British government would capture Afro-Caribbean or African women to employ them in cotton mills, Wedderburn suggests that slavery forms the economic base for the British state and economy. Moreover, he merges slaves and workers. By placing them on the same spectrum of exploitation he also subverts widespread attempts to play one group against the other. Perhaps most notoriously among contemporary English radicals, William Cobbett epitomizes 'the Negrophobe orthodoxies of English Radicalism',[17] as he juxtaposes the exploited and down-trodden British labourer with the happy-go-lucky slave: the 'wretched White slave'[18] with the enslaved 'fat and lazy Negro that laughs from morning to night!'[19]

In contrast, Wedderburn aims to engender transatlantic, trans-racial, revolutionary solidarity in his exhortations for revolution in his *Axe Laid to the Root*. Ostensibly directed to a Jamaican audience, but in fact speaking to metropolitan radicals, he employs the same double reference of slaves and British workers throughout much of this short-lived journal. Daringly, he recalls the revolutionary violence of the Haitian Revolution (1791–1804) and its fundamental socio-revolutionary overthrow of plantation slavery to call for a general overthrow of slavery and the oppressive forces of capitalism throughout the Atlantic World:

> Prepare for flight, ye planters, for the fate of St. Domingo awaits you. Get ready your blood hounds, the allies which you employed against the Maroons. Recollect that fermentation will be universal. Their weapons are their bill-hooks [...] They will be victorious in their fight, slaying all before them; they want no turnpike roads: they will not stand to engage organised troops, like the silly Irish rebels. [...] They will slay man, woman, and

16 Wedderburn, p. 114.
17 Wood, *Slavery*, p. 172.
18 William Cobbett, 'To Mr. Wilberforce', *Cobbett's Political Register*, 48: 11, 1823, pp. 641–93, here pp. 661.
19 Cobbett, 'To Mr. Wilberforce', p. 677.

child, and not spare the virgin, whose interest is connected with slavery, whether black, white or tawny. O ye planters, you know this has been done; the cause which produced former bloodshed still remains,—of necessity similar aspects must take place. The holy alliance of Europe, cannot prevent it, they have enough to do at home, being compelled to keep a standing army in the time of peace, to enforce the civil law. My heart glows with revenge, and cannot forgive.[20]

Recalling the spectre of St Domingo and the Jamaican Maroons who, after two wars with the British colonial army, achieved autonomy and freedom, Wedderburn preaches a revolutionary abolitionism rooted in slave agency.

This could not be further removed from Wilberforce's conservative Evangelical approach, which championed abolition through acts of parliament. In 1824 in a debate in the House of Commons Wilberforce conjured up the spectre of the Haitian Revolution—a 'first explosion' followed by 'dire disasters'—as he denounces revolutionary self-emancipation as 'the desperate course of taking [the slaves'] cause into their own hands'.[21] I have shown elsewhere how Wedderburn appropriates the Gothic demonization of the Haitian Revolution, of which the 'massacre of the innocent', of 'woman, child' or 'virgin', forms an essential trope, and taps into a Black Atlantic counter-discourse that turns the Gothic against the colonial masters.[22] Wedderburn further insists that the slave economy is not always based upon clear-cut racial divides but is in essence a class-based socio-economic system: even the 'black' and 'tawny' that play their part in propping up the transatlantic system of slavery have to be killed, as their 'interest is connected with slavery'. 'Interest', with its manifold meanings relating to property, business, finance, stakes and so on, subtly suggests that transatlantic

20 Wedderburn, p. 81.
21 House of Commons, 'Amelioration of the Condition of the Slave Population in the West Indies', 16 May 1824. In Hansard, https://api.parliament.uk/historic-hansard/commons/1824/mar/16/amelioration-of-the-condition-of-the (accessed 17 November 2015).
22 Raphael Hoermann, '"A Very Hell of Horrors"? The Haitian Revolution and the Early Transatlantic Haitian Gothic', *Slavery & Abolition*, 37: 1, 2016, pp. 194–200.

slavery is the primary economic engine for transatlantic capitalism, with race and racism functioning as its essential ideological levers.

In his agitation for transatlantic revolution, Wedderburn grasps the close nexus of race and class within transatlantic slavery, capitalism and colonialism. As Trinidad-born Black Atlantic Marxist C.L.R. James would later argue in his 1938 history of the Haitian Revolution *The Black Jacobins*:

> The race question is subsidiary to the class question in politics, and to think of imperialism in terms of race is disastrous. But to neglect the racial factor as merely incidental is an error only less grave than to make it fundamental.[23]

Wedderburn places this nexus of race and class within the perspective of transatlantic imperialism. As he suggests in the passage above, repressive European forces will face similar annihilation at the hands of the working classes as that which Saint-Domingue slaveholders experienced at the hands of their slaves. If the rebellious workers adopt the guerrilla tactics of maroons and slave rebels and refrain from engaging the British army in open battle, as the 'silly Irish rebels' of 1798 and 1803 did in the fight against their British colonial masters, then transatlantic 'fermentation' will indeed be 'universal'. However, although Wedderburn rhetorically and ideologically deploys the Haitian Revolution as a catalyst for a British workers' revolution, he does not reduce this slave revolution to the 'first successful workers' *revolt* in modern history', as Peter Linebaugh and Marcus Rediker suggest.[24]

'To Murder their Masters as Soon as they Please': Transatlantic Revolutionary Solidarity

Even more explicitly still, in a handbill advertising the debate of 9 August 1819 in his Soho 'chapel', Wedderburn endorses revolutionary violence as the engine of transatlantic emancipation:

23 C.L.R. James, *The Black Jacobins: Toussaint L'Ouverture and the San Domingo Revolution*, 2nd edn (London: Penguin, 2001. Original edition, 1938), p. 207.
24 Linebaugh and Rediker, *The Many-headed Hydra*, p. 319; my emphasis.

The Following Question will be
DEBATED
Has a Slave an inherent right to slay his Master
who refuses him
HIS LIBERTY?
The Offspring of an African Slave will
open the Question.[25]

As the bill suggests, again this call for slave revolution is interwoven with a call for revolution in the heady days leading up to the Peterloo Massacre (1819) in Manchester, during which army and militia forces killed dozens of peaceful working-class protesters and wounded hundreds more. In what is evidently a rhetorical question, not even worthy of debate, the bill's heading seems to justify radical-revolutionary change in Britain's government: Can it be Murder to/KILL A/ TYRANT?[26] As Iain MacCalman points out, even the Prince Regent was so concerned by Wedderburn's constant agitation for revolution and regicide that in August 1819 he sought assurances from the home secretary Lord Sidmouth, who promised the ruler that this '"notorious firebrand, Wedderburne" would be silenced by prosecution'.[27]

Ironically, it is thanks to this intense Home Office surveillance of Wedderburn that a sketch of this debate has been preserved in the ministry's archival records for posterity. With the assembly unanimously affirming the right of the slave to kill his master, 'Mr W. then exclaimed, well Gentlemen, I can now *write home and tell the Slaves to murder their Masters as soon as they please. Sd. J. Bryant*'.[28]

Speaking both as the son of a slave and a slaveholder and as the ultra-radical preacher and impoverished London tailor, Wedderburn sees the 'Slaves' who have rights to slay the 'Masters' as both chattel and wage slaves: the Caribbean slaves *and* the oppressed and exploited proletarians in Britain. Similarly, their 'Masters' are both the slaveholders and the capitalists and the repressive British government, while 'Home' seems an even more ambiguous and contested notion for

---

25 Wedderburn, p. 113.
26 Wedderburn, p. 113.
27 Wedderburn, p. 23.
28 Wedderburn, p. 115; emphasis in original.

Wedderburn the Black Atlantic radical. Is 'home' Jamaica, as he seems to infer, even after having spent his entire adult life in London? Or is it London, which would turn this exhortation into a thinly veiled call for a violent overthrow of Britain's social and political *status quo*?

A handbill in the Home Office's files on radicals goes some way to answering these questions by providing Wedderburn's version of this debate. Headed with another revolutionary threat, 'Vengence [*sic*] Awaits the Guilty', it announces a subsequent debate on the increasing political tensions in the run-up to the Peterloo Massacre (which occurred on the date set for the debate, 16 August 1819). At the bottom, the bill summarized the previous debate:

> The last Debate respecting a Slave having a Right to slay his Master who refuses him his Freedom, was decided in Favor of the Slave without a discerning Voice, by a numerous and enlightened Assembly, who exultingly expressed their Desire of hearing of another sable Nation freeing itself by the Dagger from the base Tyranny of their Christian Masters.
> *Several Gentlemen declared their readiness to assist them.*
> *The Offspring of an African who opened the debate, was highly gratified.*[29]

This is a masterpiece of satirical radicalism. Writing of himself in the third person as the 'Offspring of an African', he expresses profound satisfaction with members of the audience volunteering to assist in revolutionary slave emancipation. While this scene might be Wedderburn's fiction, the Haitian Revolution is again clearly cast as the blueprint for abolition, with the goal of creating another black nation in the Americas through the means of anti-colonial violence. With the spectre of the Haitian Revolution still fresh in the mind of the British public, endorsing the prospect of a British Caribbean colony turning, through slave revolution, into an independent black state in the mould of Haiti is a radical position unmatched in contemporary British discourse. A mere four years later the radical William Cobbett, in his popular *Political Register*, would conjure up such a scenario of Jamaica turning into a second Haiti as a vision of horror.

29 The National Archives HO/42/192.

As Cobbett suggests, this Jamaican slave revolution will continue to write the unfinished horror tale of Caribbean slave revolutions, as it 'will be a second chapter of the desolation and bloodshed of St. Domingo'.[30]

Moreover, as the handbill emphasizes, Wedderburn casts neither the French Revolution nor a mythical Albion of free-born Englishmen as inspiration for the English workers, but rather revolutionary slave resistance. Iain McCalman overlooks this ideological innovation, when he, rather dismissively, claims that Wedderburn's main goals in his speeches were 'to debunk authority and impel political action through shock, pathos or humour': 'Wedderburn's fiery extempore speeches contain little in the way of original political theory.'[31] For such a noted expert on Wedderburn, McCalman's statement can only be explained by a Eurocentric attitude that dismisses any non-European ideology as banal and inferior: the very same attitude Wedderburn set out to challenge. As Wedderburn asserts, the revolutionary fervour of the Caribbean slaves has been far superior to that of the British working class that, in the contemporary racist ideology, is deemed superior to that of the black slaves:

> One of those men who appeared to be the principal in their concern is a Mulatto and announced himself as the Descendant of an African Slave—After noticing the Insurrections of the Slaves in some of the West India Islands he said they fought in some instances for twenty years for 'Liberty'—and he then appealed to Britons who boasted such superior feeling and principles, whether they were ready to fight now but for a short time for their Liberties.[32]

Even filtered through the writings of the outraged Home Office spy the Rev. Chetwode Eustache, who complains that 'Doctrines were certainly of the most dreadful nature', we hear Wedderburn's

30 William Cobbett, 'The West India Colonies', *Cobbett's Political Register*, 48: 10, 1823, pp. 577–92, at p. 592.
31 Wedderburn, p. 25.
32 Wedderburn, p. 116.

Black Atlantic voice.[33] He throws down the gauntlet to the European racist mindset that cast people of African descent as inferior when he ironically lauds the 'superior feelings and principles' of white Britons. In particular, he attacks the claim that Britons would know more about liberty than the chattel slaves of the Caribbean who have resisted and fought for liberty ever since they were first captured and enslaved. While Wedderburn also aims to provoke his audience into action by holding up the model of the courageous Caribbean slave rebels, this transcends mere satiric agitation, to which McCalman wants to reduce Wedderburn's speeches. On the contrary, Wedderburn's position marks a theoretical advance as he points towards a Black Atlantic relocation of the axis of transatlantic liberation. For he locates the source in the struggle for emancipation, 'Liberty', not with the white Jacobins in France and radicals in Europe, nor with the slaveholding white North American revolutionaries. Instead, with him transatlantic emancipation begins with the Caribbean slave revolutionaries. In essence, he thus dismisses the American and French Revolutions, with their compromised stance towards slavery, as revolutionary models for working-class emancipation and replaces them with the Haitian Revolution. As I have argued elsewhere, this stance even challenges later Black Atlantic accounts of the Haitian Revolution, as in C.L.R. James's *Black Jacobins*, in which the slaves take their main revolutionary inspiration and cues from the French revolutionaries.[34]

While Wedderburn recasts revolutionary 'Liberty' as a *Caribbean* concept and refigures Caribbean slaves as the Atlantic's revolutionary avant-garde, he also aims to instil transatlantic and trans-racial class solidarity. This is staged in the handbill which reports how allegedly 'Several Gentlemen declared their readiness to assist' the slaves in slaying their masters. This moment of trans-racial solidarity suggests that Wedderburn's 'numerous and enlightened' working-class audience are more advanced in their attitude towards race than many of the European Enlightenment figures, who were profoundly racist and/

33 Wedderburn, p. 116.
34 Raphael Hörmann, 'Black Jacobins: Toward a Genealogy of a Transatlantic Trope', in Charlotte A. Lerg and Heléna Tóth (eds), *Transatlantic Revolutionary Cultures, 1789–1861* (Leiden: Brill, 2018), pp. 40–7.

or supported slavery.[35] Irrespective of whether this is fact or fiction, I would argue that, for Wedderburn, these moments of lower-class revolutionary identification and solidarity do form the nucleus for the future transatlantic revolution and thus a transformation of Europe's rotten, unequal society.

Dis-remembering Robert Wedderburn?
Wedderburn on Display in the 'Sugar and Slavery Gallery' in the Museum of London, Docklands

While Wedderburn is now an obscure historical figure, at least between the mid 1810s and the early 1820s he enjoyed, if not fame, at least a certain notoriety. Not only, as pointed out, did Wilberforce visit him in Dorchester gaol, but one of London's leading caricaturists, George Cruikshank, portrayed him at least twice as a central figure of a cartoon. In the first, 'A Peep into a London Tavern' (1817), we see a racially angrily caricatured Wedderburn denouncing the non-revolutionary socialist views of Robert Owen 'as just another system of slavery'. The second, 'The New Union Club' (1819), full of racist bile, constitutes a phantasmagoric orgy of cross-racial debauchery and anarchy with a voiceless Wedderburn at its centre. These political cartoons provide further proof that for some years Wedderburn was a public figure, known beyond the small circle of metropolitan ultra-radicals and their nemesis, the Home Office.

This contrasts with the lack of his memorialization at present. There are no memorials to him and he is omitted from the International Slavery Museum in Liverpool. To my knowledge there is only

---

35 Joan Dayan, *Haiti, History, and the Gods* (Berkeley: University of California Press, 1995). Emmanuel Chukwudi Eze, *Race and the Enlightenment: A Reader* (Cambridge, MA: Blackwell, 1997). Emmanuel Chukwudi Eze, 'The Color of Reason: The Idea of "Race" in Kant's Anthropology', in Emmanuel Chukwudi Eze (ed.), *Postcolonial African Philosophy: A Critical Reader* (Cambridge, MA and London: Wiley Blackwell, 1997), pp. 103–31. Louis Sala-Molins, *Dark Side of the Light: Slavery and the French Enlightenment*, trans. John Conteh-Morgan (Minneapolis: University of Minnesota Press, 2006). Sibylle Fischer, 'Atlantic Ontologies: On Violence and Being Human', *E-MISFÉRICA*, 12: 1, Caribbean Rasanblaj, 2015, http://hemisphericinstitute.org/hemi/en/emisferica-121-caribbean-rasanblaj/fischer (accessed 21 June 2015).

one museum that features Wedderburn—the Museum of London Docklands, as part of its 'London, Sugar and Slavery' gallery. This is housed in the former West India Dock, which opened in 1802 mainly to unload and store slave-produced commodities from the triangular trade. Despite the proximity of its opening to the abolition of the British transatlantic slave trade it was deeply implicated in it, for between 1802 and 1807 'twenty-two ships sailed from the dock to West Africa where they purchased more than 7,000 enslaved Africans who were transported to the Americas'.[36]

It seems fitting that such a scathing and trenchant critic of the capitalist slave economy as Robert Wedderburn should be featured in the gallery. Moreover, his agitation for revolutionary self-emancipation chimes with the key objective of the gallery to tell 'the story of self-determination by enslaved Africans to win their freedom through rebellion', as David Spence explains.[37] Particularly given his general absence in museums, the fact that Robert Wedderburn features as many as three times in the gallery is remarkable. As its co-curator Dr Tom Wareham acknowledges, 'we have a soft spot for Robert here, he was a great character.'[38] So, here, 'for the first time since his death', is Britain 'finally giving full credit to his work'?[39] The first exhibit features the only known portrait of him, the frontispiece of the 1824 pamphlet *The Horrors of Slavery* (Figure 16.1), placed next to the panel on Olaudah Equiano. This arrangement might suggest an equivalence in importance with one of Britain's most successful Black writers. However, at the same time, their stark differences in social status seem erased: Equiano, the respectable radical, who, at his death, was the richest black person in Britain, while the unrespectable proletarian radical Wedderburn (whose date of death remains unknown)

36 David Spence, 'Making the London, Sugar and Slavery Gallery at the Museum of London Docklands', in Geoff Cubitt, Kalliopi Fouseki and Laurajane Smith (eds), *Representing Enslavement and Abolition in Museums* (London: Routledge, 2011), p. 172.

37 Spence, p. 181.

38 Maev Kennedy, 'Slave Owner and Abolitionist Come Face to Face', *The Guardian*, 8 November 2007, https://www.theguardian.com/artand-design/2007/nov/08/art1?I (accessed 14 August 2018).

39 Arifa Akbar, 'Slave's Son who Inspired the Chartists Gets Credit at last', *The Independent*, 9 November 2007, p. 21.

16.1 Frontispiece to Wedderburn's pamphlet 'The Horrors of Slavery'.
Public domain. https://creativecommons.org/publicdomain/mark/1.0/

was probably buried in an unmarked pauper's grave in an unknown graveyard. The label beneath Wedderburn's image avoids any mention of his precarious socio-economic status and only the concluding sentence seems to imply that he was a working-class radical: 'Licensed as a Methodist preacher, Wedderburn used the pulpit to connect working-class ideas with the anti-slavery Movement.' Even though this description captures key aspects of his Black Atlantic political agitation, his revolutionary voice remains silenced. While all the other black abolitionists are featured with text excerpts, any quotation from Wedderburn's writings is lacking.

The second exhibit consists of a composite photograph by the white British-born artist Paul Howard entitled 'Lloyd Gordon as Robert Wedderburn' (2011). Commissioned especially for the gallery, the 'actor Lloyd Gordon' models Wedderburn,[40] as the photograph restages the adjacent oil painting of 'Portrait of George Hibbert' (1812) by Sir Thomas Lawrence. In the restaging, Howard replaces Hibbert, one of the most notorious profiteers of the enslavement of Africans, slave-trader and -holder, philanthropist, West India merchant and eight-times chairman of the West India Dock Company, with the Black Atlantic proletarian radical Wedderburn. Admittedly, this juxtaposition of the respectable epitome of British slavery with the unrespectable agitator for slave and working-class revolution could harbour some radical potential. Yet, in my opinion, this is largely wasted here. For Wedderburn, imitating Hibbert's imperious pose, seems prouder to finally have usurped Hibbert's position as Chairman of the West India Dock Company than to have overthrown transatlantic capitalism.

Crucially, Wedderburn's radical writings are again erased in the photograph. Bizarrely, it replaces his journal *The Axe Laid to the Root* with *The Poor Man's Guardian* (1831–5), a radical newspaper only founded after Wedderburn had disappeared from the political stage. This journal's deployment here seems so haphazard that Katie Donnington, in her PhD thesis 'The benevolent merchant? George Hibbert (1757–1837) and the Representation of West Indian Mercantile Identity',[41] even inadvertently corrects this image in a description of it:

40 Kennedy.
41 UCL 2013.

'Hibbert's silverware and dock designs were replaced with Wedderburn's magazine [*sic*] *Axe Laid to the Root*.'[42]

However, on closer inspection the photograph reveals an allusion to the journal's title: an axe lying on the floor. As Paul Howard explains in a blog (which also features the opening page of the first issue of *The Axe to the Root*), this '"re-constructed portrait"' of Wedderburn 'includes contemporary analogies and references to Wedderburn's achievements including an axe laid on the floor of No 1 Warehouse in Docklands, the only surviving building in London of the transatlantic slave trade'.[43] Yet, an axe laid on the floor is not the same as the axe laid to the root of exploitation and oppression, of the transatlantic slave economy. Similarly, the cane knife dangling from his hip seems more a fashionable accoutrement, like a dagger, than the work tool and primary weapon of the slaves.

What, then, of the 'contemporary analogies' Howard mentions? Michael Morris has argued that the window view with the tower of Canary Wharf looming behind the West India Dock in the background updates Wedderburn's radical critique of capitalism for the millennium: it 'suggests the connection historical slavery and contemporary global capitalism and, perhaps, the spirit of resistance that is still necessary today'.[44] While the image might indeed aim to draw these links, I would argue that its effectiveness is seriously hampered by downplaying Wedderburn's revolutionary radicalness.

Perhaps somewhat surprisingly, the final exhibit, a display for children, is the most effective, as it captures Wedderburn's complexities. In a rectangular panel bordered by a blue pattern reminiscent of West African textile, there are three flaps and an instruction: 'Look at Robert Wedderburn, the man in this [Howard's] painting [*sic*]. / Do you think he was ...The son of a rich man who owned many enslaved people / A preacher in a church? / A dangerous revolutionary'. Of course, all three of these characterizations are accurate, as is revealed when the flaps are lifted up. Ironically, in its simplicity this display captures the

---

42 Quoted in Michael Morris, *Scotland and the Caribbean, c.1740–1833: Atlantic Archipelagos* (New York: Routledge, 2015), p. 175.
43 Paul Howard, 'London, Sugar and Slavery', http://www.paulhoward.info/html/ls02.html (accessed 14 August 2018).
44 Morris, pp. 175–8.

richness and the multiple identities of the figure of Robert Wedderburn much more sharply than the other, more ambitious, representations.

As I have attempted to demonstrate, it is exactly Wedderburn's refusal to be pigeonholed into one category that vexes the academic drive for categorization. At the same time, the challenge posed by this subversive anarchic black Atlantic revolutionary, who mounted one of the first powerful intersectional critiques of capitalism that yokes class and race together, calls for further exploration by scholars, museums and activists alike.

CHAPTER SEVENTEEN

The Next Chapter: The Black Presence in the Nineteenth Century

Caroline Bressey

As the previous chapters in this collection have illustrated, during the long eighteenth century black people in Britain made up a diverse community, from activists and well-known figures such as Olaudah Equiano and Ignatius Sancho to a marginalized poor. Scholars of black history have deliberated upon what became of the descendants of these individuals during the nineteenth century. As the British Empire intensified its expansion in Africa, doctors and lawyers came to Britain to obtain professional qualifications; some remained and some returned home to become part of an imperial elite. Others railed against the Empire, creating a different network of educated Pan-Africanists who sought to challenge racial injustice. But the vast majority of the black presence would have been residing among the working classes, employed as domestic servants, nurses, groomsmen and so on. Others found work as actors, circus performers and singers. Many probably became an 'indivisible part of the urban poor', the records of their lives, as Peter Fryer described them, 'obscure and scattered' and 'for the most part forgotten'.[1] This is somewhat curious, as the Victorians were immense record-keepers, creating a mass of data, such as national census returns and hospital and asylum records, some of which

---

1 Fryer, *Staying Power*, p. 235. For further reflections see Gretchen H. Gerzina's Introduction to Gretchen H. Gerzina (ed.), *Black Victorians, Black Victoriana* (New Jersey and London: Rutgers University Press, 2003).

incorporated the developing technology of photography. All of these archives are places where histories of black people reside, though their archival traces are not always easy to identify. This is in part because, for example, though the national census provides information on employment, marital status and place of birth, a person's ethnicity was not regularly recorded, so the personal geographies of the Victorian descendants of the 'Black Georgians' are still seemingly 'obscure and scattered'. The reasons for this were also of interest to the Victorians themselves.

In March 1875 an essay titled 'The Black Man' was published in Charles Dickens's weekly periodical *All the Year Round*. The piece presented a history of 'The Black Man' in Britain from the 'quarrel' some fifty years earlier between 'Sir Walter Scott and the antiquaries' on the first appearance of 'the black man in England' to their lives in the 1870s.[2] The Black Man who was the focus of this essay was both a historical and a contemporary figure, a runaway slave, a free man, a man 'of Asia or of Africa'—and always, in the references given, a man. Written for the middle-class audience who read *All the Year Round*, the essay covers many of the themes still of interest to researchers of the black presence today: When did the first black man arrive on British shores? What did the term 'black' mean in different periods? Who were the individuals that created the need for runaway slave advertisements? And what happened to the black community in Britain after abolition?[3] The author argued that the black man of Shakespeare's time, as illustrated by characters such as Othello and Aaron in *Titus Andronicus*, was plainly 'of African blackness, without approach to olive or tawny tints—an unmitigated "nigger"'.[4] But, drawing on examples from the late 1600s, they argued that the black-a-moor could relate to 'the dark-skinned of both Africa and Asia', as illustrated by 'Hue and Cry' advertisements it presented from seventeenth-century issues of the *London Gazette*.

2 Anon., 'The Black Man', *All the Year Round*, 6 March 1875, p. 489.
3 On the readership of the periodical see Lorna Huett, '"Among the Unknown Public": Household Words, *All the Year Round* and the Mass-Market Weekly Periodical in the Mid-Nineteenth Century', 2004 Van Arsdel Prize Essay, *Victorian Periodicals Review*, 38: 1, 2005, pp. 61–82.
4 Anon., 'The Black Man', p. 489.

Run away from his master, Captain St Lo, the 21inst., Obedelah Ealias Abraham, a Moor, swarthy complexion, short frizzled hair, a gold ring in his ear, in a black coat and blew breeches. He took with him a blew Turkish watch-gown, a Turkish suit of clothing that he used to wear about town, and several other things. Whoever brings him to Mr Lozel's house in Green-street shall have one guinea for his charges.

A black boy, an Indian, about thirteen years old, run away the 8th inst. from Putney, with a collar about his neck with this inscription: 'The Lady Bromfield's black, in Lincoln's Inn Fields.' Whoever brings him to Sir Edward Broomfield's, at Putney, shall have a guinea reward.

And from the *Daily Journal*, 1728:

To be sold, a negro boy, aged eleven years. Inquire of the Virginia Coffee House in Threadneedle Street, behind the Royal Exchange.[5]

There is no reading against the grain of the advertisements in the essay, no consideration of the transatlantic journeys that brought lone children to Putney or other parts of Britain, no sense that 'being lost' might have been an active and successful form of resistance and, finally, no reflection on what kind of networks might be in place around the city to support those who ran away. The attention of *All the Year Round*'s readers was drawn to the sums that were offered for the return of these young people to their owners. They were, the author pointed out, sums similar to those offered by pet owners of the 1870s for the return of a lost dog. The observation that there was also 'something canine in that wearing of the inscribed collar by Lady Broomfield's black' implies some sense of complicity of the black child wearing the collar, despite the horrific nature and powerlessness of enslavement that many Victorians would have read or heard about through publications such as *Uncle Tom's Cabin*, as well as the tours undertaken by former enslaved Americans such as Henry Box Brown, William and

5 Anon., 'The Black Man', pp. 490–1.

Ellen Craft and, perhaps most famously, Frederick Douglass, who spoke to audiences across Britain between 1845 and 1847.[6]

Uncle Tom's Cabin would become a popular stage production in the late nineteenth century. In 1870 Bristol's new Theatre Royal advertised a revival of a production, with all the original effects, and they hoped to attract the vast audiences and overflowing houses that had attended the original performances.[7] In 1875 the theatre produced another revival, now titled 'A Night with Uncle Tom', over three nights. Though for one reporter the story had lost its political significance following the abolition of slavery in the United States, it remained 'a story of thrilling interest' and was as 'dramatic in its incidents and as emotional in its *denouement* as ever'.[8] Later that year, Jarrett and Palmer's 'Uncle Tom's Cabin Company' found itself written up in the press in a less favourable light. Alexander Brown, 'a coloured man, described as an actor' was charged at Coventry City Police Court with threatening to kill Robert Weston, another black actor.[9] Both men were part of the company performing in the city that autumn, and after a performance at the local theatre one Monday evening the pair had argued at their lodgings. Brown drew a knife, in self-defence Weston drew a pistol, and as they fought the gun went off. The pair were parted and no one was hurt, but as Brown continued with his threats he was apprehended the following day. The court's bench instructed the case to be withdrawn when Mr Jarrett agreed to have the pair separated by sending Brown to London, with the police ensuring he left town. The publicity did not seem to harm the group and Jarrett and Palmer's production company retained its popularity. In 1878 their 'Uncle Tom's Combination' toured with

6 See R.J.M. Blackett, 'Fugitive Slaves in Britain: The Odyssey of William and Ellen Craft', *Journal of American Studies*, 12: 1, 1978, pp. 41–62; and Martha Cutter, 'Will the Real Henry "Box" Brown Please Stand Up?' *Common-Place: The Journal of Early American Life*, 16: 1, 2015; and Fionnghuala Sweeney, *Frederick Douglass and the Atlantic World* (Liverpool: Liverpool University Press, 2007). For a map of the locations of Douglass' and other abolitionist tours see Hannah Murray, http://frederickdouglassinbritain.com (accessed 21 August 2018).

7 *Western Daily Press*, 15 November 1870, p. 70, p. 1.

8 *Bristol Daily Post*, 19 February 1875, p. 3.

9 *Birmingham Daily Post*, 10 October 1875, p. 5.

the 'Great American Idyl'. The company, comprising of twelve white and sixty black actors, was due to perform first at the Theatre Royal Manchester, before planned dates in Chester, Derby, Nottingham, York and Dublin.[10]

Having left the company in 1875, if Alexander Brown sought another acting job once in London *The Era* would have been a good place for him to begin his search. A weekly newspaper, *The Era* came to focus on theatres, actors, music halls and other entertainment spaces and carried advertisements for production companies seeking performers for all these stages. By the 1880s advertisements appear for 'coloured actors' to take part in 'Uncle Tom's Cabin' throughout the county.[11] In June 1882 an advertisement for 'several coloured people, male and female' was placed for immediate engagement with the Uncle Tom's Cabin company, then based at the Market Hall, Whitehaven, in Cumberland. For those who were successful long-term engagements were promised.[12] In April 1886 two more production companies were looking for similar performers.

> Wanted, for 'Uncle Tom's Cabin,' Coloured people, specialities, Dramatic Artists, and Pianiste, open 26inst.. Assembly Hall, Eccelshall, Staff.
> Wanted, Coloured People (Male and Female Jubilee Singers) Few other vacancies. Clarence Sounnes 'Uncle Tom's Cabin': T R Stockton-on-Tees.[13]

'Uncle Tom's Cabin' was not the only production looking particularly for black actors and actresses. In 1897 a touring American Sketch Company was seeking 'a Good Amateur' to join them on tour, a 'Coloured Man preferred'.[14] Andy Merrilees' Panorama of America and Canada also sought 'Ladies and Gentlemen (Coloured Persons

---

10 *The Tasmanian*, 4 January 1879, p. 13; 'THOSE JOLLY DARKIES', http://nla.gov.au/nla.news-article198899799 (accessed 22 August 2018).

11 From '*The Melodies Linger On*' by W. McQueen Pope, pp. 274–5. See http://www.arthurlloyd.co.uk/Era.htm and *The Waterloo Directory of English Newspapers and Periodicals: 1800–1900*, BL newspaper website.

12 *The Era*, 10 June 1882, p. 23.

13 *The Era*, 17 April 1885, p. 20.

14 *The Era*, 10 April 1897, p. 26.

preferred)' to perform in 1882.[15] In the same year Mr T. Wilkinson, musical director of the Grover Ex-Slave Troupe, was also looking for black performers. He had been commissioned by Grover to employ 'several Good Coloured Men' who could play, sing and dance for the Opera House in Bolton.[16] Not all adverts were so courteous in their language. The Victoria Varieties, also based in Bolton, wanted performers for all their branches, and required performers immediately for current and future dates; their request was for: 'NIGGERS, Novelties, Specialities, and Concert Hall Talent'.[17]

These advertisements give a sense of the opportunities and limitations of roles available to black people seeking work on the stage, and they challenge the observation put forward in 'The Black Man' that those who were on stage were 'only those whose complexion is obviously artificial—who are rather lamp-blacks than real blacks. Ethiopian serenaders they call themselves; singing, to the accompaniment of obstreperous instruments, now ultra-sentimental ditties.'[18] And though the 'Nigger novelties' referred to above might have been placed to attract white entertainers who performed in blackface, black performers such as William Henry Lane who also performed with blackface minstrel groups complicated these spaces.[19] Though all these roles were racialized, black individuals could find work as performers, from 'serious' roles in stage productions such as *Uncle Tom's Cabin* to performances in circuses, as lion tamers or 'wild men' in 'freak shows'.[20]

---

15 *The Era*, 10 June 1882, p. 23.

16 *The Era*, 15 April 1882, p. 23.

17 *The Era*, 10 June 1882, p. 23

18 Anon., 'The Black Man', p. 493.

19 Paul Gilmore, '"De Genewine Artekil": William Wells Brown, Blackface Minstrelsy, and Abolitionism', *American Literature*, 69: 4, 1997, pp. 743–80. Gilmore notes that Charles Dickens saw Lane perform in New York, describing him in *American Notes* (1842) as 'the greatest dancer known ... dancing with all sorts of legs and no legs', p. 754.

20 Nadja Durbach, *Spectacle of Deformity: Freak Shows and Modern British Culture* (Oakland: University of California Press, 2010). John M. Turner, 'Pablo Fanque, Black Circus Proprietor', in Gretchen H. Gerzina (ed.), *Black Victorians, Black Victoriana* (New Brunswick: Rutgers University Press, 2003), pp. 20–38.

WANTED a Steady Man as Animal Keeper. One that will enter the Lion's Den and give a performance if required. A Coloured Man Preferred.[21]

WANTED for Powell and Clarke's Circus, Ireland, to join immediately, a COLOURED MAN or WOMAN, to perform with Serpents. Railway Hotel, Town Hall-Street Belfast.[22]

Four years after 'The Black Man' was published, Miss LaLa, also known as the 'African Princess', performed in Manchester and in London at the Royal Aquarium, displaying her skills as a strongwoman, wire walker and trapeze artist.[23] But the author of 'The Black Man' did not draw attention to such arenas of popular culture. For them, black men were associated with the domestic spaces of the aristocracy and upper-middle classes, and their places in these homes was seemingly changing beyond recognition. Caricaturists represented the British nation's manners and customs through images that included the 'negro coachman, a very portly person, with powder over his curly [hair]; the negro footman, in a brilliant livery, stately of port and stalwart of body, if somewhat unshapely as to his nether limbs'.[24] Wanted advertisements show that black men did indeed seek to work in these roles. In 1857 a 'Coloured Young Man', then aged twenty-two, sought work as an under butler or footman through the *Liverpool Mercury*. He paid to ensure potential employers knew he stood at 5ft 5inches, though no mention was made of his nether limbs.[25] The 1860s provides further examples of black men seeking work as footmen and groomsmen.

FOOTMAN in a private family, or Groom and make himself generally-useful. A coloured young man. Five years' character. H.L. 19 Marylebone-lane.[26]

Wanted by a Coloured Man, a Situation as Butler, Footman

21 *The Era*, 19 October 1889, p. 19.
22 *The Era*, 17 March 1883, p. 23.
23 Marilyn R. Brown, '"Miss La La's Teeth": Reflections on Degas and "Race"', *The Art Bulletin*, 89: 4, 2007, pp. 738–65, http://www.jstor.org/stable/25067359 (accessed 10 November 2019).
24 Anon., 'The Black Man', p. 493.
25 *Liverpool Mercury*, 23 March 1857, p. 2.
26 *The Times*, 15 May 1860, p. 14.

or Valet. Four years experience at last place. Good References. Address Valentine Cottage.[27]

But, by 1875, 'The Black Man' author claimed that the 'negro footman is now rarely seen; and indeed it would appear that there has been a considerable departure of the "black man" from among us. He fills no longer the place he once occupied in our English domestic life.'[28] The roles undertaken by black people in an earlier time, performing duties within domestic households with conspicuous signs of their status in the form of a silver collar or the livery of a footman, had passed, and seemingly, for the author, the black presence had disappeared with them: 'A negro crossing-sweeper or two may remain; and occasionally there is to be encountered a black bishop.'[29] But even if their roles as footmen had altered in the changing urban landscape of the emerging modern city, advertisements from nineteenth-century newspapers show us that black men continued to seek employment in Britain as domestic servants during the 1870s and beyond.

In November 1876 a 'Coloured Man (from Canada)' placed an advertisement looking for work in the *Liverpool Mercury*; he was fifty years old, accustomed to working with horses and sought a placement in a 'gentleman's family'.[30] Further examples illustrate the continuing diversity of the black presence in Britain, one that included the descendants of those who had been part of Equiano and Sancho's Britain, while others embodied the complexities of British and other European nations' imperial expansion and emigration across the empire:

Valet or In-door servant, single-handed, Coloured man from Africa. Speaks Italian, German and English. Age 25. height 5ft 7. 12 years good person character. Disengaged April 1st. S.B. 41 Brewer-Street, Golden Square.[31]

27 *Liverpool Daily Post*, 22 February 1866, p. 3.
28 Anon., 'The Black Man', p. 492.
29 Anon., 'The Black Man', p. 493.
30 *Liverpool Mercury*, 7 November 1876, p. 5.
31 *The Times*, 16 March 1880.

In-door servant ... A Coloured Young man, age 22, speaks French and English. Half-Cast Anglo-American. Good References—H.S. 43 Bassett-road. North Kensington.[32]

Butler single-handed. Coloured man. Age 27. Been in English service 13 years. Good personal character.[33]

The advertisements placed by working people looking for work also give us insight into those who are never present in *All the Year Round*'s essay—black women.[34] They too sought work as performers and domestic servants. Women from the Indian sub-continent can be found seeking work as Ayahs, serving the British families toing and froing between imperial cities and the metropole.[35] Black women also sought to travel, looking for work that would take them from Australia to Panama, and undertook work as 'nurses' long before their important roles as nurses within the British National Health Service became established after the Second World War.

Panama. Lady would like to hear of another who would require as NURSE or otherwise, a strong, healthy Negress wishing to return.[36]

Required, by a most respectable coloured woman, a situation as NURSE to one child, or to attend an elderly lady. Would not object to travel. Highest references.[37]

These roles reflect the long history of black people's duties in white households, as highlighted in the numerous works of William Hogarth.

---

32 *The Times*, 23 November 1883.

33 *The Times*, 23 June 1886.

34 See Caroline Bressey, 'Four Women: Black women writing in London between 1880 and 1920', in Fiona Paisley and Kirsty Reid (eds), *Critical Perspectives on Colonialism: Writing the Empire from Below* (Oxford, Routledge, 2013), pp. 179–98; and 'Black Women and Work in England, 1880–1920', in Mary Davis (ed.), *Class and Gender in British Labour History: Renewing the Debate (or starting it?)* (London: Merlin Press. 2011), pp. 117–32.

35 For more on Ayahs in Britain see Rozina Visram, *Asians in Britain: 400 years of History* (London: Pluto Press, 2002).

36 *Liverpool Mercury*, 22 October 1892, p. 3.

37 *The Times*, 2 July 1885.

These examples 'The Black Man' did reference, picking out the young 'negro boy' in a scene from *Progress* and a young boy in the fourth scene of *Marriage a la Mode*, portrayed as 'a turbaned black-a-moor grinning over a basketful of antiquities and curiosities'.[38] Hogarth's works remain an important reference point in the history of the representation of black people in British art, although, as David Dabydeen noted, historians of his work before the 1980s made no reference to the many black people he portrayed. When Dabydeen published his critical engagement with Hogarth's work in 1987, this refusal to see or engage with representations of black people clearly visible in British art was 'pervasive'. As he observed,

> apart from the silence of Hogarth scholars, nothing has yet been published on the image of blacks in English art generally, and a mere handful of books exist on the broader subject of the black presence in European art, even though there are literally thousands of paintings, prints and drawings to be examined.[39]

A number of these images were brought together in 2005 when the art historian Jan Marsh curated *Black Victorians: A History of Black People in British Art*.[40] Shown in Manchester and Birmingham, it included portraits of Ira Aldridge, Mary Seacole and Olga Kaira, otherwise known as Miss LaLa.[41] The exhibition also included representations of black individuals in other forms of employment, as boxers and musicians and artists' models. The last of these occupations transformed ordinary men and women, such as Fanny Eaton, into 'mesmerising' images of blackness in the paintings they became a part of.[42] Eaton appeared as a number of characters in Victorian paintings. In one by John Everett in 1867 she formed part of a group of attendants,

38 Anon., 'The Black Man', p. 491.
39 Dabydeen, *Hogarth's Blacks*, p. 9.
40 Jan Marsh, *Black Victorians: Black People in British Art 1800–1900* (London: Lund Humphries Publishers, 2005).
41 LaLa was born in Stettin (then in Prussia, now in Poland), in 1858. She also performed in Paris at the Cirque Fernando and it was here that she was captured by Degas. See Marsh.
42 Ian Herbert, 'Airbrushed Out of History', *Independent*, 30 September 2005, https://www.independent.co.uk/news/uk/this-britain/airbrushed-out-

and she portrayed 'The Mother of Sisera', painted in 1861 by Albert Moore. These modelling jobs were one of her many roles as a working woman, wife and mother. Born in Jamaica, by the 1850s Fanny lived in London with her husband James Eaton. James drove cabs and carts and in addition to modelling Fanny was employed as a charwoman. The couple's first two children were born in St Pancras, and by 1881 the family lived in Chelsea and had expanded to include seven children, although Fanny was now a widow. At the time of the 1901 census she was employed as a cook in Oakfield, on the Isle of Wight, though by the time of the census a decade later, when she was seventy-five, she was once again in London.[43] Eaton's life shows that the black presence was not fixed in the cities, towns or on country estates; black men and women, like many of the Victorian working class, moved to find work, to support their families and kin.

The archives used by the author of 'The Black Man' are ones researchers still rely on, including the close reading of newspapers, advertisements, artworks and plays and literature for references to the black presence. Such mentions are often brief, but the tools available to gather these historical fragments together have now, in part, been transformed by the creation of digital archives, from periodicals, including *All the Year Round*, to monthly journals ('The Black Man' includes an advertisement of a 'negro boy ... to be disposed of' from a 1709 issue of *Tatler*), weekly broadsheets and penny dailies. In addition, we now also have access to the mass of data collated by the Victorian state, including national census returns. These materials form the foundation of the growing interest in family history research, and individuals of the black presence are being rediscovered through the interest of their descendants in their genealogical histories. The ongoing digitization of all these archives now makes it possible (access allowing) to draw out stories from a vast array and consider their lives among the urban poor, as a part of the urban crowd looking for work, going to or taking part in performances, as members of families, kinship and political networks, in a way that was unimaginable previously.

of-history-how-victorian-britain-portrayed-its-black-community-316099.
html (accessed 21 August 2018).
43 See Marsh, pp. 149, 162, 177, 192.

Peter Fryer concluded that as the majority of those who made up the black presence of the long eighteenth century were primarily men they married local white women, and as a result their grand-children become an indivisible part of the Victorian urban poor so familiar to readers of Dickens.[44] The advertisements drawn from digital newspapers here illustrate that the members of the community who remained worked in more diverse roles than merely crossing sweepers or sailors confined to the docks of Canning Town in London or Liverpool and other port cities such as Cardiff. There is also the way their presence in the newspaper challenges the imaginative geographies of the city, of the crowd. These men and women looking for work suggest a black presence that may have been observed but was simultaneously not present; certainly, the author of 'The Black Man' did not seem to imagine a black man or woman would be among their readers.

This may be a reflection of *All the Year Round*'s assumed middle-class readership and the assumption by the author of 'The Black Man' of a working-class black presence, but there were individuals who would have challenged such assumptions. There were the descendants of well-known eighteenth-century figures who maintained more middle-class lives, such as Equiano's daughter Johanna Vassa and the popular Shakspearian actor Ira Aldridge, who performed throughout Britain in the mid-nineteenth century. Born in New York City, Aldridge moved to Britain in the 1820s to pursue his acting career. In 1833 he became the first black man to perform Othello—an important reference point in 'The Black Man' essay.[45]

The Jamaican 'doctoress' Mary Seacole had been fêted with a summer festival and published her memoirs *The Wonderful Adventures of Mrs Seacole in Many Lands* in 1857, making her one of the few black women to publish their memoirs during the nineteenth century.[46] Following the sudden end of the Crimean War, Seacole had been left with hundreds of pounds worth of stock and unused

---

44 Fryer, p. 235.
45 For more on Aldridge see Fryer.
46 Mary Seacole, *Wonderful Adventures of Mrs Seacole in Many Lands* (London: Penguin, 2005). For a discussion of Seacole see Sandra Pouchet Paquet, 'The Enigma of Arrival: The Wonderful Adventures of Mrs. Seacole in Many Lands', *African American Review*, 26: 4, 1992, pp. 651–63.

medicines she had sold to soldiers, and returned to London ruined. As *Punch* asked:

> The sick and sorry can tell the story
> Of her nursing and dosing deeds.
> Regimental M.Ds. never work as hard as she
> In helping sick men's needs.
> And now the good soul's 'in the hole'
> What red-coat in the land,
> But to see her upon her legs gain
> Will not lend a willing her?[47]

The men she had served were keen to support her, with one writing to *The Times* observing that, while the benevolent deeds of Florence Nightingale were being 'handed down to prosperity with blessings and imperishable renown', the albeit 'humbler' actions of Mary Seacole were seemingly to be 'entirely forgotten'.[48] The response was the Seacole Fund Grand Military Festival, which ran for four days in July 1857. Over 40,000 people attended events at the Royal Surrey Gardens in South London and, according to reports, the gardens had never been thronged by a greater multitude of visitors.[49]

Aldridge had died in Łódź over ten years before 'The Black Man' was published, but his name remained a reference for theatrical reviews. In 1875 Morgan Smith, 'the celebrated coloured tragedian' was announced as a 'great African actor—the legitimate successor of Ira Aldridge' before his opening 'people's night' at the Theatre Royal in Chesterfield.[50] Francis Barber is named in 'The Black Man', but, despite the resonance of Aldridge and the place both he and Seacole held in the public sphere, neither he nor Seacole—nor other well-known nineteenth-century characters—are mentioned.

Ian Duffield advised historians in 1981 that far more work needed to be done on local histories to reveal what happened to more ordinary

---

47 *Punch*, December 1856.
48 *The Times*, 24 November 1856.
49 *The Times*, 30 July 1857.
50 *Derbyshire Times and Chesterfield Herald*, 24 April 1875, p. 5. Aldridge died in August 1867.

black people in the Victorian period.[51] Yet—and perhaps a legacy of histories such as 'The Black Man'—the histories of the nineteenth century have tended to reflect similar assumptions that by the end of the century the black presence had been reduced to small pockets of 'desperately poor' individuals composed largely of sailors living in port cities.[52] Certainly such communities existed, as illustrated by the life and work of Jacob Christian, who settled in Liverpool following his marriage to a local woman, Octavia Caulfield, in 1861. Twenty years later the couple had six children and ran a boarding house for seamen in Toxteth Park.[53] In their essay, the author of 'The Black Man' asked: 'Can it be that when it was firmly established, not so very long since, that the negro was "a man and a brother," he forthwith ceased to be a friend.'[54] Jacob Christian might well have agreed, to an extent, with this sentiment, as he worked to draw attention to the plight of black seamen in Liverpool. A seafarer before he ran the boarding house in Toxteth, Christian was concerned with his fellow men of colour, who found themselves sleeping among bales of cotton and starving when they were unable to find work onboard ships.[55]

There is still much work to be undertaken to establish how families such as the Christians experienced life in cities such as Liverpool, the activism they were engaged in and their place in local, national and international kinship networks. Liverpool's black community has a deep history, as authors such as Ray Costello have shown, but there is still much work to do. We need more studies to be undertaken in different cities, towns and villages across the nineteenth century to enable us to gauge the diversity of the black presence and by extension

---

51 Ian Duffield, 'History and the Historians', *History Today*, 31, 1981: pp. 34–6, at p. 36. As an example see David Killingray, 'Tracing People of African Origin and Descent in Victorian Kent', in Gerzina, *Black Victorians*, pp. 51–70.
52 For example see Jonathan Schneer, *London 1900: The Imperial Metropolis* (New Haven and London: Yale University Press, 1999), p. 203.
53 Caroline Bressey, 'Black Victorians and Anti-Caste: Mapping Geographies of "Missing" Readers', in Paul Raphael Rooney and Anna Gasperini (eds), *Media and Print Culture Consumption in Nineteenth-Century Britain: The Victorian Reading Experience* (London: Palgrave Macmillan, 2016), pp. 75–92.
54 Anon., 'The Black Man', p. 492.
55 Bressey, 'Black Victorians'.

British history. One avenue they may take are those opening up through the pages of digitized newspapers that enable, for example, the recovery of Jacob Christian's presence in meetings for seamen and temperance organizations. Another is the digitization of the mass of data created by the Victorians. These records of state, but also of personal networks and intimacy, are being utilized by family historians who are tracing and sharing the lives of their ancestors, directly linking the black past to our present.[56] Reconstructing the relations of family and kinship alongside those of employment and community will enable us to place black women and men within the multi-cultural communities of which they were a part and will enrich our knowledge of social interactions and cultural understandings of all the descendants of the long eighteenth century.

---

56 On family historians see Kathy Chater's contribution to this collection.

CHAPTER EIGHTEEN

Genealogy and the Black Past

Kathleen Chater

Family historians and academic scholars share an interest in rediscovering the black presence in pre-twentieth-century Britain, a research field that has grown in recent years. However, their reasons for interest in the field and their methods of approach differ, even though both sides encounter similar difficulties. Even so, they have a lot to offer each other, and it is worth looking into the ways that they can collaborate in the important recovery of Britain's black past. This chapter looks at the problems each group encounters, and suggests ways to overcome them.

Finding the Black Past

Preparations for commemoration of the 200th anniversary of the abolition of the British slave trade in 2007 brought an increased interest in the historic black presence in places around the country and there were a number of local history projects. In addition to work on the abolitionists' campaigns, these projects produced articles and publications on the black presence, drawn mainly from parish registers and other documents familiar to family historians, such as crime records. Many were just lists of individuals but some, like the Northamptonshire Black History Project (2002–5), linked sources to learn more about the lives, and some of the descendants, of people in the county. This project led to the Northamptonshire Black History Association, which is still in existence, producing publications and other educational material.[1]

---

1 www.northants-black-history.org.uk/.

In London separate projects were produced by various boroughs: Westminster, Enfield, Haringey, Hammersmith and Southwark. The London Metropolitan Archives (LMA) produced Black and Asian Londoners: Presence and Background (BAL), a database of some 2,000 references collected between 2001 and 2003 from baptism registers in its archives.[2] At this time the parish registers and other records of the City of London were housed at the Guildhall and a separate indexing project covering the City of London was set up in 2009.[3] What the outcome was is unknown and the majority of the records in the Guildhall have now been relocated to LMA. The City of Westminster still maintains a separate archive and ran an indexing project, the results of which were published in 2005.[4] Each of these projects, and all the other local activities, had its own methods of recording information, which cannot be combined to cross-reference individuals, to extract viable data or to allow a researcher easily to track mobile individuals.

From this commemoration grew other projects around the country, specifically looking at minority communities in their area and producing publications and exhibitions to spread information about them more widely. They also aimed to counter the prevailing belief that before the Windrush generation, who arrived after World War II, there were no black people in Britain. The Black Presence website has a useful list, which also includes some individuals.[5] In 2009 Jeffrey Green set up a website with brief biographies of black people living in Victorian and Edwardian Britain.[6] It is still being expanded and, while this largely improves knowledge of the variety of origins and occupations of the migrants, it is also important because he has been contacted by descendants of a number of individuals featured. They include those of William and Ellen Craft, who escaped slavery in America in 1848 and lived in Surrey before returning to the United States. Their descendants now live in both Georgia in the United States and in Britain and their

2 http://learningzone.cityoflondon.gov.uk/dataonline/lz_search.asp.
3 www.history.ac.uk/gh/baentries.htm.
4 Rory Lalwan, Sources for Black & Asian History at the City of Westminster Archives Centre (London: 2005).
5 https://blackbritishhistory.co.uk.
6 www.jeffreygreen.co.uk.

and others' experiences add an important strand to black British history.

More recently the commemorations associated with the arrival sixty years ago of the first of the *Windrush* settlers has moved earlier migrants to the background, but many of the local projects that were set up around 2007 continue. Dr Ray Costello, for example, is a community historian in Liverpool, where the black presence has a long history, and he has produced a number of publications on different aspects.[7] Audrey Dewjee, working with other local and family historians in Yorkshire, has discovered a surprising number of black people in a region without a port involved in the slave trade and she regularly originates or contributes to exhibitions in this area. There are other places that have not yet been explored because they are presumed to have no black presence or where there is no local activist to inspire awareness and interest. In Bristol Dr Madge Dresser's work has focused on slavery and ethnic minorities more generally and does to some extent bridge the gap between academia and local and family history.[8]

Beyond historic interest in black British history, there is personal involvement. Family history is a fast-growing pursuit, as the popularity of television programmes such as *Who Do You Think You Are?* attests. The exponential increase in digitized registers, other documents and long out-of-print books has made this kind of research much easier, for both genealogists and academic scholars.

7 Ray Costello, *Black Tommies: British Soldiers of African Descent in the First World War* (Liverpool: Liverpool University Press, 2015); Ray Costello, *Black Salt: Seafarers of African Descent on British Ships* (Liverpool: Liverpool University Press, 2014); Costello, *Black Liverpool*; *Liverpool's Black Pioneers* (Liverpool: Picton Press, 2007).

8 Madge Dresser and Andrew Hann, eds, *Slavery and the British Country House* (Swindon: English Heritage, 2013); Madge Dresser and Peter Fleming, eds, *Ethnic Minorities and the City c. 1000–2001* (London: Phillimore Press with Institute of Historical Research, University of London, 2007, reprinted 2009); Dresser, *Slavery Obscured*; Madge Dresser, *Black and White on the Buses: The Campaign Against the Colour Bar in Bristol* (Bristol, 2007, new edition, 2013).

Stumbling Blocks

The major problem for researchers, whether academic or genealogical, is simply official colour-blindness in Britain. Unlike in America and the colonies, colour and/or ethnicity are rarely mentioned in eighteenth-century official records unless there is some significance under the Poor Laws or the need to identify a particular individual.[9] Had Ignatius Sancho's letters not been collected and published after his death nothing would be known about his colour or ethnicity, which do not appear in any official record, such as his marriage, the baptisms of his six children, his burial and even his right to vote. From his name a Spanish or Portuguese origin might have been suspected, but it is unlikely that either he or his wife, from a family in London's Whitechapel district, could have been identified as of African origins. A further consideration is that the word 'black' was used to describe people of both African and Asian origin, as well as very dark-skinned native Britons.

In 1812 printed baptism and burial registers were introduced, which required a limited amount of information. Until then parish clerks recorded what they regarded as significant. Although this presents difficulties of interpretation and personal practice, it does provide useful information about some black individuals. The new registers asked only for names of the child and parents, abode and occupation for baptisms and name, abode and age for burials. The lives of black Victorians *should* be easier to reconstruct because of the introduction in 1837 of national registration of births, marriages and deaths, but as colour is not recorded there nor in censuses from 1841 onwards they are not recognizable, except in a handful of cases. Until 1991 it was only birthplace, not ethnicity, that was required in censuses, and of course many white people were born in British colonies. Therefore, trying to find a black person in the most complete and extensive public records of the population in the nineteenth century is virtually impossible. It is references in other places, mainly newspapers, that allow a researcher to work backwards. A further consideration, especially when researching black women (a seriously under-represented group in studies) is that they changed their names on marriage and became subsumed into their husbands' legal status.

9 Chater, *Untold Histories*, pp. 136–45.

The second problem is that the two sides, academics and genealogists, have tended to regard each other with mistrust: academics see family historians as limited hobbyists who do not grasp the full picture; family historians think that academics do not have enough knowledge of the sources to use them appropriately and therefore miss important local and legal factors. There is some truth in both views: second-rate academics start with a theory and seek out examples to illustrate it, ignoring those that do not support their supposition; second-rate family historians become bogged down in minutiae and do not look at the wider society as a whole. Often neither is rigorous enough in questioning or analysing the sources, adding what they wish was there, whether it is proof of an academic theory or proof of glamorous family forebears.

The difference in sources of funding perpetuates the divide between academic and local historians and makes it difficult for the two to work jointly. To judge from their lists of projects, academic bodies such as the Arts & Humanities Research Council (AHRC) focus on projects that foreground slavery, while the Heritage Lottery Fund, which is the most common source for local history projects, emphasizes presence within communities. This is partly because of their remits, but this divide is not helpful in encouraging cross-sectoral co-operation. In addition, funding is limited. In 2007 there was public money for local history projects in connection with the commemoration of the abolition of the British slave trade because it was topical. Since then, other anniversaries have arrived, other issues have arisen and those involved are seeking support for their areas of interest.

Revealing the Black British Presence

Although various historians mentioned the presence of black people in pre-twentieth-century Britain, this was largely as part of a more general picture, such as M. Dorothy George's *London Life in the Eighteenth Century*, published in 1925, which had a very short section on a few cases. Specific studies of the pre-Windrush black presence began later in the mid-twentieth century with Peter Fryer's 1984 *Staying Power* the most comprehensive at that time. This work, and others, has both revealed their presence and its extent (although there are still arguments about how many there were). Long-forgotten autobiographies, such as that of Olaudah Equiano, were rediscovered. Fryer, a journalist rather than a scholar, had the bright idea of contacting local record offices to ask for references, beginning the movement to look at the everyday rather than the bibliographic presence.

Academic scholars tended to interpret and re-interpret a canon of black British writers who published, or had published for them, their life histories. Some still do. These same high-profile individuals are adduced to make a point, usually on the issues of enslavement and victimhood, and from them it is extrapolated that black people in Britain were enslaved (like Equiano); were ill-treated (like Mary Prince) or were poor and struggling (like Ukawsaw Gronniosaw). The better-off are ignored or mentioned only in passing. For example, Nathaniel Wells (discussed elsewhere in this volume) was the biracial son of a West Indian plantation owner from St Kitts and became a justice of the peace, high sheriff of Monmouthshire and deputy lieutenant of the county. He also became a local master of foxhounds, which is in many ways a more telling indication of his social standing and acceptance. His colour and origins are known only through private documents and he was discovered by a local historian.[10] Cesar Picton used legacies from the family he seems happily to have served and his own keen business sense to become seriously rich. He was initially discovered by local historians from the Kingston Archaeological Society.[11] There may be many others like these whose origins and life histories require considerable research to uncover because they were relatively prosperous and stayed out of trouble. They have attracted less interest than the poor and unfortunate, partly because they are less interesting and more difficult to identify, and partly because they are regarded as exceptional. Since there are literally thousands of black people about whom nothing beyond a single reference in a single document is currently known, this is an unwise assumption.

10 Evans, 'Nathaniel Wells of Piercefield and St Kitts', pp. 91–106. Robert Wedderburn, of similar origins but rejected by his father, has been given far more attention.
11 The National Archives (TNA) PROB 11/1863/280. The Wikipedia entry is, as far as can be ascertained, accurate: https://en.wikipedia.org/wiki/Cesar_Picton (accessed 3 August 2018). The record in Kingston-upon-Thames office produced an undated booklet on him in the late twentieth century.

A number of black ministers of religion published their life stories or have been found in other documents and newspaper reports, but they have been little studied and their local impact has not been investigated because they do not fit the agenda of today's secular society. Nor do most scholars have the necessary theological understanding to assess their beliefs and significance. Although David Killingray has published a number of books and articles on the subject, black ministers are not routinely discussed in general histories of the black presence, although they might be mentioned.[12] Given the importance of religion in everyday life up to World War II, this is a regrettable omission.

Reconstructing a single individual's life is a long job and it takes an experienced genealogist about a week to explore all possible sources. Although many documents have been digitized, much work must still be done in local and county record offices. The British population has always been highly mobile and black people were no exception. Their children and grandchildren were not tied to the same place or occupations as their forebears. With other pressures, like the need to publish, academics are sometimes unwilling to undertake this kind of painstaking extended work, with no guarantee of any conclusive result at the end. A further consideration is that the reasons for black people being in Britain are very different across the centuries and scholars develop expertise in particular periods. This can be of great use to family and local historians, helping them to see their narrower interests in a wider, global perspective that may give them an unexpected insight or alternative leads to follow.

Before 1807, and to some extent up to 1834, when slavery in the British West Indian and South African colonies was abolished, the majority of black people in Great Britain arrived ultimately because of the transatlantic slave trade, such as domestics brought from the colonies. Although there was a substantial contingent who were mariners, they too were probably connected in some way to the trade, either as freed or escaped slaves or because they were hired in Africa to replace the seamen who died there. Slavery therefore becomes the dominant cause of their presence.[13]

---

12 See www.gold.ac.uk/history/staff/d-killingray/.
13 See Charles Foy's chapter on 'Black Tars' and 'Black Runaways in

After 1834 only a few seem to have come as servants to colonial residents who relocated to Britain, such as Andrew Bogle. Born a slave in Jamaica in the early 1800s, Bogle was brought to England by and worked for a member of the Tichbourne family. He became an important witness when a man claiming to be the heir to the title and fortune of the family appeared in 1866 and a long, drawn-out court case ensued. It was not finally settled until 1874, when the man claiming to be Roger Tichbourne was exposed as Arthur Orton, aka Thomas Castro.[14] Others were students and then teachers, such as Josephine and Clarissa Brown, the daughters of William Wells Brown;[15] mariners, either transitory or settled in ports, who played their part in international trade and war; or entertainers, some of whom benefited from the fashion for minstrel shows. A number fled the discrimination and violence they faced in slave-owning societies, particularly the United States after the passing of the Fugitive Slave Act in 1850, but for the majority we have no idea what drew them.

Eighteenth-Century Britain' by Stephen Mullen, Nelson Mundell and Simon P. Newman in this volume. The database is on www.runaways.gla.ac.uk.

14 Joy Lumsden, 'The True and Remarkable History of Andrew Bogle', http://jamaica-history.weebly.com/andrew-bogle.html (accessed 5 May 2018); Lord F.H. Maugham, *The Tichbourne Case* (1936); Rohan McWilliam, *The Tichborne Claimant. A Victorian Sensation* (2007). See also Jeffrey Green's website www.jeffreygreen.co.uk. Bogle had three sons living in Australia and Britain, but whether they left descendants remains unknown.

15 Josephine travelled between Britain and America and is presumed to have died in 1874 in Massachusetts. The Wikipedia entry on her is admirably cautious about what is known and what is speculative: https://en.wikipedia.org/wiki/Josephine_Brown (accessed 29 September 2015). Clarissa remained in Britain and married twice: first to Fritz Alcide Humber, in St Anne's Soho on 8 October 1855 (www. find my past.co.uk, accessed 29 September 2015), then to George Wainwright Sylvester in 1871 (https://www.freebmd.org.uk/ and TNA RG 10/4366 f. 19. She died childless in Leeds in 1874 (https://www.freebmd.org.uk/). Josephine's involvement in the abolitionist movement means that she is better recorded in published work than her sister, who pursued a very ordinary life.

The Family and Local Historians' Contributions

Volunteer researchers have been involved in most of the local projects mentioned earlier. This has some advantages. When funding dries up those who had been paid move on to other projects, but volunteers work for interest in the subject or locality so are more likely to continue participation. Family and local historians may be familiar with obscure sources that more general scholars do not know about. Local studies libraries will know of people who are researching the same or related topics. The present-day descendants of black people may have documents or even photographs and family stories passed down that supplement official records, but the stories need to be checked as far as possible. Most family history societies have members' journals that could be used to advertise for further information or to recruit researchers. The more active societies look for local projects that they can undertake. Local historians are usually also genealogists. As previously indicated, they have made a number of important discoveries about the black presence in their localities and their journals might also prove useful.

Family and local historians' experience of using the records of different centuries and different periods means they are able to work across the traditional academic boundaries. Professional genealogists, and the more experienced amateurs, also need to have an in-depth knowledge of the law at particular times on a variety of subjects that affected people according to their social status, their wealth, their religion, their occupations and stages in their life cycle: birth, schooling, apprenticeship, marriage, children, death, burial. This expertise could be harnessed by academic scholars.

My Database

Through family history I became interested in the pre-twentieth-century black presence and in doing some preliminary reading around the subject realized that, although historians often stated 'black people were …', they adduced very little evidence to prove their claims. I knew from many years of archival research in London that the records contained numerous passing references to black people who were not known to scholars and I set out to write an article. When I realized how much material there was that remained unused, I registered to do a doctorate and set up a database to extract statistical information, which might prove something, but what I was not yet certain. Initially the starting date was 1538, with the introduction of parish registers, and went on and on. My supervisor and I realized it would need to be focused on a specific time frame. Limiting it to the period of the British slave trade, would, I assumed, produce some interesting insights on how colonial assumptions about enslavement transferred to Britain.

The database gives an indication of geographical distribution, sex ratios, ages, areas of origin and, in some cases, occupations. It also includes the names of masters and sponsors, in the case of baptisms, as an indication of the social status of those by whom black people were employed. My doctorate was completed in 2007 and soon after a group of us working on the black presence made three applications for funding to put the database online so it would be available to scholars, educators and local and family historians, but we were not successful.

I still add to it on a regular basis when I come across references, either when doing my own research or when someone sends me information. There are a number of family historians who know of my interest and contribute. The database has been extended, going back to 1538 and forward to the early nineteenth century. However, recent research on the mid-nineteenth-century period shows that it would be a full-time job to extend it beyond 1834 and the ending of slavery in the British colonies in the Caribbean, as there are so many people mentioned in later nineteenth-century local newspaper reports.

The Way Forward

The British were not, of course, the only European power with slave-based colonies in the New World nor, later, in Africa. Pierre Boulle, who has done similar work in France, came to similar conclusions as mine: that there was racism in sections of society, but many hitherto unsuspected black people were living quiet lives under the official radar.[16] Interest in the pan-European experience of black people within their societies is growing and there are plans to create databases like

16 Pierre Henri Boulle, *Race et Esclavage dans la France de L'ancien Régime* (Paris: Perrin, 2007).

mine in other European countries. I hope that my database will form part of this initiative when it materializes.

In the meantime, I make the database's contents available to people with specific queries, but it is not widely accessible nor is it in a format that people could easily use to follow up references: it was not designed for that purpose. It does not, for example, have links to online sources such as Old Bailey Online, containing the *Proceedings of the Old Bailey* 1674–1913, or the British Library Newspaper Archive's website. If it were online it would be easy to add data by providing a contact address.

The database also makes it possible to identify and then, potentially, to reconstruct the lives and descendants of a limited number of people in a particular location in England and Wales. The British population has always been highly mobile and black people were no exception. Without information from a large number of case studies it is impossible to compare the typical experiences of black British people to those of the wider society. The Cambridge Group for the History of Population and Social Structure has been reconstructing aspects of historical demography for over fifty years, so a very great deal is known about British people. They have long experience in using the techniques and work of family historians to study, for example, the inheritance of jobs (and therefore class and social mobility) in general society. They might be interested in co-ordinating such a project for the black population.[17]

The Caribbean Family History Group, based in Solihull, Warwickshire, is largely focused on those descended from the Windrush and later migrant generations,[18] but there may be the possibility of widening their involvement or establishing a section for those with earlier black ancestry.

There are a number of ways that scholars and genealogists can join forces to share their knowledge and discoveries. Conferences held at universities and in local history societies and libraries could invite those doing similar work, even when they come from different research perspectives. There is already one forum where mainly amateur local historians and academic scholars are brought together with educators. 'What's Happening in Black British History', based in

---

17 www.campop.geog.cam.ac.uk.
18 caribbeanfamilyhistorygroup.wordpress.com.

Kathleen Chater

London University's Institute of Commonwealth Studies, is a bi-annual conference held in London and in the provinces that attempts to raise interest among and bring together those with interests, either professional or personal, in this topic. At this, and other gatherings, the two sides could share knowledge of possible funding sources, both from small organizations and from national fellowship organizations, and possibly even join forces as co-principal investigators and applicants. Scholars can also make a point of speaking about their own research in smaller, local locations, where they can meet amateur researchers doing related work. They could also consider using the material researched for scholarly articles to write pieces for more popular and accessible journals or for family and local history magazines. And, finally, it would be useful for both groups to recognize the reasons that such research is done in the first place: to research one's own family, to broaden the picture of Britain's past, and to reach wider audiences with this important work.

Bibliography

Achebe, Chinua. *Morning Yet on Creation Day: Essays*. London: Heinemann, 1975.

Acholonu, Catherine. 'The Igbo Roots of Olaudah Equiano', *Journal of African History*, 33, 1992, pp. 164–5.

Adams, Henry Gardiner. *God's Image in Ebony*. London, 1854.

Afigbo, Adiele E. *Ropes of Sand: Studies in Igbo History and Culture*. London: University Press Limited, 1981.

Aitken, Robbie and Rosenhaft, Eve. *Black Germany, The Making and Unmaking of a Diaspora Community, 1884–1960*. Cambridge: Cambridge University Press, 2013.

Alexander, Ziggy. 'Preface', in Moira Ferguson (ed.), *The History of Mary Prince*. London: Pandora, 1987.

Aljoe, Nicole N. 'Testimonies of the Enslaved in Caribbean Literary History', in Nicole N. Aljoe, Brycchan Carey and Thomas W. Krise (eds), *Literary Histories of the Early Anglophone Caribbean: Islands in the Stream*. New York: Palgrave Macmillan, 2018, p. 110.

Anglo, Sydney. 'The Court Festivals of Henry VII: A Study Based on the Account Books of John Heron, Treasurer of the Chamber', *Bulletin of the John Rylands Library*, 43: 1, 1960, pp. 12–45.

Anglo, Sydney, ed. *The Great Tournament Roll of Westminster*. 2 vols. Oxford: Clarendon Press, 1968.

Anim-Addo, Joan. *Haunted by History: Poetry*. London: Mango, 1998.

Anim-Addo, Joan. *Longest Journey: The History of Black Lewisham*. London: Deptford Forum Publishing, 1995.

Anim-Addo, Joan. *Sugar, Spices and Human Cargo: An Early Black History of Greenwich*. Greenwich: Greenwich Leisure Services, 1996.

Anim-Addo, Joan. *Touching the Body: History, Language and African-Caribbean Women's Writing*. London: Mango Press, 2007.

Anon. 'The Black Man', *All the Year Round*, 6 March 1875, pp. 489–93.

Anon. 'The Black Prince: A True Story being an Account of the Life and Death of Naimbanna, an African King's Son'. *Cheap Repository Tracts*, 1796, pp. 8–9.

Anon. *Historical Research Report, Predecessor Institutions Research Regarding Slavery and the Slave Trade*. Royal Bank of Scotland Group/Citizens Financial Group, May 2006, updated May 2009.

Anon. *Handlist 69: Sources for Black and Asian History*. Preston: Lancashire Records Office, 2007.

Aravamudan, Srinivas. *Tropicopolitans: Colonialism and Agency, 1688–1804*. Durham, NC: Duke University Press, 1999.

Ashbee, Andrew. *Records of English Court Music, Vol VII 1485–1558*. Snodland and Aldershot: Scholar Press, 1986–96.

Baker, Jean N. 'The Proclamation Society, William Mainwaring and the Theatrical Representations Act of 1788', *Historical Research*, 76: 193, 2003, pp. 347–63.

Baker, John. *The Diary of John Baker, Barrister of the Middle Temple, Solicitor-General of the Leeward Islands: Being Extracts Therefrom*. London: Hutchinson & Co., 1931.

Banton, Michael. 'The Coloured Quarter: Negro Immigrants in an English City', *American Journal of Sociology*, 61: 5, March 1956, pp. 497–8.

Baugh, Daniel A. *Naval Administration in the Age of Walpole*. Princeton: Princeton University Press, 1965.

Beckert, Sven. *Empire of Cotton: A Global History*. New York: Vintage, 2014.

Behrendt, Stephen D. 'Human Capital in the British Slave Trade', in David Richardson, Suzanne Schwarz and Anthony Tibbles (eds), *Liverpool and Transatlantic Slavery*. Liverpool: Liverpool University Press, 2007.

Berglund, Lisa. 'Oysters for Hodge, or, Ordering Society, Writing Biography and Feeding the Cat', *Journal for Eighteenth-Century Studies*, 33: 4, 2010, pp. 631–45.

Bermuda National Gallery. *Joscelyn Gardner Staging Mary Prince: In Her Own Words*. Hamilton, Bermuda: Bermuda National Gallery, 2016.

Bernstein, Robin. 'Dances with Things: Material Culture and the Performance of Race', *Social Text*, 27: 4, 2009, pp. 67–94.

Berrendt, Stephen D. and Hurley, Robert A. 'Liverpool as a Trading Port: Sailors' Residences, African Migrants, Occupational Change and Probated Wealth', *International Journal of Maritime History*, 29: 4, 2017, pp. 875–910.

Bialuscheski, Arne. 'Black People under the Black Flag: Piracy and the Slave Trade on the West Coast of Africa, 1718–1723', *Slavery and Abolition*, 29: 4, 2008, pp. 461–75.

Bindman, D. and Gates Jr, H.L., eds. *The Image of the Black in Western Art, Volume II: From the Early Christian Era to the 'Age of Discovery', Part 2: Africans in the Christian Ordinance of the World*. Cambridge, MA: Harvard University Press, 2010.

Blackburn, Robin. *The Overthrow of Colonial Slavery 1776–1848*. London: Verso, 1988.

Blackett, R.J.M. 'Fugitive Slaves in Britain: The Odyssey of William and Ellen Craft', *Journal of American Studies*, 12: 1, 1978, pp. 41–62.

Bloom, Edward A. and Bloom, Lillian D. *The Piozzi Letters: Correspondence of Hester Lynch Piozzi 1784–1821*. London and Newark: University of Delaware Press, 1999.

Bolster, W. Jeffrey. *Black Jacks: African American Seamen in the Age of Sail*. Cambridge, MA: Harvard University Press, 1998.

Booth, Charles, ed. *Life and Labour of the People in London*. London: Macmillan, 1903.

Boswell, James. *Life of Johnson*, Vol. I, ed. George Birkbeck Hill, rev. L.F. Powell. Oxford: Clarendon Press, 1934–64.

Boulle, Pierre Henri. *Race et Esclavage dans la France de L'ancien Régime*. Paris: Perrin, 2007.

Bourne, Stephen. *Speak of Me As I Am: The Black Presence in Southwark Since 1600*. London: Southwark Local History Library, London Borough of Southwark, 2005.

Bowen, John Wesley Edward. *Africa and the American Negro*. Atlanta, 1896.

Brand, Dionne. *A Map to the Door of No Return: Notes to Belonging*. Toronto: Doubleday Canada, 2001.

Bressey, Caroline. 'Black Victorians and Anti-Caste: Mapping Geographies of "Missing" Readers', in Paul Raphael Rooney and Anna Gasperini (eds), *Media and Print Culture Consumption in Nineteenth-Century Britain: The Victorian Reading Experience*. London: Palgrave Macmillan, 2016, pp. 75–92.

Bressey, Caroline. 'Black Women and Work in England, 1880–1920', in Mary Davis (ed.), *Class and Gender in British Labour History: Renewing the Debate (or starting it?)*. London: Merlin Press. 2011, pp. 117–32.

Bressey, Caroline. 'Four Women: Black Women Writing in London between 1880 and 1920', in Fiona Paisley and Kirsty Reid (eds), *Critical Perspectives on Colonialism: Writing the Empire from Below*. Oxford: Routledge, 2013, pp. 179–98.

Brewster Tinker, Chauncey, ed. *Letters of James Boswell*. Oxford: Clarendon Press, 1924.

Brown, Catrina and Augusta-Scott, Tod. *Narrative Therapy: Making Meaning, Making Lives*. London: Sage Publications, 2007.

Brown, Marilyn R. '"Miss La La's Teeth": Reflections on Degas and "Race"', *The Art Bulletin*, 89: 4, 2007, pp. 738–65.

Brown, P.C. and Brown, G.W. 'We Too Were in Cardiff', *The Keys*, III: 1, July–September 1935, pp. 4–24.

Brown, Vincent. *The Reaper's Garden: Death and Power in the World of Atlantic Slavery*. Cambridge, MA: Harvard University Press, 2008.

Brownley, Martine W., ed. *Reconsidering Biography: Contexts, Controversies, and Sir John Hawkins' Life of Johnson*. Lewisburg: Bucknell University Press, 2012.

Brunsman, Denver. *The Evil Necessity: British Impressment in the Eighteenth-Century Atlantic World*. Charlottesville: University of Virginia Press, 2013.

Bugg, John. 'The Other Interesting Narrative: Olaudah Equiano's Public Book Tour', *PMLA*, 121, 2006, pp. 1424–42.

Bundock, Michael. '"Pleased to Renew our Old Acquaintance": James Boswell and Francis Barber', *The New Rambler: Journal of the Johnson Society of London*. 2015–16, series F, vol. XIX, pp. 53–66.

Bundock, Michael. *The Fortunes of Francis Barber: The True Story of the Jamaican Slave Who Became Samuel Johnson's Heir*. New Haven and London: Yale University Press, 2015.

Burnard, Trevor. 'Good-bye, Equiano, the African', in Donald A. Yerxa (ed.), *Recent Themes in the History of Africa and the Atlantic World: Historians in Conversation*. Columbia: University of South Carolina Press, 2008, pp. 100–5.

Burnett, John, ed. *Useful Toil*. London: Allen Lane, 1974.

Byng, John. *The Torrington Diaries, Containing the Tours through England & Wales of Between the Years 1781 & 1794*. Reprinted London, Eyre & Spottiswoode, 1934–8.

Byrne, Paula. *Belle. The Slave Daughter and the Lord Chief Justice.* New York: Harper Perennial, 2014.

Cairns, John W. 'Enforced Sojourners: Enslaved Apprentices in Eighteenth-Century Scotland', in E.J.M.F.C. Broers and R.M.H. Kubben (eds), *Ad Fontes: Liber Amicorum Prof. Beatrix van Erp-Jacobs.* Nijmegen: Wolf Legal Publishers, 2014, pp. 67–81.

Cairns, John W. 'The Definition of Slavery in Eighteenth-Century Thinking: Not the True Roman Slavery', in Jean Allain (ed.), *The Legal Understanding of Slavery: From the Historical to the Contemporary.* Oxford: Oxford University Press, 2012, pp. 61–83.

Campbell, Gwyn. *The Structure of Slavery in Indian Ocean Africa and Asia.* London: Frank Cass, 2004.

Carlson, Elof Axel. *The Unfit: A History of a Bad Idea.* Cold Spring Harbor, NY: Cold Spring Harbor Press, 2001.

Carretta, Vincent. *Equiano, the African: Biography of a Self-Made Man.* Athens, GA and New York: The University of Georgia Press, 2005; paperback edition, Penguin Putnam, 2007.

Carretta, Vincent, ed. *Ignatius Sancho. Letters of the Late Ignatius Sancho, An African.* New York: Penguin Classics, 1998.

Carretta, Vincent. 'More New Light on the Identity of Olaudah Equiano or Gustavus Vassa', in Felicity Nussbaum (ed.), *The Global Eighteenth Century.* Baltimore: The Johns Hopkins University Press, 2003, pp. 226–35.

Carretta, Vincent. 'Olaudah Equiano or Gustavus Vassa? New Light on an Eighteenth-Century Question of Identity', *Slavery and Abolition*, 20, 1999, pp. 96–105.

Caruth, Cathy. *Unclaimed Experience: Trauma, Narrative and History.* Baltimore: The Johns Hopkins University Press, 1996.

Catherall, Gordon A. 'Bristol College and the Jamaican Mission', *Baptist Quarterly*, 35: 6, 1994, pp. 296–9.

Caudle, James J. and Bundock, Michael. *The Runaway and the Apothecary: Francis Barber, Edward Ferrand and the Life of Johnson.* Privately printed for The Johnsonians, 2011.

Cave, Kathryn, ed. *The Diary of Joseph Farington*, Vol. VIII. New Haven: Yale University Press, 1982.

Chakrabarti, Lolita. *Red Velvet.* London: Bloomsbury Methuen Drama, 2012.

Chater, Kathleen. *Untold Histories: Black People in England and Wales During the Period of the British Slave Trade, c.1660–1807.* Manchester: Manchester University Press, 2011.

Christopher, Emma. *Slave Ship Sailors and Their Captive Cargoes, 1730–1807.* New York and Cambridge: Cambridge University Press, 2006.

City of Westminster Archives. *Sources for Black and Asian History*, City of Westminster Archives Centre, 2005.

Clingham, Greg. 'Hawkins, Biography, and the Law', in Martine W. Brownley (ed.), *Reconsidering Biography: Contexts, Controversies, and Sir John Hawkins' Life of Johnson.* Lewisburg: Bucknell University Press, 2012, pp. 137–54.

Clune, John J. and Stringfield, Margo S. *Historic Pensacola.* Gainesville: University Press of Florida, 2009; revised paperback edition, 2017.

Coakley, R. Walter. 'The Two James Hunters of Fredericksburg', *The Virginia Magazine of History and Biography*, 56: 1, 1948, pp. 3–21.

Cobbett, William. 'The West India Colonies', *Cobbett's Political Register*, 48: 10, 1823, pp. 577–92.

Cohen, Ashley L. 'Fencing and the Market in Aristocratic Masculinity', in Daniel O'Quinn and Alexis Tadie (eds), *Sporting Cultures, 1650–1850.* Toronto: University of Toronto Press, 2018.

Cohen, Ashley L. *The Global Indies: British Imperial Culture, 1756–1815.* New Haven: Yale University Press, 2020.

Coke, Thomas. *A History of the West Indies, Containing the Natural, Civil and Ecclesiastical History of Each Island.* 3 vols. Liverpool: Nuttall, Fisher, and Dixon, 1808–11.

Collicott, Sylvia L. *Connections: Haringey Local-National-World Links.* London: Haringey Community Information Service, 1986.

Costello, Ray. 'A Hidden History in Liverpool: The James Family', in *North West Labour History: Black Presence in the North West.* Salford: North West Labour History Group, 1995.

Costello, Ray. *Black Liverpool: The Early History of Britain's Oldest Black Community 1730–1918.* Liverpool: Picton Press, 2001.

Costello, Ray. *Black Salt: Seafarers of African Descent on British Ships.* Liverpool: Liverpool University Press, 2014.

Costello, Ray. *Black Tommies: British Soldiers of African Descent in the First World War.* Liverpool: Liverpool University Press, 2015.

Costello, Ray. *Liverpool's Black Pioneers.* Liverpool: Picton Press, 2007.

Cotter, William R. 'The Somerset Case and the Abolition of Slavery', *History*, 79: 255, 1994, pp. 31–56.

Cox, Edward L. *Free Coloureds in the Slave Societies of St Kitts and Grenada, 1763–1833.* Knoxville: University of Tennessee Press, 1984.

Coxe, William. *An Historical Tour in Monmouthshire*. London: T. Cadell, Jr., 1801.

Cutter, Martha. 'Will the Real Henry "Box" Brown Please Stand Up?' *Common-Place: The Journal of Early American Life*, 16: 1, 2015, http://commonplace.online/article/will-the-real-henry-box-brown-please-stand-up/.

D'Aguiar, Fred. 'Mary Prince', Features: The Classics, *Penguin.co.uk*, Penguin, 2003, accessed 26 November 2003; no longer online.

Dabydeen, David. *Hogarth's Blacks: Images of Blacks in Eighteenth-century English Art*. Manchester: Manchester University Press, 1987.

Danziger, Marlies K. and Brady, Frank, eds. *Boswell: The Great Biographer 1789–1795*. London: Heinemann, 1989.

Davidson, Cathy N. 'Olaudah Equiano, Written by Himself', *Novel: A Forum on Fiction*, 40, 2006, pp. 18–51.

Davis, Bertram H. *A Proof of Eminence: The Life of Sir John Hawkins*. Bloomington and London: Indiana University Press, 1973.

Dayan, Joan. *Haiti, History, and the Gods*. Berkeley: University of California Press, 1995.

Davis, Bertram H. *Johnson Before Boswell: A Study of Sir John Hawkins' Life of Samuel Johnson*. New Haven, Yale University Press, 1960.

Dear, Eliza. *In Celebration of the Human Spirit: A Look at the Slave Trade*. Settle: Lambert's Print and Design, 2000.

DeCamp, David. 'African Day Names in Jamaica', *Language*, 43: 1, 1967, pp. 139–49.

Denning, R.T.W., ed. *The Diary of William Thomas 1762–1795 of Michaelston-super-Ely near St Fagans, Glamorgan*. Cardiff: South Wales Record Society and South Glamorgan County Council Libraries & Arts Dept., 1995. 15 November 1767.

'Deposition of Joseph Dickinson, 5 July 1732', *Bermuda Historical Quarterly*, 12: 3, 1955, pp. 82–3.

Dickens, Charles. 'The Lazy Tour of Two Idle Apprentices', *Household Words*, XVI: LVIII, December 1857.

Devine, T.M. *The Tobacco Lords: A Study of the Tobacco Merchants of Glasgow and their Trading Activities, c. 1740–90*. Edinburgh: John Donald, 1975.

Dobie, James. *Memoir of William Wilson of Crummock*. Edinburgh: privately printed, 1896.

Donovan, Kenneth J. 'Slaves in Île Royale, 1713–1760', *French Colonial History*, 5, 2004, pp. 3–32.

Drescher, Seymour. 'Whose Abolition? Popular Pressure and the Ending of the British Slave Trade', *Past & Present*, 143, 1994, pp. 136–66.

Drescher, Seymour. *Capitalism and Antislavery: British Mobilization in Comparative Perspective*. Oxford: Oxford University Press, 1987.

Dresser, Madge. *Black and White on the Buses: The Campaign Against the Colour Bar in Bristol*, Bristol, 2007; London: Bookmarks Publications, 2013.

Dresser, Madge. 'Bristol', in David Dabydeen and John Gilmore (eds), *Oxford Companion to Black British History*. Oxford: Oxford University Press, 2007, pp. 62–4.

Dresser, Madge. 'Remembering Slavery and Abolition in Bristol', *Slavery and Abolition: A Journal of Slave and Post-Slave Studies*, 30: 2, 2009, pp. 223–7.

Dresser, Madge. *Slavery Obscured: The Social History of Slavery in an English Provincial Port*. London and New York: Continuum, 2001. Reprinted Redcliffe Press, 2007 and Bloomsbury Academic Press, 2013.

Dresser, Madge and Fleming, Peter, eds. *Ethnic Minorities and the City c. 1000–2001*. London: Phillimore Press with Institute of Historical Research, University of London, 2007, reprinted 2009.

Dresser, Madge and Giles, Sue. *Bristol and Transatlantic Slavery*. Bristol Museums and Art Gallery, 2000.

Dresser, Madge and Hann, Andrew, eds. *Slavery and the British Country House*. Swindon: English Heritage, 2013.

Du Bois, W.E.B. 'The Negro in Literature and Art', *Annals of the American Academy of Political and Social Science*, 49, 1913, pp. 233–7; and in Nathan Huggins (ed.), *W.E.B. Du Bois, Writings*. New York: Library of America, 1986.

Duffield, Ian. 'History and the Historians', *History Today*, 31, 1981, pp. 34–6.

Durbach, Nadja. *Spectacle of Deformity: Freak Shows and Modern British Culture*. Oakland: University of California Press, 2010.

Earle, Thomas Foster and Lowe, Kate J.P., eds. *Black Africans in Renaissance Europe*. Cambridge: Cambridge University Press, 2005.

Edwards, Paul and Walvin, James. *Black Personalities in the Era of the Slave Trade*. London: Macmillan, 1983.

Eickelmann, Christine and Small, David. *Pero: The Life of a Slave in Eighteenth-century Bristol*. Bristol: Redcliffe Press, Bristol Museums and Art Gallery, 2004.

Elder, Melinda. *The Slave Trade and the Economic Development of 18th Century Lancaster*. Keele: Ryburn Press, 1992.

Equiano, Olaudah. *The Interesting Narrative and Other Writings*, ed. Vincent Carretta. New York: Penguin, 1995, rev. edn 2003. Also Salt Lake City, UT: Project Gutenberg Literary Archive Foundation, eBook #15399.

Este, Charles. *My Own Life*. London: Printed for T. and J. Egerton, at the Military Library, Whitehall, 1787.

Evans, John A.H. 'Nathaniel Wells of Piercefield and St Kitts: From Slave to Sheriff', *Monmouthshire Antiquary*, Vol. VII, 2000, pp. 91–106; and in *Black and Asian Studies Association Newsletter*, 33, 2018, pp. 19–49.

Eze, Emmanuel Chukwudi. 'The Color of Reason: The Idea of "Race" in Kant's Anthropology', in Emmanuel Chukwudi Eze (ed.), *Postcolonial African Philosophy: A Critical Reader*. Cambridge, MA and London: Blackwell, 1997, pp. 103–31.

Eze, Emmanuel Chukwudi. *Race and the Enlightenment: a Reader*. Cambridge MA: Blackwell, 1997.

Eze, Katherine Faull. 'Self-Encounters: Two Eighteenth-Century African Memoirs from Moravian Bethlehem', in David McBride, LeRoy Hopkins and C. Aisha Blackshire-Belay (eds), *Crosscurrents: African Americans, Africa, and Germany in the Modern World*. Columbia, SC: Camden House, 1998, pp. 29–52.

Ferguson, Moira, ed. *The Hart Sisters: Early African Caribbean Writers, Evangelicals, and Radicals*. Lincoln, NE: University of Nebraska Press, 1993.

Ferguson, Moira, ed. *The History of Mary Prince*. London: Pandora, 1987.

Fischer, Sibylle. 'Atlantic Ontologies: On Violence and Being Human', *E-MISFÉRICA* 12: 1, Caribbean Rasanblaj, 2015, http://hemisphericinstitute.org/hemi/en/emisferica-121-caribbean-rasanblaj/fischer, accessed 21 June 2015.

Fish, Vincent. 'Post Structuralism in Family Therapy: Interrogating the Narrative/Conversational Mode', *Journal of Family Therapy*, 19: 3, 1993, pp. 221–32.

Foucault, Michel. 'The Life of Infamous Men', in M. Foucault, *Power, Truth, Strategy*, ed. Meaghan Morris and Paul Patton. Sydney: Feral Publications, 1979.

Foy, Charles R. '"Unkle Somerset's" Freedom: Liberty in England for Black Sailors', *Journal for Maritime Research*, 13: 1, 2011, pp. 21–36.

Foy, Charles R. 'Compelled to Row: Blacks on Royal Navy Galleys During the American Revolution', *Journal of the American Revolution*, 2017, https://allthingsliberty.com/2017/11/compelled-row-blacks-royal-navy-galleys-american-revolution.

Foy, Charles R. 'The Royal Navy's Employment of Black Mariners and Maritime Workers, 1754–1783', *International Maritime History Journal*, 28: 1, 2016, pp. 6–35.

Foy, Charles R. 'Eighteenth Century Prize Negroes: From Britain to America', *Slavery & Abolition*, 31: 3, 2010, pp. 379–93.

Frazer, Elizabeth. *The Problem of Communitarian Politics. Unity and Conflict.* Oxford: Oxford University Press, 1999.

Frey, Sylvia R. and Wood, Betty. *Come Shouting to Zion; African American Protestantism in the American South and British Caribbean to 1830.* Chapel Hill: University of North Carolina Press, 1998.

Frost, Diane, ed. *Ethnic Labour and British Imperial Trade: A History of Ethnic Seafarers in the UK.* London: Frank Cass, 1995.

Frost, Diane. *Work and Community among West African Migrant Workers since the Nineteenth Century.* Liverpool: Liverpool University Press, 1989, pp. 111–28.

Fryer, Peter. *Staying Power: The History of Black People in Britain.* London: Pluto Press, 1984.

Galton, Bridget. 'How a Kenwood House Painting Inspired Amma Asante's "Belle"', *Ham & High*, 12 June 2014.

Gardner, Joscelyn. 'Artist Statement', in National Gallery of Jamaica, *We Have Met Before: Graham Fagen, Joscelyn Gardner, Leasho Johnson and Ingrid Pollard.* Kingston, Jamaica: National Gallery of Jamaica, 2017, pp. 22–3.

Garlick, Kenneth and Macintyre, Angus, eds. *The Diary of Joseph Farington, April 1803–December 1804*, Vol. VI. New Haven: Yale University Press, 1979.

Gaspar, David Barry. *Bondsmen and Rebels: A Study of Master–Slave Relations in Antigua.* Baltimore: The Johns Hopkins University Press, 1985.

Gerzina, Gretchen H. *Black England: Life before Emancipation.* London: John Murray, 1995.

Gerzina, Gretchen H. *Black London: Life before Emancipation.* New Brunswick: Rutgers University Press, 1995.

Gerzina, Gretchen H. 'Introduction', in Gretchen H. Gerzina (ed.), *Black Victorians, Black Victoriana.* New Jersey and London, Rutgers University Press, 2003.

'Getting Dressed in the 18th Century—Dido Elizabeth Belle (1779)', https://youtu.be/zLQXaw9GtqY.

Ghosh, Durba. *Sex and the Family in Colonial India: The Making of Empire*. Cambridge: Cambridge University Press, 2006.

Gikandi, Simon. 'Rethinking the Archive of Enslavement', *Early American Literature*, 50: 1, 2015, pp. 81–102.

Giles, Sue. 'The Great Circuit: Making the Connection between Bristol's Slaving History and the African-Caribbean Community', *Journal of Museum Ethnography*, 13, March 2001, pp. 15–21.

Gillis, John R. 'Servants, Sexual Relations, and the Risks of Illegitimacy in London, 1801–1900', *Feminist Studies*, 5: 1, 1979, pp. 142–73.

Gilmore, Paul. '"De Genewine Artekil": William Wells Brown, Blackface Minstrelsy, and Abolitionism', *American Literature*, 69: 4, 1997, pp. 743–80.

Gilroy, Paul. *The Black Atlantic: Modernity and Double Consciousness*. Cambridge, MA: Harvard University Press, 1993.

Gilroy, Paul. *'There Ain't No Black in the Union Jack': The Cultural Politics of Race and Nation*. Chicago: University of Chicago Press, 1991.

Gilroy, Paul. *After Empire: Melancholia or Convivial Culture?* London: Routledge, 2004.

GLC [The Greater London Council] Ethnic Minorities Unit. *A History of the Black Presence in London*. London, 1986.

Green, Jeffrey P. 'George William Christian: A Liverpool "Black" in Africa', *Transactions of the Historical Society of Lancashire and Cheshire*, 134, pp. 141–6.

Greene, Jack P., ed. *Exclusionary Empire: English Liberty Overseas, 1600–1900*. Cambridge: Cambridge University Press, 2010.

Gronniosaw, Ukawsaw. *Wonderous Grace Display'd in the Life and Conversion of James Albert Ukawsaw Gronniosaw*. Bath, 1770, 1712.

Hamilton, Douglas. '"A most active, enterprising officer": Captain John Perkins, the Royal Navy and the Boundaries of Slavery and Liberty in the Caribbean', *Slavery & Abolition*, 39: 1, 2017, pp. 80–100.

Harlan, Louis R. 'Booker T. Washington and the White Man's Burden', *American Historical Review*, LXXI, 1965–6, pp. 441–67.

Harris, Joseph E. *The African Presence in Asia: Consequences of the East African Slave Trade*. Evanston: Northwestern University Press, 1971.

Hartman, Saidiya. *Scenes of Subjection: Terror, Slavery and Self-Making in Nineteenth Century America*. Oxford: Oxford University Press, 1997.

Hawkins, John. *The Life of Samuel Johnson LL.D.*, ed. O M Brack Jr. Athens and London: University of Georgia Press, 2009.

Hawkins, John. *The Works of Samuel Johnson, LL.D, Together with His Life and Notes on his Lives of the Poets in Eleven Volumes, Vol. I, The Life of Dr Samuel Johnson*. London, 1787.

Hawkins, Laetitia-Matilda. *Memoirs, Anecdotes, Facts, and Opinions*, Vol. I. London: Longman, etc., 1824.

Hayden, Roger. 'Caleb Evans and the Anti-Slavery Question', *Baptist Quarterly*, 39, 2001.

Heads of Families at the First Census of the United States Taken in the Year 1790: Records of the State Enumerations: 1782–1785. Virginia. Washington: Government Printing Office, 1908.

Hecht, J. Jean. *The Domestic Servant Class in Eighteenth-century England*. London: Routledge and Kegan Paul, 1956.

Hesse, Barnor. 'Forgotten Like a Bad Dream: Atlantic Slavery and the Ethics of Postcolonial Memory', in David Theo Goldberg and Ato Quayson (eds), *Relocating Postcolonialism*. Oxford: Blackwell, 2002, pp. 143–73.

Hill, Bridget. *Servants: English Domestics in the Eighteenth Century*. Oxford: Clarendon Press, 1996.

Hill, Bridget. *Women, Work & Sexual Politics in Eighteenth-century England*. London: UCL, 1994.

Hindmarsh, D. Bruce. *The Evangelical Conversion Narrative: Spiritual Autobiography in Early Modern England*. Oxford: Oxford University Press, 2005.

Hodges, Gabrielle Cliff, Drummond, Mary Jane and Styles, Morag. *Tales, Tellers and Texts*. London: Cassell Education, 1999.

Hoermann, Raphael. '"A Very Hell of Horrors'? The Haitian Revolution and the Early Transatlantic Haitian Gothic', *Slavery & Abolition*, 37: 1, 2016, pp. 183–205.

Hofstra, Warren R. *The Planting of New Virginia: Settlement and Landscape in the Shenandoah Valley*. Baltimore: The Johns Hopkins University Press, 2004.

Hörmann, Raphael. 'Black Jacobins: Towards a Genealogy of a Transatlantic Trope', in Charlotte A. Lerg and Heléna Tóth (eds), *Transatlantic Revolutionary Cultures, 1789–1861*. Leiden: Brill, 2018, pp. 19–49.

House of Commons. 'Amelioration of the Condition of the Slave Population in the West Indies', 16 May 1824. In Hansard, https://api.parliament.uk/historic-hansard/commons/1824/mar/16/amelioration-of-the-condition-of-the, accessed 17 November 2015.

Huett, Lorna. '"Among the Unknown Public": *Household Words, All the Year Round* and the Mass-Market Weekly Periodical in the Mid-Nineteenth Century', 2004 Van Arsdel Prize Essay, *Victorian Periodicals Review*, 38: 1, 2005, pp. 61–82.

Humfrey, Paula. *The Experience of Domestic Service for Women in Early Modern London*. Farnham: Ashgate, 2011.

Inchbald, Elizabeth. *The British Theatre, Or, A Collection of Plays, Which Are Acted At the Theatres Royal, Drury Lane, Covent Garden, And Haymarket*, Vol. 7. London: Longman, Hurst, Rees and Orme, 1808.

Isichei, Elizabeth. *A History of the Igbo People*. New York: St. Martin's Press, 1976.

James, C.L.R. *The Black Jacobins: Toussaint L'Ouverture and the San Domingo Revolution*. 2nd edn. London: Penguin, 2001. Original edition 1938.

James, Stanlie M. 'Mothering: A Possible Black Link to Social Transformation?' in Stanley M. James and Abena P.A. Busia (eds), *Theorizing Black Feminisms: The Visionary Pragmatism of Black Women*. London: Routledge, 1993, pp. 44–54.

JanMohamed, Abdul. 'Between Speaking and Dying: Some Imperatives in the Emergence of the Subaltern in the Context of U.S. Slavery', in Rosalind Morris (ed.), *Can the Subaltern Speak? Reflections on the History of an Idea*. New York: Columbia University Press, 2009, pp. 139–55.

Jarvis, Michael. *In the Eye of All Trade: Bermuda, Bermudians, and the Maritime Atlantic World, 1680–1783*. Chapel Hill: The University of North Carolina Press, 2010.

Jenkinson, Jacqueline. 'The 1919 Race Riots in Britain: A Survey', in Rainer Lotz and Ian Pegg (eds), *Under the Imperial Carpet: Essays in Black History 1780–1950*. Crawley: Rabbit Press, 1986, pp 182–207.

Johnson, James. *The Life of the Late James Johnson, Coloured Evangelist: An Escaped Slave from the Southern States of America, 40 Years Resident in Oldham, England*. Oldham: W. Galley, 1914.

Jones, P. and Youseph, R. *The Black Population of Bristol in the Eighteenth Century*. Bristol: Bristol Branch of the Historical Association, 1994.

J.T. 'Samboo's Grave', *Lonsdale Magazine and Kendal Repository*, III: xxix, 31 May 1822.

Kaplan, Paul H.D. *The Rise of the Black Magus in Western Art*. Ann Arbor: UMI Research Press, 1985.

Karras, Alan L. *Sojourners in the Sun: Scottish Migrants in Jamaica and the Chesapeake, 1740–1800*. Ithaca: Cornell University Press, 1992.

Kaufmann, Miranda. *Black Tudors: The Untold Story*. London: Oneworld, 2017.

Kazanjian, David. '"Ship as Cook": Notes on the Gendering of Black Atlantic Labor', *Radical Philosophy Review*, 5: 1/2, 2002, pp. 10–25.

Kennedy, Cynthia M. 'The Other White Gold: Salt, Slaves, the Turks and Caicos Islands, and British Colonialism', *Historian*, 69: 2, 2007, pp. 215–30.

Kennedy, Maev. 'Slave Owner and Abolitionist Come Face to Face', *The Guardian*, 8 November 2007, https://www.theguardian.com/artand-design/2007/nov/08/art1?I, accessed 14 August 2018.

Kent, D.A. 'Ubiquitous but Invisible: Female Domestic Servants in Mid-Eighteenth Century London', *History Workshop Journal*, 28, 1989, pp. 111–28.

Killingray, David. 'All Conditions of Life and Labour: The Presence of Black People in Essex before 1950', *Essex Archaeology and History*, 35, 2004, pp. 114–22.

Knapp, Oswald G., ed. *The Intimate Letters of Hester Piozzi and Penelope Pennington 1788–1821*. London: John Lane, 1914.

Lalwan, Rory. *Sources for Black & Asian History at the City of Westminster Archives Centre*. London: 2005.

Lambert, Sheila, ed. *House of Commons Sessional Papers of the Eighteenth Century*. Delaware: Scholarly Resources, 1975.

Lane, Tony. *The Merchant Seamen's War*. Manchester: Manchester University Press, 1990.

Latimer, John. *The Annals of Bristol in the Eighteenth Century*. Frome: Butler & Tanner, 1893.

Langford Oliver, Vere. *The Monumental Inscriptions of the British West Indies*. Dorchester: Friary Press, 1927.

Law, Ian and Henfrey, June. *A History of Race and Racism in Liverpool, 1660–1950*. Liverpool: Merseyside Community Relations Council, 1981.

Lazarus-Black, Mindie. *Legitimate Acts and Illegal Encounters: Law and Society in Antigua and Barbuda*. Washington, DC: Smithsonian Institution Press, 1994.

Lemish, Jesse. 'Jack Tar in the Street', *William and Mary Quarterly*, 25: 3, 1968, pp. 371–407.

Lindfors, Bernth. *Ira Aldridge: The Early Years, 1807–1833*. Rochester, NY: University of Rochester Press, 2011.

Linebaugh, Peter and Rediker, Marcus. *The Many-headed Hydra: Sailors, Slaves, Commoners, and the Hidden History of the Revolutionary Atlantic.* Boston: Beacon Press, 2000.

Llwyd, Alan. *Cymru Ddu/Black Wales: A History: A History of Black Welsh People.* Wrexham: Hughes, 2005.

Locke, Gloria. *Caribbeans in Wandsworth.* London: Wandsworth Borough Council, 1998.

Long, Edward. *History of Jamaica.* London: T. Lowndes, 1774.

Lorimer, Douglas. *Colour, Class and the Victorians.* Leicester: Leicester University Press, 1978.

Lovejoy, Paul. 'Autobiography and Memory: Gustavus Vassa, alias Olaudah Equiano, the African', *Slavery and Abolition*, 27, 2006, pp. 317–47.

Lovejoy, Paul. 'Olaudah Equiano or Gustavus Vassa: What's in a name?', in Toyin Falola and Matt Child (eds), *Igbo in the Atlantic World: African Origins and Diasporic Destinations.* Bloomington: Indiana University Press, 2016.

Lustig, Irma S. and Pottle, Frederick A., eds. *Boswell: The Applause of the Jury 1782–1785.* London: Heinemann, 1981.

Lustig, Irma S. and Pottle, Frederick A., eds. *Boswell: The English Experiment 1785–1789.* New York: McGraw-Hill, 1986.

McCune Smith, James. 'Ira Aldridge' (1860), in Bernth Lindfors (ed.), *Ira Aldridge: The African Roscius.* Rochester, NY: University of Rochester Press, 2007.

McGinty, J. Walter. *'An Animated Son of Liberty': A Life of John Witherspoon.* Bury St Edmunds: Arena Books, 2012.

McGrath, Patrick, ed. *Bristol in the Eighteenth Century.* Newton Abbot: David and Charles, 1972.

McGrath, Patrick. *The Merchant Venturers of Bristol: A History of the Society of Merchant Venturers of the City of Bristol from its Origin to the Present Day.* American Society of Civil Engineers, 1975.

MacInnes, C.M. *Bristol: A Gateway of Empire.* Bristol: J. W. Arrowsmith, 1939, and Newton Abbot: David and Charles Ltd., 1968.

MacInnes, C.M. *England and Slavery.* Bristol: Arrowsmith, 1934.

MacKeith, L. *Local Black History: A Beginning in Devon.* London: Archives and Museum of Black Heritage, 2003.

MacKinnon, Dolly. 'Slave Children: Scotland's Children as Chattels at Home and Abroad in the Eighteenth Century', in Janay Nugent and Elizabeth Ewan (eds), *Children and Youth in Premodern Scotland before the Nineteenth Century.* Woodbridge: The Boydell Press, 2015, pp. 120–35

Maddison-MacFadyen, Margôt. *Mary: A Story of Young Mary Prince*. N.p.: Sisters Publishing, 2017.

Maddison-MacFadyen, Margôt. 'Mary Prince, Grand Turk, and Antigua', *Slavery & Abolition*, 34: 4, 2013, pp. 653–62.

Maddison-MacFadyen, Margôt. 'This White Woman Has Journeyed Far: Serendipity, Counter-Stories, Hauntings, and Ekphrasis as a Type of Poetic Inquiry', *Morning Watch: Educational and Social Analysis*, 40: 1–2, 2012, http://www.mun.ca/educ/faculty/mwatch/mwatch_sped13/Maddison%20MacFadyen.pdf.

Maddison-MacFadyen, Margôt. 'Toiling in the Salt Ponds', *Times of the Islands*, Fall 2008, https://www.timespub.tc/2008/09/toiling-in-the-salt-ponds/, accessed 23 July 2017.

Major, Joanne. 'Dido Elizabeth Belle—We Reveal NEW Information about her Siblings' (blogpost), in *All Things Georgian*, 26 June 2018, https://georgianera.wordpress.com/author/joannemajor/.

Major, Andrea. *Slavery, Abolition, and Empire in India, 1772–1843*. Liverpool: Liverpool University Press, 2012.

Manual of Military Law 1907, Edition 6. London: HMSO, 1907.

Marsh, Jan. *Black Victorians: Black People in British Art 1800–1900*. London: Lund Humphries Publishers, 2005.

Marshall, Peter. 'The Anti-Slave Trade Movement in Bristol', in Patrick McGrath (ed.), *Bristol in the Eighteenth Century*. Newton Abbot: David & Charles, 1972.

Mayerfeld Bell, Michael. 'The Ghosts of Place', *Theory and Society*, 26: 6, 1997.

Maynard, G. Oliver. *A History of the Moravian Church, Eastern West Indies Province*. n.p.: n.p., 1968.

Meldrum, Tim. *Domestic Service and Gender, 1660–1750: Life and Work in the London Household*. Harlow: Pearson Education, 2000.

Miller, Monica. *Slaves to Fashion: Black Dandyism and the Styling of Black Diasporic Identity*. Durham, NC: Duke University Press, 2009.

Minuchin, Salvador, 'Where is the Family in Narrative Family Therapy?' *Journal of Marital & Family Therapy*, 24: 4, 1998, pp. 397–403.

Mitchell, Robert D. and Hofstra, Warren R. 'How Do Settlement Systems Evolve? The Virginia Backcountry During the Eighteenth Century', *Journal of Historical Geography*, 21: 2, 1995, pp. 123–47.

Morgan, Philip D. 'Black Experiences in Britain's Maritime World', in David Cannadine (ed.), *Empire, the Sea and Global History: Britain's Maritime World, c. 1763–c. 1840*. New York: Palgrave Macmillan, 2007, pp. 105–33.

Morgan, Philip D. 'Introduction, Maritime Slavery', *Slavery & Abolition*, 31: 3, 2010, pp. 311–26.

Morgan, Philip D. *Slave Counterpoint: Black Culture in the Eighteenth-Century Chesapeake & Low Country*. Chapel Hill: University of North Carolina Press, 1998.

Morgan, Philip D. and Terry, George D. 'Slavery in Microcosm: A Conspiracy Scare in South Carolina', *Southern Studies*, 21: 2, 1982, pp. 121–45.

Morris, Michael. *Scotland and the Caribbean, c.1740–1833: Atlantic Archipelagos*. New York: Routledge, 2015.

Morton, Timothy. 'Blood Sugar', in Tim Fulford and Peter J. Kitson (eds), *Romanticism and Colonialism: Writing and Empire, 1780–1830*. Cambridge: Cambridge University Press, 1998, pp. 87–106.

Munday, Valerie, ed. *Enfield and the Transatlantic Slave Trade 1807–2007*. Enfield: Enfield Museum Service, 2008.

Murden, Sarah. 'Dido Elizabeth Belle—A New Perspective on Her Portrait' (blogpost), in *All Things Georgian*, 15 May 2018, https://georgianera.wordpress.com/2018/05/15/art-detectives-a-new-perspective-on-the-portraitof-dido-elizabeth-belle/.

Murden, Sarah. 'Dido Elizabeth Belle and John Davinieré, What Became of Them?' (blogpost), in *All Things Georgian*, https://georgianera.wordpress.com/2018/07/10/dido-elizabeth-belle-and-john-daviniere-what-became-of-them/.

Murden, Sarah. 'Dido Elizabeth Belle Portrait—BBC Fake or Fortune' (blogpost), *All Things Georgian*, 13 September 2018, https://georgi-anera.wordpress.com/category/dido-elizabeth-belle/.

Murden, Sarah. 'The 18th Century Fashion for Turbans' (blogpost), *All Things Georgian*, 30 January 2018, https://georgianera.wordpress.com/2018/01/30/the-18th-century-fashion-for-turbans/.

Murrin, John M. 'Religion and Politics in America from the First Settlements to the Civil War', in Mark A. Noll and Luke E. Harlow (eds), *Religion and American Politics from the Colonial Period to the Present*. Oxford: Oxford University Press, 2007, pp. 19–43.

Nash, Gary B. *Race and Revolution*. Lanham, MD: Rowman & Littlefield, 1990.

Nassy Brown, Jacqueline. *Dropping Anchor, Setting Sail: Geographies of Race in Black Liverpool*. Princeton: Princeton University Press, 2005.

New Remarks of London Or, A Survey of the Cities of London and Westminster, of Southwark and Part of Middlesex and Surrey … Collected by the Company of Parish Clerks. London: for E. Midwinter, 1732.

Newby, Evelyn. *The Diary of Joseph Farington*. New Haven: Yale University Press, 1998.

Newman, Simon P. 'Hidden in Plain Sight: Escaped Slaves in Late Eighteenth- and Early Nineteenth-Century Jamaica', *William and Mary Quarterly*, 3rd ser., digital edition (June 2018), https://oieahc.wm.edu/digital-projects/oi-reader/simon-p-newman-hidden-in-plain-sight/.

Newman, Simon P. *A New World of Labor: The Development of Plantation Slavery in the British Atlantic*. Philadelphia: University of Pennsylvania Press, 2013.

Newman, Simon P. 'Theorizing Class in an Atlantic World: A Case Study of Glasgow', in Simon Middleton and Billy G. Smith (eds), *Class Matters: Early North America and the Atlantic World*. Philadelphia: University of Pennsylvania Press, 2008, pp. 16–34.

Noll, Mark A., Hatch, Nathan O., Marsden, George M., Wells, David F. and Woodbridge, John D. eds. *Christianity in America: A Handbook*. Grand Rapids, MI: Lion Publishing, 1983.

Nora, Pierre. 'Between Memory and History: *Les Lieux de Mémoire*', in Genevieve Fabre and Robert O'Meally (eds), *History and Memory in African American Culture*. Oxford: Oxford University Press, 1994.

Northrop, Chloe Aubra. *White Creole Women in the British West Indies: From Stereotype to Caricature*. Denton: University of North Texas, 2010.

Northrup, David. *Africa's Discovery of Europe*. Oxford: Oxford University Press, 2014.

Nussbaum, Martha. *Not for Profit—Why Democracy Needs The Humanities*. Princeton: Princeton University Press, 2010.

Nwokeji, Ugo. 'Review of *Equiano the African: Biography of a Self-Made Man*', *Journal of American History*, 93, 2006, pp. 840–1.

Ogude, S.E. 'Facts into Fiction: Equiano's *Narrative* Reconsidered', *Research in African Literatures*, 13, 1982, pp. 31–43.

Ogude, S.E. 'No Roots Here: On the Igbo Roots of Olaudah Equiano', *Review of English and Literary Studies*, 5, 1989, pp. 1–16.

Oliver, V.L. *Caribbeana* Vol. 5. London: Mitchell Hughes & Clarke, 1914.

Olusoga, David. *Black and British: A Forgotten History*. London: Macmillan, 2016.

Onyeka. *Blackamoores: Africans in Tudor England, Their Presence, Status and Origins*. London: Narrative Eye and The Circle with a Dot, 2013.

Pares, Richard. *A West India Fortune*. London: Longmans, 1950.

Paterson, James. *History of the County of Ayr, With a Genealogical Account of the Families of Ayrshire, I*. Ayr: John Dick, 1847.

Peterson, Merrill D., ed. Thomas Jefferson, Writings. New York: Library of America, 1984.

Piozzi, Hesther Lynch. *Anecdotes of the Late Samuel Johnson*, ed. Arthur Sherbo. London: Oxford University Press, 1974.

Pottle, Frederick A. *The Literary Career of James Boswell, Esq.* Oxford: Clarendon Press, 1929, rep. 1965.

Pouchet Paquet, Sandra. 'The Enigma of Arrival: The Wonderful Adventures of Mrs. Seacole in Many Lands', *African American Review*, 26: 4, 1992, pp. 651–63.

Price, Jacob M. 'The Rise of Glasgow in the Chesapeake Tobacco Trade, 1707–1775', *William and Mary Quarterly*, 3rd ser., 11: 2, 1954, pp. 179–99.

Prince, Mary. *The History of Mary Prince, a West Indian Slave*, ed. Sara Salih. London: Penguin, 2004.

Prince, Mary. *The History of Mary Prince, a West Indian Slave, Related by Herself*, Introduction by Moira Ferguson. London: Pandora, 1987.

Pybus, Cassandra. *Epic Voyages of Freedom: Runaway Slaves of the American Revolution and Their Global Quest for Liberty*. Boston: Beacon Press, 2006.

Rauwerda, A.M. 'Naming, Agency, and a "Tissue of Falsehoods" in *The History of Mary Prince*', *Victorian Literature and Culture*, 29: 2, 2001, pp. 397–411.

Reed, Joseph W. and Pottle, Frederick A., eds. *Boswell, Laird of Auchinleck 1778–1782*. Edinburgh: Edinburgh University Press, 1993.

Rice, Alan J. *Creating Memorials, Building Identities: The Politics of Memory in the Black Atlantic*. Liverpool: Liverpool University Press, 2012.

Rice, Alan J. *Radical Narratives of the Black Atlantic*. London; New York: Continuum, 2003.

Ricoeur, Paul. *Memory, History, Forgetting*, trans. Kathleen Bramley and David Pellauer. Chicago: University of Chicago Press, 2004.

Rothberg, Michael. *Multidirectional Memory: Remembering the Holocaust in the Age of Decolonization*. Stanford: Stanford University Press, 2009.

Rich, Adrienne. 'When We Dead Awaken: Writing as Re-Vision', *College English*, 34: 1, 1972, pp. 18–30.

Robb, Peter. 'Credit, Work, and Race: Early Colonialism through a Contemporary European View', *Indian Economic & Social History Review*, 37: 1, 2000, pp. 1–25.

Bibliography

Robb, Peter. *Sentiment and Self: Richard Blechynden's Calcutta Diaries, 1791–1822*. Delhi: Oxford University Press, 2011.

Robb, Peter. *Sex and Sensibility: Richard Blechynden's Calcutta Diaries, 1791–1822*. Delhi: Oxford University Press, 2011.

Robb, Peter. *Useful Friendship: Europeans and Indians in Early Calcutta*. Delhi: Oxford University Press, 2014.

Rowe, Michael. 'Sex, Race and Riot in Liverpool 1919', *Immigrants & Minorities: Historical Studies in Ethnicity, Migration and Diaspora*, 19: 2, 2000, pp. 53–70.

Ryskamp, Charles and Pottle, Frederick A., eds. *Boswell: The Ominous Years 1774–1776*. London: William Heinemann, 1963.

Sala-Molins, Louis. *Dark Side of the Light: Slavery and the French Enlightenment*, trans. John Conteh-Morgan. Minneapolis: University of Minnesota Press, 2006.

Salih, Sara. '*The History of Mary Prince*, the Black Subject, and the Black Canon', in Brycchan Carey, Markman Ellis and Sara Salih (eds), *Discourses of Slavery and Abolition: Britain and Its Colonies, 1760–1838*. Basingstoke: Palgrave Macmillan and the Institute of English Studies, University of London, 2004, pp. 123–38.

Sancho, Ignatius. *Letters of the Late Ignatius Sancho, An African*, ed. Vincent Carretta. New York: Penguin Books, 1998.

Sanderson, F.E. 'The Liverpool Abolitionists', in R.T. Anstey and P.E.H. Hair (eds), *Liverpool, the African Slave Trade, and Abolition*. Bristol, 1976.

Sapoznik, Karlee Anne, ed. *The Letters and Other Writings of Gustavus Vassa (Olaudah Equiano, the African): Documenting Abolition of the Slave Trade*. Princeton: Markus Wiener Publishers, 2013.

Schneer, Jonathan. *London 1900: The Imperial Metropolis*. New Haven and London: Yale University Press, 1999.

Scott, David. 'Introduction: On the Archaeologies of Black Memory', *Anthurium: A Caribbean Studies Journal*, 6: 1, Spring 2008, article 2.

Seacole, Mary. *Wonderful Adventures of Mrs Seacole in Many Lands*. London: Penguin, 2005.

Segal, Ronald. *Islam's Black Slaves: The Other Black Diaspora*. New York: Farrar, Strauss and Giroux, 2001.

Sensbach, Jon. 'Beyond Equiano', in Donald A. Yerxa (ed.), *Recent Themes in the History of Africa and the Atlantic World: Historians in Conversation*. Columbia: University of South Carolina Press, 2008.

Sensbach, Jon. *Rebecca's Revival: Creating Black Christianity in the Atlantic World*. Cambridge, MA: Harvard University Press, 2005.

Sharpe, Jenny. *Ghosts of Slavery: A Literary Archaeology of Black Women's Lives*. Minneapolis: University of Minnesota Press, 2003.

de Silva Jayasuriya, Shihan and Angenot, Jean-Pierre. *Uncovering the History of Africans in Asia*. Leiden: Brill, 2008.

Sinclair, John. *The Statistic Account of Scotland. Drawn from the Communications of the Ministers of the Different Parishes. Volume Eight*. Edinburgh: William Creech, 1793.

Sinha, Manisha. *The Slave's Cause: A History of Abolition*. New Haven: Yale University Press, 2016.

Smith, John Thomas. *Vagabondia. Or, Ancedotes of Mendicant Wanderers through the Streets of London, With Portraits of the Most Remarkable Drawn from the Life*. London: Chatto & Windus, 1874.

Soltow, J.H. 'Scottish Traders in Virginia, 1750–1775', *Economic History Review*, 12: 1, 1959, pp. 83–98.

Sparks, Randy. 'Gold Coast Merchant Families, Pawning, Awning, and the Eighteenth-Century British Slave Trade', *William & Mary Quarterly*, 70: 2, 2013.

Speitz, Michele. 'Blood Sugar and Salt Licks: Corroding Bodies and Preserving Nations in *The History of Mary Prince, a West Indian Slave, Related by Herself*', in Paul Yongquist and Frances Botkin (eds), *Circulations: Romanticism and the Black Atlantic: A Romantic Circles Praxis Volume*, October 2011.

Spence, David. 'Making the London, Sugar and Slavery Gallery at the Museum of London Docklands', in Geoff Cubitt, Kalliopi Fouseki and Laurajane Smith (eds), *Representing Enslavement and Abolition in Museums*. London: Routledge, 2011, pp. 149–63.

Steedman, Carolyn. *Labours Lost: Domestic Service and the Making of Modern England*. Cambridge: Cambridge University Press, 2009.

Stephen, James. *The Slavery of the British West India Colonies Delineated*, Vol. 2. London: J. Butterworth and Son, 1830.

Stephen, Sir George. *A Memoir of the Late James Stephen*. Melbourne, 1875.

Sweeney, Fionnghuala. *Frederick Douglass and the Atlantic World*. Liverpool: Liverpool University Press, 2007.

Taylor, John. *Records of My Life*, Vol. 2. London: Edward Bull, Holles Street, 1832.

Thomas, Sue. 'Affective Dynamics of Colonial Reform and Modernisation in Antigua, 1816–1835', *Feminist Review*, 104, 2013, pp. 24–41.

Thomas, Sue. 'New Information on Mary Prince in London', *Notes and Queries*, 58: 1, 2011, pp. 82–5.

Thomas, Sue. 'New Light on Louis Asa-Asa and the Publication of His Slave Narrative', *Notes and Queries*, 64: 4, 2017, pp. 604–7.

Thomas, Sue. *Telling West Indian Lives: Life Narrative and the Reform of Plantation Slavery Cultures 1804–1834*. New York: Palgrave Macmillan, 2014.

Thornton, John. *Africa and Africans in the Making of the Atlantic World, 1400–1800*. Cambridge: Cambridge University Press, 1992; rev. edn 1998.

Trexler, Richard C. *The Journey of the Magi: Meanings in History of a Christian Story*. Princeton: Princeton University Press, 1997.

Turner, John M. 'Pablo Fanque, Black Circus Proprietor', in Gretchen H. Gerzina (ed.), *Black Victorians, Black Victoriana*. New Brunswick, NJ: Rutgers University Press, 2003, pp. 20–38.

Uduku, Ola and Ben-Tovim, Gideon. *Social Infrastructure Provision in Granby/Toxteth*. Liverpool: University of Liverpool, 1997.

Ukaegbu, Dorothy Chinwe. 'Igbo Sense of Place and Identity in Olaudah Equiano's Interesting Narrative', in Chima J. Korieh (ed.), *Olaudah Equiano and the Igbo World*. Trenton, NJ: Africa World Press, 2009, pp. 67–92.

Vernon, Patrick. 'Windrush Day: a fitting way to celebrate our immigrant population.' *The Guardian*, Monday 25 January 2010.

Venn, J. and Venn, J.A. *Alumni Cantabrigienses*, Part 1, Vol. 4. Cambridge: Cambridge University Press, 1927.

Visram, Rozina. *Asians in Britain: 400 Years of History*. London: Pluto Press, 2002.

Voyages: The Trans-Atlantic Slave Trade Database. http://www.slavevoyages.org/assessment/estimates, accessed 30 September 2018.

Wadström, Carl Bernhard. *An Essay on Colonization Particularly Applied to the Western Coast of Africa with some free thought on cultivation and commerce, Vol. 1*. [1794] Newton Abbot: David and Charles Ltd, 1968 reprint.

Waingrow, Marshall, ed. *James Boswell's Life of Johnson: An Edition of the Original Manuscript in Four Volumes*, Vol. I. Edinburgh: Edinburgh University Press; New Haven and London: Yale University Press, 1994.

Waingrow, Marshall. *The Correspondence and Other Papers of James Boswell Relating to the Making of the Life of Johnson*, 2nd edn, corrected and enlarged. Edinburgh and New Haven: Edinburgh University Press and Yale University Press, 2001.

Wallace, Elizabeth Kowaleski. *The British Slave Trade and Public Memory*. New York: Columbia University Press, 2006.

Walvin, James. *The Zong, A Massacre, the Law and the End of Slavery.* New Haven: Yale University Press, 2011.

Waters, Hazel. *Racism on the Victorian Stage: Representations of Slavery and the Black Character.* Cambridge: Cambridge University Press, 2007.

Wedderburn, Robert. *The Horrors of Slavery and other Writings*, ed. Iain McCalman. Princeton/Kingston, Jamaica: Marcus Wiener/Ian Randle, 1991.

Weis, Charles McC. and Pottle, Frederick A., eds. *Boswell in Extremes 1776–1778.* London: Heinemann, 1971.

Whalley, George. 'Coleridge and Southey in Bristol, 1795', *The Review of English Studies*, 1: 4, 1950, pp. 324–40.

Wheeler, Roxann. *The Complexion of Race: Categories of Difference in Eighteenth-century British Culture.* Philadelphia: University of Pennsylvania Press, 2000.

Whelan, Timothy. 'Robert Hall and the Bristol Slave-Trade Debate 1788–1789', *Baptist Quarterly*, 38, 2000, pp. 212–24.

Whitlock, Gillian. *The Intimate Empire: Reading Women's Autobiography.* London: Cassell, 2000.

Wilberforce, William. *A Practical View of the Prevailing Religious System of Professed Christians: In the Higher and Middle Classes in this Country, Contrasted with Real Christianity.* London, T. Cadell, 1829.

Williams, A.H. 'The Leaders of English and Welsh Methodism 1738–91', *Bathafarn*, 16, 1961.

Williams, Gomer. *History of the Liverpool Privateers and Letters of Marque with an Account of the Liverpool Slave Trade, 1744–1812.* Liverpool: Liverpool University Press, 2004 [1897].

Wimsatt, William K. and Pottle, Frederick A., eds. *Boswell for the Defence 1769–1774.* London: William Heinemann, 1960.

Wood, Marcus. *Blind Memory: Visual Representation of Slavery in England and America, 1780–1865.* Manchester: Manchester University Press, 2000.

Wood, Marcus. *Slavery, Empathy and Pornography.* Oxford: Oxford University Press, 2002.

Index

Index

Kennedy, Cynthia M. 245
Kenwood House (London) 161, 167, 169–70, 175, 176
Kerie, Jedidah 260
Killingray, David 337
Kiln Theatre 212
Kingston Archaeological Society 336
Knight, Joseph 87
Knight v Wedderburn 41

L'Aigrette 63
Lace, Ambrose 104
Ladies Society of Liverpool 289
Lambe, The 183
Lancashire Cotton Famine *see* Cotton Famine
Lancashire County *see* Lancaster
Lancaster
  baptisms in 187–8
  cotton trade in 180, 192, 193
  numbers of blacks 179
  slave trade in 183–4, 192, 193
  theatre in 277, 278, 290–1
Lancaster, Benjamin 254
Lancaster, Phebe 254–5, 259, 265
Lancaster Priory Church 190, 191
Lane, William Henry 320
Laporte, Pierre 280
Lawrence 74–5
Lawson, Robert 184
Lazarus-Black, Mindie 250–1
Lebenslauf 248
Lennard, E.W. (Col.) 127–8
Lester, Adrian 212
libel *see* Wood v. Pringle
Life of Dr Samuel Johnson, The see under Hawkins, John
Life of Johnson see under Boswell, James
Lincoln, Charles 223

Lindfors, Bernth 277, 280–1, 283, 284, 291
Lindsay, John 163–5, 166, 170, 173–4
Lindsay, John Edward 163
Lindsay Jr, John 175
Linebaugh, Peter 304
Liverpool
  children of African rulers resident in 100, 102–3, 104
  continuity of community 99, 1078, 110–11
  historical black presence in 99–104, 106–7
  identity formation 106, 114–15
  ignorance of black presence 99, 100, 110
  modern demographic data 116
  political engagement 110–11, 113
  theatre in 277, 278, 288–9
  Toxteth riots 106, 113
Liverpool Advertiser 192
Liverpool Concert Hall 289
Liverpool Mercury 321, 322
Lloyd George, David 109
London Gazette 216
London, Negro 77–8
Long, Edward 33, 103
Lonsdale Magazine 184
Lopez, Aaron 75
Lovejoy, Paul 57–8, 59, 60
Lyndon, Dan 18

MacCalman, Ian 305, 306, 308
McDaniel, Capt. 68–9
MacInnes, C.M. 127
  Bristol: A Gateway to Empire 127
McQueen, James 248